SIGNS AND WONDERS

Gender, Theory, and Religion

GENDER, THEORY, AND RELIGION

AMY HOLLYWOOD, EDITOR

The Gender, Theory, and Religion series provides a forum for interdisciplinary scholarship at the intersection of the study of gender, sexuality, and religion.

Signs & Wonders

THEOLOGY
AFTER MODERNITY

Ellen T. Armour

COLUMBIA UNIVERSITY PRESS
NEW YORK

Columbia University Press
Publishers Since 1893
New York   Chichester, West Sussex

cup.columbia.edu

Library of Congress Cataloging-in-Publication Data
Armour, Ellen T., 1959–
    Signs and wonders : theology after modernity / Ellen Armour.
        pages cm. — (Gender, theory, and religion)
    Includes bibliographical references and index.
    ISBN 978-0-231-17248-6 (cloth : alk. paper) — ISBN 978-0-231-17249-3 (pbk. : alk.
paper) — ISBN 978-0-231-54094-0 (e-book)
1. Philosophy and religion. 2. Philosophical theology. 3. Postmodernism. 4. Religion—
Forecasting. I. Title.
    BL51.A665 2016
    230—dc23

                                                                        2015017752

c 10 9 8 7 6 5 4 3 2 1
p 10 9 8 7 6 5 4 3 2 1

Cover design: Jordan Wannemacher
Cover image: Copyright © AP Photo/Jim Cole.

To Barbee

CONTENTS

ACKNOWLEDGMENTS

*S*IGNS AND WONDERS is both a labor of love and a work of mourning. How could it be otherwise, given the events that are its focus. Here, however, I want to acknowledge more personal dimensions to that labor and work. I owe a great debt to my friend and former colleague at Rhodes College, art historian David McCarthy, whose initial suggestions launched my education in the history of photography and visual cultural theory, and to another friend and colleague, Gail Hamner of Syracuse University, whose additional recommendations at a later stage helped round out that education. That she brought to bear on her reading of the manuscript expertise in the work of Michel Foucault was doubly helpful. On that count, I benefited enormously from careful readings by Charles Scott and LaDelle McWhorter, exceptionally fine philosophers, whose comments on early versions of the manuscript were invaluable. The opportunity in the spring of 2012 to coteach with my (now former) Vanderbilt colleague, David Rubin, a seminar in queer theory for doctoral students across the university came along at just the right time. A highlight for all of us in the seminar—and especially productive for me— was Mark Jordan's presence with us for two weeks as scholar in residence. The opportunity to think with him in person and not just through texts enriched this project in a number of ways. Readings by Sharon Betcher, Denise Kimber Buell, Patrick Cheng, Mayra Rivera Rivera, and Laurel Schneider—fellow travelers in theology and theory all—led me to and through a number of critical final revisions. This book would not be what it is without all of these generous and wonderful colleagues. That said, any shortcomings that remain are mine and mine alone.

During the long course of this project's germination, I also benefited from the responses of audiences of philosophers or religionists for various conference presentations and invited lectures. Although this project ultimately took a decidedly Foucauldian turn, I first articulated its basic problematic in a talk I was invited to give at the American Academy of Religion in one of a series of sessions devoted to the work of (now the late) Jacques Derrida, whom I had gotten to know some years earlier. That was the last time I would see him, it turns out, and I remain grateful for his expressed interest in and support for what was then a nascent project. Other obligations required that it lie fallow for a few years, but an invitation that came from Diane Perpich in 2005 to give the keynote address for the annual meeting of the Société Americaine de Philosophie de Langue Française allowed me to develop *Signs and Wonders*' key framing device in much more detail. At later stages, I benefited as well from the considered responses of colleagues and students to a lecture I gave at Katholieke Universiteit in Leuven, Belgium, my 2010 Gilberto Castaneda Lecture at Chicago Theological Seminary, and to papers I gave at the Transdisciplinary Theology Colloquium on Gayatri Chakravorty Spivak at Drew University's School of Theology and at a conference on Judith Butler and Whitehead at Claremont School of Theology. (My thanks to Judith Butler whose response to the paper I gave at Claremont was both helpful and encouraging.) As the manuscript approached completion, important opportunities for reflection and refinement came with speaking engagements at Syracuse University, the University of Toronto, Allegheny College, and as the 2014 Antoinette Brown Lecturer at Vanderbilt Divinity School. I am grateful to Lieven Boeve, Alice Hunt, Catherine Keller, Mayra Rivera and Stephen Moore, Roland Faber, Christina Hutchins, and Henry Krips, Gail Hamner (once again), Natalie Wigg-Stevenson, Eric Boynton, and the Antoinette Brown Lecture Committee for all of those invitations.

Bringing a book project to fruition requires more than authorial perseverance and collegial counsel; it also requires the labor of others behind the scenes. I am grateful for research assistance from Anna Traverse, Angela Howard McParland, and Jewly Hight. Brandy Daniels's help in preparing the manuscript for publication and her diligence in tracking down rights holders to the photographs discussed herein was invaluable. For securing or granting the permissions themselves, I thank Bobby Schindler of the Terri Schiavo Life and Hope Foundation, David Mandel of the National Center for Civil and Human Rights, Don Northup of Illinois Photo, and especially Tricia Gesner of the Associated Press. My deep gratitude, as well, goes to those at Columbia University Press who saw the book into and through production—particularly Wendy Lochner and her intrepid assistant, Christine Dunbar.

While *Signs and Wonders* was in its formative stages, I gave up the pleasures and challenges of life on the faculty of a small liberal arts college (Rhodes College) for the pleasures and challenges of life on the faculty of a divinity school at a major research university (Vanderbilt)—coincidentally, where I did my graduate work. This project benefited from the support of research funds associated with the R. A. Webb Chair at Rhodes College and the E. Rhodes and Leona B. Carpenter Chair in Feminist Theology at Vanderbilt Divinity School. Both institutions have been supportive settings for my work in other ways, as well—not least in the opportunities both provided for rich and formative interactions with students and faculty alike. I single out for special mention two important interlocutors and friends who died during the course of this book's genesis: my former colleague at Rhodes, the fine Shakespeare scholar Cynthia Marshall, and my former professor at Vanderbilt, the exceptional philosophical theologian Edward Farley. *Signs and Wonders* bears traces both affective and intellectual of their influence—I hope in ways that honor their memories.

As always, I am deeply indebted to my family for their support and inspiration: my parents, Rollin and Mary Anne Armour; my brothers, Rod and Steve; Steve's wife, Jo Smith; my partner of almost thirty years, Barbee Majors; and all of the wonderful animals with whom we've shared our households. Without reading a word of it, Barbee knows better than anyone the labor, love, and loss that this book embodies. I dedicate *Signs and Wonders* to her. May her unfailing love, deep wisdom, and wry sense of humor continue to sustain me for many more years to come.

July 2015
Nashville Tennessee

SIGNS AND WONDERS

INTRODUCTION

Making Space, Marking Time

T HOSE OF US who trade in contemporary continental philosophy are supposed to be able, at the drop of a hat, to tick off the
various symptoms of modernity's demise: the death of the subject, of credible metanarratives, of reason and truth. If we happen to be
philosophical theologians, we are then pressed to state whether we think
religion (as a set of metanarratives that assert claims to ultimate truth) is
a collateral casualty or whether religion might be poised to make a come-
back. If we happen to be feminist or queer philosophical theologians, we
are further pressed to articulate whether (and, if so, how) our particular
field of inquiry is aided or hindered by modernity's passing.[1]

These expectations arise because many of those philosophers we study
and deploy are supposedly caught up in the wide net cast by the postmodern. Yet in many instances, they themselves are explicitly wary of association with such epochal claims—both on behalf of their own work and in
general. This is true, for example, of the philosophers whose work is featured prominently herein: Michel Foucault, Jacques Derrida, and Judith
Butler.[2] For the record, I share their wariness—not because I think subjectivity, metanarratives, and claims for truth and justice are actually secure,
but because I think the relationship between "modernity" (or certain

things we pull out as its hallmarks, including these) and our time and place is not well captured by "post."

This is particularly true of our relationship to religion, whose "return" is said to both mark and be made possible by modernity's ostensible end. Not surprisingly, such claims often reflect the standard narrative of the effect of modernity's emergence on religion. According to that narrative, the advent of modern science and history replaced religion as the arbiter of truth with autonomous human reason. Religion was shunted to the side as a matter of (largely private) belief, whereas the public square became increasingly secular. Certain theologians and philosophers of religion have suggested that the erosion of confidence in reason might open the space for a renewed, if grudging in some quarters, respect for religion. At the same time, religion has reasserted its claim on the public square in vocal and visible, if not always welcome, ways. To cite only the most prominent on the U.S. scene, the religious right emerged as a singularly potent political force in the eighties, a place it continues to occupy (although, with the advent of the Tea Party movement, not without some competition). And violent Islamist movements of various sorts (including but not limited to al-Qaeda) promise to be an ongoing source of global disruption for some time to come. Although we identify these as signs of modernity's end, we often do so from within a modern framework. Whether benign or virulent, the return of the religious is the return of reason's opposite: faith, belief, and the a/rational, if not the ir/rational.[3] Finally, to speak of religion's return presupposes a clean line between the secular and the religious, an assumption that a number of scholars have called into question in recent years.[4]

Making Space: Signs and Wonders

Given this assumption, however, a case can be made that we have come to occupy a distinctive relationship toward certain impulses, notions, concepts, and ways of being that in some sense can be characterized as "modern." In what follows, I will trace the emergence in modernity of a "fourfold" made up of man, his divine other, his animal other, and his raced and sexed others placed in a certain configuration. Man occupies the center, while his others surround him like a network of mirrors that reflect him back to himself, thus securing his sense of identity and of mastery—over self, over nature, and over his others. This fourfold has served to channel forms of power that are specific to modernity issuing in certain forms of knowing, doing, and being that we now inhabit, often without thinking. This system is showing signs of strain, as we'll see; these signs may indicate its imminent passing, but that remains to be seen. And we are struggling to bear up under the strain—and perhaps give birth to whatever will take its place.[5]

I speak of a fourfold, a term I get from the philosopher Martin Heidegger, for several reasons. First, like his fourfold (mortals, divinities, earth, air[6]), this fourfold is more than merely the sum of its parts. Each enfolds and opens onto the other; we cannot think one without implying the others. I say *enfolds* here to mark certain peculiar features of fourfolds. It may seem as though we are talking about distinctly different kinds of beings: beings that die (mortals, man, his animal, sexed and raced others), beings that don't (divinities), a planet located solidly beneath our feet, and the more ephemeral atmosphere "above" it. It may seem, as well, that the elements of these fourfolds are easily separable one from the other. After all, mortals dwell on the earth while divinities occupy a more spiritual realm, don't they? And did I not just say that man sits at the center of the hall of mirrors composed of his others? Heidegger's readers know better—to dwell on earth is both spiritual and material. It invokes and involves—enfolds, really—the transcendence figured by divinities and air.[7] Similarly, man and his others are not dots connected by straight lines that form a quadrilateral, no matter how complex or contorted. The mirrors that secure man in and to himself are the reflective side of that thinnest of membranes that, as we'll see, simultaneously joins and separates man and each of his others. Recall, as well, how a hall of mirrors works. What one sees reflected depends on the mirror into which one is looking and what else is reflected there, or not. Depending on the specific context, certain elements of the fourfold come into view, while others slip into shadow. It will become clear in what follows that the fourfold functions like a set of vectors that refract rather than reflect whoever (or whatever) enters into it. That refraction is a critical element in how those it targets come to be who or what they are.

I use Heidegger's terminology for other reasons, as well. Although the terms of my fourfold are at once more pedestrian and less freighted than Heidegger's, we are no more accustomed to thinking through it than we are his more esoteric fourfold. Yet, I hope to demonstrate that my fourfold, like his, gives shape to our being-in-the-world prereflectively. It is habitual and affective, not just ideological; it exercises a centripetal pull on those caught in its sway (including arguably, Heidegger, but that's a tale for another day).[8] That centripetal pull manifests not only in ideas and beliefs but also in quotidian practices. So, just as constructing a high-rise presupposes (and might be said to violate) mortals dwelling on the earth, placing a dog collar and leash around a Muslim prisoner's neck presupposes and violates the line between human and animal that runs through our grammar of religious and ethnic difference. Finally, like Heidegger's fourfold, mine points in the direction of an ontology that, while ultimately more Foucauldian and Butlerian than Heideggerian, has roots in his thinking of *ontos*—and thus what he calls Being—not as a static property or an enduring substance, but rather as dispersion and gathering, concealment and unconcealment, profoundly temporal and historical.[9] *Signs and Wonders* presses toward an ontology that acknowledges rather than obfuscates finitude and vulnerability, including the finitude and vulnerability of this fourfold itself. This marks a difference between the status of my fourfold and Heidegger's. If his has a specific historical or epochal provenance, it goes unspecified, so far as I am aware. If anything, it seems more akin to a primordial structure or emplacement with which, like Being, we have lost touch. Recovering access to it or contact with it is key to the recovery of what of our long enthrallment to the forgetfulness of Being has cost us.

What follows herein, however, is no exercise in recovery—nostalgic or otherwise.

It is, rather, an inquiry into certain events that expose, I will argue, the regime that the fourfold has produced as simultaneously constitutive of our time and place and threatening to give way. I draw on resources in French and French-inflected philosophy in my attempt to understand and respond to that to which these signs and wonders bear witness. I focus on four events that captured Americans' attention between the fall of 2003 and late summer 2005: the consecration of the Rt. Rev. V. Gene Robinson as bishop of the Episcopal diocese of New Hampshire (chapter 3), the Abu Ghraib prison scandal (chapter 4), the Terri Schiavo case (chapter 5), and Hurricane Katrina (chapter 6). Although I believe I am the first academic to consider them in concert, I am not the first to turn a scholarly lens their way. In the immediate aftermath of each event, a veritable torrent of scholars from a wide variety of disciplines in the humanities and the social sciences found themselves compelled to write about one or another of these events.[10] Indeed, portions of some of the analyses herein were first born in that frenzy of immediate response. A potential reader might well ask what justifies resurrecting these events from the proverbial dustbin of (especially recent) history. What remains to be said about them? Although the events themselves may have receded into memory for many of us, the issues they raise—philosophical and theological as well as social, ethical, and political—remain salient. The advantage of a few years of historical distance, I believe, can help us see past the immediate pain and trauma—or jubilation, for many of us, in the case of Bishop Robinson's consecration—in these events to deeper issues that lie beneath, issues that have hardly gone away. Debates continue over the status of lesbian, gay, bisexual, transgender, queer/questioning, and intersex (LGBTQI) people not only in U.S. society but also around the globe—and Christianity is in the thick of it, as the ongoing controversy (which ranges from a high boil to a low simmer) within the Anglican Communion demonstrates. Robinson's retirement from his position in the church is not likely to bring this controversy to an end any sooner (indeed, his announcement in May 2014 of his divorce exacerbated it). The photographs from Abu Ghraib trade on Orientalist views of Islam and of Muslims that continue to run deep in Western culture. Anti-Islamic sentiment seems to have reached a new virulence in the wake of September 11 and the wars that followed it. Ongoing resistance to the construction of a mosque here in the Nashville area and, in 2010, of an Islamic community center in lower Manhattan near Ground Zero was anchored in crude stereotypes and vicious rumor—and local and national politicians and self-appointed spokespersons for Christianity remain poised to fan the flames of Islamophobia. That *those* flames can erupt into violent acts of terror was brought home to us in the 2011 bombing and murderous rampage in Oslo, Norway. If the advent of the Arab Spring brought new hope for democracy in the Middle East, subsequent developments in Libya and Egypt—not to mention Syria and Iraq—often raise the specter in the United States, at least, of emergent Islamist states. New Orleans and the rest of the Gulf coast continue to rebuild and repopulate in the face of the continued threat of hurricanes potentially worsened by climate change, but those efforts were set back in 2010 by the worst environmental disaster in U.S. history: a catastrophic oil spill in the Gulf following the explosive demise of an off-shore oil rig owned by BP. The Gulf Coast will be dealing with the consequences of that disaster for some time to come, and yet offshore drilling has resumed and our appetite for "our own" oil seems only to increase even in the face of the growing evidence of climate change's catastrophic effects. Since then, the United States and the world have faced other "natural disasters"—the tsunami off the coast of Japan that caused the catastrophic failure at the Fukushima Daiichi nuclear plant (2011); Hurricane Sandy (2012), which devastated much of the northeastern United States; and record-setting catastrophic flooding in Colorado (2013) and in the Midwest (2014). As of summer 2014, the southwestern United States has faced several years of record-setting heat waves, droughts, and fires. And the aftermaths of all of these events are ongoing. I place "natural disasters" in scare quotes to signal that these events, like Katrina, result from a complex interplay between human action (or inaction) and the natural world. Although many of us prefer to deny it, the consensus among climate scientists is that with the climate warming, these events herald a new normal that, unless the human appetite for fossil fuels is contained, will be catastrophic. Passage of the Patient Protection and Affordable Care Act (H.R. 3590, commonly and pejoratively known as "Obamacare") was imperiled by claims (false, it turned out) that "death panels" would decide the fates of the infirm and terminally ill.[11] Although the Supreme Court has, as of this writing, allowed so-called Obamacare to stand as the law of the land, its opponents remain determined to see it repealed or at least dramatically undercut.[12] And debates continue over how to finance programs like Medicaid, Medicare, and Social Security that sustain the lives of the elderly and the poor either in their current forms or some other. Meanwhile, families and health care professionals struggle daily with the ethical and theological challenges that arise as they make decisions for severely injured and ailing loved ones. The case of Marlise Muñoz—a Texas paramedic who was kept on life support for two months after being declared brain dead against her family's wishes (and her own) to try to preserve the life of her fourteen-week-old fetus—grabbed headlines in January 2014, raising different, but related, questions about our ability to manage life and death.[13] In other words, although the events I analyze herein are singular, the deeper realities they index have long historical roots and pose challenges to us that show no sign of ending. Read together through the fourfold, they showcase its continued salience as an organizational schema even as they exhibit signs of its inadequacy to the task.

My approach to these events will be distinctive in yet another way. I frame my analysis of each of these events through photographs. I do this for a number of reasons. Still or moving photography played a central role not only in the Abu Ghraib scandal (launched as we all know by the circulation of photographs of scenes of prisoner torment taken by U.S. soldiers) but in the other events as well. U.S. citizens witnessed the immediate aftermath of Hurricane Katrina on television as the events unfolded. Certain photographs taken by news photographers captured in powerful ways the horror and loss experienced by Gulf Coast residents in Katrina's immediate wake. A home movie of Terri Schiavo made in her hospice room figured prominently in the political controversy over her fate. A still from that movie—a close-up of Ms. Schiavo's face—crystallized for many the complexities of her situation. The consecration of an Anglican bishop may make the local paper on occasion, but rarely is it deemed worthy of national (much less international) attention. And yet Rev. Robinson's consecration attracted not only coverage in word but also in photographs. For those reasons, I will focus my discussion of each event through specific images—visual images that verge on the iconic, which I suggest concentrate the event's impact in a particularly powerful way.[14] But it is not just the content of these photographs that connects them to this project; as I'll show in chapter 2, the visual technologies that produced them are part and parcel of modernity and its putative end and were integral to the fourfold's emergence and its subsequent deployment.

Marking Time: After Modernity

The preceding section may have provided some introduction to the signs and wonders at which the title of this project hints, but it has probably only raised questions about the subtitle. "Theology After Modernity" seems to take as *fait accompli* modernity's end; yet I have just expressed my skepticism about that notion. "After" has another connotation—as much spatial as temporal—that of following or coming after. It is primarily that sense of "after" that I want to call upon here. In what sense are we following after modernity—caught up in and by ways of thinking, being, and doing that it brought to birth? It may be, of course, that the potency and even shape of these ways of being, thinking, and doing are eroding and even dying out. If so, are these losses we should mourn or celebrate? And what other ways of being, thinking, and doing do we want to come to be in their place?

I take my orientation to this epochal question from Foucault. For some, this may be surprising. After all, if any of the philosophers I mentioned seems most easily tethered to the version of postmodernity of which I am suspicious, it would seem to be him. As Amy Allen has noted, both fans and detractors alike have understood the import of Foucault's work as sounding the subject's death knell.[15] Moreover, his oeuvre consists in large part of inquiries into the emergence of modern institutions (the clinic, the prison, the asylum) that undercut their claims to be (in any simple sense, at least) improvements over what came before. Although incarceration is undeniably less spectacularly violent than drawing and quartering, it does its own violence to the incarcerated (and I am not speaking here of prisoner abuse, but of the goals and mechanisms of orderly prison life). Who has done more than Foucault to expose the dark underside of justice, morality, and truth—and, in the process, to give the lie to modernity's metanarrative of unceasing progress grounded in the exercise of reason?

To some degree, this sketch of Foucault's oeuvre rightly describes its aims and effects. I align myself, however, with Foucault scholars like Allen and Todd May (among others)—and ultimately, with Foucault himself—in rejecting reading his methods' or his work's ultimate import as breaking with modernity.[16] Certainly, these projects reflect critically on certain aspects of modernity with the aim of exposing their limitations and, in many instances, moving beyond them. That very posture, however, is deeply indebted to modernity, as Foucault himself acknowledges in an essay written toward the end of his life entitled "What Is Enlightenment?"

In that essay, Foucault suggests we think of modernity as an attitude rather than an epoch, one that has from its inception had to struggle against "countermodernity." This attitude, which he traces back to Kant, is "a mode of relating to contemporary reality; a voluntary choice made by certain people; in the end, a way of thinking and feeling; a way, too, of acting and behaving that at one and the same time marks a relation of belonging and presents itself as a task."[17] It is embodied in critical investigation of the past in the service of furthering freedom. At the center of this modern attitude and its deployment—for both Foucault and Kant (although not necessarily in the same way)—is "man" (*l'homme*) as both its object and subject. On the one hand, "man" is the source of critical reflection; the capacity for critique lies within him and is exercised by him. On the other, man is also its object. Critique is aimed—by both Kant and Foucault—at cultivating man's capacities vis-à-vis what would restrain them, contain them, and shape them in particular ways. But here, of course, they part ways. Critique (aimed at establishing the ground of knowing, doing, and judging) leads Kant to posit a transcendental subject, a subject that becomes a centerpiece of modernity.[18] Critique (aimed at understanding how we come to know, do, and be) leads Foucault to posit subjectivity as product and project rather than ground.[19] Critique, as Foucault employs it, is not aimed at separating the universal wheat from the particular chaff—certainly one trajectory for its deployment (by Kant and others)—but at the specific and particular. Its approach to the past is archaeological in method and genealogical in aim; that is, it seeks to identify and understand the historical contingencies that shape us and to sift through those contingencies in search of (equally contingent) possibilities for doing, thinking, and being otherwise. It yields, then, what Foucault calls here an "historical ontology of ourselves" composed of the constitutive effects of certain formations of knowledge and power in specific ways of doing, being, and thinking.[20] Indeed, in other late writings, Foucault suggests that his entire oeuvre could be read as various attempts to account for the emergence of the modern subject. I situate *Signs and Wonders* within that framework in several ways. For one, it extends and expands that project. As I will argue in what follows, although Foucault never speaks in such terms, one can trace the emergence of the fourfold in the composite picture of man's emergence provided by Foucault's oeuvre and certain scholarship prompted by it. Such projects are necessarily plural ("attempts" rather than "attempt"); any particular approach, including this one, is inherently limited. Whatever it enables us to see and understand, it inevitably will obscure other realities about our time and place.

It would be possible, of course (in theory, at least), to establish the fourfold's viability some other way. I turn to Foucault for these purposes for at least two reasons. I think Foucault's approach to the past grants the fourfold the status appropriate to this project in both its diagnostic and remedial aspects. This is not an exercise in the history of ideas as it is commonly understood. That is, I will not in these pages trace the development of the *ideas* of man, animal, the divine, race, gender, and sexuality in the modern era. Such a project is utterly beyond my ken. Rather, I simply want to establish the fourfold as a legitimate and useful heuristic device for thinking about *our* time and place and some of the challenges that beset us. Hence, seeking a Foucauldian ground for its legitimacy seems apt. Foucault's methods interrogate the past, but their import (indeed their aim) is to illumine the present. The first volume of Foucault's multivolume history of sexuality, for example, starts not with the ancient past but with a query about the way we in the late-modern West present our relationship to our past.[21] Why, Foucault asks, in the opening chapter entitled (in the English translation) "We Other Victorians," do we tell ourselves—and with such vehemence—that we are liberating ourselves from a past history of sexual repression? This volume contains several chapters that at least resemble the work of an historian, but it also includes chapters entitled "Method," Domain," and "Periodization"—chapters in which the author draws out the philosophical implications of this historical work. Instead of giving us the history of sexuality per se (a project that assumes we know what sexuality is), Foucault relates the history of sexuality's emergence as concept and, more important, as an organizational feature of (modern) individual, familial, and political life. Seen in that light, the story of liberation from repression that so dominates contemporary discourse about sexuality is called into question.[22]

But the mode of that calling into question needs further elaboration. In "Foucault's Ironies and the Important Earnestness of Theory," Mark D. Jordan calls our attention to the ironic tone and strategic writing practices in which Foucault engages.[23] These practices effectively draw us "other Victorians" (or, following the original French, "others, Victorians") into a text that plays off of the double meaning of *histoire* ("history" and "story") in French. This volume—and, I would argue, the other texts of Foucault's on which I will draw herein—are "histories of the present."[24] That is, they make of "history" a "story" that, in tracing and tracking "what happened," weaves a narrative that shows us who we are and how we got here, a story that implicates us in the telling and the being told. This does not mean that fiction masquerades as fact in Foucault. Nor are Foucault's *histoires* intended as entertainments or diversions—or, like bedtime stories, to console and reassure. Hardly. These are *histoires* that, like the photographs on which my analysis centers, call us to what Foucault calls *askesis*, a discipline of attending and undergoing that aims at transformation—of ourselves and, if it's not too much to dare, of the world we inhabit.[25] In referencing *askesis*, I do not mean to invoke dour visions of self-denial and self-flagellation. There are pleasures to be had here—not least, as Jordan points out, the pleasures of knowing, which Foucault indulges and which beckon us into undertaking the work. These plea-sures, however, also mark our subjection by and to what Foucault's work reveals. And the possibilities, such as they are, of transformation not only mark the limits of our knowing but also hold out the promise of pleasures yet to come. These pleasures will not come unmixed with pain and, above all, uncertainty. But access to them requires that we submit ourselves to the process of undergoing through a disciplined attentiveness that will, if it succeeds, unmake us—that is, cause us at least to see ourselves and our time(s) and place(s) differently and thereby potentially open up ways to be and do differently. Accessing those ways of doing and being, I suggest, entails a shift from vision, the sensory mode so focal to *Signs and Wonders*, to touch, a move that transpires organically as these chapters unfold. I make that turn not because touch is free of the taint of modernity and its fourfold; it is not. As we'll see, both senses are deeply imbricated in the signs and wonders I attend to here—in their form as well as their content. Touch is essential to taking photographs (e.g., the shutter's click) and to viewing them; we sometimes (literally) touch them, they sometimes (metaphorically) touch us. Moreover, touch figures centrally in the events referenced in all of the photographs that anchor this project. As we'll see, it limns a site of vulnerability and connection that is easily exploited but that also calls forth modes of care.

Finally, a word about theology, including what I take it to be and how it will function in what follows. In no small part in adaptation to modernity's demands, theology has become an academic discipline; it is the province of scholars who have submitted themselves to years of spe-cialized training in reading, writing, and thinking that culminates in the awarding of a so-called terminal degree (the doctorate). But, as Edward Farley has argued, reading, writing, and thinking were understood by our premodern forebears in theology as undertaken in service of the pursuit of wisdom (*sapientia*) that could inform ordinary (Christian) living.[26] The pursuit of wisdom included not only practices of reading and writing, but also of contemplation, a practice to which Wendy Farley has committed herself in a very disciplined way over several decades and to which she recently has explicitly (and very gently) beckoned us.[27]

Signs and Wonders, then, mines what might seem an unlikely conver-gence of the (putatively) post- and premodern, a convergence marked by the notion of *askesis* to which I already referred. This book could well be approached as a contemplative exercise of sorts, one that asks readers to slow down and pay close attention—to photographs they have likely seen before, to what they open up and open onto (including the events they reference), to what they reveal about our own formation. These processes of making and unmaking are, I shall argue, in need of reformation. I shall point toward certain resources within Christian theology that can aid in that reformation, but resources are surely to be found elsewhere as well. Certainly neither *askesis* nor contemplation are of exclusively Christian—or religious—provenance. Contemplative practices are embedded in most religious traditions—and certain philosophies, as well. Indeed, Foucault's turn to *askesis* reflects his work in ancient Greek and Roman philosophical traditions from which Christian theology adopted and adapted many of its own practices.[28]

That said, this book *is* an academic work, an exercise in the scholarly discipline of constructive philosophical Christian theology. Rooted in critical reflection on the contents of Christian ideas and claims and informed by philosophical insights, it seeks to enable the articulation of theological positions that respond to the contemporary situation. One might, then, be tempted to read this book as a form of Tillichian correlationist theology in which culture provides the questions that theology must answer. Indeed, one might so position many (but by no means all) of the theological engagements with postmodernity insofar as "postmodernity" poses specific and distinctive challenges to which theology must respond.[29] But, for one thing, I do not accept the overly neat division—and the asymmetrical relationship—between "culture" and "theology" that such a reading seems to imply. As will be clear, I trust, from what follows, theology is embedded in culture and vice versa; indeed, I am not at all confident I could say where one starts and the other begins. For obvious historical reasons, what counts as Christian theology (concepts of God, Christ, sin, and the like)—even in its earliest forms—is redolent of the cultural context in which it came to be. In return, thanks to Christendom and its legacy, Christian concepts, figures, and tropes shape many aspects of contemporary culture, although often without being recognized as such. Christian theology is a form of cultural capital that is available not only to those who identify as Christian but also to anyone conversant with Christian-inflected contemporary culture.[30] Indeed, as I think we will see, Christian theology in that sense is in the cultural air we breathe, the cultural water we drink. It is, in fact, *this* form of Christian theology—Christian theology as cultural capital—that will be my focus. It is the theology in the air we breathe and the water we drink that I seek to bring to light and subject to critical (and constructive) reflection. But, as my comments above on *askesis* suggest, I hope, the kind of critical reflection that I will deploy is Foucauldian in several ways. For one, whatever constructive theological insights I offer in this text are as contingent as the context to which they seek to respond. That includes their relationship to modernity in all of its complexity. I would no more claim to have escaped its grasp than Foucault did. Like Foucault, I see this project as offering enlightenment and pursuing freedom, if you will, and such offers are made and pursuits are undertaken not by claiming to have escaped the conditions of modernity but by the *askesis* of plunging deeper into it and the questions of its putative end.

CHAPTER ONE

MAN AND HIS OTHERS

A History of the Present

Classical thought, and all the forms of thought that preceded it, were able
to speak of the mind and the body, of the human being, of how restricted
a place he occupies in the universe, of all the limitations by which his
knowledge of his freedom must be measured, but . . . not one of them was
ever able to know man as he is posited in modern knowledge. Renaissance
"humanism" and Classical "rationalism" were indeed able to allot human
beings a privileged position in the order of the world, but they were not
able to conceive of man.

—Michel Foucault

T HIS CHAPTER TRACKS the emergence and formative effects
of the fourfold of man and his others in modernity through the
work of the philosopher Michel Foucault. My reading of Foucault
takes off from his suggestion that much of his oeuvre could be taken as
various attempts at accounting for the emergence of the modern subject,
for whom he reserves the term "man."[1] The reading I offer of Foucault
herein shows that man's emergence is simultaneous with and made possible by the other elements of the fourfold: his sexed and raced others, his
animal other, and his divine other. I make this case by drawing together
Foucault's archaeological investigation into epistemic change in *The Order
of Things* and his genealogical investigations into the emergence of disciplinary power and biopower (specifically *Discipline and Punish*, the first
volume of his *History of Sexuality*, and certain of his recently published
lectures at the Collège de France). I also engage with the work of Foucauldian scholars who have critiqued, nuanced, and extended Foucault's
analyses. Together, these scholarly trajectories yield an account of modernity as *episteme* and *ethos*; that is, an order of knowing, doing, and being.
The modern *episteme* produces and comes to rely upon Man (capital-
ized henceforth when used in this specifically Foucauldian sense) as both

subject and object of knowledge, of external and self-discipline, and of normalization. As we will see, the fourfold is integral to Man's emergence at the center of the nexus of the particular forms of knowledge and power that constitute the warp and woof of the modern *episteme* and *ethos*.

Here, we begin in earnest the process of *askesis*, an undergoing I described in the introduction. Like the spiritual disciplines that *askesis* calls to mind, disciplined attention to the (un)makings tracked herein aims at transformation. Familiar (spatial and temporal) landmarks that have heretofore assured us of who we are and of our place in the world may recede from view, or our orientation to them may shift. The path by which the fourfold will emerge in what follows may seem indirect, at times. The elements of the fourfold are not signposts; they lack the regularity of form and appearance that characterizes interstate highway signage, for example. Nor do they appear all at once, fully formed and fully visible. Recall that I've described the fourfold as a hall of mirrors. What one sees reflected depends on where one stands; but what one sees is equally dependent on what lies outside one's immediate line of sight—including the other mirrors in the hall. This chapter tracks the fourfold's appearance and effects in relationship to the modern order first of *things* and then of *humanity*. Man comes to take center stage in each, but primarily in relationship to his divine and animal others in the first, and his raced and sexed others in the second. As I will show, however, these orders overlap. Tracing those overlaps will allow the reflective (and refractive) labor of the fourfold to come fully into view.

A few topographical reflections on how time will be (re)marked and space (re)made in and on this Foucauldian terrain to help (re)orient us. The shift from Renaissance to Classical to modern *epistemes* will be important in what follows. How exactly these *epistemes* map onto conventional periodizations of European history writ large is a question I will not address in any detail here or elsewhere. I do, however, want to alert the reader to certain features of *epistemes* and their relationship to time— and thus of epistemic change. Movement from one *episteme* into another happens piecemeal, here and there, in fits and starts, for the most part. Thus, although the terminology may be somewhat anachronistic, think of epistemic change as a matter of morphing from one to the other rather than of either gradual (logical, linear, or progressive) development or of radical endings and dramatic beginnings Some changes will seem minute indeed; comparable, perhaps, to the change in the size of beach dunes over the course of a week. Only to the attentive eye will the movement of sand from one spot to another be noticeable. In other cases, change seems more dramatic; seismic, even, we might say. In these cases, strikingly distinctive structures and concepts appear—and, with them, distinctive material practices of knowing, thinking, being, and doing. The conditions of epistemic change apply, as we'll see, to the fourfold itself as well as to the *episteme* in which it comes to be.

To speak of knowing and thinking as material practices may seem counterintuitive. After all, while the objects we know and think about are often material (books, paintings, plants, bugs, furniture), the frameworks and concepts by means of which knowing and thinking take place (which can become objects of knowing and thinking themselves) are not. At least, so common sense would seem to suggest. Foucault, however, would argue that the frameworks and concepts are not just means-by-which we study material (or nonmaterial) things; the frameworks and concepts produce what we know and think. I do not mean by this that by thinking about a rose, I can make one materialize out of nothing; rather, I mean that the framework within which I consider the rose will materially effect what I see as the rose; what features I highlight, which I ignore; and the meaning I find in those features. These material effects are not limited to the objects of knowing and thinking; they affect the one doing the knowing and thinking, as well. Epistemic shifts produce material changes in knowers and thinkers; in their relationships to what they know and how, in their sense of their place in the order of things and of humanity. The knower and thinker of the Renaissance (or Classical) *episteme* is not the knower and thinker of the modern *episteme*. For this reason, Foucault reserves the term, "man," for the modern knowing and thinking subject.[2]

Foucault also comes to see that knowledge is inseparable from power; not so much in the sense of the familiar adage, "knowledge is power" (i.e., the more we know, the more we can control) but in a much more pervasive sense. The production of knowledge, the framing of what is knowable, is one of the chief forms power takes. Understanding this requires that we think of power in more complex terms than we are used to. Power is not only—or even primarily—coercion or domination, nor is it solely the province of governments or judicial systems or their functionaries. Power operates on, in, and through the body politic writ large; through its institutions, to be sure, but also in, on, and through groups and individuals. Power is, then, first and foremost productive—of the subjects said to wield it (whether kings or scientists), of the objects said to bow to it (whether serfs, flora, or fauna), of the schemata that order them and their relations to one another. That includes human beings and the institutions that govern them, nourish and sustain them, oppress and constrain them. We come to be who we are in and through our interactions with one another and the institutions that shape our world. Those interactions can be malignant or benign, violent or gentle, but they are ubiquitous. We can and do capitulate, cooperate or resist, but capitulation, cooperation, and resistance are all part of the network of relations that constitutes power (it is, quite literally, a grid).[3]

Modernity as *Episteme*: The Order of Things

Originally published in French as *Les mots et les choses* (*Words and Things*), the explicit subject of *The Order of Things* is the human sciences—that is, those sciences that consider human beings as users and producers of language (e.g., philology), of labor and exchange (economics), and as occupiers of a particular place in the natural order (physiology, psychology, biology). These sciences do not appear out of a vacuum, of course; they are made possible by larger cultural shifts. It's tracing those cultural shifts—changes in the ways Europeans understood the relationship among things and, significantly, the relationship between words and things—that occupies the bulk of Foucault's analysis. And central to the account he offers is the emergence of the subject (and object) of the human sciences, Man. Indeed, one could argue that the primary artifact uncovered by this archaeological exercise is Man—as both knowing subject and known object.

But why speak of this project as an archaeology rather than a history? The English translation includes a foreword not present in the original French edition that tackles this question directly. *Order* is not, Foucault tells us, a project in the history of science—at least, as such projects are usually carried out (in France, anyway). Those projects take as their objects the "noble sciences, rigorous sciences, sciences of the necessary" and trace the progress of discovery while attending as well to what eluded scientists at a particular time.[4] They are, in other words, histories of the work of the scientific consciousness and its limits (construed as what it could not know at the time), which Foucault calls science's "unconscious." In these histories, science's unconscious is a negative; it is "that which resists [science], deflects it, or disturbs it."[5] *The Order of Things* differs on all counts. First of all, it includes in its scope academic disciplines, the human sciences, whose claim to the title "science" is contested. These "sciences" do not admit to the same regularity of method and purity of data that constitute mathematics or physics, for example; thus, whether their history constitutes a history of science is a matter of debate. Second, *The Order of Things* is a "comparative study"—that is, rather than remaining inside the boundaries of one scientific field, it considers together the sciences of language, human labor, and economic exchange, as well as of nature. Finally, *The Order of Things* reveals what Foucault calls the "positive unconscious" of the sciences: the largely unexamined and unthematized organizing principles, if you will, that enabled these fields to *produce* what they knew and how they knew it; a set of "rules of formation" shared by those studying nature, human labor and economic exchange, and language—largely unbeknownst to any of them.[6] Foucault adopts the term "archaeology" to describe his method of approach, and the term captures well what *The Order of Things* yields. Foucault unearths, if you will, an epistemological scaffolding erected in and by these fields of study that produced the artifacts they subjected to analysis and shaped the larger framework of that analysis.[7] That scaffolding (*episteme*) becomes visible only in hindsight. It is not the deliberate, intentional production of any particular scholar or field, but rather it reflects deep and lasting—even epochal—shifts in ways of knowing—that is, in ways of thinking, seeing, doing, and being.

From Nature to Life

Although Foucault does not thematize it this way, the fourfold is central to his account of the emergence of Man in *Order*. To be specific, shifts in the relationship between human and divine being, human and animal being, are part and parcel of the emergence of a new (modern) order of things out of its (Renaissance and Classical) predecessors. Within the Renaissance *episteme*, knowledge was essentially divination; discerning in things their place within a divinely established order. That order followed a logic of correspondences; the cosmos was a series of concentric mirrors linking God, human beings, the natural world, and language. So, the seven orifices on the human body reflected the seven planets (and vice versa). The nutritive systems of plants and animals both run from below ground to above (the venous system was thought to be rooted in the belly and directed primarily toward the heart and head). Earth's rocks are analogous to bones, its rivers to veins, and its bodies of salt water to a bladder. The same logic governed the relationship between language and the material world. Words named things because they were divinely endowed to correspond to the things they name. Emplaced in and by this logic were the elements of what would become the modern fourfold: human beings, animals, and divinity. Human beings were understood to reside in the middle of that set of concentric circles linking and separating not only heaven and earth but also animality and divinity. Like animals, they sense and labor. Like God, they know and speak. Their mediating role is reflected in their role as divinizers. Their ability to decipher the divinely ordained order in things and in language mirrors a divine power.

In the seventeenth and eighteenth centuries, this order of words and things begins to morph. A gap appears between God and the order of things and between words and things. Human beings—as knowers and namers—come to greater prominence. These changes are reflected in the emergence of new sciences—natural history and philology—whose very existence signifies the end of an order reflective of an eternal sameness to one disrupted by time and space. God remains the ultimate source of the order of things, but "nature" (*la nature*) comes to constitute the site where that order resides and "language" (*le langage*) the human tool used to communicate that order. Both are, to some extent, unruly objects of divine order insofar as nature and language are subject to time and thus change. Although ultimately nature's divinely oriented *telos* toward perfection will have its way, climate changes or natural disasters can take nature off course for a time. Both *telos* and its disruption will register on the surface of things: in the flowers or fruits plants produce (or fail to produce), in whether animals are pawed or hooved (and the changes thereto). Discerning the order implicit in nature is no longer a matter of divinization but now of the exercise of divinely given gifts of perception and judgment. Natural historians used those gifts to map the similarities and differences visible on the surface of things and thereby discern the order implicit in the ebbs and flows of nature.

Knowing in the Classical *episteme* is less secure than in the Renaissance. Relying on human judgment to find order increases the possibility for error. It is perhaps, then, no surprise that the process of knowing itself—of sense perceptions, of imagination, of memory, "all of that involuntary background which is, as it were, the mechanics of the image in time"—becomes an object of study after 1750.[8] So also the means of communicating knowledge: language. Words were no longer directly linked to things by divinely grounded correspondence, but by human perception and judgment. Like nature, language comes to be understood as affected by time and space. Hence, the emergence of the science of philology, the comparative study of language.

In the modern *episteme*, an order of things emerges that reflects shifts in all of these areas. "Life (*la vie*)" (*bios*) replaces "nature" as the space in which things are known; biology replaces natural history as the taxonomic order of things. Things are divided into organic and inorganic; things that are born, reproduce, and die and things that do not. If nature was primarily horizontal in orientation, life is primarily vertical. Whereas nature was a grid of visible similarities and differences, access to the similarities and differences among (especially living) things requires going beneath the visible surface and plumbing the depths below (think anatomy and dissection here). If nature provided a relatively stable space for taxonomies to reveal themselves to a knower with the requisite patience, the teeming profusion of the regional and relatively autonomous forms of being that comprise life fragments that space. The new order that arises is constituted by cleaner lines that distinguish (living) things from one another (e.g., vertebrates from invertebrates), but the spaces between things remains open—and necessarily so. Life is not only a taxonomic structure, but a force or power made manifest in things. The same force that propels a particular form of life in its sovereign autonomy, its discontinuity with other forms, also requires its communion with its larger environment. Living requires exchanges that cross the line separating any particular form of life's inside from its outside (think breathing and eating).

This new spatial schema entails and enables a reconfiguration of time, as well. "Natural history" is replaced with nature *as* history. It might seem that natural history and biology share the notion that things develop, but development's place in the larger order of things differs considerably in each. For natural historians, development revealed the complexity of the preordained order of nature. The development observed in any particular thing made manifest a teleology and temporality outside the thing itself. When finitude becomes the order of things, time and *telos* become internal and particular; each living thing bears within itself the (inherited) seeds of its own becoming and its own eventual demise.

The perception of the relationships among things and between words and things changes, as well. If the order of things in the Classical *episteme* was basically horizontal, the modern order of things is now vertical. Invisible to the things themselves, it requires the steady labor of a new kind of knower in order to appear. Comparison of similarities and differences continues to be key, but function becomes the category that gives them meaning. Discerning function requires plumbing the depths of things—not in search of a divinely ordained underlying ground of resemblance or an overarching developmental teleology but to find each thing's particularity.

From God to Man

If the Classical *episteme* brought human beings as knowers and namers closer to God (as source of order) than in the Renaissance, Man essentially replaces God in the modern *episteme*, according to Foucault. Man looks into the depths of things to determine what makes them tick. He brings order out of the chaotic mass of things in discerning the laws that govern the otherwise murky forces that produce things, exchanges, and words. In that sense, Man replaces God as the knowing subject. But Man is not God's equal. Man appears in the space hollowed out for him among living beings, objects of exchange, and words. On the one hand, he is counted among the living, he participates in exchanges, he uses words. In that sense, his place is among things; he is subject to the laws of nature, exchange, and language that constitute the modern order of things. On the other, as the one-who-knows things—and, more important, the order of things—he stands above and outside of things. According to Foucault, "Man, in the analytic of finitude, is a strange empirico-transcendental doublet, since he is a being such that one finds in him knowledge (*connaissance*) of that which renders all knowledge possible."[9]

The human sciences put Man's doubleness on display. Man is both the knowing subject and known object of these sciences; thus, he provides both their empirical data and knowledge and analysis of that data. In addition, the human sciences themselves follow the twin imperatives of the empirical and the transcendental. Economists track and aggregate the data of labor and exchange, drawing from this data observations about Man's economic behavior per se. Linguists track the content and rules of the languages Man uses, and from that data, seek to establish patterns of linguistic behavior per se. Physiologists track the data and function of our body's biological systems, and from that data seek to make projections about life span and vulnerability to disease. Thus, the human sciences are simultaneously grounded in the empirical and the transcendental. But Man also seeks to know *how* he knows and to understand the conditions that make knowing possible. This becomes the central project of modern philosophy from Descartes forward—with Kant as arguably its centripetal figure.

It might seem as though these two trajectories of knowledge—the empirical and the transcendental—could go on without any reference to or need for one another. Yet philosophy is from time to time pulled in the direction of empiricism (e.g., Comte) and the sciences of exchange, language, and life raise questions that they leave unanswered about the constitutive conditions of Man's existence. At the intersection of the empirical and the philosophical, certain specific human sciences appear: history, psychoanalysis, and ethnology (an early term for the study of specific peoples or *ethnoi*). These sciences take as their object of study the ones *who* exchange, speak, and live. They seek to give an account of *how and why* they exchange, speak, and live. What are the conditions that undergird and give rise to exchanging, speaking, and living?

Each of these sciences highlights the ramifications of the analytic of finitude for knowing Man and knowing what Man can know. Ethnology exposes Man's finitude by demonstrating to him the variety of social schemata that both found and limit his knowing, being, and doing. Neither mere chronology or the tracing of the outworking of providence (both notions of considerable antiquity), modern history embodies the analytic of finitude as *historicity* comes to constitute the very being of life, labor, and language. Despite its relatively late provenance, Foucault gave to psychoanalysis a privileged spot among the human sciences. In investigating what lies at the edges of law, labor, and language, it lays claim to an account of what gives rise to them. And that account—centered as it is in death and desire—is particularly redolent of the analytic of finitude.

Thus, Man's ability to know is simultaneously heightened and called into question in the modern *episteme*. Before, not knowing was nothing more than the occasional failure to see correctly. In the modern *episteme*, not knowing structures knowing. Yes, the sheer variety of things presents an enormous challenge to knowledge; that so much of what makes things what they are is hidden from immediate view presents another challenge.

But more to the point, the knower himself is constituted by built-in limits. Man's knowing-about depends on elements that are anterior in space and time to his knowing; any particular instance of knowing is contingent on "the spatiality of the body, the yawning of desire, and the time of language," as Foucault puts it.[10] Man understands himself as fixed in and by time and space. That fixation constitutes simultaneously the conditions required to know anything at all and the *limits* of knowing (things *and* the order of things), even as it prompts the desire to know more and better. In turn, the specific limits of his knowledge—the conditions specific to human finitude—become objects of study themselves. Thus, a vertiginous quality attends not only the project of trying to know *life* in all of its forms but also—and perhaps especially—the life of the one-who-knows, Man. The truth of Man—the truth of truth—remains caught in this constant oscillation between the empirical and the transcendental in the modern *episteme*, Foucault claims. We make repeated attempts to escape it, to bring it to an end—most notably, by positing experience as that to which our knowing must be accountable. But even *this* turn turns back on itself; experience, after all, is situated and sedimented. Man is, then, both product and project of constant speculation and specularization; caught in a hall of mirrors reflecting himself back to himself and in so doing, reconstituting himself as (un)grounded ground of knowing.

Of the elements of the fourfold, my account of *The Order of Things* has focused primarily on the roles played by Man and his divine other in and as the genesis of the modern *episteme*. They are hardly alone in this hall of mirrors, however. It is noteworthy that an encounter with textual animals—Borges's description of a taxonomy of animals he claims to have found in "a certain Chinese encyclopedia"—helped launch Foucault down the line of inquiry that became *The Order of Things*.[11] More to the point, however, one hallmark of the shift from the Classical to the modern *episteme* is the displacement of plants as emblematic of the natural order in favor of animals. In the Classical *episteme*, Foucault argues, plants were paradigmatic of the order of things—and one can understand why. The plant wore its place in nature on its sleeve, so to speak. The shape of its branches, leaves, flowers, and fruit rendered it "a pure and transparent object for thought as tabulation [*pensée en tableau*]," Foucault writes. But once being is conceived in terms of *bios* and finitude, animals come to the fore because "the animal maintains itself at the borders of life and death [*aux confins de la vie et de la mort*]."[12] Animality is constituted by finitude in the form of threats from the outside (predators and the like) and from the inside. Whatever its immediate cause, death overtakes the organism from within, ultimately from its innermost depths.

The fourfold is a hall of mirrors, recall, in which reflections not only multiply but also reflect and refract one another. Indeed, it is that refraction that produces Man, that empirico-transcendental doublet. Within the modern *episteme*, then, animals come to take up their place as one of Man's mirrors—one in which Man sees himself reflected as both like and unlike his image. Like animals, Man lives and dies; unlike animals, Man *knows* that he lives and dies.

Modernity as *Episteme* and *Ethos*: Ordering Humanity

These reflections and refractions set the stage for the emergence of the element of the fourfold that has yet to make its appearance: Man's raced and sexed others. Tracing its emergence requires moving from one Foucauldian method of doing *histoire* (archaeology) to another (genealogy). It will take us into certain of Foucault's genealogical projects and beyond them to work by other scholars inspired by that method and those texts. Foucault takes the term "genealogy" from Nietzsche. Genealogies track the descent or lineage of something or someone—a particular person or family, or in Foucault's hands, sexuality, the prison, the asylum. As is often the case with its more commonplace cousin, the family tree, Foucault's genealogies belie any claim to purity of origin or inevitability of destiny. They trace the generally a-teleological—even random—events that eventually consolidate in the present object of interest. That Foucault's genealogies focus on sites where morality matters is not coincidental, given genealogy's Nietzschean roots. Like Nietzsche's genealogy of morals, Foucault's genealogies undo the pieties in the *histoires* we have come to tell ourselves about who we are and how we got here.[13]

Foucault describes the doing of genealogy as a practice of disciplined and patient attention to what (actually) was in all its messiness. Thus, the turn off the archaeological path and onto the genealogical continues our process of *askesis* as tracing and tracking (un)makings described in the introduction. That turn will offer us the opportunity to consider the modern *episteme* as *ethos*, as an epochal shift that, by producing new ways of knowing, produced as well new ways of individual and collective being and doing. Life, it will turn out, is not only something Man seeks to know, but also something Man seeks to manage.

To this point, we have marked Man's emergence as (a certain kind of) knower as a correlate to changes in the order of things, but people are more than knowers; they are workers, family members, citizens, students, and patients. These ways of knowing, doing, and being were produced by and remain embedded in systems and institutions large and small that are distinctively modern. Those systems and institutions also produced and continue to rely on the taxonomies of human beings that code for what we know as "race" and "sexuality." Becoming a modern subject requires taking up one's (proper) place in relationship to those taxonomies, a project coextensive with modernity's goal of not just knowing but managing life—especially human life. A specific form of power (and knowledge) emerges to serve that end, which Foucault dubs biopower.[14] In target and in form and aspect, biopower differentiates itself from those forms that predate and are marshaled to serve it, which Foucault calls sovereign power and disciplinary power. Directing itself at "man-as-living-being," biopower seeks to manage and cultivate (human) life.[15] In its manifestation as biopolitics, it enlists sovereign and disciplinary power in the service of this aim. As we'll see, the fourfold channels modern forms of power and knowledge giving shape to modern biopolitics.

To this point, I have used these terms *sexuality* and *race* as though their meanings were self-evident and singular—in themselves and in the work of Foucault and those who engage him on these topics. Nothing could be farther from the truth. That I could do so reflects a long and troubled history that all of these works interrogate and lay bare in various dimensions. That history is not unrelated to the insights Foucault offers in *The Order of Things*, as we shall see. Epistemic shifts—particularly the shift into modernity—are integral to the meanings and social force that race and sexuality have assumed. Race and sexuality have become axes in a modern taxonomic structure that attempts to contain and constrain human beings in all their variety (or at least as much variety as our taxonomies acknowledge). Like those discussed in *The Order of Things*, the effects of this taxonomic structure are more than epistemological; rather, this classificatory grid materially affects our being and doing as well as our seeing and knowing.

Of course, differentiating between human beings on grounds that read as "sexual" or "racial" to us is not unique to modernity—or to the West, at that.[16] Nor is it the case that only in modernity do some deem themselves superior to others on those grounds.[17] Morphological differences like skin color, genital configuration, and eye shape, for example, were deemed socially and politically significant well before modernity's advent. As was the case with the modern order of things, so too the modern order of human beings is not created *ex nihilo*, but rather it reflects a morphing of what precedes it into something different.[18] This order arises as a result of a confluence of factors and practices and serves a variety of ends. That race and sexuality are the taxonomic axes and vectors of identity formation that we take them to be is an effect of the modern *episteme*; both of what it repurposes from its past and what it invents. As with the modern order of living things, the modern order of humanity runs deep, not just wide. Surface differences index deeper features of who we are—that is, the features intimately linked to and redolent of finitude.

Empowering Modernity

The crucial differences between modern race and sexuality and their predecessors are a manifestation of biopower's formative impact, so I begin by delineating it in relationship to its predecessors. All three forms of power saturate the social fabric in which they are embedded. That is, each operates through a network that not only links state and citizen or ruler and ruled, but also runs throughout the various institutions that make up a given social context (e.g., its systems of government, jurisprudence, commerce, education, its families). They differ from one another in important ways, however. Sovereign power, Foucault argues, concentrated power in the hands of a monarch who, together with his (or her) subjects *en masse*, comprised the sovereign's corporate body. Within that system, power took the form primarily of domination (power over)—a power that granted to the monarch the right to kill his or her subjects, a power exhibited in particularly graphic form in public executions. The account of the drawing and quartering of a would-be regicide that opens Foucault's genealogy of disciplinary power, *Discipline and Punish*, places sovereign power on graphic display. As Foucault notes therein, executions play an important role in the maintenance of the sovereign corporate body. If the point were to simply eliminate the threat posed by the would-be assassin, any form of killing would do—and there would be no need for public spectacle. But simply eliminating an immediate threat isn't the point; it is the (re)assertion of the king's power over the corporate body he forms with his subjects. Execution as (tortuous) spectacle reminds the king's subjects of their proper place, as, *en masse*, subject to his (absolute) rule and his (absolute) will. Subjects matter only in the collective, not individually; the specific body being drawn and quartered could just as easily be another.

Biopower's other predecessor, disciplinary power, is more diffuse and seemingly benign than sovereign power, as evidenced in the emergence of the modern prison. As drawing and quartering is to sovereign power, so incarceration is to disciplinary power. Although both ultimately target the larger social body through specific individuals, incarceration replaces the individual's public destruction with his or her (quite literal) re-formation through various disciplinary practices and techniques evident in its architecture, its social structure, and its treatment of prisoners. The French title of *Discipline and Punish, Surveiller et punir*, provides an important clue to a major aspect of disciplinary power: surveillance. Prison advocate (and philosopher) Jeremy Bentham designed the ideal prison as a panopticon. At its center he envisioned a round tower inhabited by guards with visual access to each and every cell arranged in rings around the tower. The architecture is echoed in the practice of interrogation—aimed (within the prison) not at determining guilt or innocence but at unearthing and treating the underlying cause of criminal behavior, delinquency, and undertaken by scientists and doctors expert in it rather than lawyers and judges. Punishment, in other words, is directed toward rehabilitation, toward the ultimate restoration of the prisoner to the larger social body. Rehabilitation might start with the external imposition of discipline (enforcing a set schedule of interrogation, work, and other edifying activities), but the press from outside aims to arouse and instill self-knowledge and self-discipline. Success means adapting oneself to carceral existence: internalizing delinquency as one's self-identity, working to re-form oneself by conforming to prison discipline, becoming what Foucault calls a "docile body [*un corps docile*]."[19] The carceral system may exemplify disciplinary power, but its reach extends throughout modernity's social fabric; its dominance was cemented with the rise of industrial capitalism and republican democracies. Its exercise permeates not only prisons and the military but also schools, the workplace, and the domestic sphere. The docile bodies that disciplinary power aims to produce are ideally suited to those systems and the institutions in which they are embedded and to a context constituted by democracy, industrialism, and capitalism.

The term *docile body* should not be taken to suggest a nascent mind–body dualism—either in Foucault's analysis or in the disciplinary regime itself. Rather, the body serves as the route to the mind (or, better, the self). Regulating bodily location and regularizing movement—whether in the prison, the dormitory, or the factory—is a process of re-formation that works on the self through the body. One comes to be a model prisoner, a proper schoolboy, an efficient worker through in-corporation, internalizing disciplined movements into one's own embodied routine until they become second nature. Consider the origins of the factory assembly line, for example. Time and motion studies were employed to determine the precise bodily movements needed to manufacture the most products in the least time with the fewest workers. Would-be workers subjected themselves to a rigorous regime that taught them to move in these precise ways, thus producing the specific docile body—man-the-(literal) machine ["*L'Homme-machine*"], Foucault says—suited to the specific task at hand.[20] But think as well of a seemingly utterly benign setting, the school. Students learn not only "reading, writing, and arithmetic," as we say, they are schooled in the (self-)discipline of sitting quietly at a desk, of raising a hand to speak, of working in solitary silence or in cooperative groups.

While it conscripts sovereign power and disciplinary power into its service (and torques them in the process), biopower is distinct in target, form, and aspect from both of its predecessors. In lieu of the sovereign's right to kill, biopower pursues its goal of managing life by enabling some to live while allowing others to die. If disciplinary power yielded "an anatomo-politics of the human body," biopower yields "a biopolitics of the human race."[21] Exercising sovereignty now in the name of the people rather than the king, biopower works on and through the individual (aided and abetted by disciplinary power). Its ultimate targets are populations, its aim the survival and flourishing of the (human) race.

Biopower thus reveals its roots in the modern *episteme*. The (human) race is a form of life; it is constituted, like all modern life forms, by historicity and finitude, by its own internal teleology. For the race to flourish, we must know what makes human beings live and what causes them to die; thus, biopower issues in new forms of knowledge (e.g., statistics and statistical analysis) and bends other forms (e.g., physiology) to its will. These forms of knowledge create new objects of knowledge (rates of birth, disease, and death) that are, in turn, tracked within and across populations. These ways of knowing become ways of (individual and collective) doing and being, as well, as disease is medicalized and public health is pursued. Draining swamps and planning cities, mounting campaigns to prevent disease and treating disease (in the modern clinic, hospital, or asylum) all manifest biopower's aim to manage life so the race will flourish.[22]

Biopower's interest in managing life manifests in a new relationship to death, as well. Death recedes from the public into the private realm; a reflection, Foucault suggests, of sovereign power's demotion, if you will, by biopower. Instead of a transition from the power of one sovereign to another (from the monarch to God), death now constitutes the outer limit of life and thus of biopower's reach. But biopower stretches itself as far as it can toward its limit—to extend life (for some, at least) but also to manage dying in ways that serve the race. Biopower thus colludes with sovereign power to consign certain people to death either by passively standing by (e.g., allowing disease to run its course in certain populations) or by actively targeting certain populations (think eugenics)—those deemed to threaten the flourishing of the race—for extinction.[23] As LaDelle McWhorter argues, modern (biopolitical) racism is first and foremost a racism *for*. In the name of nurturing the (human) race by eliminating what threatens it, it activates and animates racisms *against* certain human populations. Modern race and sexuality, then, will turn out to be more than vectors of identity; they are also crucial conduits for modern (biopolitical) racisms both for *and* against. Tracing their genealogy will take us back through some of the temporal and spatial terrain traversed in the previous chapter. Because many of its more important developments occurred in Europe's (former) colonies—including the United States—we will travel to certain of those locations, as well.

Modern (Race and?) Sexuality: A Genealogy

Ten years after the publication in France of *Les mots et les choses*, Foucault published the introduction to what he originally envisioned as a six-volume work on the history of sexuality.[24] The introduction was entitled—tellingly, for our purposes—*La volonté de savoir* (The will to know). There is a kind of double—or even triple—entendre to the French title. As I noted earlier, the book takes its mark from its contemporary setting; it puts in question the narrative about sex that had become commonplace in the sixties and the seventies. At the time, we claimed to be finally liberating sex—and thus ourselves—from a long period of repression initiated by our Victorian forebears. They didn't want us *talking* about sex, much less engaging in it—beyond the amount and type needed for the reproduction of legitimate offspring; indeed, they didn't want us to *know* much about sex *at all*. Repression served the needs of the labor market well (by ensuring a steady stream of workers), but it was not healthy. Thank goodness we had begun to recognize that fact and rouse ourselves from this slumber.

Foucault dubs this narrative "the repressive hypothesis," and proceeds to challenge all of its assumptions. Instead of a will not to know, Foucault documents a pervasive will *to* know. In place of a repressive silence, Foucault documents the proliferation of speech. The procreative married couple is of considerable interest, but what Foucault called the *dispositif de sexualité*[25] extends its gaze well beyond their bedroom to those of their children and, further, to adults whose erotic investments and adventures are not confined to the marital bed. The *dispositif's* interest is indeed aimed at containment and control, but in the service of ends other than the production of laborers.

One of biopower's chief manifestations and products is what Foucault calls *scientia sexualis*, the science of sexuality, a peculiarly modern and Western creation. This science essentially produces "sexuality" as both its object of study and as the essence of who human beings are. Distinct from the science of reproduction (although dependent on it for legitimacy), *scientia sexualis* renders sex "not only a matter of sensation and pleasure, of law and taboo, but also of truth and falsehood"—that is, a particular form of knowledge.[26] That form of knowledge should look all too familiar to readers of *The Order of Things;* although Foucault didn't name it as such, *scientia sexualis* bears all of the hallmarks of a human science—one centered on the empirico-transcendental doublet that is Man. Pursuing the truth of sex required empirical knowledge (of bodies, what they did, and with whom or what), but that knowledge alone did not constitute the truth of sex. Locating that truth is no easy task, it turns out. The truth of sexuality is hidden from view—not only or in the first place from those who would study it but also from those who embody it. Getting sexuality to tell its truth was seen to require elaborate mechanisms of inquiry, including interrogation (and its counterpart, confession) and deeper bodily investigations. This research eventually produced sexuality's truth in several forms: as a complex taxonomy of the various forms sexuality takes (constructed along the axes "perverse" and "normal"); as a corresponding set of sexual personages or characters;[27] and, finally, as the most intimate aspect of who we are, the most foundational, and the most unruly. Like the modern order of things, *scientia sexualis* both reorders the old and invents the new. Erotic desires, acts, and objects, of course, had been around for quite a while, and they were sometimes organized by an identitarian logic in other times or places and according to other taxonomies.[28] *Scientia sexualis* reorders these elements into a new taxonomy that eventually coalesces as a distinctive understanding of subjectivity. Sexual acts express desires that reside in and arise out of the depths of our selves. Sexuality is who—and what—we are. Modern subjectivity *is* sexual subjectivity.

Recall, however, that biopower's ultimate interest isn't merely taxonomic; it is productive and functional. It seeks to nurture the evolution of the (human) race. Because "sexuality exists at the place where body and population meet," Foucault writes, it proved to be a useful tool in both positive and negative racisms.[29] If biopower and sovereign power came together at the boundary between life and death, biopower and disciplinary power joined forces in the formation and management of the *dispositif de sexualité*. Together, they subject sexuality to both discipline and regulation: discipline for the sake of the individual (to prevent the consequences of debauchery), regulation for the sake of the species (because debauchery begets degeneracy, which in turn begets more debauchery). Medicine becomes the key technology for disciplining and regulating sexuality. Via the *dispositif de sexualité*, itself animated by *scientia sexualis*, biopower produced a population of sexualized subjects subjected to and by a therapeutic regime aimed at securing individual, familial, and societal health through the proper management of sexuality.

Going deeper into the introduction to Foucault's history of sexuality may have given us insights into modern *sexuality*'s biopolitical origins, but it seems to have offered us no insight (yet) into those of modern race. That might not surprise some readers, especially in theology. Those familiar with the groundbreaking work of Cornel West in *Prophesy Deliverance* or womanist theologian Kelly Brown Douglas in *Sexuality and the Black Church* are certainly well aware that Foucault's work can be productively *applied* to issues of race and raced sexuality, but both West and Brown Douglas had to turn to other resources to develop the potent genealogies of U.S. race and racism that are central to their projects.[30] For one thing, as Douglas notes, Foucault's eyes are firmly fixed on Europe. Shifting one's gaze to the United States—or, as we shall see, to other European colonies—requires frameworks and knowledge specific to those locales. Moreover, although race puts in a frequent appearance in *History of Sexuality, Vol. I*, the text of Foucault's that figures most prominently in Brown Douglas's work, it does not get anything close to the microscopic attention that sexuality receives. Nor is Foucault specifically concerned with the black–white divide that is Brown Douglas's focus. Thus, she can assert with some justification that Foucault "virtually ignores" race therein.[31]

More recently, however, a number of scholars (including theologian J. Kameron Carter) have argued that placing *History of Sexuality, Vol. I* in conversation with lectures Foucault gave at the Collège de France around the time that he was writing that volume requires reevaluating race's significance to that project.[32] Published in France in 1997 and in English translation in 2003, we now have access to carefully edited transcripts of those lectures (previously available in their entirety only on audiotape in a Paris research library).[33] The lectures collected in the first volume (entitled "Society Must Be Defended") are those particularly closely linked in time and subject matter to *History of Sexuality, Vol. I*. In them, Foucault traces a genealogy of modern (European) racism as both the goal and product of biopower and biopolitics and sexuality serves as its central axis. Recent work by philosopher LaDelle McWhorter and anthropologist Ann Laura Stoler allows us to see what can happen when Foucault's analytic frames enriched by material from the lectures are engaged anew in analyses of race and sexuality in Europe's colonies and in the United States. Singly and together, these scholars perform a valuable service for my project (and for Foucauldian studies) in providing both erudite and, in some instances, critical readings of his work on these matters and, most important, in nuancing, developing, and extending that work in directions that Foucault did not fully pursue or see.

Beyond Intersectionality

It has become commonplace to speak of the relationship between race and sexuality (along with other vectors of identity like gender and class) in terms of "intersectionality." Intersectionality, however, hardly begins to describe the deeply intertwined nature of sexuality's relationship to race in modernity's racisms both for and against, LaDelle McWhorter observes in *Racism and Sexual Oppression in Anglo-America: A Genealogy*. Although her focus is on the United States, the genealogy she reconstructs begins where colonialism originates: in Europe. Before the Classical era, "the races" referred to peoples who shared a common ancestry, history, and language. So, for example, in Britain after the Norman Conquest, the Normans and the Saxons were considered races. The Saxons justified their umbrage against the Normans—using what Foucault calls "race war" discourse—not via a natural superiority signaled by morphological differ- ence, but on the basis of the enemy's presence where it did not belong. It was simply not right that the Normans should occupy Saxon land.[34]

That race became a morphological category—based in observable dif- ferences in skin color, eye shape, and hair texture, for example—reflects the work of Classical natural historians, McWhorter argues. The natural historian Linnaeus notes that, like all species, the human species comes in varieties—four, to be precise: Americanus, Europaeus, Asiaticus, and Africanus. In keeping with the Classical *episteme*, he reads this taxonomy off of differences manifest on the surface of human beings (skin color, hair texture, eye shape). Like variations in any other species, they index not deep differences in character, lineage, or status (as they will later), but differences in geography and climate. (In fact, Linnaeus does not use the term *race* for these variations.) Kant provides the key turning point in emergent modern morphological race and (positive and negative) racisms. Noting skin color's resistance to change upon moving from one climate or locale to another, Kant posits morphological differences as immutable and characterological. They may be reinforced by climate and geography, but they are fundamentally hereditary, he claims. Where Linnaeus saw (four) natural variations, Kant sees (four) *races* ("white," "Negro" and two oth- ers whose names and content vary[35]) that he ranks in order of relative superiority and inferiority.[36]

Although Kant represents a crucial turning point, seventeenth-century colonial Virginia—not Europe—is really the birthplace of modern mor- phological and political race and racism, McWhorter argues. The con- cerns that drove this transformation in the discourse and practice of race were political and economic, not simply epistemological, and manifest the mutual imbrication of power and knowledge. Virginia's elite employed racialized discourses and practices to divide and conquer the laboring classes. The planter class deployed race war discourse to sow seeds of division and distrust (and thus undercut any sense of solidarity) between laborers of European lineage and their counterparts of African descent.[37]

They restricted the right of self-defense and the right to vote to those of European descent, a practice justified by an emergent doctrine of the superiority of Europeans to Africans signaled by morphological differences. Institutionalized in law and its enforcement as well as in more informal modes of interaction, (morphological) race and (morphological and political) racism mutually (in-)formed one another as ways of knowing and doing became ways of being.

But these forms of race and racism are not yet fully the concept of race—or the practice of racism—so critical to the modern *episteme* and *ethos*. Biopolitical race and racism, McWhorter argues, required the historicizing of the human organism as a form of *life* (*bios*) defined by its function and possessed of its own internal and natural momentum that develops, declines, and eventually dies; a pattern of development and decline that can be tracked and normed. By the 1850s, McWhorter argues, "the absorption of race into function and development, was complete."[38] By providing channels for weeding out deviance, biopolitical race and the racisms that it underwrote were now ready to serve biopower's goal of preserving the (human) race.

Not only was the ideology and practice of modern race and racism biopolitical; so, too, were its effects. The exemplars of humanity, it turned out, were primarily to be found in a limited segment of it: those of northern European ancestry. Constituting the core of what eventually became the white race (in the United States), "the Nordics," as McWhorter calls them, justified their exemplary status on the basis of their accomplishments.[39] It was this race, after all, that was responsible for the great achievements of the modern era, including industrialization, capitalism, and democracy. Surely, then, the Nordic race was destined to continue its steady march of progress and to ever more firmly establish its dominance over the inferior races. These races, so the story went, eventually would die off—victims of their own inherent weaknesses, vulnerabilities, and excesses. But, in the meantime, they represented a threat that needed to be managed, if not eradicated. Thus, racism *for* issued in racism *against*—against the abnormal. Sin against the sovereign, if you will, is replaced by failure to measure up to the norm. Although abnormals were certainly to be found among the Nordics (indeed, McWhorter shows that Nordic abnormals were the first targets of this form of racism), they constituted a much higher proportion of the other races: the Irish, and people of African, Asian, and southern European descent (including Jews and Catholics).[40] Thus, it wasn't long at all before these races became targeted *as* abnormal and were subjected to the more vicious and violent forms of biopower. The abnormal was to be slowly but surely eliminated—allowed to die off in most cases, but more actively pursued where necessary through practices like lynching and forced sterilization.

Although abnormality purportedly manifested in a variety of ways (laziness, wastefulness, weak constitutions, intellectual ineptitude), erotic desires and behavior—what we now call "sexuality"—came to be seen as its principle symptom and as the chief source of danger to the Nordic race. Abnormality manifested itself most markedly as excessive sexual desire, wrongly directed desire, and the inappropriate behaviors that issued therefrom. Thus, sexuality became a primary mechanism through which abnormality was managed—that is, discovered and contained or eliminated and guarded against in the first place. The emergent human sciences became agents of biopolitical racism as individual human beings were essentially dissected into parts and systems and subjected to measurement and assessment. Scientists measured the size and shape of noses and of genitalia, the angle and shape of foreheads and of skulls; they developed ratios of arm length to body length and leg stride to leg length. Large flat noses and protruding foreheads signaled inferior intellect and stunted development—findings "confirmed" by tests that measured one's "intelligence quotient." The size of one's genitalia was correlated with the degree of one's femininity or masculinity. Lesbian genitalia were determined to be oversized, a reflection in their case of sexual inversion (an overdose of masculinity) and issuing in their failure to conform to heteronormative familial and social norms. The genitalia of people of African descent were also purportedly larger than "normal," a "fact" that corresponded with their allegedly outsized sex drive. Bodily abnormality reflected abnormal desire, and both in turn issued in social abnormality—families that failed to live up to the norm, thus in turn (re-)producing a new generation of abnormal bodies with abnormal desires.

Of course, those well versed in critical race theory in various fields will recognize many of these phenomena. As Carter has reminded us, the sciences of phrenology and physiognomy were at the heart of Cornel West's genealogy of modern racism (itself inspired methodologically in part by Foucault).[41] The significance of genitalia (and other sexualized body parts) is nowhere more visible than in the case of the so-called Hottentot Venus (Saatjie Baartman), powerfully analyzed as early as 1985 by Sander

Gilman (and a case to which we'll return in chapter 2).[42] And, of course, Angela Davis and others established some decades ago the centrality of the claim that people of African descent possess (or, better, are possessed by) an outsized sex drive to racist ideology and practice from slavery forward. Moreover, that racism in all of its manifold forms was established and maintained to serve the cause of white supremacy is an insight all of these earlier accounts of modern racism share, as well.

McWhorter's analysis confirms and deepens these insights particularly by tracking the history of U.S. racism (for and against) in minute detail, a history in which eugenics is prominent. Originally imported into the United States from Europe, eugenic science and the managerial practices it undergirded had much in common with those used in Nazi Germany. Indeed, the term *racism* was coined to distinguish U.S. eugenics from Hitlerian eugenics, she notes. Hitlerian eugenics were "racist" because they sought to promote one race (Aryans) at the expense of others. U.S. eugenicists sought to distance themselves from Hitler by claiming that they sought to promote normalcy regardless of race. What we have come to think of as the "normal family," an economically secure unit made up of mom, dad, and their (well-adjusted) kids, replaced the Aryan race as the explicit target of population management. It was also the primary mechanism through which normality was nurtured and protected—among the Nordics and their descendants, at any rate. The normal family may seem a racially neutral target, but given political and economic realities (also manifestations of modern racism), it wasn't—especially in the first two-thirds of the twentieth century, McWhorter argues. Attributed to an inherent lack of fitness, failures by black or immigrant families to measure up to the standard of normalcy reflected a political and economic system—itself a manifestation of modern racism—aligned against them in multiple ways.

It is important to remember, though, that just being descended from Nordics was no guarantee of normality; the presence of the poor and the perverse among them was proof of that. Nor did lineage provide any immunity from degeneracy.[43] That danger faced Nordics and their descendants at every turn and sexuality was a particular site of vulnerability. Thus, marriage—and sex within marriage—became a particular target of biopower and biopolitics. American eugenicists and their intellectual descendants sought to encourage reproductive marriage between Nordics of "good stock" (and discourage it otherwise) via antimiscegenation laws and the forced sterilization or institutionalization of unfit Nordics.

Containing, managing, and cultivating "healthy" sexuality within "good stock" marriages became a key aspect of biopower and biopolitics. Achieving and maintaining sexual and emotional satisfaction for both marital partners was deemed critical not only to reproductive life but also to productive life; to the stability of the family unit and of the state; and, ultimately, to the progress of the race.

Incorporating Modernity: Managing Life in the Colonies

So far, I have focused my account of the emergence of modern race and racisms at the macro-level, both conceptually (biopower) and mechanically (*scientia sexualis* and biopolitics writ large). Central to those dynamics is a differentiation between "us" and "them" that centers on sexuality as distinguishing the normal from the abnormal, the degenerate from the healthy (in body, mind, and morality). *Signs and Wonders*, however, is a project in a particular form of *askesis*—of slow, disciplined attention to processes of (un)making in which we are entrained. Fulfilling the promise inherent in that project requires moving from the macro- to the micro-level, to an inquiry into the inculcation and incorporation of biopower by those under its sway. I begin that turn here by way of the work of a another scholar whose work both critiques and expands Foucault's insights: the anthropologist and (post)colonial theorist Ann Laura Stoler. Like a number of scholars of (post)colonialism, Stoler has been engaged with and by Foucault's work since the early nineties. She is hardly alone in finding Foucault's oeuvre to be remarkably generative—even more so, in her case, with the recovery of the Collège de France lectures.[44] Like Brown Douglas, however, she found Foucault's Eurocentrism—which, the reader will recall, persists in the lectures—troubling and limiting, although the specific arena of her concern differs. The genealogies of race and racism offered in the lectures make only passing (if suggestive) reference to Europe's imperial adventures, in her view. What would come into sight, she wondered, if one considered Foucault's genealogy of race (and sexuality) from the perspective of the history of colonialism? The fruits of that labor are borne out in *Race and the Education of Desire: Foucault's* History of Sexuality *and the Colonial Order of Things* and *Carnal Knowledge and Imperial Power: Race and the Intimate in Colonial Rule*. Her years of study of Dutch colonial archives coupled, in *Carnal Knowledge*, with recent ethnographic research among Javanese who were formerly domestic workers in Dutch colonial households, provide for a deep, thoughtful, and sometimes critical engagement with Foucault on these matters.

Turning to European colonial projects that parallel in time McWhorter's America broadens yet further our knowledge of the repertoire of race and sexuality in modernity. It returns us as well to an exploration of the role of the family in modern (biopolitical) racism for Stoler's analysis focuses on "the intimate"—the realm of the domestic, the quotidian. Who slept with whom (and where), the children produced by such unions (or lack thereof), the practices by which families and households were constituted or denied constitution were arguably the central sites for the production and management of (flesh and blood) men and their (flesh and blood) sexed and raced others in colonial contexts. As we'll see, there are a number of parallels between the colonies and the United States.

That European colonialization was a racist enterprise and the policing of sexual and familial mores and practices a major focus of colonial regimes is certainly well documented. But it is commonly assumed, Stoler argues, that these aspects of colonialism were European exports imported lock, stock and barrel into the colonies and imposed on the colonized. Against that commonplace view, Stoler argues that the colonies were "laboratories of modernity" in which what became central features of the modern order were worked out.[45] She describes an open circuit between metropole and colony where currencies of various sorts circulated. A major project and product of this exchange is what Stoler calls "the bourgeois self."[46] Race and sexuality are central axes of its construction, a task that invoked colonized (raced and sexed) others as simultaneously support and threat to this subject's making and securing. Thus, she calls the colonies "taxonomic states" whose administrators were charged with defining and policing the lines demarcating the European colonizer from his others.[47] For a number of reasons, as we shall see, those lines were more often confounding and contested than clear; they made for permeable and even fluid boundaries. Thus, the taxonomy intended to structure colonial society was never entirely stable; one's location within it could shift and change as the taxonomic categories themselves shifted and changed in tandem with the larger sociopolitical context. Yet it always served the same goals: marking out the colonizer from the colonized, the rightfully dominant from the rightfully subordinate. And the organization of sexual, family, and affective life was essential to that project whatever form it took.

Colonialist taxonomies organized the populations of a given colony—both indigenous and imported—by taking a number of features into account. Somatic color was among them, but only and always as interlaced with national background, class status, lineage, and gender. Being of Dutch parentage and white skin was not sufficient for one to count unequivocally as European, for example, in the Dutch Indies. Poverty or indigency signaled a lack of self-mastery, which called into question a Dutch male's claim to manhood. A Dutch woman involved in a sexual relationship (licit or not) lost her status as European—legally, when and where mixed marriages were allowed, by reputation otherwise. At certain points in the history of the Dutch Indies, Japanese, African, and Chinese immigrants counted as "Europeans" over against the Javanese.[48] And children born of one Dutch and one native parent—no matter what they looked like—created particular concern and consternation for colonial authorities.

Together, all of this illustrates that race in the taxonomic state was more than skin deep. To the degree that skin color mattered, it was as an (often unreliable) index of the true locus of race, character. Yet, character was neither directly visible nor directly accessible in itself; it was made manifest in one's way of living, of behaving. Racial taxonomies themselves are forged (made and made up) out of all of these factors—gender, class, lineage, character, behavior—taken as vectors of an underlying essence. To the degree that the categories themselves change—along with the criteria for determining the category to which one belonged—racial taxonomies, the identities that comprise them, and the lines that separate one from another, are revealed as projects and projections rather than straightforward and disinterested descriptions. This is true of European colonials, the primary target of taxonomic denomination, as well as their (raced, sexed, and) colonized others.

As in the United States, sexuality in the taxonomic colonized state served as both race's central manifestation and as a mechanism for managing (or attempting to manage) colonial populations. On the basis of her extensive research in colonial archives, Stoler argues that no single aspect of colonial life received more (anxious) attention from colonial administrators than sexuality. Central to the colonial order of things was who *should* sleep with whom. This proved an unruly business at best; indeed, managing the consequences of who *actually* slept with whom gave colonial administrators no end of trouble. Thus, changes in colonial taxonomies register with particular profundity—and pathos—in changes in the definitions of colonial families and in their household arrangements.[49]

At first, Dutch colonials were all men who were actively discouraged (and often outright prohibited) from marrying and starting families during the period of their service. Marriage and family obligations would distract colonists from the task at hand, administrators believed. Moreover, Dutch women's delicate constitutions were deemed particularly vulnerable to the dangers of a tropical climate and geography, thus they were forbidden to even go to the colonies in the first place. Instead, colonial men were encouraged to meet their sexual and domestic needs—safely and cheaply, note—through concubinage with native women.[50] (These women also served as convenient sources of indigenous knowledge.) Only in the nineteenth century was marriage allowed and even encouraged (though tightly regulated). By that point, almost 50 percent of European men living in the Indies were cohabiting with Asian women.[51]

It was the importation of eugenics along with Dutch women into the colonies, however, that brought colonial marriage and family to the forefront of colonial concern. Like other imperialist Europeans, the Dutch justified their right to rule by claims to an innate superiority of character over that of those they colonized. According to Stoler, self-mastery—the ability to properly channel and limit desire (sexual and economic) and to rule emotion with reason—demonstrated the colonial subject's fitness to rule others. But as the effects of biopower and its conception of the human as a form of *bios* came to be felt, the line that delineated superior from inferior came to seem more vulnerable. Europeanness was simultaneously (and somewhat paradoxically) an innate endowment and subject to contamination. Thus, it required both protection and active cultivation. Inferiority of character was as contagious as inferiority of "blood"; thus, too much (and too intimate) contact with colonized peoples was dangerous. Marriage (to European women, at least) and family (if produced by said marriages) became central to both evidencing and nurturing superiority—and to protecting against degeneracy. Thus, marriage and the production of children came to be encouraged, initially among the colonial elite but eventually among the lower level functionaries, as well.

As in the United States, the family—as sexual, economic, and affective unit—came to be a major site where modern racism (for and against) trained its eye and its disciplinary efforts. The true measure of Europeanness lay in "how [colonials] conducted their private lives—with whom they cohabited, where they lived, what they ate, how they raised their children, what language they chose to speak to servants and family at home."[52] This display took the form of proper European dress, behavior, and food consumption—all of which demonstrated mastery over oneself, one's desires, and one's appetites, as well as one's subordinates and surroundings. But these desires needed to be cultivated and protected from native contagion and contamination.[53] To that end, for the first time in the history of the Dutch colonial project, private family space was cordoned off within the larger household and access to this space by native laborers was strictly limited.

Gender mattered to this enterprise. Colonial men were expected to manifest self-mastery in all that they did. Concern for the installation and maintenance of European manhood and womanhood, for the making of colonial boys and girls into European men and women, was central to the colonial household. The colonial wife was charged with the task of making the home a delightful haven for her husband (as a prophylactic against any attraction to native life) and a school in Europeanness for her children. Colonial wives were equipped with manuals in household management and child rearing—and, in some cases, explicitly trained in those practices believed to best ensure the cultivation of the self-mastery necessary to successfully master others. Because of their vulnerability, children's contact with indigenous caretakers—and indeed, with all things native, including food and clothing—had to be carefully restricted lest the allure of familiarity set them on the path to racial ruin. To prevent their charges from becoming too attached to their "natural" smell, colonials required native nursemaids and nannies (*babus*) to bathe regularly and, in some cases, to live in the colonial household rather than with their own families.

Nothing illustrates the fragility of Europeanness more, however, than the belief that the longer Europeans stayed in the colonies, the less resistant they became to contagion. At a certain age, Dutch colonial children were sent back to the homeland where the process of inculcating Europeanness was taken over by extended family, in some cases, or by the staff of boarding schools designed for the purpose. Colonial policy limited the length of stay for colonials in general—and for segregating and often deporting colonials who evidenced signs of degeneration either through illness, acquired disability, poverty, or dissolute behavior. Though purportedly less vulnerable than colonial women or children, colonial men were not immune to the degeneracy that overexposure to native life could inaugurate. Virility was deemed so critical to the British colonial project, for example, that policies of early retirement and repatriation were established. According to Edward Said (quoted by Stoler), "no Oriental would witness a colonial man suffer the effects of old age," nor would a European colonial "ever . . . see *himself* mirrored in the eyes of the subject race, as anything but a vigorous, rational, ever-alert young Raj."[54]

Remarking Space, Remaking Time: Modernity and the Fourfold

The aim of this chapter was to establish the fourfold of Man and his others (divine, animal, raced, and sexed) as a useful and legitimate heuristic device for marking modern time and space. Some readers may be surprised (and perhaps disappointed) to have reached its concluding pages without receiving a map of the modern (biopolitical) taxonomy of human beings. Our reading of McWhorter and Stoler has made it clear, I trust, that there is no single such taxonomy. How human beings are categorized and organized varies with time and space. Labels lose their pertinence or change in meaning as the context changes. (This point and its relevance will be brought home in subsequent chapters.) I hope, however, that the analysis presented herein has broadened readers' awareness of the varieties of forms taxonomies and what they organize have taken and thus can take. It can be difficult to think outside the boxes of the taxonomic structure of sexuality and race that we inhabit (although ours is shifting and changing even as we speak).[55] Idiot, moron, and pervert are mere insults for us, but they were once much more than that; they were personages—and racialized and sexualized ones at that. This, I hope, brings home a major point this chapter seeks to make. What divides Man from his raced and sexed others under modern biopolitical racism is, at bottom, neither race or sex per se, but rather it is the line that separates the normal from the abnormal—a line that runs straight through modern biopolitical race and sexuality.

It also may seem from my analysis to date that Man and his others are not really quite a *fourfold*. The reader will recall that the order of *things* featured Man and his divine and animal others, while the order of *humanity* foregrounded his raced and sexed others. If these are merely parallel planes that organize different aspects of modernity as *episteme* and *ethos*, then what would justify speaking in terms of a fourfold? Yet much binds the order of humanity to the order of things. Recall that underlying both orders is *bios*, the (meta)physical substance, we noted earlier, that undergirds modernity as *episteme* and *ethos*. Whatever else Man and his raced and sexed others are, they are living beings. On the one hand, as *human* beings, Man and his others constitute a distinctive species within *bios'* taxonomic structure, but recall that the lines that separate kinds of *bios* from one another are not rigid boundaries. Readers familiar with animality's centrality to racist rhetorics will not be surprised to know that to be designated abnormal marked a precipitate slide from the human toward the animal. So, for example, McWhorter notes (in passing) that the sexuality of abnormals was often described as more animal than human. According to some of her sources, abnormal sexual desire was set in motion by animal-like motives. Whereas normal (human) sexual desire is aroused by and teamed with affection for one's partner, affection was said to be absent in the sexual bonds of abnormals. Incapacity for affection extended to their children, who were viewed—by their parents, according to biopolitical regimes, but quite certainly by those regimes themselves—more as litters or broods.[56] It is perhaps no coincidence then that some of the mechanisms by which abnormal sexuality was held in check (sterilization, for example) were drawn from practices of animal husbandry.

Recall also that the shift from nature to life involved a double displacement of God. Man-the-knower displaces God as the source of knowledge of the order of things. Knowing nature meant perceiving, despite occasional movements off course, the overarching divine teleology propelling all of the natural order ever forward. Knowing life, however, meant peering into the depths of things to find the internal *telos* unique to each form of life. The *logos* of *bios* is essentially godless—that is, it evidences only one thing common to all (each, though, in its own way): finitude. Bio-logic is easily visible in the orders of humanity we have seen emerge in modernity. Conceived as a singular species, what motivates and mobilizes the race's progress toward full self-realization is not a divinely ordained *telos*, but that which constitutes humanity as a specific and distinctive form of life. Realizing that teleology is not a matter of divine providence, but of human management through the exercise of bio-disciplinary power. And insofar as that teleology meets its limit in finitude—of each human being, but also potentially of the species—the stakes are high.

To displace, however, is not necessarily to replace; it is certainly not to make disappear. That belief in God could no longer be *assumed* in modernity does not mean that such belief—much less what we call "religion" (which is both more and less than belief)—disappeared.[57] One need only recall the impact of the notion of Manifest Destiny on U.S. expansion (with its displacement of Native Americans) or Max Weber's thesis linking Protestantism to capitalism to appreciate the mutual imbrication of Christianity and modernity. Indeed, religion—both in general and in terms of specific traditions—is, as we'll see in subsequent chapters, also deeply embedded in the modern *episteme* and *ethos*. As much recent literature in religious studies has noted, religious difference is one of the axes of the taxonomies applied to a diverse humanity in modernity, an insight that will be crucial to subsequent chapters.[58] Religious difference is caught up in modernity's racial and racist logics and the biopolitical regimes that enact and embody it.[59]

Although neither focuses on religion in any systematic way, this insight is borne out in both McWhorter's and Stoler's work. In eighteenth-century colonial Virginia, McWhorter notes, "white" was shorthand for "Christian and European" (vs. African and pagan). The ever-changing taxonomy of race she tracks includes, as I noted, Jews and Catholics as racialized categories. That Christianity aided and abetted colonialism is well known (and will be key to my argument in subsequent chapters), although Stoler argues that Christianity played a relatively minor supporting role in the Dutch Indies. Not surprisingly given its role in colonial projects, Christianity shows up in and around the shifting landscape of the regulation of intimate relationships in her work. The original 1617 decree against intermarriage between colonials and colonized was cast in terms of Christian versus non-Christian, not European versus native, the terms used in the 1848 law legalizing intermarriage.[60] Moreover, belief in Christianity was one of the "cultural competencies" that marked the European as such.[61] That the education of "European" children was insufficiently "Christian" was a central concern to colonial functionaries in 1874.[62] Perhaps most chilling is a footnote in *Carnal Knowledge* that attests to frequent mention (in the documents of the local Dutch Indies eugenics society) of the basic compatibility between Christianity and eugenics.[63]

◆ ◆ ◆ ◆ ◆ ◆

Our reading of Foucault has established modernity as *episteme* (a way of knowing) and *ethos* (a way of doing and being). As *episteme*, modernity produces new orders of knowing with new taxonomies that ground them—and, as we'll see in the next chapter, new ways of seeing. Taxonomies do more than merely allocate, delineate, and describe; as conduits of power as well as knowledge, they mold, induce, and produce the objects that they order. These modern taxonomies created by the fourfold are both creations of and channels for the exercise of biopower and disciplinary power. (Indeed, to denote their mutual imbrication in and through this taxonomic deployment, hereafter I will use the locution bio-disciplinary power when and where they come together.)[64] The chapters that follow trace and track the specific effects of bio-disciplinary power channeled through the fourfold; first in and through the invention and deployment of photography and then in and through specific sets of (quite recent) photographs and the events they index.

As we'll see, the human beings targeted in and by the exercise of bio-disciplinary power come to know, be, do, and see in relationship to that taxonomy. I do not mean to imply that human beings are mere blank slates that can be made to bear the imprint of whatever master comes along. I say "in relationship to" to make space for resistances and capitulations of all sorts—successful or not, visible or not, conscious or not, willing or not. For the crafting of human beings into particular taxonomic objects is a complex and interactive project. To be sure, bio-disciplinary power can certainly take dictatorial, violent, and other immediately coercive forms; we will witness some egregious examples in the chapters to come. But it works on us routinely in much more subtle, seemingly benign, even gentle ways—in ways that encourage us to go along to get along (as we say), to take ourselves under our own wing as objects of self-discipline. In other words, bio-discipline works on us from the inside out as well as from the outside in, a point that later chapters will bring home. Of course, the degree to which one is subject to bio-disciplinary power's gentle or more violent exercise will depend on one's location (or allocation) within a given taxonomic structure. The particular techniques of power applied to produce (flesh and blood) men certainly differ from what goes into the production of their (flesh and blood) raced and sexed others, but men are as much products of bio-disciplinary power as their raced and sexed others.

A few concluding observations about the "Man" at the heart of our fourfold: just as Man occupied a distinctive place in the modern order of things, so also in the modern order of humanity. Man is both object and subject of the knowing, being, and doing that takes place under their aegis. He comes to be the (idealized) subject of modernity in and through becoming the object of bio-disciplinary power—and the others of the fourfold are integral to his becoming. This is more than a claim that Man's role in relationship to the modern taxonomies that guide and guard modernity as *episteme* and *ethos* is marked out in contrast to his others, although it is that. Rather, it is a claim about the distinctive nature of the relationship between Man and his others under modernity's aegis. Recall that Man is both projection and project. If mastery of self, nature, and others is central to Man as epistemic and ethical project, then the success of that project requires his others—both to acquire and to demonstrate mastery. To the degree that they are necessary to that project, his others also threaten it. Man as master may displace God, but God remains as the standard of mastery against which Man can never quite measure up. That Man's others simultaneously ground and threaten the project of achieving mastery is particularly clear in Man's relations to his sexed and raced others. The capacity for self-mastery (of desire and appetite, of style and affect) sets Man apart from these others—and his animal other. Successful cultivation of self-mastery demonstrates one's fitness for domination of those same others. But the lines between Man and these others are not rigid boundaries that are easily maintained and policed. Each of the sites where mastery is to be constructed is vulnerable, as Stoler's account of colonial intimate space demonstrates. Moreover, although he periodically tries to deny it, Man shares with his sexed and raced others his humanity—both as *bios* and as *ethos*—and with animal others his finitude and historicity (and perhaps more). It is no wonder, then, that so much anxiety and uncertainty surrounds the production of (flesh and blood) men. The reader will recall that, in the modern order of things, Man-the-knower is constitutively marked by limits: of knowledge, of time and place, of finitude. So also in the modern order of humanity, mastery is a fraught project that bespeaks Man's vulnerabilities, fragilities, and limits as much as his strengths. It is to that fraught project that the signs and wonders to come bear witness.

CHAPTER TWO

PHOTOGRAPHY AND/AS BIO-DISCIPLINE

Photographic Askesis

"Our era . . . prefers the image to the thing, the copy to the original, the representation to the reality, appearance to being"—and we know it.
—Susan Sontag (quoting Ludwig Feuerbach)

The body itself is invested by power relations through which it is situated in a certain "political economy," trained, supervised, tortured if necessary, forced to carry out tasks, to perform ceremonies, to emit signs. Power is exercised in, and not just on, the social body because, since the 19th century, power has taken on a capillary existence.
—John Tagg

Spectatorship (the look, the gaze, the glance, the practices of observation, surveillance, and visual pleasure) may be as deep a problem as various forms of reading . . . visual experience or "visual literacy" might not be fully explicable on the model of textuality.
—W. J. T. Mitchell

THE PREVIOUS CHAPTER traced the emergence of the fourfold of Man and his others (animal, divine, sexed, and raced) in and through Foucault's analyses of modernity as both *episteme* and *ethos*, as an order of knowing, being, and doing. Man and his others came into being as both project and product of a peculiarly modern form of power and knowledge (i.e., bio-disciplinary power) and became one of its organizing frames. Future chapters will trace the ongoing effects of the fourfold in the exercise of bio-disciplinary power—and evidence of fractures within what it has built—in certain events in the recent past. Each chapter will, I trust, add depth and dimension to the fourfold in whole and in part even as it takes us deeper into the *askesis* of its (and thus our) unmaking. Largely because photography (moving or still) played such a critical role in these events, I will frame my analyses of the events themselves through certain of those photographs that crystallize with particular profundity and power the events and their aftereffects. In this chapter, I will argue that the fact that photographs possess such salience witnesses to and reflects photography's relationship to modernity. Indeed, in both form and content, photography is intimately bound up with bio-disciplinary power and the emergence of the fourfold—that is, with modernity as *episteme* and *ethos*.[1]

That I use photographs in this way marks something of a departure from philosophical theology's largely textual focus. Thus, another aim of this chapter is to establish a way to "read" the photographs in question, a way to interpret them that takes seriously medium and message, form and content. On the surface, this might not seem terribly significant or complicated. First of all, photography is simply (it seems) one among many technologies of the visual. I would not be the first philosopher or theologian to take up the topic of the visual—or to draw on visual images.[2] No undergraduate history of philosophy survey would omit the myth of the cave in Plato's *Republic* or Descartes's image-laden thought experiments in the *Meditations*, just to mention a couple of particularly salient examples. Many of the major names in contemporary continental philosophy likewise attend explicitly to the visual—as image, as a mode of becoming subject, as emblematic of and endemic to our culture. Bergson's *Matter and Memory*, Merleau-Ponty's *Phenomenology of Perception*, Deleuze's work on cinema, Derrida's occasional foray into art (including a small volume on photographs) are only some of the more obvious examples.[3] Indeed, that religious motifs focused on the visual (idol and icon) feature centrally in the work of Jean-Luc Marion, one of the most influential scholars to bridge that contested border between continental philosophy and theology, arguably reflects the legacy of both disciplines.[4] Before literacy was widespread, Christianity relied on visual arts and architecture as a means of lay education. Yet both Western philosophy and theology are ambivalent about the value—and trustworthiness—of visual imagery and, indeed, of vision itself. Absent the proper light (the Good), Plato's cave dwellers confused shadows with reality. And the very invisibility and unknowability of infinitude cemented Descartes's confidence in its (i.e., God's) existence. Central to the schisms between Eastern and Western Christianity and between Protestantism and Catholicism were different evaluations of visual imagery's proper role in and for Christian faith, evaluations mobilized around the motifs of idol and icon. Iconoclasm's suspicion of the visual also took root in Western culture at large, including academic treatments of visual images, according to W. J. T. Mitchell, a trend he seeks to counter in his work.[5]

To turn to visual imagery in an inquiry into modernity and its end, however, is to enter into another set of debates. Some have claimed that modernity's end (or near end) is constituted by a sea change in the relationship between visual images and truth. In his famous and influential Situationist treatise, *The Society of the Spectacle* (1967), Guy DeBord argues that the forces of commodification endemic to late modern capitalism have created a culture in which we prize the image over the thing itself.[6] Jeans may all be denim pants, but we'll pay $200 for a pair of 7 for All Mankind (to use a contemporary example) instead of $50 for a pair of Levi's. The falsity of the system is revealed in the endless process of obsolescence of the former fetishized object and its replacement with the latest and newest (e.g., before 7 for All Mankind, there was Calvin Klein). Subsequently, in *Simulacra and Simulation* (1981; 1994 in English translation), Jean Baudrillard marks the end of modernity with the utter triumph of the *mere* image (the simulacrum) over reality.[7] The distinction between the real and the simulated has itself disappeared; the simulated *is* the real. These claims have met some resistance, of course. Given how rarely visual images appear in mass media without accompanying text, Roland Barthes rejects describing us as wholly captive to "a civilization of the image—we are still, and more than ever, a civilization of writing, writing and speech continuing to be the full terms of the information structure," he claims.[8] And Foucault explicitly rejects DeBord's claim arguing that ours is a culture of surveillance not spectacle.[9]

From a twenty-first-century perspective, the technologies and practices that gave rise to such claims—television, cinema, and mass advertising, for example—were only precursors of what was to come. The relationship between the real and the virtual has only become more complex—and the line between them seemingly less clear—in the digital age. One has only to consider the effects of digital technologies in film (and photography, about which more later) and the popularity of video games (especially those played in online virtual communities) and "reality" television to see why many find compelling DeBord's and Baudrillard's positions.

In recent years, W. J. T. Mitchell and Jacques Rancière, among others, have argued (in somewhat different keys, if you will) for less apocaplytic and more nuanced understandings of the role visual images play in our culture.[10] Visual imagery is newly ubiquitous at all levels of Western (really global) culture, but its hold isn't monopolistic either in form or content. All media are mixed media, Rancière notes; although the visible and the sayable are different registers of signification, we might say, they are mutually dependent. So, Rancière's "imagetexts" and Mitchell's "pictures" are both verbal and visual. That said, Mitchell has argued for a "pictorial turn" (following after Richard Rorty's linguistic turn, both thematically and temporally) in contemporary culture, including academia. In addition to the influential works of Baudrillard, DeBord, and Foucault, Mitchell notes a new interest in visual imagery in philosophy and the emergence of the hybrid academic field of "visual culture."

The pictorial turn is evident in recent world events, as well, Mitchell argues, in *What Do Pictures Want?* The current War on (or of) Terror is, in part, a war of images.[11] Al-Qaeda targeted the World Trade Towers because of what they (literally) stood for: the formidable concentration of global capital (financial and cultural) in the United States. And the United States fought back with its own (carefully controlled and disseminated) images, including the destruction of Saddam Hussein's statue in Baghdad. Both are examples of iconoclasm as what Mitchell calls "iconoclash" and are replete with religious overtones. For al-Qaeda, the World Trade Towers were idols, not icons; to topple and dismember Saddam Hussein's statue anticipates his literal toppling and dismemberment to come, thus exposing him as idol not icon.

Insofar as these claims and counterclaims frame their interest in visual images as a concern about the relationship between visual image and reality, they may seem to have little to do with photographs—especially those I will be discussing. After all, those photographs, at least, seem to be nothing more—and nothing less—than straightforward records of actual events as witnessed by the photographers themselves. Indeed, although these indictments may target the uses to which photography is put, they seem to have little purchase on the photograph itself. For isn't *every* photograph—at its base, at least—merely a record of what was (of a that-there-then)?[12] Can I not, then, simply take these particular photographs as things present-to-hand, available in their mere thingness, useful precisely because they are what they appear to be: unmediated records of what-actually-was?

A survey of scholarship on photography, however, suggests that photography—as a technology and as a form of visual imagery—from the outset has had a complicated relationship to truth. That relationship cannot simply be reduced to the equation of truth with the real *or* the simulacrum, although it may tell us something about why claims like those of DeBord and Baudrillard have gained purchase (and why they provoke resistance, as well). But the complexity of what I will call photographic truth extends beyond questions of reference—that is, questions about the photograph's adequacy to the material reality it represents. Photographic truth is not simply another form of what Heidegger has called truth as correspondence—in this case, between image and thing rather than word and thing. Rather, photographic truth is a form of truth as *aletheia*, concealment and unconcealment—not in the quasi-mystical sense of Heidegger's clearing, but in the more Foucauldian sense of epistemic truth. Just as how we (think we) know affects what we know, so too how we (think we) see affects what we see—materially. That we think of the photograph as a straightforward copy of that-there-then reflects a complex series of shifts in the modern "scopic regime" in which photography's invention and use is embedded.[13] The modern scopic regime is central to the modern *episteme* as described in the previous chapter. Indeed, as Martin Jay reminds us, the epistemic shifts that Foucault describes are also shifts in scopic regimes. Modernity, then, yields not only a new kind of epistemological and ethical subject, but also a new kind of visual subject. And the new way of seeing that this subject embodies is embedded in and enabling of the new way of knowing, being, and doing that constitutes modernity as *episteme* and *ethos*. The advent of photography marks a critical juncture in the emergence of the modern visual subject. Photography's role in the modern scopic regime is intimately tied to bio-disciplinary power's emergence and exercise—and the fourfold that channels it. In turn, the exercise of bio-disciplinary power is critical to the establishment of what I will call photographic truth. Indeed, we could speak of an emergent *scientia visualis* as analogous to *scientia sexualis*. The emergence of the fourfold of Man and his others is intrinsic to the establishment and exercise of photographic truth—and vice versa—and to photography's imbrication in bio-disciplinary power.

As in the previous chapter, I begin with Man's emergence—now as the subject (and object) of the modern *episteme* as scopic regime. Jonathan Crary, whose work features prominently herein, calls the modern visual subject "the observer."[14] As we'll see, the human sciences—particularly that of physiology—in tandem with developments in visual technologies play a central role in this scopic shift. Thus, the modern scopic regime's emergence is both enabled by and enabling of the observer's emergence as subject and object of knowledge. Once again, as in my account of *The Order of Things*, Man's divine and animal others appear first on the scene, reprising the roles they played in the last chapter. Just as Man displaced God as knower, so too the observer will displace God as viewer. To displace is not to replace; the observer, like Man-the-knower and unlike God, is constituted by finite embodiment with all of the limits thereto appertaining. The observer also reprises Man-the-knower's empirico-transcendental doubleness; he is simultaneously subject and object of observation. Thus, as finite *bios* and observable object, the observer is the reflection of his animal other.

Photographic truth consists not only of how we come to see, but also of what we see—what we subject to the camera's eye. The camera's use as an instrument of bio-disciplinary power is central to the establishment of its claim to present that-there-then. Here, Man's sexed and raced others come to the fore as the mirrors reflecting Man back to himself and securing his sense of mastery (over himself and his others). Thus, the camera serves as a mechanism of subjection active in the production of the fourfold of Man, his sexed and raced others, and his animal other as a channel for bio-disciplinary power.

Modern Seeing

I did not make note of it in the previous chapter, but the first chapter of *The Order of Things* features Foucault's analysis of a visual object, the famous painting by Diego Velázquez, *Las Meninas* (1656), a reproduction of which graced the cover of the original edition of *Les mots et les choses* (and the 1973 Vintage paperback edition of the English translation). The painting is a dazzling display of a circuit of spectatorial positions: the artist, the artist's models, and the viewer(s) are all at one and the same time rendered by Velázquez visible, if not necessarily or in any simple sense present, as observed and observer. I'll have more to say about Foucault's treatment of the painting in due course, but for now let me simply note that its prominence in *The Order of Things* signals the importance of the visual in the epistemic shifts that are *Order*'s primary concern. Let me substantiate that claim by revisiting—from the perspective of the visual—the epistemic shifts into and out of the Classical *episteme* that I traced in the previous chapter. Recall that the Classical *episteme*'s emergence is marked by a profound shift in the relationship between words and things. Previously grounded in a divinely ordained order of correspondence that directly linked words to things, words lost their immediate connection to things becoming instead tools that mediated human knowledge of things. As a result, direct visual perception took on a new prominence as *the* mode of access to truth. Recall that the tables produced by natural historians map things according to the similarities and differences visible on their surfaces. "The triumph of natural history was thus the triumph of a new visual order," Jay writes, at the expense of the other senses.[15]

Recall as well that God recedes to the background in the Classical *episteme*. Although still posited as the ultimate source of the order of things, access to that order comes through human perception conceived, Jay reminds us, as "an observing eye" that is subject of but not to natural history's tabulations.[16] The peculiar position of this spectatorial eye is captured well by Velázquez in "Las Meninas" as parsed by Foucault in *Order*'s opening pages. Most significant to the painting's status as emblematic of Classical vision is Velázquez's depiction of a reflection in the small mirror that hangs on the painted room's back wall. The mirror reflects the images of a man and a woman—otherwise absent from the scene—who are reflected back to themselves as they look at the scene before them. These are, Foucault tells us, King Phillip IV and his wife, Mariana, the rulers of Spain. Only they are in the position of being able to truly see the painting—to truly comprehend it. Significantly, they themselves are outside the scope of representation. Their peculiar absent presence (or the peculiar presence of their absence) signals the situation of the spectatorial subject within the Classical *episteme*. The spectator exercises sovereignty over the viewed object, which places the spectator firmly outside the scope of the visual. As Jay puts it, within the Classical *episteme*, "the seeing subject can only be inferred, not perceived directly."[17]

This changes in the modern scopic regime. The emergence of the modern order of things, recall, is marked by nature's replacement with life (*bios*), the displacement of a divinely directed singular teleology with teleologies internal and particular to each form of life. Time in the form of finitude and historicity becomes the stage upon which these teleologies play out. A new kind of knower, Man, takes up his place at the center of the modern order of things. Insofar as knowing things in this new order requires plumbing beneath their surface into what lies hidden beneath, Man is a new kind of seer, as well. But unlike the spectatorial eye of the Classical scopic regime, Man is implicated in the modern order of things. As a form of life, he bears within himself his own *telos*. Like all forms of life, he is subject to the conditions of finitude. Man is, then, this strange empirico-transcendental doublet; simultaneously knower and known, seer and seen, subject of and subject to the emergent sciences of physiology and biology. Thus, Man is simultaneously subject of and subject to bio-disciplinary power.

Jonathan Crary traces the emergence of the modern scopic regime and its visual subject in *Techniques of the Observer*. Emerging between 1810 and 1840, this subject, dubbed by Crary "the observer," is produced out of an assemblage of an emergent empirical science of vision (and theories related to it) and new visual technologies constructed to exploit that new understanding of vision. The observer is the product of emergent physiology's quest to know the body, a quest that proceeded by dividing up the body into multiple isolable mechanical systems, including those connected to each of the senses (hearing, sight, touch, taste, smell).[18]

The significance of this shift is perhaps most clearly perceived against the backdrop of Jay's account of the early modern understanding of vision. The invention and rediscovery of perspective in the Renaissance coupled with emergent Cartesianism already had resulted in what he calls "the denarrativization of the ocular."[19] From "an intelligible text (the book of nature)" that, if properly read, revealed a divinely established order, the world became an "observable but [in itself] meaningless object."[20] Space became a neutral container and time a series of moments each the same as the other, in essence. Together, space and time constituted the matrix in which things appeared. In a shift reminiscent of *The Order of Things*, God is displaced as source of order and primary observer of the visual. In the words of John Berger, "the visible world is arranged for the [human] spectator as the universe was once thought to be arranged for God."[21] But this spectator is neither God nor Man. Contained along with the objects of its vision in space and time, the spectatorial I/eye is a disembodied and utterly generalized figure. Its function is simply to see what appears in front of it. Light provides clarity and self-transparency to the singular unblinking I/eye rendering its vision objective.

The advent of new visual technologies distinguishes the modern scopic economy from its predecessor. The first of these technologies is the camera obscura (literally "dark room"), a simple technology used by painters to enable closer resemblance between their artistic renderings and their objects; in other words, to ensure greater verisimilitude. The camera obscura is essentially a box (often as large as a room) that directs light through an aperture onto a reflective surface, thereby producing (in reverse) the precise image of its object. Crary's text includes a seventeenth-century etching showing the camera obscura in action, as it were.[22] The artist stands off to the side facing the surface on which he is working. Rays of light (depicted as straight dark lines) enter the room through a round hole cut in its rear walls. The rays of light produce on the opposite wall the image the artist aims to reproduce. Tellingly, it is that act of production that is the etching's focus, not the artist's reproduction. The etching testifies to the emerging visual subject that Crary describes. The artist, depicted alone in the confines of the camera obscura, prefigures the modern observer as simultaneously the subject and object of vision. On the one hand, he holds the brush in his hand; the painting to come will be his product. On the other, its production requires his submission to the discipline of the camera obscura as the purveyor of visual truth. Visual truth, note, lies outside the artist's body; its objectivity guaranteed by the anonymous and utterly disinterested mechanism of the camera obscura.

In addition to technological innovations, the emergent human science of physiology enables what I've called *scientia visualis*. As scientists learned more about how human vision worked, the locus of vision moved from the impersonal to the personal. Whereas space and time were previously understood as constituting the container holding both spectator and visual object, they move into the human body, which became vision's space–time container, if you will. Visual truth, then, is rendered profoundly subjective—finite and perspectival—rather than infinite and objective.[23] This change reaches its apex in the findings of physiologist Johannes Müller who demonstrated that visual objects could be produced by any number of mechanical operations on the retina, including chemical or circulatory agents internal to the eye.[24] Thus, there is no necessary connection between what we see and what's real. Severed from an immediate relationship to reality, vision is rendered vulnerable not only to distortion but to self-generated illusion.

These discoveries made possible a new set of visual technologies that simultaneously exposed and exploited the vulnerabilities and capacities intrinsic to the human visual mechanism. Among the best known and most emblematic of these technologies is the stereoscope, which drew on the latest scientific understanding of binocular vision. Scientists had determined how human vision produced a single three-dimensional image out of the two slightly different images received by each eye. The stereoscope essentially reproduced this experience, thus turning vision back on itself. Specially made two-dimensional cards inserted into the stereoscope contained two slightly different versions of the same image (mimicking the slight differences in what each eye sees). Viewing them through the stereoscope produced the illusion of depth and perspective where there was none.[25] In return, this melding of human and machine gave the viewer complete possession of its visual object, something that eluded "natural" vision. The stereoscope, however, was no parlor trick designed to remain hidden from view; quite the contrary. The inventors of the stereoscope made no attempt to disguise the fact that their viewing machine manipulated vision to provide its visual pleasures. Indeed, it was precisely the explicit riff on natural vision that the stereoscope provided that eventually helped make it the ubiquitous feature in Victorian bourgeois homes that it became (and, Crary suggests, explains the popularity of stereoscopic pornography).

The significance of Crary's account lies in its demonstration of *scientia visualis* as a discipline that forms the seer into a new kind of visual subject. Developed primarily to entertain, these technologies turn seeing into spectacle. But, in the process, these technologies train, produce, and deploy the modern visual subject as empirico-transcendental doublet by subjecting the observer to disciplinary power. In stepping up to the stereoscope, one inserts oneself into a complex visual scenario. The production of the stereoscopic image replicates and requires one's active embodied gaze, but yielded up to the discipline of another's technological mastery. This, Crary argues, is the situation of the observer. On the one hand, vision is cut free from its premodern fixed context and rendered autonomous and singular; it is specific to *this* body at *this* site. Yet the very same conditions that ground vision's autonomy also render the observer observable. As a result, the observer is simultaneously subject and subjected—the putative master of all he surveys (and that's quite a lot, it will turn out) *and* the object of disciplinary power. Thus, Foucault and DeBord are both right, Crary argues: modernity is simultaneously a culture of surveillance and spectacle.

Photographic Truth: Seeing Is Believing

The invention of photography—machines that used chemicals and mechanical lenses to turn light into a representation of what appeared in front of them—constitutes a signal moment in the evolution of the modern scopic regime. The immediate precursors to film photography, the daguerreotype and the calotype, were invented in France in the early decades of the nineteenth century.[26] The early use of these machines and the initial reception of the visual artifacts that they produced reflect a context in which painting was the predominant visual medium of the day. Photography was greeted, either with enthusiasm or dread, as the fulfillment of the desire for realistic visual reproduction launched in the Renaissance. Some saw in photography the imminent death of painting—in several senses. Might the skill and discipline required to produce a painting be replaced by the ease of clicking the shutter, thereby essentially bringing about the end of the artist? Might the enticement of (relatively) instantaneous (re)production rob painting of its audience? Walter Benjamin famously argued that the promise of endless reproducibility meant the end of the "aura"—of originality and singularity—that surrounded works of art before the age of mechanical reproduction (*pace* the title of his influential essay).[27] Others welcomed photography on the grounds that it would free painting to pursue other goals and forms, a pursuit realized, some argue, in the turn toward abstraction that came to characterize modernist painting (and sculpture).

This anxiety about the consequences for painting of photography's advent distinguishes the two media on the basis of a difference in the relationship between medium and master. On the one hand, to the degree that photography promised to give the viewer verisimilitude, it seemed to threaten painting, at least insofar as verisimilitude was its object.[28] Yet painting retained its claim to be "art," and thus to occupy the "high" side of the divide between "high" and "low" culture (to which photography was initially consigned, although not without resistance). That claim centered on the perceived role of the artist versus the photographer. Where the painter wielded paint and brush to realize a uniquely creative vision on the canvas, the photographer simply pointed and shot what appeared in front of the camera. Photographs required no artistic hand or vision—or so it seemed.[29]

Our analysis of the modern scopic regime complicates this division between art and photography. On the one hand, the photographic camera is more than the namesake of the *camera obscura*. True, as (mere) mechanism, it seems to promise disinterested objectivity. It will capture whatever is in front of it when the shutter clicks. And, with that click, the conditions of the photograph's production disappear, as Abigail Solomon-Godeau notes. But the conditions of its production are more complex both mechanically and artistically, if you will, than this narrative allows. Insofar as the photograph is a product of chemical (or now digital) interactions with light, it *is* that-there-then; according to Barthes, it is a literal *memento mori*.[30] But, as Solomon-Godeau reminds us, the photograph is not a mere *reproduction* of what was visible that-there-then; it reduces "that" to "this." Three dimensions become two, binocular and perspectival vision becomes monocular and flat, the viewfinder (aided by standardized sizing and framing) excises a precise quadrangle out of a much larger and messier three-dimensional scene.[31] The vibrant differences and subtle nuances of color are translated to their chemical or digital analogues—or in some cases transubstantiated, we might say, into black and white (ironically, the genre of photography that registers as the most "objective"). Finally, the photograph itself is always subject to manipulation. Photoshop may have rendered ubiquitous the means to exploit more easily that feature of (especially digital) photography, but the possibility and actuality—and awareness of same—has been there from the start.

Of course, the lens must be directed, the shutter must be clicked; it is only because—and insofar as—the photographer observed that-there-then that the photograph makes any referential claim. But the photographer is more than a mere extension of the camera-as-mechanism. The role the photographer plays in the production of photographic truth is more complex. For one thing, the photographer selects "that" not "this" as worthy of the click. That a particular photograph is available for viewing by others represents further acts of selection (intentional or accidental)—by the photographer him- or herself; sometimes by editors, publishers, or curators; or by miscellaneous others who come into possession of a certain photograph (or who refuse possession by passing over or passing by).[32]

Recall that the shift into the modern scopic regime is, in part, a shift in the locus of time and space from outside the visual subject to inside. Photography embodies that shift realized. The temporality and spatiality of the photograph presupposes the temporality and spatiality of the photographer's body—and, subsequently, the bodies of the photograph's viewers. Photographic truth as I have described it so far, then, is emblematic of modern visual truth as finite and perspectival. And yet . . .

The attribution of direct referentiality to photography was neither automatic nor immediate; rather, its claim to referentiality had to be established—and learned. "The history of photography," Solomon-Godeau writes, "is not the history of remarkable men, much less the history of remarkable pictures, but the history of photographic uses."[33] That history, as John Tagg notes, is often local, contingent, and particular (as we'll see).[34] The linchpin in this history, Solomon-Godeau demonstrates, is "photography's equivocal status *in* and *as* representation."[35] It owes a debt to the real, but it is inescapably *re*presentation. Thus, photographs are "as highly mediated and as densely coded as any other kind of picture."[36] And it was in and through being put to use as a mechanism of the exercise of bio-disciplinary power—also an "invention," recall, of the nineteenth century—that photography accumulated what Tagg calls (after Barthes) its "reality effect"—that is, its reputation for giving us simply that-there-then unadulterated and pure.[37] Simultaneously shaped by and undergirding bio-disciplinary power, photography served as an essential tool in the production of human taxonomies and the new forms of subjection they enabled. In turn, looking at such photographs trained their viewers in how to see and what to see—emplacing them within the fourfold of Man and his others. It is the sum total of this circuit that runs between the that-there-then and photography that constitutes photographic truth.

Man the Master

Photography's initial subject matter, predominately landscapes and portraits, also reflected its emergence into a painterly context—and a context of emerging industrial capitalism.[38] Early photographic landscapes generally depicted pastoral scenes of the local countryside, which were valued as a respite to the pressures of urbanization and emerging industrialism. The invention first of flexible film (and later of cheap portable cameras like the Brownie) eventually democratized access to photography, enabling it to become more and more ubiquitous at all levels of society.[39] Initially, however, photographic portraiture was, like its painterly counterpart, available only to the wealthy. Although taking a daguerreotype was considerably less time consuming than painting a portrait, the experience for the subject of the daguerreotype was still somewhat akin to sitting for a portrait. The technology required fairly lengthy exposure to light of the chemicals on the metal plates to produce the image. As a result, subjects of portraiture had to remain very still (and various rigs were developed to invisibly hold their heads still). Photographic portraiture, like painterly portraiture, functioned to solidify its subject's rightful claim to high socioeconomic status. Thus, the practice of photographic portraiture drew on the doubleness inherent in the modern visual subject (as observer and observed)—literally reflecting Man back to himself and securing his sense of mastery and superiority. Photography's reproducibility, however, enabled new practices. The calling cards traditionally left by upper-class people at one another's homes in lieu of a face-to-face visit were eventually replaced with *cartes de visites*: miniature reproductions of the would-be visitor's photographed portrait. As the number of photography studios grew and the cost of being photographed dropped, *cartes de visites* and other forms of self-referential photographs became more widely available—at least to the upwardly mobile.

Photography's deployment as a mechanism to assert and secure Man's status as masterful subject did not stop with portraiture, but extended to other subject matter—matter redolent with the elements of the fourfold. Historian Graham Clarke describes the use of the camera by natural historians like Buffon, Lamarck, and Cuvier to document and catalog natural objects, thereby extending and consolidating Man's displacement of God as site and source of knowledge of nature.[40] With colonial expansion, landscape photography expanded its repertoire to include scenes—and occasionally people—from exotic locales. Compilations of such photographs into books like Francis Firth's *Visits to the Middle East* enabled the so-called armchair tourist to travel through places he (or she) might never see in person. Extending Man's line of sight into places otherwise unseen by Western eyes effectively affirmed his place at the center of the world.

That Firth's volumes focus on the Middle East reflects that locale's place at the heart of armchair tourism. According not only to Clarke, but also to

Jay and Solomon-Godeau, the Middle East was a particularly popular subject of this form of photography. This was not a matter of mere curiosity,
but is intimately connected to European (in this case French) imperialism
and colonialism, a resonance captured in the term "photographic orientalism" originally coined by the famous curator and scholar of photography,
Robert Sobeieszek.[41] In a paradigmatic instance described by Solomon-
Godeau, the photographer August Salzmann was hired in 1855 by Louis
Ferdinand de Saulcy to accompany him on an expedition to Jerusalem.[42]
De Saulcy hoped (unsuccessfully, it turns out) that Salzmann's photographs of Jewish, Christian, and Muslim holy sites would provide con-
vincing proof of the accuracy of dates he posited for their construction.
For this project, de Saulcy (and Salzmann) received state funding, one
of a large number of photographic missions that the French government
sponsored as part of what Solomon-Godeau describes as the nineteenth
century's "passion for documentation."[43] "Photography," she writes, "was
understood to be the agent par excellence for listing, knowing, *and possessing*, as it were, the things of the world. . . . [It] was the technical analogue
to the absolute belief in the legibility of appearances" expressed philo-
sophically in Comte's positivism and aesthetically in realism.[44]

Note here the link once again between a form of visual image—in this
case, the photograph rather than the stereoscopic image—and possession—
this time run through the alleged immediacy of photography's referentiality. Against that backdrop, the fact that Salzmann's photographs are all but
devoid of people resonates doubly. On the one hand, it belies the claim of
mere immediacy. Because of the length of time required to expose a calotype, it was unable to freeze motion; thus, Salzmann had to wait for—or
engineer?—a time when the façade he wished to photograph was unpopu-
lated. On the other, whether intended or not, the absence of people also
presents to the viewer a land seemingly available for occupation or conquest. Indeed, Solomon-Godeau notes that Francis Wey, a French art critic
who encouraged his government to invest in photographic expeditions like
Salzmann's, called such trips "*conquêtes pacifiques*," a term rendered deeply
ironic by the fact that Salzmann's trip occurred during the Crimean War,
undertaken supposedly to "defend the holy places."[45]

To this point, our discussion of photographic truth has focused on photography's use in the establishment and consolidation of Man as master—
of nature, of his household, of exotic lands and peoples, and of himself.

By subjecting himself to the photographic disciplines exemplified in *cartes de visites* and armchair tourism, aspirants to Manhood learn how to see and know it and, to some extent, to be and do it. Bio-disciplinary power, however, aims not only—or even primarily—at those at or near the top of the West's social hierarchies but targets all of us. The uses of photographs in situations closer to our time and place allow us to see more clearly photography's role in the exercise of bio-disciplinary power channeled through the fourfold in a more cumulative way. Photography is critical to the establishment of the modern taxonomic social order discussed in the previous chapter—and to the creation and installation of the personages it organizes, personages assembled via the triangulation of sexuality, race, and animality.

Recall that bio-disciplinary power is (positively and negatively) racist in both aim and effect. That is, in the service of the (human) race, it nurtures and guards the lives of those deemed most valuable in part by protecting them against those deemed threatening to the race's survival and success. "Bio-disciplinary" bespeaks the modes and mechanisms in and through which this hybrid form of power is realized and exercised, modes and mechanisms that manage populations to enforce normalization. As McWhorter argues, modern racism is racism against the abnormal; it becomes anti-black or anti-immigrant racism (racism as we usually think of it), for example, as abnormality comes to be associated predominately with non-Nordics. In all of its forms, modern racism is endemic to the modern state; bio-discipline takes political form as biopolitics.

We must not forget, however, that bio-disciplinary power is first and foremost productive not repressive, or better, that its exercises in repression serve certain productive ends. Recall that it is in the service of its overarching aim of guarding and nurturing (human) life that bio-disciplinary power is exercised. It targets human being (individually and collectively) *as* a specific form of *bios*, one by McWhorter's account that is constituted by an internal dynamism that propels it toward domination, but is checked by disease, atrophy, and death. In other words, human being's status as a form of life simultaneously grounds and threatens its pursuit of domination. Thus, nurturing and shepherding the race requires disciplining human *bios* by targeting individuals and populations. That targeting is done through the fourfold of Man and his others, I have argued, with photography as one of its modes and mechanisms. Moreover, it is in and through its bio-disciplinary usage that photography's claim to represent reality was established. Thus, photographic truth is itself a creation of bio-disciplinary power and its fourfold.

Photography and/as Bio-Discipline

Take, for example, the practice of using photographs as evidence. Although it may seem that such uses of photography simply exploit the realism intrinsic to the camera, Tagg makes it clear that the "evidential force" of photography is an archival creation.[46] Rather than an innate capacity of the camera, realism is a self-reflexive discursive code established through repeated practice of "controlled and limited recall of a reservoir of similar 'texts.'"[47] The production of photography's reality effect is part and parcel of the emergence of managerial and disciplinary techniques associated with new institutions established through bio-disciplinary power (the prison, the asylum, hospitals[48]) and the sciences that went with them (sanitation, comparative anatomy, psychology). The "evidential force" of photography lies not in its ability to *reflect* the ideologies expressed in these institutions, but it is consolidated by and through its use in their material operation. Photography is one of the managerial and disciplinary techniques and technologies annexed and thereby decisively shaped by bio-disciplinary power.[49]

I will focus here on two particular sites in Tagg's account: in the use of photography in a paradigmatic example of what we would now call "urban renewal" and in the development of what we've come to call the "mug shot." Significantly, for my purposes, each draws on the conventions of photography's artistic antecedents, landscape painting and portraiture. Moreover, each manifests different aspects of bio-disciplinary power at work. The first of these sites, the clearing of an Irish ghetto in Leeds, England, embodies some of the same dynamics as the instances of photographic orientalism discussed previously. In the name of "public health," photographs of (temporarily emptied) spaces and places help to mobilize actions that separate a population of Man's raced and sexed others from the land or space it occupies. The photographic antecedent of the second site, the creation of the mug shot, is portrait photography deployed now to create and contain a new subject, the delinquent. Both sites illustrate the establishment of photographic truth as a (self-referential) process of materialization.

As the population of Irish immigrants grew in Leeds, the immigrants tended to concentrate in a particular area of the city known as Quarry Hill. The association of immigrants with disease and disorder aroused concerns among some in the governing classes that Quarry Hill might become (if it wasn't already) a breeding ground of disease that could spread to the native English population. A movement began to clear the slum of its inhabitants in the name of urban hygiene. An elaborate series of photographs of Quarry Hill that purported to document evidence of disorder played a significant role in the decision to clear it. These photographs, along with other visual documents (maps of Quarry Hill, of Leeds; renderings of what might replace the dwellings there), are part of the archival record of the debate over Quarry Hill's fate. Although there is no evidence that those who made the decision ever actually visited Quarry Hill (or, at least, undertook such an expedition as part of their deliberations), the weight of the real registers here in lengthy debates over not only the meaning and significance but also the veracity of the photographs. One might assume that the photographs spoke for themselves, but the archival record shows that they did not. Met with suspicion from the beginning, the slum photographs—unlike other visual documents brought to bear on the issue—required the supplement of explanations from Medical Officer of Health Dr. James Spottiswoode Cameron, who was apparently present when many of the photographs were taken. Indeed, Cameron's testimony served as a tutorial in how to "read" photographs—how to contend with the inevitable selectivity imposed by camera angle and framing, with what any photograph (intentionally or not) omits. Whatever resistance his colleagues had to photographic truth was eventually overcome and Quarry Hill was cleared of its inhabitants and their dwellings razed. This exercise of bio-disciplinary power in its rawest form rendered literal what many of the Quarry Hill photographs seemed to represent. For like Salzburg's photographs of Jerusalem's holy sites, most of these photographs, too, were utterly devoid of people. Thus, they anticipated the reality they helped to create.

Bio-disciplinary power conscripted into its service photographic portraiture as well as landscape photography. Indeed, we have already seen evidence of that in the production of *cartes de visites*. But while the *cartes de visites* perpetuated the conventions of formal portraiture in proclaiming and reinforcing one's elite social status, the creation of the mug shot served bio-disciplinary power's interest in the identification and containment of abnormality. Here, as in the case of Quarry Hill, we witness the establishment of photographic truth as a process of codification and materialization. A good mug shot—one with evidentiary value—is no accident, Tagg makes clear. Police archives document the evolution of standards for it and the establishment of practices that will yield it. Achieving the appearance of objectivity and neutrality required the right production values, police ultimately conclude. Too lavish or too spare and the photograph's claim to objectivity suffers. In the end, responsibility for producing photographic criminality was placed in the hands of a cadre of professional police photographers trained in the "how-to's" of this photographic practice.

Like the Quarry Hill photographs, the mug shot anticipates what it purports to document. Recall from chapter 1 that our account of disciplinary power centered on the emergence of the modern prison. Within that context, disciplinary power is employed through the carceral process to produce (and hopefully rehabilitate) a new form of subjectivity, the delinquent. The delinquent, recall, is more than someone who has committed a criminal act; the delinquent has come to understand the crime as an expression of his or her character *as* delinquent. Ideally, he or she then becomes engaged in the process of self-remaking that organizes prison life (incarceration as reformation) with the aim of becoming fit to rejoin society. The mug shot inaugurates the carceral process as one of characterological cultivation within a panoptical system. In Tagg's words, it delivers "the [delinquent] body made object; divided and studied, enclosed in a cellular structure of space whose architecture is the file-index; made docile and forced to yield up its truth; separated and individuated, subjected and made subject."[50] Its truth, like that of the Quarry Hill photographs, materializes well after the fact, in the subsequent creation of the delinquent him- or herself through the processes that constitute incarceration.

Quarry Hill and the mug shot may be emblematic of photographic truth as bio-disciplinary mechanism and product, but they are far from the only sites where we can see this relationship at work. Tagg identifies several other institutions—the asylum, the clinic, the factory, for example—as sites where photography served bio-disciplinary power's ends. Thus, these are sites where the fourfold of Man and his others is mined and manipulated in the forging of new social taxonomies of human beings through the installation and consolidation of the new personages they organize into actual embodied subjects. These are sites where the lines between the normal and the pathological were established and policed. Above all, these are sites where the human being—as a particular form of *bios*—is managed in pursuit of racisms both for (the normal and normative) and against (the abnormal and non-normative).

The photographic practices in asylums, like those of the mug shot, appropriate the conventions of portrait photography. Photographed full on, the mad or insane are "subjected to an unreturnable gaze; illuminated, focused, measured, numbered and named."[51] Every gesture or feature captured in the photograph received careful scrutiny as a signifier of realities hidden within the photographed subjects. In the practice of emergent psychiatric medicine, Tagg demonstrates, a picture was worth a thousand words. Photographs were used not only to organize and classify disease but also to diagnose. More efficient and accurate than an in-person exam, doctors claimed to be able to determine from even the briefest glance at the right photograph the essence of a patient's problem and how to treat it.

Among the most poignant, pointed, and pertinent examples for our purposes, though, are found in photography's conscription by *scientia sexualis*. Recall from chapter 1 that abnormality was defined and tracked through studies in comparative anatomy. Morphological differences—in the shape or size of foreheads, arms, heads, or genitalia, for example—signaled one's proper place on the scale of (ab)normality. Bodily abnormality tracked and reflected characterological abnormality and thus social abnormality. Sexuality was the primary site and symptom of abnormality and certain populations—not coincidentally, those of Man's raced others—were eaten up with it, as it were. The asylum and the clinic served biopower's interest in furthering the race by diagnosing, treating, and thus containing (if not eradicating altogether) sexual abnormality. Photography, it turns out, played a significant role in this process.[52]

Take, for example, the account of the work of the Committee for the Study of Sex Variants provided by historian Jennifer Terry in *An American Obsession: Science, Medicine, and Homosexuality in Modern Society*.[53] Founded in New York City in 1935, the committee was composed of (mostly medical) experts of various sorts—most of whom were, Terry notes (although without comment) liberal protestants—who volunteered their time and expertise to investigate what they took to be the burgeoning population of homosexuals in New York. Employing the latest in medical science and technology (including X-rays as well as photography), the committee "sought to establish the distinguishing characterological and physical qualities of the 'sex variant'."[54]

I focus on this particular instance in part because it highlights bio-disciplinary power's complex and ambivalent relationship with its subjects and objects. Up to this point in my account, it may seem as though bio-disciplinary power is a form of domination via (photographic) subjection, my anticipatory protestations to the contrary. Those caught in the cold clinical stare of its diagnostic eye—a captive audience, to be sure, given the institutionalization of *scientia sexualis* in asylums, prisons, and clinics—had little choice but to conform to its demands. This study, however, shows us another side of bio-disciplinary power's work on us. Unlike previous studies, whose subjects came primarily from those contexts, this study successfully recruited significant numbers of self-acknowledged gay men and lesbians as volunteer subjects. This fact reflects the efforts of two self-avowed homosexuals who recruited these volunteers on behalf of the researchers: Jan Gay, a lesbian journalist with a long-standing interest in the science of homosexuality, and Thomas Painter, a gay man and a graduate of Union Theological Seminary. (Both were integrally involved in the study, although neither conducted any of the formal research.) The study also was financed in part by wealthy gay donors. From her research in the archive, Terry concludes that many of the volunteers were drawn to the project's explicit aim to come to know homosexuality better. They saw promise in the researchers' explicit desire to avoid cant and prejudice, their commitment to the use of proper science, and their interest in assuaging widespread antipathy toward "inverts." The report ultimately issued in the committee's name, however, espoused explicitly eugenic aims; it sought to understand homosexuality to better contain its spread (if not eliminate it altogether).[55]

Of the more than 100 volunteers, many were of immigrant stock (including two of Cuban descent), eight (four men, four women) were African American, and two were Jewish. The final report includes data on eighty subjects (forty men, forty women) deemed by the researchers the "most informative" cases.[56] The data include extensive (edited) interviews done by psychiatrists, including reports from extensive (and often invasive) medical examinations that include detailed sketches of the genitalia of several of the women, and full frontal, nude photographs taken of the third of the subjects who permitted them.[57] The photographs "were explicitly intended to supplement other physical data and to act as diagnostic instruments for correlating body form with behavior," Terry writes. To serve the project of constructing a "typical . . . sex variant body," faces are obscured and names are omitted, thus rendering the photographed bodies generic and anonymous. Following the conventions of medical textbooks, these photos are "encoded as morbid" by their placement as an appendix to the narrative report.[58]

By Terry's account, however, the committee's project of establishing a clear etiology of homosexuality visible on the body of the sex variant subject fails, victim of its own internal incoherence. The bodies themselves exhibited too much variability to render them stable and reliable diagnostic tools. That so many of the subjects studied came from non-native stock (European or African) or "unstable households" was deemed not incidental to their abnormality.[59] Thus, the etiology of homosexuality remained complex and mysterious. But those conclusions hardly brought an end to the eugenic project; if anything, they widened and broadened it in the directions familiar to us from McWhorter. The lessons of the committee's report were aimed ultimately, after all, not at abnormals but at normals. If sex variance cannot be easily identified, it cannot be easily contained. Thus, it represents an even bigger threat to the race than it seemed at the outset of the committee's work. As the editor of the final report puts it, "As long as sex mating continues to be irrational, constitutionally predisposed sex variants are to be expected."[60] The solution: the family. But not just *any* family, the one constituted around "middle class white companionate heterosexual marriage, which . . . guided [the virtues of pleasure] toward responsible and genetically sound reproduction."[61] At the head of such families, we find the bourgeois subject familiar to us from Stoler. Charged with claiming mastery over his body and its desires, he demonstrates said mastery and thus his suitability for headship by rationally choosing an appropriate "mate."

It would be a mistake, however, to think that photography served the policing of (ab)normality only when put to formal use by governmental or medical agencies—or that it was only conscripted for this purpose in the twentieth century. My return to Stoler is more than fortuitous here on both counts, for *Carnal Knowledge* is liberally illustrated with photographs taken of (and presumably by) late-nineteenth-century colonials *en famille* in the Dutch Indies. Included are photographs of colonial families (in whole or in part); native servants; and, in a number of instances, servants and colonials together. The latter, in particular, represent in photographic form the liminal space between Europe and Java that the colonials occupied. The effect of the staging of these photographs is to (re)assure viewers (which would likely include the colonials and perhaps even the servants themselves) that proper order is maintained. Take the second photograph that appears in Stoler's book, for example.[62] The clothing worn by mother and children displays the family's Europeanness. But the tropical foliage—and the presence of a native servant—signals the exotic setting. That the husband/father is dressed in native garb like the servant standing behind him represents in photographic form the liminal space between metropole and colony that the colonials occupied—a liminal space, Stoler's analysis also demonstrates, that the metropole perceived as threatening the achievement of true manhood and womanhood. Reproduced on the same page as the family photograph is a *carte de visite* for the patriarch of the family—now wearing more European clothes.[63] Recall that, by convention, the *carte de visite* featured a portrait of its subject alone and functioned to establish said subject's manhood (or womanhood). Here, the colonial stands confidently at ease behind a waist-high Javanese counter resting his folded arms on a small stack of books, his helmet at his left elbow, a walking stick propped up against the table's right end. Seated cross-legged and barefoot in front of the table—thus framed by its elaborate decoration—is a turbaned male servant. Like its metropolitan counterparts, this *carte de visite* assures its recipient of the card bearer's elite status—indicated here by his visual and positional domination of the native servant. Together, these photographs embody the would-be truth of the colonial order—and the vulnerability of that truth to contamination.[64]

One need not travel to the colonies, however, to encounter such regimes involving Man and his sexed and raced others either live or in photographs; one could find them right here at home—in the form of public lynchings, as noted in the prior chapter (a topic to which we'll return later), or in the seemingly more benign (or at least less spectacularly violent) freak show. In these contexts, spectacle and surveillance come together as mechanisms aimed at consolidating normalcy; thus, both are examples of bio-disciplinary power at work. The freak show, a staple of American entertainment from the mid-nineteenth through the mid-twentieth centuries, was a traveling exhibition of living human beings whose bodies set them apart in some way. They were far more than mere curiosities, as disability theorist Rosemarie Garland Thomson demonstrates.[65] The freak show was a "cultural ritual that dramatized the era's physical and social hierarchy by spotlighting bodily stigmata that could be choreographed as an absolute contrast to 'normal' American embodiment and authenticated as corporeal truth."[66] Looking (or perhaps better, staring[67]) at these bodies on display was "to the masses what science was to the emerging elite: an opportunity to formulate the [normal] self in terms of what it was not," she writes.[68] So, freak shows included people with what are now categorized as disabilities (giantism, dwarfism, microcephaly, missing or shortened limbs, etc.), with sexually ambiguous bodies ("hermaphrodites," hirsute women, hairless men), or whose bodies blurred the border between human and animal (the frog man, the leopard child).[69] The truth of (ab)normality was available for viewing, observable to the naked eye. For those unable to attend the shows in person, photographs of the shows—including *cartes de visites* of freaks produced by some of the best known photographic studios of the day—were widely circulated and collected. Like the spectators of the live shows, what I will call freak photography enabled its consumers to cut their bio-disciplinary teeth by visually dissecting the curiosities on display.[70] Thus, the visual dissections of the freak show and freak photography are kin to those embodied in the committee's report and other exemplars of *scientia sexualis*.

Although bodily anomalies certainly caught Nordics in the dynamics of what Garland Thomson calls "enfreakment," of particular interest were the extraordinary bodies found among non-Nordics.[71] A few of the most infamous freaks are still known to us by name or visual image (photograph or sketch). They include Europe's so-called Hottentot Venus (Saatjie Baartman, recall); her American counterpart, Julia Pastrana (a Mexican Indian billed as "the Ugliest Woman in the World"); the "Siamese" [conjoined] twins, Chang and Eng Bunker; and one of a number of so-called missing links, a microcephalic black man named William Henry Johnson. Garland Thomson's account focuses on the careers of Baartman and Portman, a focus that brings formative bio-disciplinary power's concern with sexed and raced deviance into sharp and painful relief.

Bodily signs of such deviance marked, as well, the slippery slope toward animality. The moniker assigned Baartman, "Hottentot Venus," alerted spectators to look for bodily manifestations of raced and sexed deviance, thus positioning Baartman on the border of the bestial. "Hottentot" was the European term for the most "primitive" species of human; the size and shape of Baartman's buttocks, typical of her San tribe but not of Europeans, signaled her alleged sexual deviance and incipient animality. Wearing a flesh colored garment that clung to her buttocks, Baartman was paraded silently in and out of a cage by her minder. Money was collected from the crowd, a surcharge added for the privilege of touching her. Pastrana's comely breasts, stocky shape, thicker facial features, and unusual hairiness mixed features of normative femininity and masculinity, humanity and animality. In addition to being displayed for public consumption, Pastrana was also the object of scientific inquiry as an article from the well-known British medical journal the *Lancet* attests.[72] Garland Thomson astutely notes the mix of quasi-anthropological detail (a reference to Pastrana's "feminine singing voice" is particularly striking) with scientific tone in the author's description of Pastrana, which she quotes at some length.[73]

The freak show marks a critical transition point in the modern *episteme* and *ethos*, and thus in biopower's emergence and consolidation. Before modernity, Garland Thomson argues, extraordinary bodies were seen as marvelous if disturbing wonders and portents; they were considered evidence of God's control over nature.[74] The sense of wonder and mystery evoked by the freak shows reflects the residue of this view of the extraordinary body even as the challenges freakish bodies posed to spectators evidences bio-disciplinary power's will to know. But it is the demise of the freak show that marks the epistemic shift with particular clarity. Freak shows largely disappear from the scene around 1940, notes Garland Thomson, a casualty of the ascendance of medical science. Extraordinary bodies lose entirely their ability to inspire wonder and become instead problems to be solved, objects of scientific knowledge and medical treatment. Scientists sought to "fix" extraordinary bodies—to eliminate deviance and disability by treating its effects and, where possible, by tracking down and eliminating its causes.

The treatment of the bodies of Baartman and Pastrana after their deaths exemplifies this transition. Both had relatively short careers as living freaks, but extended postmortem careers as public scientific specimens. Virtual dissection became literal dissection in Baartman's case; her body was carved into its requisite pieces and her preserved genitals (the ultimate bodily signature of her sexed and raced deviance) were made available for public viewing. Indeed, they resided in the collection of the Musée de l'homme in Paris until 2002 when, nearly ten years after Nelson Mandela requested it, they were repatriated to South Africa and interred.[75] After Pastrana died giving birth to a child (who looked like her), her husband/manager sold both bodies to a Russian scientist who embalmed them. The husband/manager was so impressed with the results that he bought the bodies back from the scientist—for more than his original selling price—and put them back on tour. His death in 1884 did not end the practice of their exhibition, as the remains changed hands (often illicitly) for a number of years after. Last exhibited publicly in 1972, according to Garland Thomson, the remains are still an object of medical speculation. As recently as 1993, scientists were pressing for testing of Pastrana's skull, hair, and teeth to determine the cause of her abnormalities.[76]

Taking Stock I: Photographic Truth and/as Askesis

To this point, I have offered an account of the emergence and consolidation of photographic truth. Against the assumption that the truth of photographs lies in the self-evident immediacy of their relationship to what they represent, I have argued for a more complex and multivalent understanding. That we take the reality referent of photography for granted reflects our immersion in the modern scopic regime. At the center of that regime's emergence is its generation of a new visual subject, the observer (Crary), who is simultaneously subject and object of this new regime. Photographic truth is essential to modern panoptical culture, "that modern play over bodies, gestures and behaviour which is the emergence of the so-called 'science of man' and the constitution of the modern state."[77] Moreover, photography's claim to (re)present that-there-then rests on its function as a transfer point for bio-disciplinary power. Photographic truth was established through its use in showing its subjects and objects their truth, a truth granted them—indeed, instilled in them—by bio-disciplinary power in both its malign and benign manifestations. Thus, photography is integral to what Tagg, following Foucault, calls the culture of surveillance at the heart of bio-disciplinary power.

In the modern *episteme,* Man's status as empirico-transcendental dou-blet positions him as both subject and object not only of knowledge but also of management. As the one-who-manages, Man aspires to God-like status. But, like his raced, sexed, and animal others, Man is finite *bios* and, as such, is subjected to (and made the object of) bio-discipline.

So far, I have focused on photography's use in the production and management of abnormality and thus on bio-disciplinary power's less than benign manifestations. Recall, however, that Tagg named the fac-tory as a site of photography's use to serve bio-disciplinary power. Indeed, early motion picture photography (more pictures of motion than pic-tures that move, it turns out) was critical to one of industrialization's sig-nal accomplishments: the creation and production of the assembly line worker. The inventor of this photographic technology, Eadweard Muy-bridge, claimed to capture what the naked eye could not see: fluid move-ment dissected into precise stages and elements.[78] Initially contracted by a racehorse owner to resolve a longstanding question about the gait of horses (whether, at any point during a gallop, all four feet touched the ground), Muybridge developed his technique (and apparatus) by photo-graphing various animal bodies in motion.[79] However, his most famous collection of photographs (bearing the telling title *Animal Locomotion*) includes photo-series of human bodies in motion, as well: a (white) man swinging a tennis racket, another diving off a diving board, a (white) woman dancing, and another descending a staircase, for example.[80] Dis-playing these photographs alongside similar series of a sow walking, a horse galloping, and a dog running blurs the line between human and animal. As in other forms of photographic dissection, Man's others—his animal others, in this case—reflect Man back to himself now as a form of *bios.* When Muybridge's project came to the attention of Frank and Lillian Gilbreth, pioneers in the study and engineering of human motion, they saw its potential as a tool for increasing the efficiency and productivity of human *bios* in enterprises like housework and factory work. Notably, they applied Muybridge's techniques to the motions of factory workers to pro-duce bodily choreographies in which assembly line workers were trained, thereby forming themselves into the kinds of docile bodies needed for industrial production.[81]

Recall that I have described *Signs and Wonders* as an *askesis,* a disci-plined attending-to in pursuit of transformation—a slow (un)making of our sense of self, world, and our place in it. It is, like Foucault's *histoires,* a history of the present. We are the scions of the *histoire* of photographic truth; its truth is our truth. In our most ordinary having-to-do-with the world, we are subjected to photographic truth. This is a manifestation of what Heidegger called "thrownness."[82] We find ourselves always already in a world not of our own making, affected by it in ways we rarely notice. That world is shaped and sustained by bio-disciplinary power—as are we. This does not mean we are utterly and thoroughly determined by it; where there is power, there is resistance, remember—in which photography also figures, as we'll see. But our knowing, doing, being, and seeing is a constant and mostly unconscious negotiation with bio-disciplinary power—often channeled through the fourfold. I trust it is clear, by now, that the fourfold is not a set of ready-made identities; instead, it functions as a set of vectors that refract rather than reflect whoever (or whatever) enters into it. To know, to do, to be, and to see is to take up one's place in the social order that it has produced. Thus, we are all caught up in the fourfold's constant and vertiginous specularization.

Photographic *Signifiance*: How Photographs "Move" Us

This chapter has yet to attend fully to its ultimate aim—that is, to provide some guidance on how to read the photographs to come. How to read is more than a question of what to look for. It is a question of attending to *how* photographs signify and to what. I want to pose this as a question of photographic *signifiance*. A neologism coined by Julia Kristeva and picked up by Barthes, *signifiance* turns on its head our ordinary notion of what's involved in wresting meaning from things. That ordinary notion posits the thing (a photograph, say) as an object standing over against a clearly defined subject, the interpreter. The act of interpretation is essentially an act of decoding, of exhibiting or attaining mastery over the object by gradually stripping bare its layers of meaning until there is no more to say. *Signifiance*, on the other hand, posits a much messier and more complex understanding of interpretation, one that entrains subject and object in a process of meaning making that is more abyssal than masterful.[83] Our account of photographic truth, then, has already started us down the path of inquiry after photographic *signifiance*. Just as photographic truth proved to be anything but self-evident, so also photographic *signifiance*. And just as coming to know photographic truth required working through the various layers of its establishment, so also for our further inquiries into photographic *signifiance*. As we have already begun to see, the surface of a photograph—its visual content—draws us into a world of immeasurable depth and complexity. That world includes not only the immediate events that the photographs reference (the specific that-there-then of each photograph), but their larger context, including the philosophical, theological, and sociopolitical concerns at the heart of *Signs and Wonders*. But it also includes modes and mechanisms by which we have come to know the photographs in question and the events they reference. That certain photographs hold special significance reflects their embeddedness in the various news media whose coverage was critical in our attempts to come to terms with the events the photographs reference; hence, I pay particular attention to photojournalism in what follows. In taking up the photographs that constitute the signs and wonders of the chapters to come, I extend the process of *signifiance* that the photographs' publication inaugurated. I take up my place as one in a long line of journalists, activists, volunteers, and scholars who responded to the photographs and to the events they reference in some way. This network includes, of course, those in the photographs and those immediately affected by those events.

No attempt to read these photographs would be complete without taking account of their capacity (and the limits thereof) to "move" us—that is, to evoke an emotional response or to inspire action. Many people around the world were horrified by the photographs from Abu Ghraib, for example. Of that number, some were moved to acts of protest of various sorts. Prolife and disability rights activists made (what they perceived to be) Terri Schiavo's cause their own as did state and national legislative bodies. And many Americans who watched coverage of Hurricane Katrina on television were outraged by the Federal Emergency Management Agency's pathetically slow and inadequate response; some even got in their cars and went to help. These responses were not universal, of course. Others seemed quite unmoved by the Abu Ghraib photographs dismissing them as mere "fraternity pranks" (Rush Limbaugh) or the work of "a few bad apples" (Donald Rumsfeld). Still others appropriated them for pornographic use. And let's not forget that the photographs also likely prolonged and expanded the War on Terror by moving others to join the cause of violent Islamism. Terri Schiavo's situation prompted a good many of us, apparently, to craft living wills and designate medical powers of attorney, in many cases to protect ourselves against the agenda of prolife activists. Katrina's devastation moved Pat Robertson to declare it a sign of God's wrath against a morally lax (read "gay friendly") New Orleans. I would not claim that the photographs *themselves* were the sole cause of these movements. But what is it about photographs—and ultimately about these photographs in particular—that might have contributed to them?

"Iconic" Photographs

I am hardly the first to raise such questions about photographs—or even about certain of these photographs in particular. These questions have been circulating in and around academic and critical discussions of photography for quite some time. I will not presume here to chronicle that discussion in its entirety; I will, however, call on some of its most prominent voices for insights that I will use to address these questions and thus further craft an approach to reading the photographs to come. Attending to these questions will take us beyond the account of photographic truth that has constituted the bulk of the labor of this chapter. That account has attended primarily to what art historians and visual culture theorists call photography's "indexical" dimension—that is, to its evidentiary production values and uses. But such scholars also speak of photography's "iconic" dimension—that is, its ability to transcend the hold of the "reality effect," which would limit photographic signification to the merely (or mostly) mechanical capturing of that-there-then.[84]

The term "icon" originates, of course, as a term for religious art—that is, for visual images that stand in for (because they open access to) the divine. As I noted earlier, Benjamin famously claimed that the ability to mechanically reproduce images robbed art of its "aura" of originality and authenticity, which secular art had inherited from religious icons. That aura resided in the artwork's distinctive relationship to time and place; in the specificity of its origin and substantive duration, in the "testimony" it offered to its history.[85] Photography's acceptance into the realm of high culture rested on its ability to lay claim to features associated with other kinds of visual art. In the capable hands of certain photographers, early-twentieth-century art critics finally had to admit, the camera yielded to

aesthetic values; notably to a formalism congruent with modernist painting and sculpture (e.g., think Alfred Stieglitz's famous photographs of the
New York skyline).[86] Steiglitz's photographs took the New York skyline
beyond a mere record of one building's proximity to another. In shooting
the skyline from just this angle in just this light with just this apparatus
and using just this developmental process, the juxtaposition of line and
form, of foreground and background, of shades of dark and light signaled
more than a mere record of that-there-then. A certain beauty—sublimity,
even—emerged out of the skyline; the photograph represents the skyline
as simultaneously ephemeral and monumental, as an icon, if you will, of
modernity.

With the emergence soon after of professional documentary and com-
mercial photography, the claim to iconicity quickly outgrew its limitation
to art photography.[87] One has only to think of such familiar photographs
as Dorothea Lange's "Migrant Mother" (1936), featuring a Depression-
era migrant worker mother and her children, or Associated Press photographer Hyunh Cong "Nick" Ut's "Accidental Napalm" (1972), a
photograph of a group of children running down a Vietnam road after
their victimization by a U.S. napalm attack, whose central focus is a naked
little girl screaming and crying, to understand why.[88] These photographs
are, first of all, iconic in the quasi-religious sense; they stand in for the
larger events they reference (the Depression, the Vietnam War) because
they open onto the larger significance these events have taken on in historical memory. It is fitting that Robert Hariman and John Louis Lucaites
include both of these photos in their superb study, *No Caption Needed:
Iconic Photographs, Public Culture and Liberal Democracy*.[89] That said,
it may seem a categorical mistake to speak of these photographs as possessed of an iconic dimension in the more aesthetic sense. After all, the
very term *documentary* bespeaks evidentiary intent—and indeed central
to the impact of these iconic photographs is their claim on that-there-
then. That claim, as we'll see, rests on the account of photographic truth
provided previously. Professional documentary photographs, however,
like art photography (and mug shots), rely on convention and composition. Although it may not have been shot in a studio, Hariman and
Lucaites show that "Migrant Mother" is as thoughtfully composed a
photograph as most studio portraits. Lange carefully selected, shaped,
and shot this particular that-there-then in accord with the conventions
established for documentary portraiture over the course of some thirty

years or so of its practice. Given the conditions of war photojournalism, Nick Ut's photograph cannot be the carefully composed study in portraiture that is "Migrant Mother." Indeed, were it to attempt to be so, it would violate the conventions of photojournalism, which seek to avoid the "taint of artistry," as Susan Sontag puts it, like proper lighting or too much attention to composition.[90] The very immediacy of "Accidental Napalm"—its capturing of its subjects-in-action—is a hallmark of compelling news photography (it won the Pulitzer Prize) and reflects Ut's own well-honed skills at quickly selecting, framing, and shooting that-there-then under stressful conditions. Both photographs also transcend their that-there-then in ways quite similar to Stieglitz's New York skyline. As Hariman and Lucaites show, the particular juxtapositions of figure and gesture, light and dark, foreground and background that are integral to the staying power of these photos are the work of *artistes* skilled in the conventions of their genre.[91]

But there is more to documentary photographs' iconicity than professional skill and mastery of generic conventions. We speak of these photographs as iconic in part because of their affective dimension, what I described earlier as their ability to "move" (provoke an emotional response and motivate to action) their viewers. Although the noun "affect" has been part of the vocabulary of psychologists and psychiatrists for quite a while, it has recently become an object of interest and even theorization in broader academic circles. Affect theory attends to what and how we are moved; how and what emotions—positive or negative, blissful or painful—arise in us in response to events mundane or consequential and what they prompt us to do.[92] Such attending brings to light the degree to which we are deeply embedded in and multiply connected to our world and to others who inhabit it with us, a point to which I'll return in later chapters. Affect theory occupies a complex position in relation to (post)modernity. On the one hand, its heritage lies in the human sciences, a distinctively modern enterprise. On the other, it resists or overturns certain modern assumptions. For example, to the degree that Cartesianism focuses on the cognitive acts of a self-contained subject, affect theory is profoundly anti-Cartesian in the priority it grants to emotive response and in its (mostly implicit) ontology. Affect theorists also are careful to distinguish affect from emotion. Whereas emotion refers to states of feeling (prompted, to be sure, by external events) that are internal to the individual subject, affect travels in that liminal space of contact between self, world, and others.[93]

Iconicity and Affectivity

Affect theory may be relatively new to the humanities in general, but concern and interest in what moves us certainly isn't—particularly to studies of photography. As early as 1981, Barthes's landmark study *Camera Lucida: Reflections on Photography* distinguished between two modes of photographic meaning: *studium* and *punctum*.[94] The *studium* is the social content and context that we have absorbed that we see reflected in the photograph—in other words, its subject matter. We respond to the *studium* with detached acknowledgment; we may like or dislike the photograph, find it more or less interesting, but it doesn't truly move us. The *punctum*, on the other hand, is what certain photographs provoke in us; it is a puncture or prick that arouses a strong emotive response. That response is often provoked not by the focal element of a photograph but by a random detail that simply happens to be part of its that-there-then. It is also, Barthes asserts, a subjective response that says as much or more about the viewer as about the photograph itself.[95]

Likewise, Sontag has argued that there is nothing intrinsic to photography itself that *guarantees* that any given photograph—even photographs of atrocities—will evoke sympathy or outrage. "For photographs to accuse, and possibly to alter conduct, they must shock," Sontag claims; they must provoke in viewers a struggle to assimilate what they see *as* truly that-there-then. Sontag notes that photographs of atrocities—she mentions those of the Bosnian war, but those of the current conflict in Syria also confront the same dilemma—are routinely denounced by some as fakes.[96] At the same time, photography necessarily aestheticizes its that-there-then, and sometimes a photograph's beauty has an anesthetic effect on the viewer.

But photography's limited ability to "move" us is not simply a matter of shock versus aesthetic production values, if you will; it is also—perhaps primarily, even—a matter of a photograph's context. Sontag takes up briefly *Without Sanctuary*, the touring exhibition of lynching photographs organized in 2000 (to which I'll return in chapter 4). The very same photographs that moved many of their original white viewers right past acknowledgment of suffering to self-congratulatory self-assurance about their (white) supremacy—and thus to circulate the photographs as souvenirs of same—in this new context now moves contemporary viewers to horror, grief, and, for some whites at least, guilt. That context certainly includes the new setting in which these photographs are viewed: a thoughtfully curated—researched, ordered, guided—exhibition put on display for somber ends in places and spaces (museums, galleries) built for this purpose. But it also includes the complex history of race relations in the United States as that history has unfolded in the decades since the photographs were made. Indeed, as Sontag points out, it's in part the history of the original responses to the photographs that moves contemporary viewers now—and to very different ends.[97]

Hariman and Lucaites's overarching interest in iconic photography is in pursuing and articulating the conflicted, ambivalent, and ambiguous role photojournalism plays in liberal democracy. The photographs they deem iconic are exclusively the work of professional photographers (photojournalists mostly) that were widely circulated beyond the original sites of their publication (indeed, circulation both signals and cultivates iconicity). They reference events—crises, not coincidentally—of major political significance to which they have a special relationship. The title of the book is apt, as the photographs it features need no caption; they remain instantly recognizable decades after their initial publication. Most are known for their political impact (and all rightly claim it), an impact grounded in their ability to both arouse and manage affective response.

Cultivating that capacity is intrinsic to the aims and purposes of documentary photography, the photographic genre to which photojournalism is typically consigned. Documentary photography emerged as part of the social reform movements of the nineteenth and twentieth centuries; thus, its emergence is of a piece with the exercises of bio-disciplinary power that produced Quarry Hill.[98] Photographic surveillance and dissection of (ab)normals, recall, established the camera's claim on that-there-then; its claim, in other words, to document the real. As John Tagg shows in *The Disciplinary Frame*, documentary photography draws on that claim, but deploys the camera and its products in the service of a different form of subject formation. Rather than installing, policing, and managing (ab)normality through photographic surveillance, documentary photography aimed to shape its viewers into "civic subjects of liberal democracy."[99] Thus, as Tagg puts it, documentary photography's truth claims "rested on a populist rhetoric—an emotionalized drama of witness—that worked to wed its audiences to its realism, its viewers to its look, sealing them into its system of enacted truth."[100]

"Migrant Mother" exemplifies this genealogy. Lange was one of a cadre of professional photographers employed by what became the Farm Services Administration (FSA) and tasked with the job of documenting the suffering of the victims of the Great Depression. That project served a larger purpose—that is, generating support for the various relief programs of Roosevelt's New Deal by arousing sympathy for the suffering poor and ultimately, as Tagg argues, for the New Deal state and its policies. The FSA photographs were, then, propaganda; they were more benign and democratic in aim, certainly, than Leni Reifenstahl's films, say, but propaganda nonetheless. And, as Hariman and Lucaites document, "Migrant Mother" worked—at least, up to a point. Selected to accompany a story in the San Francisco newspaper demanding relief for pea farm laborers, it helped move people to contribute to those relief efforts.[101] But photography can also prompt civic subjects to turn against their government. Ut's photograph provoked in many American viewers a searing guilt for the suffering inflicted on innocents by a war that came to epitomize U.S. overreach—and thus a righteous anger over the war conducted in our name. Guilt and anger motivated some to become involved in antiwar protests; indeed, "Accidental Napalm" is often credited with accelerating the growth of that movement and thus intensifying the pressure on the U.S. government to bring the war to a close, which it finally did a few years later in 1975.

Can "Snapshots" Be Icons?

My discussion thus far of iconicity has focused exclusively on professionally produced photographs. Four of the photographs on which we'll focus in subsequent chapters—those of Gene Robinson's consecration and of the aftermath of Hurricane Katrina—fit within this category. The other photographs—those from Abu Ghraib and those of Terri Schiavo's face—do not. They are, respectively, souvenir snapshots and stills from a home movie (family snapshots, in a sense).[102] Both kinds of photographs are literal *souvenirs* (mementoes, remembrances; *se souvenir* = to remember in French). Certain family photographs are, like the lynching photographs, souvenir photographs in the narrower sense; that is, they are mementos of public events, times, and places, although the stills of Schiavo's face are not. That we commonly refer to these photographs as "snapshots" signals their generic difference from photojournalism. "Snapshots" are the work of amateurs; they may seem, then, more "mechanical" or automatic than either documentary photography or photojournalism—especially with the advent of the point-and-shoot camera. For now, however, I want to demonstrate the applicability of the categories of photographic *signifiance* with which we've been working—indexicality, iconicity, and affectivity— to snapshots. Leaving aside iconicity for the moment, snapshots exemplify the indexical, but they open onto the affective. We pull out our cameras and point and shoot to capture a particular that-there-then. An event's emotional significance often prompts us to point and shoot, to be sure, but even snapshots taken with mere documentary intent can move us in certain contexts. So, for example, a photograph of my mother and me standing in the yard of the house of our Punjabi hosts in Patiala, India, in 1969 evokes in me the emotional resonances of my family's five-month stay in Asia when I was ten years old—an event that was, for me, life changing.

Recall that Barthes argues that a given photograph's ability to wound, if you will, is more subjective than objective. Indeed, the focal example he offers of the distinction between *punctum* and *studium* is his response to a photograph he came across after his mother's death, a snapshot of her as a much younger woman standing in a garden. He had no recollection of the that-there-then of the snapshot; he knew neither the garden or what his mother looked like at that age. And yet it moved him to tears, he reports, in a way that no photograph that actually represented her *as* he recalled knowing her did.[103] Sontag's observations about the lynching photographs confirm that souvenir snapshots can generate collective affect, as well. That the same is true of family photographs (in certain situations, at least) is confirmed by the role played by the stills of Terri Schiavo's face in the controversy over her case. But can we speak of an iconic dimension to snapshots—in either the aesthetic or the quasi-religious sense?

A partial answer to that question can be broached with reference to Sontag's earlier work, *On Photography* (1977). There, Sontag takes up the question of the significance of family and souvenir snapshots (they come together in what she calls "tourist photographs").[104] The questions I've posed presume that we allocate snapshots to the sphere of the private versus the public, the singular versus the shared, an allocation that

Sontag calls into question. Snapshots, she argues, are "mainly a social rite, a defense against anxiety, and a tool of power."[105] It is no coincidence that photography emerges as "a rite of family life" at just the time when "that claustrophobic unit, the nuclear family, was being carved out of a much larger family aggregate."[106] Family snapshots serve "to memorialize, to restate symbolically, the imperiled continuity and vanishing extended-ness of family life."[107] Tourist photographs, as well, blur the boundary between private and public. Let's take as an example a snapshot I took of my partner by the banks of the Merced River in Yosemite National Park on the July 4 weekend in 2009. On the one hand, this photograph is deeply private; it documents that "we" (my partner and I) were "there" (Yosemite) "then" (July 2009). On the other hand, it's quite public. We were hardly the *only* people there then, the busiest weekend of Yosemite's very busy tourist season. Our places were immediately taken, in fact, by a busload of tourists who proceeded to photograph one another in more or less the same spot and same position (smiling, facing the camera, backs to the spectacular scenery) that my partner had occupied a moment earlier. Certainly, my photo is unique, but all of the photographs taken there that day serve the same purpose—to prove that "we were there" (if I may riff off the name of an old Walter Cronkite show). As Sontag argues, just as family photographs signal our grasp on a past to assure us of our status in the present, so also tourist photographs. They signal that we know a photogenic site when we see it, which (re)assures us that we matter. Thus, family and tourist snapshots—even of people the viewer has never met—can transcend their that-there-then.

To the degree that aesthetic iconicity is a matter of conformity to generic convention, then, like documentary photographs or photojour-nalism, snapshots are legible to anyone trained in their conventions. Indeed, Marianne Hirsch claims that, even in the seemingly private space where we view our own family snapshots, we are objects of what she dubs the familial gaze. That gaze naturalizes certain ideologies of family that are to be reincarnated in and through the conventions of family photog-raphy.[108] Margaret Olin adapts the Hindu concept of *darshan* to describe what we seek from tourist and family photographs. We take tourist and family photographs to "bask" in them as one does the sun. Only pho-tographs that are relatively generic (e.g., my photo of my partner) can serve that purpose. "If you see the image, you cannot bask in its gaze," she writes.[109]

But can snapshots be iconic in the full sense of the term? Can they stand in for (because they open onto) events of *public* significance or is that capacity limited only to professional documentary photographs? The Abu Ghraib photographs themselves provide an answer to that question. Although Hariman and Lucaites defer any judgment about which, if any, of these photographs will become fully iconic, W. J. T. Mitchell argues that two snapshots have become so, at least for our time and place.[110] One features a pyramid of naked prisoners; the other an Iraqi prisoner draped from head to calf in a fringed blanket or shawl standing on a box with arms outstretched and apparently wired to an electrical source that remains outside the frame.[111] Mitchell spends considerably more time on the latter, even giving it a proper name (if not quite a title), "Hooded Man on a Box"—and rightly so, given "Hooded Man's" subsequent role in what Mitchell calls "the Abu Ghraib archive."[112] Other photographs documenting the abuse at Abu Ghraib have been widely circulated, but "Hooded Man" is the primary one that has been taken up—in a variety of ways and by professionals and amateurs alike—in the making of protest art, Mitchell notes (recall that circulation and citation both indicate and enable the achievement of iconicity, according to Hariman and Lucaites).[113]

Although some (but not all) of the photographs I will discuss in what follows may not need captions now,[114] I will not claim that they have met the high standard Hariman and Lucaites set for iconicity, although they exhibit many of its characteristics. Excepting Mitchell's claim for "Hooded Man," it is too soon to say what photographs(s) if any will emerge as icons of the events these photographs reference. For one thing, the relationship between these particular photographs and the political movements in and around the events they reference is ambiguous. What movements they may have prompted or strengthened were, as my earlier brief description indicated, hardly univocal in intent or unilateral in effect. Moreover, we cannot know now what significance subsequent generations will grant to those events. They may be replaced in historical memory by other natural disasters, war crimes, personal tragedies-cum-political dramas, and ecclesiological milestones—or by other kinds of events entirely. What interests me, however, is another dimension of these photographs' iconic potential: the access that they offer into the specific theological, philosophical, social, and political issues at the heart of *Signs and Wonders* and of our time and place. Each of these photographs highlight dimensions of those issues—in and through the events that they reference, to be sure—and each in a distinctive way.

Admittedly, then, my selection of these photographs from the archives of which they are a part is somewhat idiosyncratic. Hariman and Lucaites, however, note in their introduction that people they happened to talk to about this project while it was under way—friends, family, people they met on airplanes—always remembered the photographs in question. The same is true for the photographs I've selected. Inevitably, people to whom I've described this project (and there have been quite a number of them in the years of its gestation) nod in recognition when I mention the photographs in question. They may need the prompt of a brief description to recall one or another of them, but their quick responses indicate its almost immediate availability to memory—and, in most cases, the recollection is laden with affect. Their reactions mirror my own and suggest that the photographs in question assert a claim on our attention—an arresting claim, even—to which we should attend. This claim lies at the heart of iconicity and is something these photographs share with those in *No Caption Needed*.

In their opening chapter, Hariman and Lucaites offer a set of "axioms" that articulate the sources of this claim on us.[115] Critically for my purposes, they acknowledge that iconic photographs do not hold a monopoly on the features they identify. These features are present in whole or in part in much photography, especially photojournalism, and other forms of visual imagery; iconic photographs simply exhibit them in concentrated form. Indeed, several of these characteristics echo prior aspects of our discussion. For example, Hariman and Lucaites note that iconic photographs use a conventional visual vocabulary rooted in the "middlebrow arts such as landscape or portrait painting," recalling our earlier discussion of photography's painterly background.[116] That vocabulary includes artistic, political, and social codes of various sorts; codes that iconic photographs communicate with particular economy and power. Such photographs show us civic identities, social behaviors, and social contexts that are often familiar to us from everyday life. Thus, they mirror who we are, who we wish we were, and who we hope we are not, individually and collectively, a claim that recalls the role of freak photography, colonial family snapshots, and those of sexual deviants in the production of photographic truth.

Of particular import are what Hariman and Lucaites's axioms contribute to our understanding of photographic affectivity. In what they anticipate will be their most controversial claim, Hariman and Lucaites assert that iconic photographs do more than prompt us to act; they "act" themselves. The photograph itself constitutes a performative space in which the embodied gestures and facial expressions of photographed subjects create an affective relationship with the viewer. Because iconic photographs arise out of situations of social conflict or crisis, that relationship often involves "civic pride or outrage."[117] Indeed, iconic photographs are circuits of political affect, to borrow a term from John Protevi.[118] By "concentrat[ing] and direct[ing] emotions," iconic photographs serve as "aesthetic resources for performative mediation of conflicts," the authors of *No Caption* assert.[119]

As the chapters that follow will show, the photographs that are their focus exhibit these same characteristics. They draw on established aesthetic and social codes: the generic conventions of photojournalism and souvenir snapshots; social codes of embodied gendered, racial, ethnic, and religious performance. Gesture and facial expression (or its obscuring) are critical to their affective import. Because each of them arises out of a situation of social and political conflict or crisis, their affective charge is social and political, a distinctive mix in each case. Thus, each chapter will attend to the role of the photograph in question as an "aesthetic resource" in the messy business of political and social conflict. Notice, however, that I do not say "conflict *resolution*." That is, in part, because even if the *specific* conflict each photograph references has been resolved (Terri Schiavo was allowed to die, Gene Robinson served as bishop until his recent retirement, torture has supposedly been taken off the U.S. military's table, the Gulf Coast is rebuilding), the underlying political, social, and civic conflicts that they index have not been. Moreover, the photographs and the conflicts that occasioned them expose a deeper set of challenges that we are only beginning to acknowledge and live into. These challenges are as much philosophical and theological as social and political and are my ultimate focus in *Signs and Wonders*.

Photographic *Signifiance* and/as *Askesis*

I have positioned this project as an *askesis*, an engagement in disciplined attentiveness aimed at transformation. In coming to see ourselves and our time and place differently, I hope to open up ways for us to know, be, and do differently. I have proposed this particular ascetic exercise as a kind of unmaking; a patient destructuring, if you will, of certain aspects, at least, of bio-disciplinary power's role (channeled through the fourfold) in what has made us who and what we are. That way of describing the project aligns well with photographic *signifiance*. My account of photographic truth in the first part of this chapter excavated the role of photography in peculiarly modern forms of subjection—that is, both the making and managing of modern subjects. As a mode and mechanism of the exercise of bio-disciplinary power framed and focused by the fourfold, I argued that photography was a critical tool in the creation, installation, mainte-nance, and policing of modern ways of being, knowing, seeing, and doing.

But my account of photographic truth centered on photography's index-icality, not its iconicity or affectivity. Are these other dimensions of pho-tographic *signifiance* involved at all in subjection? Certainly, photographic iconicity and affectivity trade on indexicality. That "Migrant Mother" and "Accidental Napalm" need no caption rests as much on their claim to rep-resent that-there-then as on the aesthetics of their composition. More to the point, however, that these particular photographs moved their viewers in the ways they did presumes viewers' prior formation through subjection in, to, and by modern visual culture and its ways of seeing. That form of subjection would include the conventions that underwrite photographic truth, such as the social codes and visual grammars that photographs often cite. Of particular import in "Migrant Mother" and "Accidental Napalm," for example, are the social codes of gender, race and ethnicity, class, age, and nationality as features of embodied—and properly performed—sub-jectivity. Those codes inflect and are inflected by the visual grammars of religious and popular iconography the photographs also reference. Those visual grammars reflect the organizational schema of the fourfold; thus, all three dimensions of photographic meaning—iconicity and affectivity as well as indexicality—channel bio-disciplinary power.

If, however, our account of photographic truth focused on photog-raphy's role in establishing and consolidating the modern social order through which bio-disciplinary power (as biopolitics) manages us, atten-tion to affectivity and iconicity complicates photography's social role. Pho-tographs may move us, but they do not necessarily move us all in the same direction or to the same extent. Recall that "Accidental Napalm" helped mobilize and intensify antiwar activism by arousing viewer sympathy, pity, and outrage. Despite the initial uproar that the Abu Ghraib photographs created, many commentators subsequently noted their ultimate failure to rally any support for prosecuting the architects of Bush administration policies for the treatment of detainees.[120] Of course, these differences are to be expected; the photographs in question differ in many ways, as do the wars they reference. But how might our understanding of photographic *signifiance* need to be reconfigured to incorporate what we might call photographic ambivalence into our understanding of photographic subjection? Such a reframing is critical to my overarching ascetic project as an intervention in (but not an overcoming of) the exercise of bio-disciplinary power run through the fourfold. Given its totalizing reach, I cannot claim to intervene from outside bio-disciplinary power, yet I will claim some purchase on it, purchase that comes through photographic subjection, not in spite of it.

Recall Tagg's claim that the New Deal state deployed documentary photography in the service of creating the citizenry it needed to support its goals and aims. The Israeli scholar Ariella Azoulay makes a related but more comprehensive claim about photography per se, a claim that I find helpful in situating the chapters to follow.[121] Although she does not (and perhaps would not) use these terms, Azoulay presents photography as a form of political and ethical subjection. It opened a new and uniquely modern form of civil life, she argues, one that "modified the way in which individuals are governed and the extent of their participation in the forms of governance."[122] One of those modifications, of course, is photography's appropriation by and assimilation into the system of surveillance I tracked earlier, as Azoulay acknowledges. But as we've seen, some photographs double back on the state as a form of critique that motivates political resistance. This aspect of photographic practice—and its limits—lies at the heart of her project.

Azoulay argues that photography is first and foremost not a technology or a form of seeing, but a tacit civil contract between viewers ("spectators," she calls them), photographed subjects and objects, and photographers. Like the social contract posited by Hobbes as the ground of civilization as we know it, the photographic contract is a fiction, of sorts. There is no formal document signed by our forebears committing us all to its terms. Rather, "contract" bespeaks the social constitution of photographic practice that, for all practical purposes and largely without conscious consent, binds those under its sway. Its artificiality comes into view only when we encounter photographic neophytes—those who have not been exposed to photographs before and thus must be trained in their conventions.[123]

Given the ubiquity of the camera, any of us can (and most of us likely will) occupy any or all of those positions (photographer, photographed subject, spectator) at some point.[124] In taking up any one of them, we effectively sign on to the photographic contract subjecting ourselves to its terms. In so doing, we are made photographic citizen-subjects with all the rights and responsibilities thereto appertaining, so to speak. The photographic contract links all who come into the camera's purview in an abyssal network of responsibility. Photographer, subject, and spectators share responsibility for the photograph, but none is its master. The subject—willing or unwilling, knowing or unknowing—catches the photographer's eye. The photographer focuses the camera's lens, but also concedes to what it allows to be seen and shot. The photograph that results issues its mute demand to be properly seen, a demand spectators can ignore or take up in a variety of ways.

Margaret Olin's recent *Touching Photographs* also attends to the social and communal dimensions of photography in a way that fits well with the account of photographic truth and *signifiance* I have offered here. Borrowing a concept from the sociologist Pierre Bourdieu, she suggests we think of photography as a *habitus*; that is, as a set of practices—posing for, shooting, and especially viewing—in which we have been inculcated and which we (faithfully or not) repeat. Those practices vary with photographic genre and context, as we've seen; photographic *habitus* is flexible enough to include professional photography (artistic or journalistic) as well as amateur photographic practices (family photography, souvenir photography). So also the various modes and media through which photographs "touch" us, from formal museum exhibitions—where they "touch" us only by "moving" us—to situations in which we might both be moved by and physically touch them. These situations include selecting which printed photographs to put in a family album or reading the newspaper.

Thinking of photography as a *habitus* focuses our attention once again on the process of subjection. We are made subjects by subjecting ourselves (consciously or, more often, unconsciously) to disciplinary regimes of seeing, knowing, being, and doing. In my case, those various forms of subjection include not only my habituation into photographic mores but also my formation as a philosophical theologian. Let me close this chapter by explicitly bringing that disciplinary subjection to bear on the reading of the signs and wonders that is to come. Iconic photographs, Hariman and Lucaites argue, follow certain familiar aesthetic conventions, including those drawn from "the middlebrow arts such as landscape and portrait painting," "popular iconography," "representational realism," and simple design.[125] The depiction of suffering in "Hooded Man on a Box," "Migrant Mother" and "Accidental Napalm" is central to their iconicity (and affectivity). As Sontag observes, "the iconography of suffering has a long pedigree" that includes a lineage grounded in Christian art.[126] Hariman and Lucaites note that "Migrant Mother" recalls Christian iconography of the Madonna and Christ child. Similarly, Mitchell sees echoes of depictions of Christ in "Hooded Man," a reference it shares with Kim Phuc's posture and the position of her arms in "Accidental Napalm."[127]

In the introduction, I resisted any clear division between theology and culture, noting that the deep intertwining of Christianity in the West's history (and Christianity's history in the Western world) renders a clean delineation of one from the other difficult, if not impossible. As a result, although few contemporary Westerners are truly literate in Christian theological traditions, they are conversant in certain Christian tropes (visual and literary) that are widely available and frequently deployed as cultural capital. We saw evidence of that early in our discussion of photographic *signifiance*. Christian iconography is a central feature of the visual grammars of suffering that "Migrant Mother," "Accidental Napalm," and "Hooded Man" cite. While "Migrant Mother" recalls the pathos of the *Pieta*, both "Accidental Napalm" and "Hooded Man" call to mind various artistic representations of Christ. Those citations are central to each photograph's claim on iconicity.[128] But the connection between theology—and religious discourse in general—and photographic *signifiance* encompasses photography itself, not just its visual content.

Photographs and/as Theology

I want to suggest that photographs themselves are a form of what I'll call theological cultural capital. That is, even absent explicit religious references, photographs function according to a logic with deep religious—even theological—roots.[129] As a form of cultural capital, photography services a variety of forms of social ritual—public and private, collective and individual.[130] Performativity, a category central to photographic *signifiance* and *habitus*, lies at the heart of scholarly accounts of ritual and ritualization.[131] Formal rituals (the Catholic mass, say) and everyday bodily practices (brushing one's teeth, say) inculcate ways of knowing, doing, seeing, and being through learned bodily performances of practices that signal one's subjection to communal norms.

Recall Hariman and Lucaites's claim for photographic performativity. Photographs are performative spaces wherein photographed subjects cite through gesture and facial expression visual social codes and iconographies. Photographic performativity is a critical dimension of photographic subjection—that is, the formation and management of delinquents, inverts, and freaks as well as masterful men, submissive servants, and docile workers—not to mention proper husbands and wives, mothers and fathers, daughters and sons.[132] When we pose for, shoot, or simply glance at photographs—of ourselves or of others known or unknown to us— we participate in photographic ritual practices. Through said participation, we subject ourselves to bio-disciplinary power trained on us through the fourfold of Man and his others by the camera's lens. Photography (en)trains us in the modes of seeing, knowing, doing, and being that are integral to the modern *episteme* and *ethos*.

But there is more to the theo-logic of photography than its ritual function. The very category of iconicity itself is of theological provenance, recall, and like its theological counterpart, photographic iconicity is figured in terms of transcendence of the immediately visible and sayable.[133] Moreover, Tagg roots *Disciplinary Frame* in the insight that all attempts to confine photographic meaning to specific disciplinary regimes inevitably meet their limit in photographic excess. Attempts to crop out unwanted detail leave traces of that detail. Photographs intended to promote civic values evoke resistance to those very values. W. J. T. Mitchell's most recent foray into visual culture theory *What Do Pictures Want?* offers a provocative way of thinking about photographic transcendence and excess—and, more important, of approaching it. By "pictures," he means images or objects that appear in a variety of media (the visual arts, photojournalism, fiction, and nonfiction writing of various genres). His choice of the quotidian term *picture* calls attention first to the ubiquity of visual imagery. Speaking of pictures also disrupts the divide between high and low culture in alerting us to what connects the poet William Blake's visual images to a Spike Lee film—and what differentiates them from one another.

What Do Pictures Want? reinforces important aspects of the analysis I've offered in this chapter. The book makes good on the title in many ways; Mitchell treats pictures *as if* they were desiring things—perhaps even living things—metaphorically, of course. Inquiring after what pictures want places front and center the *demand* that photographs place on us—that we look, and in and through looking, interpret and respond. Pictorial desire as framed by Mitchell is abyssal. "To ask what do pictures want? is not just to attribute to them life and power and desire, but also to raise the questions of what it is they *lack*, what they do not possess, what cannot be attributed to them."[134] Significantly, Mitchell locates pictorial affectivity in lack, not plenitude—now from the side of the picture rather than the viewer.

But another dimension of Mitchell's proposal also bears directly on this project, and that's the role religion plays, a role that reframes iconicity. In treating photographs as (if they were) living things, Mitchell quite deliberately and self-consciously (if somewhat ironically) courts associations with animism, a quality of so-called primitive religions. Animism names the propensity to endow inanimate objects with not only life but divine life. Within animistic traditions, trees, rocks formations, and so on are icons; they are portents of divine intent to be tended and attended to. It is a commonplace that "primitives" fear photography, he notes; to take someone's picture is to steal their spirit and bring them one step closer to death. We (post?)moderns like to think that we're past that, but Mitchell insists that we are not. As proof, he cites a pedagogical exercise practiced by a colleague that plays off of Barthes's response to the photograph of his mother that I referenced earlier. The colleague asks each of his students to bring to class a photograph of his or her mother. Once in class, the colleague asks the students to cut out their mothers' eyes. Without exception, Mitchell reports, the students refuse.[135]

Of course, one person's icon is another person's idol; Mitchell notes that the history of iconoclasm is rife with such distinctions and their sometimes violent enforcement (recall the discussion of iconoclash earlier in this chapter). Mitchell differentiates his aim in pursuing what pictures want from iconoclasm. Iconoclasm is, at its root, profoundly skeptical often of the visual in general, but always of certain visual images in particular. The iconoclast seeks to expose the idol behind the icon, in other words. In contrast, Mitchell aligns his approach with Nietzsche's "sounding of the idols." He seeks not to determine the truth or falsehood of pictures, but to hear them out, if you will, and to approach them in ways that allow them to resonate in all of their complexity. To sound out these idols—to ask what *these* pictures want—is to inquire after their role in bio-disciplinary power as channeled through the fourfold. What do these signs and wonders have to tell us about what circulates between and among those of us who are subjected by and to the current disciplinary regimes? What do they tell us about our past, our present, and our future? It is to that task that I now turn.

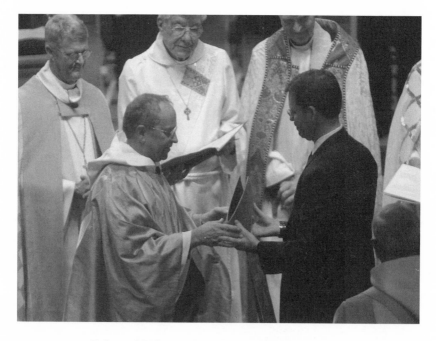

FIGURE 3.1 Episcopal Bishop Gene Robinson is handed his miter by his partner Mark Andrew during his consecration ceremony in Durham, New Hampshire, on Sunday, November 2, 2003.

CHAPTER THREE

BIO-DISCIPLINE AND GLOBALIZATION

The Crisis in the Anglican Communion

"WITH THE CEREMONIAL laying on of hands by a cluster of bishops, the Rev. V. Gene Robinson was consecrated the next bishop of New Hampshire and the first openly gay prelate in the Episcopal Church U.S.A. on Sunday, laying the groundwork for a split in the American church and a break with fellow Anglican churches abroad."[1] So began the front-page story about this event as it appeared in the *New York Times* on November 3, 2003. Two photographs accompanied that story. Appearing on the front page was a photograph (not reproduced here) of an act of dissent to Robinson's consecration. In it, the Rev. F. Earle Fox responds to the ceremonial query about objections to Rev. Robinson's consecration by "read[ing] an explicit list of what he said were gay sexual practices" as another colleague listens.[2] The second photograph in the *New York Times* (figure 3.1) features Rev. Robinson's then-partner (now ex-husband) Mark Andrew, handing him his miter as the consecration concludes. It was relegated to the paper's interior pages where the story continued. For reasons that I hope will become clear shortly, instead of using the *New York Times* front-page photograph in this chapter, I have included a photograph from the Episcopal News Service that captures the scene described by the opening line of the *New York Times*

FIGURE 3.2 The Most Rev. Frank T. Griswold III places his hands on the head of Gene Robinson as bishops gather on Sunday, November 2, 2003, during the consecration in Durham, New Hampshire.

(AP PHOTO/JIM COLE)

article (figure 3.2). In what follows, I "read" this archive as an imagetext (recalling Jacques Rancière's terminology from chapter 2). I move back and forth between the photographs and the news story to limn the photographs' indexical, iconic, and affective dimensions—first, in relationship to the events they document and then in relationship to the larger concerns of this project (as signs and wonders, in other words).

First I examine the photograph of the moment of consecration (figure 3.2). Like the news story it represents, it positions its viewers above and outside the fray. The vantage point from above allows us to look into the "cluster" of participating bishops, most of whom appear to be, like Rev. Robinson, white middle-aged (or older) men dressed in the rather opulent ritual garb of the episcopacy.[3] With one exception (a dark-haired man on the far right with glasses), none of the faces are visible to us; all attention is

focused on what is happening at the front of the room. All stand at rever-
ent attention—all but the presiding bishop (whose hands rest upon Rev.
Robinson's head) with hands clasped or folded in gestures of prayer or
contemplation, some holding printed liturgies. As they encircle Rev. Robinson, who kneels before the presiding bishop, they form their own small
world. We are witnesses to an event simultaneously private and public, contemporary and historical. The flow of energy—power, even—around and
through the circuit formed by these bodies in formation is palpable. One is
caught up in and by a sense of reverence that demands a respectful silence.

Figure 3.1, taken after the moment of consecration itself, is more intimate both in content and in angle of vision. We find ourselves almost
level with the principals of the ceremony along with (we know from the
caption), Mr. Andrew. Dressed in a business suit, Mr. Andrew is handing
the newly consecrated bishop his miter as those presiding look on with
benevolent smiles. The photographer has caught the very moment of the
exchange as the new bishop and his partner's fingers touch, a gesture that
reads as tender familiarity tempered by the solemnity of the occasion.

The photographs document a ritual that, with its set liturgy, has been
performed hundreds if not thousands of times in much the same way since
the founding of the Church of England in 1534 (or at least since this particular form of the ritual was authorized). And, given the spread of Anglicanism through the good offices of its missionaries—aided and abetted
by British colonial expansion—it is one that has been performed in many
times and places around much of the globe. But *this* consecration makes
history, as we say. The new bishop may be a white middle-aged man like
most of those who surround him, but he is gay; he is the first openly gay
or lesbian priest to be consecrated a bishop in the Anglican Communion.
The focus of the story, however, is less on the consecration itself than on
the political storm it was expected to unleash both in the United States
and around the world. Although met with great celebration by the 4,000
or so in attendance by the ceremony's conclusion, the story tells us that,
led by Rev. Fox, Episcopal dissenters had departed for a prayer service
elsewhere. Their departures hint at the conflict to come. Globally, the
New York Times delineates two major sides in that conflict: the numeri-
cally small (1.9 of 80 million Anglicans worldwide) but "established"
American church pitted against "what were once the mission churches of
the developing world" led by the 17 million strong Church in Nigeria.[4]

Considered against this backdrop, the photographs read somewhat differently, and their iconic dimensions—their ability to "stand in" for the

events they index—open up a distinctive perspective on the fourfold of Man and his others. On the one hand, the fact that an openly gay man is welcomed into this circle of power, reverence, and benevolence signals what many celebrated on that day. On the other hand, the very same photograph that reads to some as a sign of progress that moves them to celebrate reads to others as a disastrous calamity that moves them to acts of resistance and revolt. Indeed, the photograph of Robinson's consecration anticipates the terms of the conflict to come. It will be theological, pitting the weight of theological tradition against innovation. It will be theopolitical, pitting the wealth, power, and needs of the "established" churches within the Communion against the size, promise, and needs of the former mission churches. It will be biopolitical, pitting progress in the normalization of homosexuality against the specter of colonialist racism. And it will take place on a global landscape shaped by bio-disciplinary power, but whose contours are changing under the pressures of shifting alliances and allegiances within the Anglican Communion and beyond.[5]

This reshaping heralds a remaking of space that is captured well by literary theorist Gayatri Chakravorty Spivak's concept of planetarity. In *The Death of a Discipline*, Spivak critically evaluates her discipline, comparative literature, exposing through the mundane (the book opens with a set of academic memos) and the sublime (Spivak's usual combination of literary analysis and theoretical counterpunch) this discipline's imbrication in not only academic but also global politics.[6] Born in response to an emergent postcolonial sensibility and emblematic of that movement's political aims of attending to "the other" on "the other's" own terms, it nonetheless finds itself caught in the gravitational pull of nationalisms evident in its mapping of literary traditions according to nation-states and in its own Americanism: privileging "America" as a haven for the multicultural.

Spivak's suspicion of comparative literature's geopolitics resembles my suspicion of attempts to neatly separate Christianity from (Western) culture. As our query into photographic truth and photographic *signifiance* showed, although Westerners are not necessarily fluent in Christian traditions, the wide circulation of certain Christian tropes through various cultural media like the visual arts make them widely available as potent signifiers. For example, the "Hooded Man's" iconic status rests in part on that photograph's citation of Christ's crucifixion. I argued further that, even absent explicitly religious content, the purposes that photographs often (but not always) serve render them a form of theological cultural capital. Spivak similarly positions comparative literature in relationship to globalization. It participates—unwittingly and perhaps unwillingly—in globalization, which Spivak describes as a grid-like mapping of the world as a network for the circulation of capital (of all kinds, including cultural). Globalization is, arguably, colonialism's unruly heir. Colonialism involved relatively centralized movements of economic, cultural, and human capital from metropole to colony largely via nation-states and their surrogates. Although these categories of capital moved in both directions, the specific forms capital took differed considerably. Colonial powers extracted from their colonies raw material, exotic curiosities, and unskilled labor—largely to the colonizers' benefit. In an asymmetrical exchange, colonial powers exported to the colonies financial capital, "civilization," and managers—also resources turned to the colonizers' benefit. The globalized order of things (and humanity) is less centralized and more multidirectional. Capital of all sorts moves back and forth between and within the so-called First World (heirs of the colonial powers) and the Third (or Two-Thirds) World (much of it formerly subject to colonial powers), and the entities that primarily manage and benefit are more diffuse.[7] Non-state actors such as multinational corporations and terrorist networks, for example, have their colonialist analogues (the East India Company comes to mind) but are central to globalization. Financial wealth still concentrates—for now, at least—primarily in the First World, but the global economy creates scarcity and excess in both Worlds at the micro- as well as macroeconomic levels.

Spivak proposes planetarity as an alternative (although not a direct opposite) to globalization.[8] If globalization seeks exhaustive mapping of the world via an economy of sameness subject to the desire for ownership, the planet is an (im)possible alterity that we inhabit on loan, she says. Planetarity renders our home, the earth, *unheimlich*—literally, unhome-like ("uncanny" in English).[9] Behind the place we take for granted lies a (non)place that gives place: a planet that both makes possible and undoes our mappings of its surface into a globe. Thus, planetarity offers no secure and well-known terrain across which we can stride confidently, but rather an unstable landscape of shifting ground, at once familiar and unfamiliar, with fissures opening beneath our feet as we attempt to navigate it. The effects of those fissures on this landscape and those who populate it are, not surprisingly, ambivalent.

Our practice of *askesis*, in this chapter, will focus on practices of geographical and political (un)making, if you will, funded by the exercise of bio-disciplinary power and channeled by its fourfold. Our access to these practices will come by tracing the contours of this shifting landscape and tracking the movement of various forms of capital across it. These events in the global Anglican Communion open onto certain challenges and opportunities that these (un)makings pose to our time and place.

America's Culture War Goes Global

It did not take long for the seismic impact of Robinson's consecration to be felt across the Anglican Communion, composed of some eighty-five million members distributed among thirty-eight provincial Churches (and six dioceses or churches outside the provinces) in more than sixty-five countries across the globe.[10] This extraordinary event exacerbated old fractures and created new ones.[11] Rifts have appeared within local parishes, between parishes and their home dioceses, and between and among the provincial churches.[12] But, like actual earthquakes, the conditions for this fracturing and fissuring lie in terrestrial changes set in motion some time before. Robinson's consecration certainly exacerbated the controversy within the Communion over homosexuality, but it did not inaugurate it. That conflict had been brewing for some years, if not decades, but took central stage in Anglican life at the 1998 Lambeth Conference, the decennial gathering of Anglican bishops from around the globe. Although those who organized Lambeth 1998 planned to deal with several issues that affected the Communion (including international debt and poverty), the conflict over homosexuality virtually took over. As sociologist (and now Episcopal priest) Miranda K. Hassett notes in her fine ethnographic study of the conflict, "Lambeth 1998" is now synonymous with the contentious debate on that topic that occurred there.[13] The debate culminated with the passage of a resolution that, although perhaps less drastic than many present feared, sought to proscribe further progression toward acceptance of homosexuality. Against that backdrop, the subsequent consecration of the Rt. Rev. Robinson reads as either a courageous stand for justice or an egregious violation of Anglican unity. It has precipitated talk of schism (and schismatic acts, as we'll see) as well as calls for disciplinary action (although, given Anglican polity, that would be difficult). The roles played by the non-Western Anglican provinces—especially those located in former British African colonies—have drawn particular attention. Many see in Lambeth 1998 and what has followed from it evidence of Philip Jenkins's claim that we are witnessing the inevitable rise of a "next Christendom," a "global Christianity" headquartered in the so-called Third (or Two-Thirds) World.[14] This diagnosis assumes a map that divides the Communion into two relatively monolithic regions, the "global South" and the "global North," and two relatively monolithic positions, "liberal" and "conservative."[15] Like fellow scholar of global Christianity Lamin Sanneh, Jenkins argues that substantive differences in social and historical context give Southern Christianity—especially in Africa—a distinctive theological shape.[16] If, to use Sanneh's terminology, Northern Christianity must reckon with a context that is largely post-Christian if not postreligious, African Christianity confronts the complex realities of a postcolonial context that is much more akin to the worlds of the biblical writers. Tyrannical or corrupt governments that offer few reliable services for their constituents, economic struggles, and the need to establish one's place among a variety of religious traditions are everyday realities for many African Christians. Thus, elements of biblical thought (supernaturalism, martyrdom, apocalypticism) that many modernist Northern Christians have come to regard as historical curiosities are living modes of faithfulness for Southern Christians. For these reasons, Jenkins expects this new Christendom to be more theologically conservative on the whole, a reality to which Northern Christians will have to accommodate.[17]

There is certainly much to be learned from Jenkins's and Sanneh's analyses, but, at the level of popular conversation, they are applied to the Anglican controversy in ways that risk oversimplification. For one, both regions contain more internal diversity than the map allows. The Episcopal Church in the United States is arguably ground zero for the controversy; American parishes and dioceses unhappy with the direction the Church is moving have sought to separate from it. Southern Anglicans' views on sexuality are not monolithic either. Bishop Terry Brown of Malaita (of the Province of Micronesia), an openly gay (and celibate) man, has edited an anthology of essays by Anglicans and Episcopalians from across the global South—several of them members of sexual minorities themselves—that belie any claim that Southern Anglicans speak with one voice on this issue.[18] Bishop Musonda Trevor Selwyn Mwamba of Botswana identifies three different orientations among Africans toward the issue, which he labeled as conservative, liberal, and moderate.[19] Archbishop Njongonkulu Ndungane of the Province of the Church in Southern Africa welcomed Bishop Robinson's consecration with prayers of support and congratulations. Retired Ugandan Bishop Christopher Ssenyonjo saw the event as "God's way of making the church come to terms with homosexuality."[20]

Tracking Capital: Global Anglicanism and Its Colonial Roots

Whether the conflict will result in full-blown schism remains to be seen, but it is already remapping and realigning the Communion in substantive ways. New alliances of advocates for and against full acceptance of lesbian, gay, bisexual, and transgender (LGBT) persons[21] have formed that have created new links from South to North, metropoles to former colonies. The alliances have not escaped the legacy of colonialism, which determines the map's cartographic divisions. The Church of England became a global communion in and through the expansion of the British Empire from North to South. Human, financial, political, and theological capital is distributed asymmetrically between the South and the North, reflecting a colonialist pattern. The South is wealthiest in human capital. Of the thirty-eight provinces of the Anglican Communion, twenty reside in the global South, but those twenty house a substantial majority of the Anglican Church's population. Insofar as the controversy pits essentially two Northern provinces (Canada and the United States) against most of the provinces of the global South, the conflict resembles the struggle between David and Goliath. Consider the Episcopal Church's small size in comparison to the Anglican Church of Nigeria, whose former archbishop, the Most Rev. Peter J. Akinola emerged frequently as a primary spokesperson on behalf of Southern churches, and the asymmetry looms larger.[22]

Consider financial capital, however, and the asymmetry cuts differently. Economic resources continue to move primarily from North to South via Northern (indeed, Episcopal) largesse, as it has since colonial times. No surprise, then, that the specter of colonialism hangs over this controversy. In an official document, Akinola speaks of "unilateral actions taken without consulting the wider Communion" on the part of the Northern churches as just the latest evidence of "a new imperialism": actions taken by materially advantaged churches without regard for their impact on the materially disadvantaged.[23] For some Southern Anglican bishops, then, resistance to greater openness toward gays and lesbians is an anti-imperialist and anticolonialist stance. Although the Episcopal Church has continued to provide financial support to the larger Communion and its missions, some primates in the global South have refused Episcopal financial support in the wake of Robinson's consecration. And some Episcopal parishes and dioceses have ended their financial support of specific Southern enterprises over the same issue.[24]

At the heart of the controversy are charges of theological imperialism. The Northern churches stand accused of imposing a new theology on the Southern churches. That charge is made, however, in the name of the original imperial theology, as an interview with then Archbishop Akinola by Ruth Gledhill, religion correspondent for the London *Times*, demonstrates. Gledhill writes, "The irony is not lost on [Akinola] that he is attempting to preach a gospel back to England that was brought to his country by English missionaries in the mid-19th century." Quoting Akinola, she writes, "The missionaries brought the word of God here and showed us the way of life. We have seen the way of life and we rejoice in it. Now you are telling me this way of life is not right. I have to do something else."[25]

I do not presume to know all that the former archbishop had in mind as "the way of life" that the missionaries taught, but his viewpoint conjures for me the various levels of that conflict that I named earlier: the theological (tradition versus innovation), the theopolitical ("established" churches versus their former missions), and the biopolitical (one "way of life" versus another). If together those call to mind colonialism's past, the context in which this interview appears—the London *Times* is one of the many newspapers owned by Rupert Murdoch's now-infamous conglomerate News International—recalls the globalizing landscape on which this conflict takes place. Tellingly, whatever Akinola intended to *in*clude in "the way of life," it is clear that he intended to *ex*clude same-sex relationships. I turn my attention first, then, to the present, to tracking and tracing the significance of that exclusion for our time and place through these various levels of the current conflict.

That the controversy—globally and locally—is waged over "homosexuality" reflects bio-disciplinary power's global reach. The analysis offered in chapter 1 lends claims by Akinola and other Southerners that homosexuality is a Western import—and a recent one, at that—a certain (limited) credence.[26] "The homosexual," recall, is one of the personages that populates the taxonomy of sexual subjectivities created by *scientia sexualis*, itself the product of the modern West's major innovation, according to Foucault, bio-disciplinary power. Recall, as well, that bio-disciplinary power was racist in both aim and effect. In seeking to advance the (human) race, it sought to eliminate abnormality, which, in the United States, was found running rampant through the non-Nordic population according to McWhorter. According to Stoler, colonial expansion extended bio-disciplinary power's reach into the Dutch colonies. Against the view that colonial powers simply exported to the colonies their way of life (to borrow Akinola's phrase) fully formed, she argues for the colonies as "laboratories of modernity."[27] Considered against that backdrop, resistance to the embrace of homosexuality by the Anglican Church can claim to be an antiracist and anticolonialist gesture.

But let me be clear here. "Homosexuality" may be a Western import, but same-sex relationships are not—certainly not in Africa, the forefront of Southern Anglican resistance. Historian and former Anglican missionary Kevin Ward notes that, although the historical record of precolonial sexual mores is murky, evidence is strong that same-sex relationships have always existed in African societies (in various forms and with varying degrees of acceptance or rejection). They have not been understood, however, within the framework of sexual essence, as they have in the modern West.[28] Although he cautions against taking this research as definitive for all times and places on the African continent, Ward cites David Greenberg's taxonomy of African sexualities. Greenberg distinguishes at least three forms of same-sex relationships: transgenerational, transgenderal (one partner adopts the dress or habits of the opposite sex), and egalitarian (similar age, similar gender identity).[29] That these forms of same-sex relations no longer exist is itself a result of colonialist imposition. Same-sex relations were initially made illegal in many African colonies by colonial powers.[30]

Extending to African British colonies, Stoler's read of the relationship between the Dutch colonies and bio-disciplinary power is helpful here. Recall that metropole and colony were connected by an open circuit through which bio-disciplinary power circulated—channeled, I argued, by the fourfold. The account of Stoler in chapter 1 focused on the production in colonial laboratories of what Stoler calls the bourgeois subject. Targeted by the fourfold of Man and his others, colonials took on that form of subjectivity by subjecting themselves to ways of knowing, being, and doing that enabled them to incarnate proper manhood and womanhood. These practices included properly ordering and managing their colonized others. Importing Stoler's framework into this context shifts our focus from the colonizers as the fourfold's targets to the colonized. The terms of bio-disciplinary power's exercise, however, will remain markedly familiar.

Colonialism, like slavery, was justified in part as a civilizing project directed at improving the state of the colonized. In British colonies like Nigeria, Rwanda, and Uganda, the Anglican Church took on an important role in that project. To civilize was to Christianize and to Christianize was to resexualize. Reorienting indigenous religious practices and beliefs toward Christianity entailed reorienting sexual and familial practices toward Western (Victorian) mores. That meant remaking indigenous subjects into sexual subjects via the exercise of bio-discipline baptized in Christian theology. Same-sex relationships were not the only ones in need of what we might call Christian (bio)discipline. Polygamy, too, was deemed deviant and strongly discouraged across Africa, at least officially (although in practice the Church was and remains more tolerant, according to Ward). Although they allowed polygamous families to participate in all other areas of ecclesial life, Ugandan Church authorities withheld access to the sacraments as a mechanism of enforcement.[31] The current controversy over homosexuality is not the only place where the effects of Christian (bio)discipline can be seen in African Anglicanism. Although in proportion to Uganda's population, the Anglican church is quite large (40 percent in 1991), only a small minority of participants are communicants. This is so not only because of the history of polygamy but also because, until 1973, the Church would baptize only those children born to parents who had been married in the church.[32]

That the Anglican controversy—locally as well as globally—takes place within the terms established by Christian (bio)discipline, suggests that, at least to some degree, these particular experiments in modernity worked; the postcolonized have adopted the normative ways of knowing, being, and doing created by bio-disciplinary power and enforced here by Christianity.[33] But the circuit between metropole and colony that brought this about remains open. Capital of all sorts—infused, clearly, with bio-disciplinary power—continues to circulate through it. The patterns of its circulation, while they still reflect colonialist legacies, are also changing as new alliances form between Southerners and Northerners. Although they pose no substantive challenge to the reign of bio-disciplinary power, they circulate it in ways that hold out both promise and peril.

New Alliances: (Neo)Colonialism, Globalization, or . . . ?

The activist role taken by Southern—particularly African—primates in the controversy is often seen as evidence of the shift of theological and political capital from the North to the South following the changing demographics of Christianity.

If so, this is a shift that Northern traditionalists (largely Episcopalian dissidents) think works to their benefit. They report that they find common cause with Akinola's assertion that a progressive stance on homosexuality is not in itself the problem, but rather the deeper theological differences over biblical authority and church tradition that it indexes. Thus, they appear to find in their Southern colleagues welcome allies for the resurgence of an Anglicanism more conservative not only on sexual mores but also on theological matters.

That the controversy over homosexuality moved from backstage to center stage in the Anglican Communion at Lambeth 1998 was no accident, as Hassett demonstrates. A series of conferences held in advance of Lambeth by Episcopal dissidents with Southern bishops and primates laid the groundwork for this controversy's new centrality. Financed by Northerners, these conferences resulted in the investment of theological and political capital to forge new alliances across lines of geography, race, and class. Predictably, these new alliances have been met with vocal resistance from Northern progressives, resulting in the immediate aftermath of Lambeth in what Mary-Jane Rubenstein calls a "perfectly triangulated charge of colonialism."[34] Traditionalist Southerners, as we've seen, accused progressive Northerners of once again imposing their values on the South. Traditionalist Northerners, trading on Southern charges of neocolonialism, denounced progressive Northerners for cultural insensitivity. Progressive Northerners denounced traditionalist Northerners, in turn, for essentially buying the loyalty of traditionalist Southerners.[35]

Yet, as Hassett argues, beneath the charged rhetoric of colonialism, global Anglicanism is being reconfigured as a result of new alliances between North and South. Rather than the inevitable and natural consequence of globalization, the alliance between Southern and Northern traditionalists is its Anglican instantiation. Her fieldwork has allowed her to render in rich detail the alliance between Northern and Southern traditionalists and its effects. Although hardly unaffected by the legacies of colonialism, Hassett argues that the traditionalist alliance is genuine and serves the interests of both sides (which are not necessarily the same). She traces its transformative effects at the structural, congregational, and personal levels. Since Lambeth 1998, new formal networks that link Northern and Southern traditionalist Anglicans have been constituted particularly around Northern dissatisfaction with the Episcopal Church.[36] A number of the American parishes that want no truck with the Episcopal Church sought episcopal oversight from primates in the global South, which Akinola (among others) was particularly happy to supply despite strong criticism that it violates Anglican polity.[37]

Hassett's extensive fieldwork (which concluded in 2002) included Anglican communities in Rwanda and in the United States. The promise inherent in the traditionalist alliance is particularly evident in her account of a dissident Episcopal congregation that she calls St. Timothy's, which is now overseen by a bishop in Rwanda. This congregation has taken its new provincial affiliation quite seriously. Led by lay members who have visited Rwanda, many in the congregation have become advocates for such issues as ending poverty in Africa that *Rwandans* define as critical. A closer affiliation with Africa has also yielded emergent practices of self-criticism around anti-African racism (what connections, if any, are made to anti-African *American* racism is not clear, according to Hassett). These are surely moves that progressive Anglicans would welcome, indeed, to which they would aspire. They have long seen themselves as the advocates for their Southern coreligionists (although the degree to which their coreligionists share that view is questionable, Hassett notes). That these moves come at the expense of a progressive stance on sexuality affirms a critical insight that Jenkins and Sanneh share. Both stress that Southern Christianities are becoming truly indigenous creations that do not conform neatly to Northern political or theological alignments.[38]

Yet some Northern and Southern progressives have taken advantage of the open circuit between metropole and former colonies to find opportunities to work together. In contrast to the highly organized networks created by traditionalists after Lambeth, progressive alliances remain, as best as I can determine, more ad hoc. As in the traditionalist Anglican alliance, financial and human capital play critical roles, although on a much smaller scale. If the traditionalist alliances are global and formal, progressive alliances are more local and personal. They are constituted and managed primarily by individual laypersons and clergy with connections to other individual laypersons and clergy. Para-church organizations dedicated to promoting LGBT causes within the Anglican Communion, including both Changing Attitudes U.K. and Integrity USA provide some institutional support and connections. Changing Attitudes has had a program in Nigeria since at least 2007, although threats against the director of Changing Attitudes Nigeria, Davis MacIyalla, are believed to have led him to seek asylum in the United Kingdom.[39] In 2001, with Ssenyonjo's support, a Ugandan Anglican priest and his wife (whose ministry with youth led them to get involved) founded a local chapter of Integrity.[40] According to its current vice president for national affairs, Rev. Jon Richardson, Integrity USA maintains a small endowed fund specifically to support work in Uganda, but to avoid confusing its Northern constituency, it now leaves most of the fundraising for work in Uganda to Ssenyonjo and his colleague, Rev. Canon Albert Ogle (Richardson's predecessor who resigned to work more closely with Bishop Ssenyonjo).[41] Individual parishes are involved as well, as hosts for the African visitors, but I have been unable to determine whether any of those parishes have the kinds of ties to their Southern coreligionists that St. Timothy's has cultivated—or what effects, if any, whatever ties do exist have had on parishioners' minds and hearts.

The progressive alliance, too, is affected by the conflict's colonialist past. Indeed, Hassett credits anti(neo)colonialism as the primary force behind the Southern church's resistance to homosexuality. Southerners' perception of the conflict as forced on the South by the North renders suspect close ties between Southern and Northern progressives. As one symptom, Hassett notes that the Ugandan house of bishops denounced the founding of Integrity Uganda as "an outside plant."[42] What effect that is having on the efficacy of Southern LGBT activism is impossible to assess from this distance; that Bishop Ssenyonjo has continued to seek Northern support suggests that, in his view, the risk of guilt-by-association is worth running.

That progressive Northerners have responded to requests for assistance from their Southern counterparts is certainly commendable and can be credited as anticolonialist gestures themselves. How much support Southern progressives will be able to count on from their Northern counterparts is not clear. The Episcopal Church has continued to move forward officially with pro-LGBT policies. In 2012, it approved a liturgy for same-sex unions (to be used only with one's bishop's approval) and added gender expression to its nondiscrimination policy. When civil same-sex marriage became the law of the land in the United States in June 2015, the General Convention passed resolutions allowing priests to perform same-sex weddings and provided rites for them.[43] However, in recognition of the fact that many remain conflicted about these matters, the Convention also left it up to individual bishops to decide whether to allow same-sex weddings in his or her diocese and left individual priests free to refuse to perform them.[44] The ongoing conflict in the American church and what it augurs may continue to draw Integrity USA's resources toward home and potentially away from the global South. Moreover, the nature of the connections that link Northern and Southern LGBT organizations make the progressive alliance potentially fragile, it seems. Often forged originally through personal contacts between Northerners and Southerners, according to Rev. Richardson, the progressive alliance remains dependent on those contacts.

That this is the case may reflect larger trends among progressive Northern Anglicans that have distanced them from Southern Anglicanism. Willis Jenkins argues that, in general, progressive Anglicans have responded to prior charges of colonialism largely by withdrawing from mission activity in Africa and elsewhere. What mission activity persists tends to take the form of sending money rather than people, he claims.[45] This is perhaps understandable given that the history of colonialist (and postcolonialist) interventions by Northerners—including progressives—is indeed rife with evidence of collateral damage, but it is not free of colonial contamination.[46] For one thing, it perpetuates the asymmetries in capital and potentially in influence described previously. In addition, the relative dearth of human contact creates and perpetuates ignorance about the lived experience of African Anglicans. As a result, Jenkins argues that Northern progressives are not as attuned as they need to be to the specific circumstances that shape the African provincial churches' perspectives on homosexuality. That concern is borne out in accounts of the reactions and responses of Northern progressives both pre- and post-Lambeth 1998, which come off often as hapless at best and patronizing and racist (in effect if not intent) at worst. In contrast to traditionalists, progressive Northerners were caught flat-footed at Lambeth 1998, according to Rubenstein.[47] Despite warnings by Bishop John Shelby Spong, there were no parallel advance attempts at organizing alliances even among Northern progressives, much less across the lines that divide the North and South. Although individual Northern bishops spoke against retrenchment on the issue of homosexuality, they could only react; they were not prepared to tackle the issue in any collaborative or constructive way. Indeed, the water was already poisoned for them before they arrived. Bishop Spong raised the ire of many in the South when, just before Lambeth 1998, he described African Anglicans as "superstitious, fundamentalist Christians" who have "moved out of animism into a very superstitious kind of Christianity—[and have] yet to face the intellectual revolution of Copernicus and Einstein."[48] One of the more public attempts to mend fences between North and South is perhaps particularly telling. In 2002, the Cathedral of St. John the Divine enthroned Archbishop Akinola. The day's events concluded with an announcement from bishops Mark Sisk and Griswold (presiding bishop of the Episcopal Church, who presided at Robinson's consecration) and Akinola of "plans to sponsor a 'Nigerian Chaplaincy' in ECUSA" that will "pay for Nigerian clergy to come to America 'in an effort'—these are Akinola's words—'to bring people back into the Church of God.' "[49] Rubenstein's conclusion is worth quoting *in toto*:

> And when they come, the Anglo-American Left will no doubt cry colonialism—only to find themselves face to face with the very Oxford Bibles and Victorian gender codes that justified their *ancestors'* transcultural moral impositions a mere century ago. Who, in good faith, can say that she or he is colonized? Who—with an African archconservative sitting on the throne of an almost pagan cathedral in New York, amid the silencing liberal rhetoric of 'different contexts,' as promises to deploy evangelical ground troops to the Church of Satan mix with assurances of 'universal salvation' from three bishops looking disturbingly like one another's warrant chiefs— can say anything at all?[50]

Since Lambeth 2008, traditionalists have proceeded to pursue institutionalization without breaking formal ties with the Communion, but in ways that have fractured the Episcopal Church. Lambeth 2008 was preceded by a gathering in Jerusalem of Northern and Southern traditionalists called the Global Anglican Future Conference (GAFCon).[51] That meeting gave birth to the Anglican Communion of North America (ACNA), a confederation of dissenting Episcopal dioceses and parishes, and to the Fellowship of Confessing Anglicans, an international body dedicated to the vision of Anglicanism upheld at GAFCon. These networks remain in place, although not without conflict. ACNA is apparently divided over the issue of women's ordination, so it allows individual bishops—who must be male, according to its Constitution and Canons—to decide the matter.[52] Disputes between the Episcopal Church and dissident parishes and dioceses over ownership of property are now working their way through the U.S. legal system. So far, the courts have decided mostly in favor of the Episcopal Church.[53] If that pattern continues, dissidents will continue to have to devote financial and personal capital to brick-and-mortar building. What impact this potential drain on resources will have on their alliance with the Southern churches remains to be seen.

Whatever threats the alliances face, the stakes are high at the moment not only for Anglicans but also for LGBT people in the global South regardless of religious affiliation—particularly in Nigeria and Uganda. After circulating for several years, draconian legislation that would impose severe punishments on those accused of homosexual conduct (or of knowing about homosexual conduct) passed in Nigeria and in Uganda in 2014.[54] Nigerian and Ugandan AIDS organizations and LGBT organizations, including Integrity Uganda and Changing Attitudes Nigeria, were and continue to be courageous and vocal in their opposition to and critiques of this legislation, despite threats (sometimes realized) of violence.[55] Already a problem, extrajudicial violence against LGBT people increased in the wake of the legislation, leading many to seek asylum in neighboring African countries, the United States, and elsewhere.[56] The Ugandan constitutional court overturned the legislation some months later (on a technicality), but the government began gearing up to consider a new version of it soon after (although nothing has passed to date).[57] Tellingly, the only concern that those gathered at the 2014 meeting of GAFCon's leadership expressed about the original legislation and its aftermath pertained to the effects of international backlash in reaction to it.[58]

Well before it passed, the legislation had caught the attention of secular human rights organizations as well as major Western powers, thus likely exacerbating the association of pro-LGBT activism with neocolonialism. The International Gay and Lesbian Human Rights Commission, Human Rights Watch, and the United Nations took up the cause of defeating this legislation and ending violence against sexual minorities in these countries. When the legislation was signed into law, Secretary of State John Kerry and President Barack Obama denounced it and, along with other Western powers, the United States imposed a number of sanctions on Uganda, although not (yet) on Nigeria—for, I suspect, complex reasons.[59] But traditionalists are not immune to charges of neocolonialism from indigenous activists. Indeed, LGBT activists in Uganda have charged American evangelicals who have active ministries in these countries—including Revs. Scott Lively and Rick Warren—with actively supporting the legislation as well as with helping to foment a more virulent form of homophobia. Indeed, according to a 2014 article in *Mother Jones*, there is strong evidence of Lively's active role in shaping the legislation.[60] Rev. Kapya Kaoma, an Anglican priest and researcher with the U.S.-based think tank Political Research Associates, indicts the African branches of mainline Protestantism (including Anglicanism) alongside the ministries of Lively and Warren.[61] Although Warren has (under some pressure) disavowed connections to the Ugandan legislation, Rev. Lively has yet to do so.[62] Moreover, Lively remains the object of a U.S. lawsuit alleging his connection to the death of prominent LGBT activist David Kato.[63] And behind it all, it appears, is American money and American politics. A number of sources have documented the role of conservative donors, foundations, and think tanks in fomenting ecclesial dissension not only in the Episcopal Church but also among United Methodists and in the Presbyterian Church (USA) as a way to advance their political goals.[64]

Indeed, who *can* say anything at all?

Planetarity, (Post)Modernity, and the Fourfold

The account given in the previous section of the Anglican controversy over homosexuality surely renders the globe *unheimlich*. The fissures and fractures in the landscape scarred by colonialism and being reshaped by emergent globalization reveal a Spivakian planet beneath. The earth gives (us) space on which we enact our spatializing (and temporalizing) schemas only to find them undone by others to whom the earth also gives space. Finding a point of orientation on this changing landscape is difficult; it is hard not to feel a bit unsteady on one's feet. Let me attempt a reorientation, at least for my readers, by situating this account within the larger framework of our time and place as provided in the first chapter.

The controversy within the Anglican Communion is certainly, in some respects, particular to its specific history and its polity. But those particularities are not cleanly or clearly separable from larger dynamics. For one thing, the *mutual* imbrication of Anglicanism, colonialism, and globalization affirms my reluctance to separate Christianity from culture. Not only is (Anglican, but not only Anglican) Christianity itself a network for the circulation of capital (financial and human, cultural and political), but also it is connected to—and even embedded in—political and social entities (nation-states, faith-based nongovernmental organizations, etc.) that are nodes in the larger network of the global economy through which capital of various sorts circulates.

I also opened this project by troubling the notion of postmodernity. Clearly, if the "post" is understood as marking a break with modernity—specifically, with its notions of subjectivity, of truth, of the metanarratives in which these artifacts are situated—then I trust this chapter adds additional support to my claim that this break is not yet a fait accompli. That the culture war over homosexuality has gone global suggests that we remain deeply embedded in and beholden to *scientia sexualis*, itself a creation of modernity. The controversy is over whether to normalize homosexuality or not, and neither Anglican progressives nor traditionalists appear to be interested in challenging the notion of sexual subjectivity itself. Indeed, this is true of the larger debate over homosexuality.[65] Most if not all of us—however we identify in the spectrum of possibilities indicated by the acronym LGBTIQ (lesbian, gay, bisexual, transgendered or transsexual, intersexed, queer or questioning), whether we are confirmed secularists or avowed religious believers, and wherever we align ourselves on the spectrum of the current "culture war" over homosexuality—continue to seek the truth it offers us, a truth that holds out the promise of a secure self-identity and communal home. We continue to give ourselves over, and often without question, to the regime of sexual subjectivities spawned by *scientia sexualis*. Our pursuit of justice for LGBTIQ people more often than not relies on and reinforces what Foucault called the *dispositif* of sexuality. That said, that we can see sexuality *as* a *dispositif* arguably positions us differently in relationship to it than our forebears. I do not think this position is best described as "post," however, not only because we remain in its grip but also because that critical scrutiny is itself deeply beholden to the so-called Enlightenment project.

Of particular interest to me, however, is what this critical analysis reveals about Christianity's relationship to this *dispositif*—and to the possibilities (such as they are) of living differently within it (if not, for now at least, beyond it). It is noteworthy that religious communities—especially Christian communities—are particularly prominent sites of the conflict over homosexuality, a conflict waged with particular virulence therein. What accounts for this? That religious communities would be deeply interested in properly channeling sexuality is of a piece with the role bodily practices play in their formation and maintenance, Mary Keller and Jeremy Carrette argue.[66] Bodies are invoked and involved in the ritual processes of (un)making (baptism, confirmation, confession, worship) that create Christian subjects. It is perhaps more than coincidental that rituals—of ordination, consecration, and marriage—figure prominently in this "culture war." But I suspect that Christianity's status as a chief funder of resistance to LGBT inclusion is specific to the particular history of its relationship to *scientia sexualis,* a history whose outlines Foucault traces in the *History of Sexuality, Vol. 1.*[67] We return, then, to that volume supplemented now by the work of historian and ethicist Mark D. Jordan in his groundbreaking work, *The Invention of Sodomy* and other texts.[68]

The Roots of (Christian) Bio-Discipline: Sodomy and Its Discontents

Although ultimately displaced as the proper domain for dealing with sexual matters, Christianity provided both a key method for *scientia sexualis* and fallow ground for its primary product, the sexual subject, to take root. The emerging science of sexuality appropriated the Church's key strategy for handling sex, confession, transferring it from pastoral practice to scientific inquiry and thus from a logic of sin and redemption to the pursuit of (ab)normality. Begun as a practice centered on monastic contexts, with the Lateran Council of 1215, confession became required of lay Christians as well. The ostensible targets of confession also underwent considerable expansion when it came to sexual matters. At first, sexual sins were treated very much like other sins. One can find in early Christian penitential manuals lists of sexual acts named, one after the other, with little attempt to differentiate them. These acts were, like all sins, objects of ecclesial juridical authority and penitential practice. One confessed having perpetrated a given act, a corresponding penance was imposed, and performing it absolved the sinner, thus essentially wiping the slate clean.

But the status of *certain* sexual sins began to change within the monastic context, according to Jordan. Jordan traces sodomy's evolution in medieval theology from *sodomia*, one among other sexual sins, to a particularly problematic sin, and eventually to "sodomy," the essence of a personage, "the sodomite."[69] The account he narrates is not one of simple and straightforward development. For one thing, the meaning of *sodomia* is difficult to pin down. This is more than a problem in translation (though it is that, as well); it is a problem with the term's expansion and contraction in meaning and with the interplay of silence and speech in and around it. In some cases, Jordan argues that *sodomia* seems to have functioned as a catchall term for all sexual sins (although the specifics are more often assumed rather than spelled out). Many sources refuse to define *sodomia*, as if to do so is to conjure it up or invite it in. It's as though speech is unnecessary. Like pornography now, medieval church authorities should know *sodomia* when they see it. Its meaning, however, comes to coalesce around specific practices of homo-sex—but primarily to practices between men.[70] I speak of "homo-sex" here to mark the space between *sodomia* and modern "homosexuality," a space constituted by, among other things, a (temporary, as it turns out) gap between acts and character.

The gap does not survive the medieval period. Confession within monastic circles focused originally on sinful acts (sexual and otherwise). Sodomitic acts between monks became objects of particular concern, Jordan suggests, because they were perceived as constituting a temptation specific to and particularly dangerous both for the aim of monastic life (union with God) and its organizational structure. The solitary dimension of monastic life made sins of self-pleasuring (e.g., masturbation) particularly tough to resist. Conversely, its communal dimension provided too many opportunities for monks to pleasure one another and to form overly intimate relationships. Sexual sins, then, threatened the monk's status before God and the bonds within the community. Confessing acts performed came to be seen an insufficient prophylactic measure, and so confessors were directed to press beyond acts to the desires that motivated them. Nonvolitional acts (e.g., spontaneous erections, nocturnal emissions, sexual dreams) also became objects of inquiry—again, not simply for their own sake, but as routes to the desires that underlay them.

Deviant desires eventually came to be taken as evidence not just of the sinful nature shared by all humanity after Adam, but of a specific kind of nature: the sodomite. Jordan describes sodomy's move from one among a list of sexual sins (and a vaguely defined one, at that) to "a brand that burns condemnation into certain acts. It burns into them as well the presumption of a stable essence, a sameness found wherever the acts are performed."[71] The sodomite was irredeemable, unchangeable; once a sodomite, always a sodomite—and a sodomite to one's core. What constituted sodomitic acts, then? Everything a sodomite did. How to rid the community of the threat posed by the sodomite? There was only one solution: excision altogether. The object of confession changed once again: from policing deviance to rooting out deviants.

The alert reader will have discerned elements in sodomy's career that prefigure *scientia sexualis*. Confession may serve a different master, but its practice is aimed toward a similar object: inquiries into acts and desires serve as entry points into one's character.[72] Like sexuality, sodomy hides itself—not only from those in authority, but also from sodomites themselves. Yet the search for its truth, no matter how difficult or elusive, must go on. After all, it serves a higher imperative. Yet these two taxonomic categories are not, for all that, the same. The sodomite is not a homosexual; for one thing, as noted previously, the label was applied primarily to men. Moreover, the sodomite is, at bottom, a religious personage located in a Christian taxonomy governed by a logic of sin and redemption; sodomy indexes one's proximity to the demonic and distance from the divine. Homosexuality, by contrast, indexes one's distance from the normal and proximity to the pathological (although clearly residue from its predecessor carries over into this new logic). The homosexual's identity was as total and totalizing as the sodomite's. Encompassing body and soul, if you will, homosexuality's causes were deemed to lie in nature *and* in nurture. As Foucault puts it, recall, the term "homosexual" named "a personage: a past, a case history [*une histoire*], a childhood, a type of life [*un caractère*], a life form; a morphology also, with an indiscreet anatomy and possibly a mysterious physiology."[73] At the heart of this sexual identity lies the notion of perversion as inversion; the homosexual is possessed of (and produced by) "an interior androgyny, a hermaphrodism of the soul."[74] Sexual deviance, in other words, expresses gender deviance, itself likely linked to sexed deviance (although the specific bodily signs and symptoms and the nature of their connection to homosexuality remained mysterious).[75] Like sodomy, homosexuality was "the insidious and indefinitely active principle" of all of that personage's actions. Homosexuality's existence had implications not just for the individual, his family, and his community, but also for human nature itself. If the sodomite was "a temporary aberration, the homosexual was now a species," Foucault writes, that needed to be codified, identified, contained, and controlled.[76]

On the one hand, the displacement of Christianity by *scientia sexualis* fits a standard metanarrative of modernity, one that identifies it with an ever-increasing drive toward secularity and corresponding diminishment (or eradication altogether) of religion. On the other, however, *scientia sexualis* would not have taken the form it did were it not for Christianity. Indeed, traces of Christian theology and practice remain visible not only in its formative history but also its ongoing practice—a practice that, as we've seen, continues to this day around the globe thanks in no small part to the legacies of what I have called here Christian (bio-)discipline. Acknowledging this history has implications for how we might respond to the global dimensions of the controversy over homosexuality within Christian communions. It is tempting to see opposition to homosexuality in formerly colonized locations as symptomatic of a systemic ignorance (or stubborn rejection) of modern insights. Indeed, it is to some (including some Northern Anglican progressives, as we've seen) of a piece with a more pronounced emphasis on biblical literalism, supernaturalism, and theological "conservatism" that characterizes the Christianity of the formerly colonized. The account I have offered in this chapter cautions against seeing modernity as the solution. For one thing, the North is reaping the fruits of its colonialist seeds when, as Carrette and Keller put it, Southerners advocate "a modernist, heterosexist orientation," one in which, ironically, "homosexuality becomes the new primitivism."[77]

Moreover, I would submit that better acquaintance with what predates modernity—both in the North and the West—may even hold a key to a more progressive future for gender and sexual diversity within Christianity (and those territories that feel its touch). I say this not because premodernity was diversity's utopia; it was not. For example, although three decades of historical research has uncovered evidence of times, places, and circumstances in Africa as well as in early Christendom where same-sex relationships—although primarily between men—were accepted and even celebrated or sanctioned, the overarching trajectory is largely negative on same-sex love, especially between women.[78]

I see philosophical and theological promise in this history, however, in the challenges it poses to the very terms of the current debate and in its ability to denaturalize our current understanding, and more important, lived practice of subjectivity as sexual subjectivity. This history makes us aware of the inexorable effects of time and history on everything we touch and treat. To speak of sexuality, of gender, of sex—of male and female, masculine and feminine, homosexuality and heterosexuality—is to speak within and out of a particular *histoire*, one that we have inherited and for which we are now responsible.[79] Lived bodies are products of their *histoires*, of nurture as well as of nature, if you will. This is not to say that bodies are mere inert matter that culture shapes at will; bodies are complex entities in and of themselves and as sites of interaction with their environment (natural, cultural, and historical; local and global), as we will continue to see in later chapters. The *histoiricité* (if I may play off of the dual meaning of *histoire*) of bodily existence offers us no easy answers to any of the dilemmas that confront us. The burden of our *histoiricité* will not be so easily set aside. It is in working through the dilemmas of our present in light of the perils and promise of our past that the hope of living into a more just future resides.

Those dilemmas are not limited to this particular global "culture war"; they appear in other wars, as well, both metaphorical and literal. In the next chapter, we turn our attention to another context: that of the so-called Global War on Terror. Simultaneously a war of visual spectacle and of "boots on the ground," we focus on a particular convergence of both forms of this war, the Abu Ghraib scandal. We will once again take our mark from a pair of photographs, in this case, two of several in a much larger "archive" that figured most prominently in the scandal. These photographs are "iconic" in that they open onto the events they reference (in this case, mistreatment—many would say torture—of so-called detainees by U.S. soldiers) and onto the larger context that gave rise to those events. Our practice of *askesis* will take us deeper into the globalizing terrain, the scars of colonialism it bears, and the Spivakian planet beneath that have concerned us here—traversed again through religious difference (now around the figure of the Muslim as "other"). The practices of (un)making that we will track and trace will be both global and local, theological and photographic. They will involve and invoke subjection (willing and unwilling) to bio-disciplinary power channeled by the fourfold of Man and his others, his raced and sexed others, his divine other, and, more prominently than in this chapter, his animal other.

CHAPTER FOUR

REGARDING THE
PHOTOGRAPHS OF OTHERS

Abu Ghraib and/as Bio-Discipline

Can one divide human reality, as human reality seems to be genuinely divided, into clearly different cultures, histories, traditions, societies, even races, and survive the consequences humanly?
—Edward Said, *Orientalism*

The torture scenes in Baghdad were organized to be photographed.
—Stephen Eisenman, *The Abu Ghraib Effect*

All photographs are vehicles of identification and disavowal.
—Shawn Michelle Smith, *Lynching Photographs*

I F ANYTHING CAN evoke the unstable landscape of planetarity beneath a globe we thought we knew, it would be the events of September 11, 2001, and their still-unfolding aftermath. Members of al-Qaeda, a militant Islamist organization headed then by Osama bin Laden, hijacked four airplanes turning them and all that they contained (passengers, crew included) into airborne suicide bombers. A passenger revolt prevented one from reaching its target in Washington, D.C., crashing that plane into a Pennsylvania hillside instead (killing all aboard). But the other three found their intended targets, the Pentagon and the two World Trade Towers in New York City. In response, the United States launched what then-President Bush and his administration dubbed the Global War on Terror (GWOT). The spatial and temporal limits of this war remain impossible to fix even now—more than a decade after September 11 and long after Bush's successor, President Barack Obama, dropped the term from his lexicon. But there is surely no question that its impact can be traced in certain unmakings and remakings of and on our globe and its inhabitants. The fissures and fractures that it has exploited or caused, covered over or sought to repair are literal and figurative; local, regional, and global; and personal, communal, and political. Thus, we have yet to see the end of this global war, much less of the terrors it both inflicts and seeks to ameliorate, a point brought home in a different way with the release in December 2014 of the 500-page summary of the Senate Intelligence Committee's review of the controversial Central Intelligence Agency's (CIA) interrogation techniques and their results (about which more anon).

GWOT is arguably a uniquely visual war. As noted in chapter 2, W. J. T. Mitchell has described this war as an instance of "iconoclash." In its spectacular visibility, GWOT is iconographic and iconoclastic, a war of "shock and awe" (the tagline for the U.S. invasion of Iraq in March 2003) waged in and through images of all-too-real violence and death.[1] Al-Qaeda targeted the Twin Towers and the Pentagon as icons of U.S. global military and economic dominance. In turn, the images of the towers' destruction have come to stand in for the assault of September 11 in all its dimensions. As Mitchell demonstrates, the relationship between image and reality in this war of images is (as always) ambiguous. Photographs of the dismantling of Saddam Hussein's statue may have spectacularly prefigured his overthrow, but photographs of then-President Bush beneath a "Mission Accomplished" banner on the deck of an aircraft carrier anticipated a victory never fully realized.[2]

War-as-(sporadic)-spectacle threatens to distract us from its more everyday forms, most of which remain largely invisible to us. The first front in GWOT was the war launched in Afghanistan, where bin Laden was headquartered, shortly after September 11. What has already become our "longest war" was launched with little fanfare. Apart from the successful assault on bin Laden himself in 2011, it has produced nothing by way of memorable visual spectacle. But more to the point, as the Senate report documents, GWOT has been prosecuted on more clandestine fronts, and there are several. Through "extraordinary rendition" and a network of so-called ghost prisons or black sites, the Bush administration conducted interrogations (sometimes by proxy) unfettered by constraints (such as they are) that would apply on U.S. soil. GWOT has spawned an ever-expanding and largely privatized "industrial-intelligence complex" tasked along with the CIA, the Federal Bureau of Investigation (FBI), and the National Security Administration (along with military intelligence offices) with gathering information that can thwart potential attacks on "the homeland," a network that is all but invisible to the U.S. taxpayers who fund it.[3] Under President Obama, drone strikes—remote bombings of suspected terrorist enclaves by unmanned planes guided by stateside pilots—increased exponentially, yet the damage to lives and property has gone largely unseen by us.[4]

Of course, all of these events have coincided with the tremendous growth in the use of cell phones and access to the Internet and with the development of new technologies and new ways of sharing information. The camera is, if anything, even more ubiquitous whether on cell phones or in private and public surveillance networks. Recall that photography is essential to modern panoptical culture, "that modern play over bodies, gestures and behavior which is the emergence of the so-called 'science of man' and the constitution of the modern state."[5] Panoptical culture is in full bloom. That we inhabit a culture of surveillance—including self-surveillance—was made clear in the use of "crowd sourcing" to identify and track down the perpetrators of the bombing at the 2013 Boston Marathon.[6] Law enforcement authorities requested and received terabytes of video footage and still photographs from spectators and racers, as well as private and public surveillance networks. Sifting through that amount of data would have required untold numbers of man hours, as they say, but with the aid of facial recognition software developed with the support of the CIA's venture capital fund, law enforcement agents were able to sort through that data in two days and identify the two suspects, Dzhokhar and Tamerlan Tsarnaev, brothers of Chechen descent. Still photos or screenshots were made public shortly thereafter and the public was enlisted to help locate the suspects. After a fierce gun battle that resulted in the death of the older brother, Bostonians were told to "shelter-at-home" as a search continued for Dzhokhar, who had fled the scene. The event ended somewhat less spectacularly when a Watertown resident left his home after the lockdown was lifted and saw blood on the tarp covering his boat in the driveway. Dzhokhar was found clinging to life as a result of a number of gunshot wounds (including one that appeared to be self-inflicted) in the boat and was arrested and taken to the hospital for treatment. Eventually, he was brought to trial on federal charges of use of a weapon of mass destruction and sentenced to death.

The long-term results of GWOT are impossible to predict, but its imbrication in a series of unmakings and remakings of our globe and its inhabitants is unmistakable. In what follows, I focus on a singular instance of (un)making and remaking set in motion by a set of souvenir snapshots that Mitchell has dubbed "the Abu Ghraib archive."[7] In the spring of

2004, CBS News first broadcast (censored versions of) photographs of abuse by U.S. military personnel of detainees held at Abu Ghraib, an Iraqi prison that had been repurposed as a U.S. military prison. Those photographs were a small subset of a much larger archive (more than 270 photographs and 19 videos, according to *Salon.com*). The *New Yorker* broke the story in print form in an essay by Seymour M. Hersh, which turned out to be just the first of many attempts by journalists to follow the trail of the abuses the photos documented. Congress and the military also undertook investigations that confirmed the allegations of abuses at the prison that, in the minds of many, amount to torture. A small number of soldiers found to be directly responsible for abuses (including those in the photographs to follow) were court-martialed or discharged, but those who put in place the policies that not only allowed but also allegedly authorized such treatment went unprosecuted and largely unpunished.[8]

Taking up the Abu Ghraib photographs means not only a shift in photographic genre (from professional photojournalism to souvenir snapshots) but in photographic affect, as well. Instead of the awe and reverence signaled by the photographs of the Rt. Rev. Robinson's consecration, these photos evoke their own kind of shock and awe—and, for many viewers, shame and outrage. Instead of photographs of ritual celebration, we must contend with photographs of ritualized pain. Indeed, the title of this chapter plays on Sontag's book *Regarding the Pain of Others* (2003) that I discussed in chapter 2. Written in the wake of the war in Bosnia, Sontag takes up the question of what happens when we "regard" the pain of others in photographs. Please hear the *double entendre*: regarding (in reference to) regarding (looking at) photographs. The choice of terminology is deliberate—and important. To look can imply a certain immediacy, casualness, and brevity in one's encounter with the visual object. To regard implies a more sober, lingering, and mediated encounter. Regarding invites our considered reflection on what it means to look at, look into, and perhaps even look through photographs of others—and allow them to look (back) at us. That is appropriate, one would think, for a topic like the pain of others. But regarding the particular photographs of others in pain at issue here requires that we press beyond the immediacy of the pain and its infliction to the discursive conditions that made it possible in the first place. There is, moreover, more to the "otherness" of those in pain here than simply that they are "not me." And that otherness inflects the pain that these photographs put on display.

I invoke Sontag here not only because of the title but also because her essay allows us to reprise important elements of our discussion of photographic truth, *signifiance,* and spectatorial responsibility from chapter 2. "Everyone is a literalist when it comes to photographs," Sontag says.[9] That is, we all tend to take photographs—especially certain genres of photographs—to be nothing more (and nothing less) than a representation of a certain that-there-then "captured," as we say, by the camera's lens. But she also reminds us that photographs' claim to refer to a real that-there-then is often contested. Photographs can be staged and manipulated, for one thing. And the same photograph can be claimed for opposing political views. Both sides in the Bosnian conflict, for example, claimed the same photograph of Bosnian children killed by bombs as evidence of the others' war crimes. And the very same photograph can "move" us in entirely different ways. Serbs and Croats both reproduced that picture to rally support—and likely both succeeded. "No 'we' should be taken for granted when the subject is looking at other people's pain," says Sontag.[10] Facing up to what I have called photographic ambivalence implicates spectatorial responsibility in ethical ambivalence, as well. As Sontag explains, "One can feel obliged to look at photographs that record great cruelties and crimes. One should feel obliged to think about what it means to look at them, about the capacity actually to assimilate what they show."[11]

Taking up spectatorial responsibility requires attending to the ways we are made and unmade by photographic subjection. Photography (en)trains us in the modes of seeing, knowing, doing, and being that are integral to the modern *episteme* and *ethos.* When we pose for, shoot, or simply glance at photographs—of ourselves or of others known or unknown to us—we subject ourselves to bio-disciplinary power trained on us through the fourfold of Man and his others by the camera's lens. In *No Caption Needed,* Hariman and Lucaites argue that photographs are performative spaces wherein photographed subjects cite through gesture and facial expression visual social codes and iconographies. Photographic performativity is a critical dimension of photographic subjection—that is, the formation and management not only of those paradigmatic Foucauldian subjects, delinquents and homosexuals, but also of proper husbands and wives, mothers and fathers, daughters and sons. Photographic performativity also speaks to the effects certain photographs have on the body politic. We speak of certain photographs as "iconic," that is, as opening onto the events they reference and their larger significance in particularly powerful and efficient ways. Such photographs are circuits of political affect that arise out of situations of social conflict or crisis. According to Hariman and Lucaites, they "concentrate and direct emotions," thus serving as "aesthetic resources for performative mediation of conflicts."[12]

Into the Archives: Abu Ghraib and Lynching

The Abu Ghraib photographs (or at least those initially released in the spring of 2004) were without doubt a singularly disastrous—some might say traumatic—event in the GWOT's prosecution.[13] I reference trauma with some trepidation. Certainly, I, like many Americans, was horrified and repulsed what was being done in our name, neocon pundits' apologias for the U.S. soldiers who were immediately responsible notwithstanding. And by "in our name" I mean the names of America, democracy, freedom. This response—an inversion, perhaps, of shock and awe—in turn has provoked the reminder that such acts are nothing new but yet provide a further example of "man's inhumanity to man," as we say. And those reactions have in turn provoked the demand that we not erase the historical specificity of these particular atrocities in the rush to increase the number of shoulders on whom the mantle of responsibility falls. Part of staying with the specificity of these images involves remembering the difference between the damage done to "our name(s)" and the all too real trauma experienced by the Iraqi prisoners depicted in the photos (and by other victims of brutal subjugations at Abu Ghraib and elsewhere)—an insight that the tone of righteous indignation that the photos often evoke sometimes obscures.[14] Indeed, exactly how "we" are positioned by the photos—indeed, exactly who "we" are—will be central questions of this chapter.

In the weeks and months immediately after their release, journalist Mark Danner argued that the public had known for some time—even before the photos were made public—that the Bush administration was pursuing these kinds of policies. The photos added no new information, really, and in some ways became a substitute for the real problem. Noting the absence of a powerful public outcry against these policies, Danner says, "We must look squarely at the photographs and ask, is what has changed only what we know or what we are willing to accept?"[15]

As for the images in the archive themselves, they have taken on a life of their own—far beyond that intended for them by their creators. In addition to their circulation (to various ends) in cyberspace, the images were quickly taken up into acts of artistic resistance in various locations around the world, including the Middle East as well as Western Europe and North America. Although the soldier-photographers reportedly threatened to show the pictures to prisoners' families as an extension of the staged humiliations, they were initially circulated among the soldiers, their families and friends, as personal photos—souvenirs, if you will— well before the photos became public. Indeed, this similarity in intention as well as in subject matter has prompted Hazel Carby, Dora Apel, and others to link the Abu Ghraib photographs to lynching photographs, an insight with which I will spend some time here.[16]

But to compare is not to equate, as Apel and Carby, in particular, insist; it's to attend carefully to similarities and differences in content and context. Particularly salient are the photographs from both archives that include victims and spectators, as we'll see. Although both archives index scenes of torment, the differences in those scenarios require our attention. Only a few photos in the Abu Ghraib archive—at least, the portion that most of us have seen—come close to the gruesome sight of mutilated, burned, or hanged bodies that are the stock in trade of lynching photographs. But both archives largely leave unseen the torments and tortures that precede the clicking of the shutter and the pain and loss they inflict on the victims, their families, and communities. In addition, what links these photographs, I would argue, is accessed best through photographic *signifiance* or iconicity—that is, what these photos stand in for and open up and how they "move" us (or fail to). And that has everything to do with both archives' relationship to bio-disciplinary power.

Like the Abu Ghraib archive, the full record of lynching photographs (and attendant artifacts) is unknown; we have access only to pieces of it. Significantly, a portion of the lynching archive that belonged to a private collector, a white Southern gay man named James Allen (who was motivated to collect them by his own experience of oppression at the hands of white men) became a curated exhibition in 2000—just a year before September 11 and four years before the abuses at Abu Ghraib came to light.[17] Originally mounted and curated by a small gallery in New York City, the exhibition attracted such attention that it circulated (in different forms each time) to several other exhibition spaces around the country drawing exceptional crowds each time. Although no longer on display in brick and mortar venues, it lives on in virtual form online and, in abbreviated form, in a published volume.[18] The exhibition and its virtual and material heirs are entitled "Without Sanctuary," a title that, I'll suggest later, evokes its deeply complex effects on viewers.

Spectacle Lynching and/as Bio-Discipline

Most lynchings took place in relative secrecy and involved only a few killers, but others were staged as public spectacles complete with media coverage (including photographs) before and after. These events drew large crowds of white spectators—men, women, and children—who came to witness the violence itself or to share in its triumphant aftermath. In some cases, the spectators arrived by special passenger trains commissioned just for this purpose. Indeed, the role of modern technologies (and emergent consumer culture) in the practice of spectacle lynchings leads historian Grace Elizabeth Hale to claim them as "a peculiarly modern ritual," one that played an important role in what she calls the making of whiteness as a collective identity.[19] In addition, McWhorter deemed lynching a form of "state facilitated terrorism" that enabled whites to realize more fully their "evolutionary supremacy, reproductive potential, and self-proclaimed civil singularity."[20] Yet elements of spectacle lynchings, in particular, may cause some to question the modernity of lynching. For one thing, spectacle lynchings call to mind premodern executions like those described by Foucault in the opening pages of *Discipline and Punish*.[21] Not only were they staged before large crowds, but like the drawing and quartering Foucault describes, the victim's eventual death was preceded by lengthy and elaborate tortures. The graphic violence of spectacle lynchings, like their premodern precursors, were designed not just to punish wrongdoers but also to secure a certain social order; here, too, the specific identity of the victim was of secondary consideration. Historian Leon F. Litwack reports that if, as sometimes happened, the wrong person was mistakenly apprehended—or the right one was unavailable—the lynching would proceed with whoever was unfortunate enough to be at hand. Although black women and their children (and the rare white woman) were sometimes deliberately targeted, more often, they were victims-by-proxy served up as surrogates in the intended victim's absence. The lesson inherent in such substitutions wasn't lost on the black community. As one of its members observed, "one Negro swinging from a tree will serve as well as another to terrorize the community."[22]

Recall, however, that sovereign power does not disappear when disciplinary power (and subsequently biopower) come on the scene. Rather, it is enfolded into bio-disciplinary power and channeled through the fourfold of Man and his others. Spectacle lynchings exemplify this mixture of forms of power. In modernity, recall, sovereign power aligns with the people, not the monarch. That lynchings were largely extrajudicial (often aided and abetted by government authorities) illustrates this shift. Lynch mobs acted as self-appointed representatives of the people in appropriating to themselves sovereign power to kill. When lynch mobs came for prisoners, jailers often offered little or no resistance. In addition, perpetrators were rarely even identified, much less prosecuted, for the murders they had committed. If they investigated at all, local authorities typically attributed the crimes to "persons unknown" despite evidence to the contrary, including photographic evidence. Finally, what prosecutions did occur took place before all-white local juries, and thus lynchings went unpunished.

The rhetoric that justified lynching evinces bio-disciplinary power's role—as channeled through fourfold—in its practice. That spectacle lynchings involved sexual mutilation (castration was commonplace and lynched women were similarly subjected to breast and genital mutilation) traded on biopower's attribution of deviance to black sexuality.[23] As we saw in chapter 1, excessive desire (imputed to black women, especially) and desire for inappropriate objects (black men for white women, especially) indexed African Americans' putative residual savagery that was manifest as well in their alleged intellectual and moral deficits. Those deficits purportedly rendered blacks largely incapable of holding their disordered desires in check, making them an ever-present threat to the (white *qua* human, recall) race. Protecting white women—from whose wombs would issue the race's next generation—from this threat provided a central justification for lynching. The task of protecting white women fell to white men, of course. Thus, lynchings figure white masculinity as "the epitome of Victorian genteel manhood" even as the acts themselves demonstrated a "hard, virile, masculine brutality."[24]

Although there is evidence that some whites found spectacle lynchings profoundly disturbing, others were not shy about expressing their disregard for black lives taken through lynching—and often in animalistic terms. [25] A governor of Georgia reported his amazement at learning that, to many of his fellow Georgians, the "slaughter" of a black person amounted to "nothing more than the killing of a dog." Just to the south, a white Floridian equated the lynching of black people with killing fleas.[26] This lesson in animality was not lost on black people. Litwack cites a black Southerner of the time, "In those days it was 'Kill a mule, buy another. Kill a nigger, hire another,'" further exhibiting the fourfold's effects as a channel for bio-disciplinary power.[27]

Tracking the specific forms of torture and torment to which victims of lynching were subjected in comparison to incarceration exhibits additional dimensions of the particular convergence of disciplinary power and biopower that it embodies. Recall that, if disciplinary power seeks to produce "docile bodies" suited to modern life, biopower seeks the flourishing of the species. Disciplinary power targets the individual through his or her body, while biopower targets populations through the individual. Together, they entrain their human subjects in forms of knowing, being, seeing, and doing that serve those ends. Like incarceration, lynching seeks to protect the community from internal threats. But where the carceral system targets the individual soul through the individual body, spectacle lynchings target populations through an individual body. And where subjection to the routines of carceral life aims to (re)form a criminal into a docile delinquent, lynchings aim to produce a docile black population through the ritualized torture and death of one of its own. Like carceral disciplines, spectacle lynchings yield a distinctive anatamo-politics of the body. Instead of *in*carceration, lynching practices *ex*carceration; the threat posed to the race by blacks is extracted through ritual slicing and dicing, dismembering and mutilating, and hanging and burning a particular black body.

Recall, however, that biopolitical racism serves biopower's aims in a particular way: racism-against serves racism-for. As a number of historians of the practice have argued, spectacle lynchings consolidated white dominance of the social, economic, and political order. The anatamo-politics of excarceration serves that goal by (quite literally) incarnating white supremacy in, on, and through the black body, rendering legible another dimension of the fourfold's effects. I say "incarnation" quite deliberately, as lynching hereby begins to reveal its underlying theo-logic. Recall that emblematic of modernity's emergence is Man's displacement of God as master. What historian Hale describes as the ritualized choreography of spectacle lynchings embodies this displacement.[28] Snatching the victim from his or her home or jail cell, extracting a confession of crimes real or imagined, subjecting the victim to bodily torments of all sorts before the final act of slaughter installed whites as masters over (black) life and death. The ritual concluded with the sourcing of lynched bodies for souvenirs— eyes, ears, penises, fingers, toes, locks of hair, pieces of skin, bits of bone. Like the relics of medieval saints, lynching souvenirs were often put on public display. But if saints' relics pointed toward an order of things under God's control, lynching souvenirs reminded their viewers that whites were in charge. Not only who lives and who dies, but the manner of that living and dying, was a matter of white sovereignty; a sovereignty that, as we'll see, laid claim to divine sanction, and exercised itself virtually without limit—although not without resistance.

The Lynching Archive: Spectacle and/as Subjection

It may seem as though spectacle lynchings direct bio-disciplinary power only toward the black population, but that is not the case. To be sure, this population was directly targeted by lynching's malevolent violence, but consolidating white supremacy also required disciplining white people into their proper roles. Visual subjection—including photographic subjection—was critical to spectacle lynching's bio-disciplinary effects on white people. More critical, arguably, than to their disciplinary effects on the black population at large. Unless inadvertently caught up by them, black people rarely witnessed spectacle lynchings—and for good reason.[29] To attend was to risk one's own lynching. But black people didn't need to see spectacle lynchings first-hand to feel their effects.[30] As Richard Wright puts it, "Indeed, the white brutality that I had not seen was a more effective control of my behavior than that which I knew," a sentiment echoed by many others.[31] In fact, spectacle lynchings were arguably organized by *and for* white viewers. Seeing white men (and sometimes women) torture and kill black people taught other white men—and white boys—their proper roles of (proto) mastery. Viewing the violent and deadly consequences of sexual desire that (putatively) crossed the color line tutored white women and girls in the proper direction of their own desires—and where and how to direct blame if they got caught doing otherwise. It reinforced their consignment to the pedestal as passive and pure objects of white male protection and patronage.[32] And these were lessons that the white population by and large took to heart, if not in every instance readily or easily.[33]

Photographs of spectacle lynchings were essential to the events' effects on the white community. The taking of photographs—whether by amateurs or professionals—was as significant to the ritual of spectacle lynching, according to Allen, as "torture or souvenir grabbing."[34] Not only did such photographs "document the consolidation of a white supremacist mob," writes Smith, "they also performed it."[35] Indeed, they rendered in unmistakably visual and visceral terms the making of white supremacy as an embodied phenomenon.[36] The presence of white spectators in so many of these photographs directly returning the camera's gaze without the slightest trace of shame, embarrassment, or guilt documents lynchings' success. Their publication and circulation—in newspapers, as postcards, between family members and friends—widened and deepened the reach of bio-disciplinary power through the opportunity provided for photographic subjection of their white viewers.[37] Indeed, antilynching activist Walter White bemoaned the ease with which "an uncomfortably large percentage of American citizens can read in their newspapers of the slow roasting alive of a human being in Mississippi and turn, promptly and with little thought, to the comic strip or sporting page."[38] Hale credits this particular convergence of photography and journalism, spectacle and consumption, with a critical role in the long history of the making of whiteness as a cross-regional identity, one founded on lynching as, in White's words, "an almost integral part of our national folkways."[39]

Whatever its success in disciplining both black and white populations, lynching never occurred without resistance—including among white people (though they often were motivated more by concerns about white lawlessness than black suffering). Outrage within the black community, in particular, motivated a courageous and persistent antilynching campaign (whose most prominent spokesperson was Ida B. Wells-Barnett), which, in turn, sowed the seeds of the modern civil rights movement.[40] Although it failed to produce either tougher enforcement of pertinent current law or successful passage of federal antilynching legislation, the antilynching movement claimed the moral high ground and excoriated the brutality of lynching, eventually forcing white racism to pursue its goals largely by other means.[41] The lynching archive played a critical role in that endeavor.[42]

I turn now to consider that archive in more specificity. I focus on the career of three copies (of copies) of a particularly "iconic" lynching photograph; one that, in its early incarnations, embodies white supremacy, but in later (and different) contexts, excoriates it. I attend to the photograph's indexical and iconic dimensions and to each copy, in turn, as a performative space—that is, a site that generates, concentrates, and directs political affect. I close my inquiry into the lynching archive with some reflections on the exhibition ("Without Sanctuary") and the book (*Without Sanctuary*) as performative spaces that shape the import of lynching photographs for a contemporary audience. This exercise in photographic *askesis* will, I hope, prepare us for a fuller reading of the Abu Ghraib archive in relationship to bio-disciplinary power.

"Pictures Do Not Lie": Reading "Bo pointn to his niga" [*sic*]

As befits the genre of souvenir photography, the lynching archive consists of professional as well as amateur photographs, some converted to postcards, some framed, many bearing proprietary marks of those who circulated them. A studio photographer named Lawrence Beitler took the photograph on which I'll focus here after a lynching held in Marion, Indiana, on August 7, 1930. I select this photograph for its iconicity— both what it stands in for and opens up—with regard to lynching as past practice and current legacy. One of the most famous and well-published photographs of lynching, it appears in two different forms in *Without Sanctuary* (on facing pages), both of which I discuss here.[43] Both are reproduced in *Imagery of Lynching* and in Smith's *Photography on the Color Line*. It features prominently in *Lynching Photographs,* as well.[44] This time, the unadorned print (this one without the place and time notation), is joined by two other reproductions, both from newspapers of the day. A telling sliver focused on the white spectators in the foreground graces the cover of *Lynching Photographs* foreshadowing the volume's concern with the ethical implications of white spectatorial responsibility, in particular; an issue to which I'll return in due course. I begin with what we might call the *ur-photograph* of this series (figure 4.1), a print from the original negative inscribed with the date and location of the event it represents. Most of the photographic space is occupied by a large group of white spectators circulating through the scene. In the background,

FIGURE 4.1 A photograph of the lynch victims Thomas Shipp and Abram Smith hanging, surrounded by white spectators in Marion, Indiana on August 7, 1930. This photograph was taken by Lawrence Beitler, a studio photographer, and has appeared in numerous publications on lynching, including *Without Sanctuary*.

suspended above the heads of the crowd, hang the bodies of the two victims (Thomas Shipp and Abram Smith). Their clothes are ripped, dirtied, and presumably bloodied; a sheet (a Klan robe, according to Allen's notes in *Without Sanctuary*, a feed sack according to Wood) takes the place of missing pants on Smith's body: "not unlike the loincloth in traditional depictions of Christ on the cross," Allen observes.[45] A young couple in the lower left corner stands out from among the gathered throng. Their clothing and demeanor contrast strikingly with the dead men. Dressed as if for a date (the young man sports a white shirt and tie, the young woman a sleeveless dress), the two smile into the camera as they stroll through the crowd, not a hint of perturbation on their faces. Just to the right of center, positioned precisely between the two dead bodies, a mustachioed white man wearing a hat looks commandingly into the camera and points. This canonical gesture (Apel calls it "the 'finger of God' gesture") implicates

FIGURE 4.2 Beitler's photograph of lynch victims Thomas Shipp and Abram Smith hanging, surrounded by white spectators, including one pointing to the victims, in Marion, Indiana on August 7, 1930, here appears framed with the caption "Bo pointn to his niga" [*sic*] and a lock of one of the victims' hair.

him as the photographer's accomplice positioned just there to direct the viewer's gaze above the crowd to the lynched bodies that occasion its convergence.[46]

Beitler's photograph proved quite popular. Allen reports that thousands of copies were printed of it over the course of ten days; each sold for $0.50.[47] One such copy, framed and double matted, appears on the facing page to its *ur-photograph* in *Without Sanctuary* (figure 4.2). As Apel notes, the spectators, presented now in full length, become the focus of this apparently uncropped version.[48] This version of the photograph is a personal souvenir, the property apparently of an acquaintance of the pointing man. A caption printed by hand on the left corner of the inner mat immediately below the photograph identifies him as "Bo pointn to his niga" [*sic*]. Framed on the left corner of the outer mat of the photograph is a lock of hair presumably from one of the victims. The inclusion of this relic chillingly cites a common practice in family photography of the time. According to Smith, mourners often memorialized a deceased beloved in precisely this way.[49] The inclusion of the lock of hair doubles down on the photograph's indexicality and its iconicity. On the one hand, as Smith argues, its presence literalizes Roland Barthes's description of the photograph as a memento mori. It performs Bo's (and by proxy the photograph's owner's) mastery over "Bo's niga" as forever a fait accompli; his is a death embalmed in a photochemical reaction on paper doubly matted and framed with its signatory relic behind glass. The citation of a practice of photographic mourning further literalizes biopower's racism-for and -against as a matter of life and death—who gets to live and who must die. And yet, that same citation, I would argue, manifests photographic ambivalence that opens to the viewer another interpretive possibility that may or may not realized: someone—certainly not Bo, certainly not the collector, certainly not the mob that murdered them or the white community that took pleasure in it—might mourn these dead young men. Indeed, Wood reports anecdotal evidence that lynching photographs served as private memento mori for the family and friends of victims.[50] In opening onto what Judith Butler would call the victims' grievability, "Bo pointn at his niga" preserves the trace of the victims' humanity even as it closes the door on their liveability. [51]

That Beitler's photograph also took on a journalistic life of its own reflects an important shift in the public role of lynching photographs. In the early decades of the lynching era, Wood reports, newspapers—especially local newspapers—whether black or white owned were reluctant to publish lynching photographs given the potent and multivalent affective charge (particularly intense where the lynchings occurred) they carried.[52] That had changed by 1930, thanks in no small part to antilynching activism, as we'll see. According to Smith, several local or regional Indiana newspapers received advanced notice of the lynching and sent their own photographers to the scene. She reports, however, that those newspapers that chose to run a photograph used Beitler's photograph, not one of their own.[53] Several black-owned newspapers, including *The Chicago Defender* also ran the photograph.[54] The contrast between two such imagetexts is striking. The *Anderson Daily Bulletin* places the photograph on the front page under the headline "MARION IS QUIET AFTER DOUBLE LYNCHING." The headline reassures readers that order has been restored—although whether by or despite the lynching is unclear—which the article describes as "vengeance" for the rape of a white woman and murder of her white male companion.[55] The photograph's publication in the *Defender*, on the other hand, effectively transforms it from a souvenir of legitimate white power into an exposé of white brutality—and of what lies behind it. "Pictures do not lie," the article that accompanies the photograph says, according to Smith. "Although members of the mob . . . couldn't be identified according to the officers, here is a picture which shows plainly any number of the guilty persons." [56] Indeed, the caption indicts the lynchers, "a mob of Ku Kluxers, church members, women and businessmen," and the Marion police who not only "made no resistance to the lynchers," but also "assisted in fanning the flames of hatred by hanging the shirt of one of the dead men in the jail window all day" before the evening the lynching took place.[57] Smith claims that, seen in this context, the photograph's evidentiary significance is inverted. Instead of an "object lesson" in "vengeance" against alleged black brutality, it becomes an object lesson in "vicious murder" and the system that supports it, justifies it, and allows it to go unpunished.[58]

Of particular note, though, is the title given in the caption: "AMERICAN CHRISTIANITY." That the practice of lynching is indicted in theological terms calls our attention to the photographs as a form of theological cultural capital. The accompanying article excoriates a supposedly "Christian" nation—the very same nation that "spends millions to Christianize other countries"—for allowing and enabling this kind of torture. "Christian America's" culpability is now visible to "all the world" which, in turn, "points with scorn" at its double standard, the *Defender* concludes.[59] The true "barbarians," the *Defender* implies, are not only the lynchers and the spectators but also their numerous enablers, including the state authorities who turn a blind eye to evidence of the perpetrators' identity and the white community that, actively or passively, endorses the practice of lynching performed in its name. Many, if not most, of all of those responsible were, after all, Christians, as theologian James Cone points out in his recent book, *The Cross and the Lynching Tree*.[60] Indeed, what the *Defender* calls here "lynching picnics" were sometimes held on Sundays after church. Litwack reports that a lynch mob in Morganton, North Carolina (1889) "held prayer services" before proceeding with the business at hand.[61] Here, our foray into the lynching archive opens onto the deeper Christian theo-logic of lynching as reflected in and by these photographs and what they index.

As the title indicates, Cone's reflections on lynching and its legacy are prompted by an uncanny resemblance between the cross and the lynching tree, between the practice and significance of Christ's crucifixion and of America's history with lynching. His reflections take off from the powerful convergence of race and religion in that history. That convergence is manifest in the ritual of lynching itself, recall, which like the public executions it replaces, exhibits a deeply Christian theo-logic. That white Christians would willingly and even jubilantly subject blacks to cruciform torments and ultimately death is, on the one hand, not at all surprising. Whites have shown themselves quite adept at racist theo-logic, as the history of slavery and colonialism have shown. Indeed, white dominance is grounded in a version of manifest destiny in which America—and the white race—is "called by God to bear witness to the superiority of 'white over black',' Cone writes.[62] That superiority is expressed in terms that reveal a Christian theo-logic as a motivating force in biopolitical racism. Historian Philip Schaff of Union Theological Seminary (1870–1893) asserts the rightful dominance of "the Anglo-Saxon and Anglo-American" on the grounds of "fitness" and "character."[63] A Southern governor and senator deems lynching to be a "divine right of the Caucasian race."[64] Wood brings home the point arguing that Southern evangelicalism's notions of sin, redemption, and retribution gave lynching much of its symbolic and affective charge. Its violence reads as "terrifying retribution ordained and consecrated by God against the black man's transgressions."[65] Antilynching activist Walter White found it "exceedingly doubtful if lynching could exist under any other religion than Christianity."[66]

If white Christians failed to see it, the resemblance between the cross and the lynching tree was not lost on black people. Indeed, the black community found in that resemblance both some degree of solace and a platform for antilynching activism.[67] Cone cites a particularly powerful painting that appeared in the National Association for the Advancement of Colored People (NAACP) newspaper, *The Crisis*, called "Christmas in Georgia." It depicts a lynching of a black man "held up with the silhouette image of Christ" as the white mob hangs him from a tree. Posted on that tree is a sign: "'Inasmuch as ye did it unto the least of these, My brethren, ye did it unto Me."[68] Those who crafted this image effectively turn Christian biopolitical theo-logic on its head, using it to indict those it benefits and inspire those it harms to political resistance.

"Without Sanctuary" and Spectatorial Responsibility

It should be clear by now that context matters to photographic performativity: to what we see in photographs and how they move us—and in what direction. I close this discussion of the lynching archive with some reflections on what it evokes when it is encountered in "Without Sanctuary" (and *Without Sanctuary*). Both in place and time, this context is significantly different from that in which lynching photographs were originally viewed. If the very existence of the archives testify to an unambivalent desire to look—indeed a right to look (to borrow from Nicholas Mirzoeff[69])—as an exercise in white domination, the prospect of looking at the archive many decades later was much more complicated, perhaps especially for white viewers. On the one hand, the large audiences who came to see the exhibition at its various sites testifies to a need or desire to see— one spawned, I suspect, as much by our racial history as despite it. Yet the photographs both compel and repel the contemporary viewers' gaze; one can imagine that many wanted to look away. For these are photographs that (in some cases literally) look back at their viewers—and for white viewers in particular (especially those who don't identify or want to be identified with white dominance), this creates an ethical conundrum. As disturbing as the horrific violence they depict, Apel argues, are the depictions of the white mobs in so many of the photographs. We are shocked at the brazenness with which our look is returned by those who witnessed and in some cases committed the horrific acts the photographs document. Yet we are also implicated in and by the photographs—compelled as if by Bo's pointing finger to look at what has been done in our name. And "what has been done" includes the taking and circulation of the photographs themselves. Viewing "Without Sanctuary" prompted feelings of shame and guilt (a focus of Apel's analysis in her contribution to *Lynching Photographs*), but it also prompted some scholars and cultural critics to question the value of placing these photographs before the public once again—particularly in the aestheticizing context of a curated exhibition (or art book). Although some saw in it the opportunity to start a new conversation about race, others feared—or saw no point in—the dredging up of long-standing (black) anger and (white) guilt, of indulging relatively newly minted white shame or guilt if it would attach only to the past and not to the present. Others, however, invoked the mantra of Holocaust survivors—"never again"—and that familiar adage that those who don't know their history are doomed to repeat it. The title of the exhibition, "Without Sanctuary," aptly captures the exhibition's multivalence. On the one hand, read as a good caption to what the photographs index, it accurately describes the situation of lynching victims who found themselves without refuge. On the other, it also captions the iconic and affective dimensions of these photographs: to what the exhibit opens up and opens onto and how it moves contemporary viewers. That certainly begins with shame and guilt, anger and outrage, sorrow and grief in response to the horrors of lynching, but it also extends to the larger history of racism and colonialism that gave birth to those horrors—a history formed by bio-disciplinary power and its fourfold. The lynching archive offers its viewers no sanctuary from confronting at least some of that history. But the title also widens the question of spectatorial responsibility: who is left without sanctuary in the present? That the practice of spectacle lynching has faded away does not mean the sentiment and system that motivated it have disappeared. McWhorter reads its decline as simply an indication of its replacement by other mechanisms of bio-disciplinary control now grown sufficiently robust. And one doesn't have to think hard to come up with candidates for such mechanisms. Cone, for example, argues that "the lynching of black America is taking place in the criminal justice system . . . [which] Michelle Alexander correctly calls . . . 'the new Jim Crow'."[70] The asymmetrical effects of incarceration—and the death penalty, for that matter—on the African American population are well documented, if not widely acknowledged. And yet our appetite for incarceration has only grown in recent decades.[71] What forms of suffering—as and less immediately violent—do we allow to go on in our names?

In the concluding pages to *The Cross and the Lynching Tree*, Cone connects, if only briefly, the abuses at Abu Ghraib with lynching noting that, while many whites were shocked to learn of them, most blacks were not. After all, he writes, "we have been the object of white America's torture and abuse for nearly four hundred years."[72]

Cone's observation brings us back to the Abu Ghraib archive and to the forms of (un)making that it embodies and engenders. I focus on two photographs from it that, while perhaps not as "iconic" (in the colloquial sense) as "Hooded Man," circulated widely in the aftermath of the archive's discovery—one even generating, as "Hooded Man" did, its own protest art. Through what they index, these two photographs open up and onto the questions and issues that motivate this project in ways that allow us to build on the insights into bio-disciplinary power and its four-fold gleaned from our inquiry into the lynching archive.

"Pictures Do Not Lie" Redux: Lynndie Pointing to Her Muslims

Just left of center in figure 4.3, a female U.S. soldier (Pvt. Lynndie England, we know now) fully clothed and standing upright holds the business end of a leash. She gazes down the leash toward the unnamed male detainee at its other end lying on his side naked on the floor, his face obscured by editorial alteration, his genital area completely exposed to the camera's gaze. The effects of the fourfold of Man and his others—divine, raced and sexed, and animal—on the (un)making of England and her detainee are anything but straightforward. England's clothing—military

FIGURE 4.3 This is an image obtained by the Associated Press, which shows Pfc. Lynndie England holding a leash attached to a detainee in late 2003 at the Abu Ghraib prison in Baghdad, Iraq.

(AP PHOTO)

issue t-shirt, camouflage pants, and boots—effectively androgenize and anonymize her to a degree. If holding the leash and looking down on the detainee makes England the detainee's master, her posture (body angled away from rather than toward the leashed prisoner) suggests some ambivalence, perhaps, on her part to fully occupying this position. (Indeed, she claims that she was ordered to take up this position by Cpl. Charles Graner, her then boyfriend and the scene's master-choreographer.) Although morphologically male, the detainee's position as the one mastered—and by a *female* soldier, no less—strips him of the mastery associated with maleness. Collared and leashed, as well as naked, the detainee is rendered "animal" in contrast to Pvt. England's (hu)man(ity). And yet, insofar as these (un)makings trade in gender and species inversions, they trade *on* what resists those inversions: England's (white) womanhood, the detainee's (Iraqi) manhood remain legible even if *sous rature*.

The second photograph (figure 4.4) repeats these inversions in apportioning now a gleeful form of mastery to England and abject subordination to, in this case, three detainees—all naked and hooded and posed in various positions of subjection.[73] Whether its choreographers intended it to or not, the tableau calls to mind visual representations—often featuring monkeys—of the old adage "see no evil, hear no evil, speak no evil." At the photograph's center, one detainee sits atop another. The detainee whose body serves as a human chair faces the wall behind them, his ability to see further obscured by his hood. A second detainee sits upright and facing the camera, perched on the first detainee's upper back and shoulders, his legs spread wide enough to fully expose his genitals and still maintain his balance. His hands are linked behind his head; only the hood prevents him from seeing. The third detainee kneels on the floor to the human chair's left, his hip supporting the human chair's left knee. Although positioned facing the camera, the kneeling detainee's hooded head is bowed toward the floor, ears covered by his hands, rendering him unable to see or hear. What words any of the three might utter would likely fall on deaf ears whether the hoods muffled them or not. To the right of this threesome, England—fully clothed and fully mobile—grins as she looks straight into the camera. In an eerie reprise of Bo's "finger of God" gesture, she points her right index finger directly at the seated detainee's penis as she gives (it? the whole scene?) a thumbs up with her left hand.

Taken together, these tableaux purport to strip the detainees of their humanity, reducing them—like the lynching photographs—to bestialized

FIGURE 4.4 This is an image obtained by the Associated Press, which shows Pfc. Lynndie England posing with naked detainees with bags placed on their heads in late 2003 at the Abu Ghraib prison in Baghdad, Iraq.

(AP PHOTO)

(racialized, sexualized, animalized) and forcibly, if temporarily, disabled (blind, deaf, and dumb) flesh. Stephen Eisenman credits the hoods, in particular, for this all-but-totalizing effect.[74] The hoods hide from view these detainees' faces, to be sure, but traces of their humanity remain legible both in what these photographs leave visible and in what they obscure.[75]

In figure 4.3, the awkward posture of the leashed detainee registers the unnaturalness, if you will, of this position of animalized submission and his resistance to it. In figure 4.4, the seated detainee's knees bow inward—perhaps to secure his balance, but possibly a gesture of modesty. The contact between the kneeler's hip and the human chair's knee will, for some of us viewers, channel sympathy—the two detainees for one another and their compatriot, and ours for them. Most moving, though, may be the kneeling detainee, whose posture and gesture registers the humiliation of the threesome's subjection—doubly so, given the likelihood that his posture and gesture were choreographed by his tormentors—and their collective embarrassment or shame. He seems to call for a sympathetic response that he does not expect will come.

What links these photographs to the lynching archive, however, resides primarily in what they open up and open onto: what simultaneously exceeds the quadrangular frame of the photograph itself and is implicated in it. Taking up spectatorial responsibility for the Abu Ghraib photographs requires tracking and tracing the larger discursive systems embedded in and embodied by bio-disciplinary power channeled through the fourfold of Man and his others to which they give access and to which they subject their viewers.

Like the lynching archive, the Abu Ghraib archive trades in certain theo-logics that serve bio-disciplinary racism in both its positive (racism-for) and negative (racism-against) aims. As noted earlier, Mitchell argues that "Hooded Man's" iconicity is traceable in no small part to a Christian iconography of suffering. In posture and gesture, the hooded man echoes depictions of Christ's crucifixion. One can indeed read the two Abu Ghraib photographs I consider here through a theo-logic of (involuntary) vicarious suffering—the detainees must suffer both for the sins of their terrorist brethren *and* to secure the safety of the American public—but only up to a point. Eisenman, an art historian, sees in the Abu Ghraib photographic archive allusions to a *pathosformel* (pathos formula) that, although it includes Christian art, runs through the entire history of Western art from the ancient Greeks onward.[76] Like the crucifixion, this *pathosformel* depicts sufferers as acquiescing to (and, in some cases, even taking pleasure in) their own pain-in-subjection to those in power. But whereas the crucifixion is ultimately redemptive, this *pathosformel* is ultimately about nothing more or less than utter domination, with "the supposed bestiality of the victim" serving to justify "the crushing violence of the oppressor."[77]

The lynching photographs, which Eisenman touches on briefly, arguably exhibit this mix of Christian theo-logic and Western *pathosformel* to
serve bio-disciplinary power's racism-for and racism-against run along the
black–white axis. Against that backdrop, I find another element of Eisenman's analysis suggestive. In the final chapter of *The Abu Ghraib Effect,*
he offers a brief discussion of the Orientalist roots of the treatments to
which the Abu Ghraib detainees were subjected. Might we then, consider the Abu Ghraib archive under the rubric of photographic Orientalism (per chapter 2)—that is, as deploying the Western *pathosformel* and an
Orientalist theo-logic in the service of bio-disciplinary racism? Although
I focused only on landscape photography in my earlier discussion, the
label "photographic Orientalism" itself extends to photography a term
first applied in art historical circles to sculpture and painting, including
portraiture. The photographs under discussion here do not repeat the
romanticized stylistic conventions of nineteenth-century Orientalist art.
They trade in a much cruder visual vocabulary,[78] but one that is equally
redolent of the discursive regime of Orientalism.

Photographic Orientalism Redux

According to Edward Said's magisterial (Foucauldian inflected) study,
Orientalism is a form of knowing and managing the Arab–Muslim other.[79]
A creation of modern European scholars, primarily (but also redolent of
currents in medieval thought), Orientalism took on a political life in the
service of colonialist expansion. This discursive field undergoes shifts and
changes at the level of academic and political discourse (what Said calls
"manifest Orientalism") but retains much the same shape in its general
features (what he calls "latent Orientalism"). Latent Orientalism's effects
are part and parcel of the current global political landscape, including the
GWOT, as Said makes clear in the preface to the 2003 edition.[80] In Said's
account, modern colonialism, imperialism, (pseudo)biological and philo-
logical racism give the West's treatment of Muslim and Arab others its
peculiar shape—and vice versa. Orientalism justified the conquest of the
Near East on the basis of a natural inferiority of the population and culture
of the (heathen) Orient to the population and culture of the (Christian)
Occident. (Here, the work of Gil Anidjar in *The Jew, the Arab: A History
of the Enemy* provides an important supplement.)[81] Anidjar argues that

"Europe" is a theopolitical identity composed by the triangulation of the three Abrahamic religions: Judaism, Islam, and Christianity.[82] Christianity occupies the privileged center shored up by its excluded others, which are aligned on a grid formed by the dual axes of "religion" and "politics." Islam is pure politics, not religion—and a politics based on submission. Following the trajectory laid out for it by the Abrahamic, Islam finds its "natural" home among a "people," the Arabs, whose essential desire is for absolute submission. That they so desire calls into question their essential humanity—marked after the Enlightenment by the mutually grounding features of rationality and freedom—providing ontological justification of not only their empirical subjection but also their constitution as a perpetual political enemy.

Grounded in nineteenth-century schemata that divided humanity into two races (the Aryan European and the African Oriental), Orientalism asserted "the separateness of the Orient, its eccentricity, its backwardness, its silent indifference, its feminine penetrability, its supine malleability" all of which justified its need for "western attention, reconstruction, even redemption."[83] To the degree that nineteenth-century Orientalism, in particular, credited Islam as the source of the cultural and racial characteristics of the Arab Near East, it conflated (pseudo)racial difference with religious difference thereby adding yet another layer of justification to the Near East's political subordination. Indeed, like white supremacy, Orientalism also manifests a certain Christian theo-logic that, according to Said, positioned Islam as, at best, a pale imitation of Christianity and, at worst, a subhuman threat to (Christian) civilization. Well before the advent of modern bio-disciplinary power and its fourfold, Christian theologians had associated Muslims with hypersexuality and animality. Maximus the Confessor, writing c. 630 C.E. after the Arab invasion of Europe, lamented seeing "our civilization laid waste by wild and untamed beasts who have merely the shape of a human form."[84] Later medieval writers claimed that, during Ramadan, Muslims fasted all day and then engaged in all forms of sexual and gastronomic indulgence at night.[85] Put in modern bio-disciplinary terms, "the Oriental man was first an Oriental and only second a man," Said writes.[86] Furthermore, "since the Oriental was a member of a subject race, he had to be subjected: it was that simple."[87] That "his" subjection is figured through sexual transgression as well as gender and species inversion echoes the rhetoric and practice of lynching (and of white supremacy in general), as we've seen, albeit in a different key.

Like the lynching photographs, the Abu Ghraib photographs make manifest the workings of bio-disciplinary racism as racism-for and racism-against—now aimed (directly) at Iraqi Muslims rather than black Americans and (indirectly) their putative American masters. Here, too, bio-disciplinary power is channeled through the fourfold of Man and his others—sexed and raced, divine, and animal. Drawing on Orientalism's theo-logic, religious difference is racialized, sexualized, and animalized by and in a choreographed ritual of dominance and subjection aimed at securing mastery over the "detainees" and subduing the threat they purportedly pose to the race.

Of course, like the lynching photographs, the Abu Ghraib photographs "move" their viewers in various ways depending, in part, on context. Although their circulation was apparently intended to further consolidate U.S. dominance over its enemies, once the photographs leave the circuit of viewers for which they were intended, their effects proliferate and diversify well beyond that intent. Like lynching photographs, the Abu Ghraib photographs inspired acts of protest—and protest art[88]—around the world. But these acts of protest were, if anything, more ambivalent in their effects than the forms of protest that the lynching archive helped to engender. Might this be related to the hold bio-disciplinary power exerts over us? Into what modes of seeing, knowing, doing, and being do *these* photographs of "others" in pain seek to entrain us? How does bio-disciplinary power channeled through the fourfold of Man and his others work through these photographs to (un)make their viewers? What resources might they simultaneously provide to resist such entrainments and (un)makings?

Our inquiry into the lynching archive showed us that the *practice* of torture was primarily directed toward disciplining blacks into subjugation, but the *photographs* of lynching primarily served to discipline whites into domination. To better understand our current relationship to bio-disciplinary power and its fourfold, I will focus this inquiry into photographic subjection on those to whom the photographs would accord a position of mastery—that is, the *beneficiaries* of Orientalist racism. That is an ever-widening circle, as we've seen, beginning with the soldiers at Abu Ghraib themselves, their families and friends (the audience to whom the photographs originally were circulated and for whom, it appears, they *really* were intended), and now, arguably, Americans in general.

Abu Ghraib and Spectatorial Responsibility

That both archives associate subjugants with animality and dominants with (hu)man(ity) offers a conjunction between them and the fourfold that I propose to highlight here. Drawing on Jacques Derrida's essay, "The Animal That Therefore I Am (More to Follow),"[89] I track the spectatorial positions that the Abu Ghraib photographs, in particular, open up with regard to both (putative) mastery and (disavowed) vulnerability through the link between Man and animal. Derrida opens the essay by invoking an experience that, no doubt, many of us whose households include cats have had, but probably haven't thought about: what happens when your cat looks at you—naked—in the bathroom? For Derrida, at least, this experience is accompanied by shame and embarrassment—especially if the cat has a frontal view. Before whom or what is he ashamed? Animals, after all, are supposedly distinct from humans because they are not naked. More to the point, they don't know that they are naked; thus, they are not ashamed. (The allusion to the story of the Garden of Eden in Genesis is intentional and becomes a theme later in the essay.)[90] Conversely, cloth-ing is considered proper to the human. It is intrinsically connected to other distinctively human proper(ties): technicity, consciousness, and con-science. It is as though the abyssal gaze of his cat reflects Derrida back to himself as the man that he is at least supposed to be. He writes, "the gaze called animal offers to my sight the abyssal limit of the human: the inhu-man or the ahuman, the ends of man, that is to say the border crossing from which vantage man dares to announce himself to himself, thereby calling himself by the name that he believes he gives himself."[91]

This border between man and animal is first and foremost a linguistic site in several senses: language creates the border (man "corrals a large number of living beings" under this one term, "animal" and does so by naming).[92] Language is also what man has that he claims the animal lacks. Derrida coins a neologism for this linguistic site: *l'animot*. Derrida writes, "Men would be first and foremost those living creatures who have given themselves the word that enables them to speak of the animal with a sin-gle voice and to designate it as the single being that remains without a response, without a word with which to respond."[93]

This terrain, where man separates himself from the animal, is perhaps the founding site of philosophy, Derrida says, noting that philosophy seems to take for granted—and reinforces, for the most part—this fundamental division, at least on the surface. In the past 200 years, however, we have been living through a tectonic shift, of sorts, in man's relationship to the animal. Symptoms of this shift include the macroscopic and microscopic changes in what was once called animal husbandry—the development of incredibly efficient and deeply invasive technologies of animal breeding, feeding, slaughtering, and processing that produce maximum pounds of tender meat at minimum price for human consumption; the use of animals in scientific research; the usually unintended but no less dramatic animal "genocides" (Derrida's term, and its use is part of the problematic of the essay) from human damage to the environment (and human attempts to repair the damage); and so on.

These changes produce reactions in the human body politic, as well (the animal rights movement, the slow food–organic food movements). And they register at the philosophical level. Derrida recalls Jeremy Bentham's famous call to change the terms of the question regarding the line between human and animal. The question isn't whether animals know, think, speak, and respond (are of the genus *zoon logon echon*), but do they suffer?[94]

Although some will quibble and want to use different terms for animal versus human suffering, the answer clearly is yes. Derrida asks us to spend some time with this tectonic shift: thinking it through threatens to unground *l'animot*. The very terms of the question shift from one of possessing (or not) certain powers and abilities to a question of passivity and powerlessness—*impouvoir*, if you will (the French captures the nuance better), of sufferance, of undergoing and going under. And our animal mirror, in this case, I think, shakes *us* up by reflecting the *impouvoir* that resides within us.[95] The opposite of mastery, to be sure, that hallmark of modern subjectivity.

Derrida is not proposing here that there *is* no difference between man and animal after all, that would be to ignore the abyssal gaze with which the essay began. "The animal looks at us, and we are naked before it. Thinking perhaps begins there," he writes.[96] But he does want us to ponder for a while—to stay with, as it were—the sympathy evoked in us by this brief recollection of these horrific tableaux. We are engaged in a war over pity between those who acknowledge this experience of compassion (feeling-with) and those who don't. What Derrida wants us to think *is* the abyssal border itself. There is no simple or clean line separating "man" from "animal." Obscured by *l'animot* are the multiple differences within "the animal" as well as within "the living." Not to mention the multiple lines of continuity and discontinuity between "us" and "them."

The Abu Ghraib photographs under discussion here figure "us" versus "them" as "man" versus "animal"—but how successfully? Consider these images through the lens of Bentham's question that repositions the line between man and animal: do they suffer? Most of us would answer, yes. Part of what disturbs (some of) us about the photographs is imagining that the detainees' suffering goes either unnoticed or is enjoyed by the soldiers, supposedly our representatives in Iraq. Yet Orientalist views called into question whether Orientals suffered, according to Said—an insight that renders even more sinister Rush Limbaugh's comparing of these tableaux to fraternity stunts.[97]

To the degree that the images allow us to imagine ourselves in the position of the prisoner on a leash or the kneeling detainee, the line between "us" and "them" erodes. But that is not the only spectatorial position that the images offer up to us—especially to Americans. This is done in my name, after all. Can I—no matter how much I might want to—distance myself from the U.S. soldiers outside the frame? The one(s) who took the picture(s)? The one(s) who invented these particular scenarios? Aren't "I" contaminated by "them?" In participating in rendering the Iraqi prisoners less-than-human, don't they, too, call into question the border between man and animal? Do not the mute gestures of the Iraqi prisoners in these photos evoke the abyssal border between who we human beings like to *think* we are and what we are *all* capable of—particularly "us" white Americans? Here, the comparisons to the lynching photographs become particularly salient. Contemporary viewers—especially white viewers, Cone's observation suggests—are caught short by their (our) forebears' easy comfort in the presence of such violence. And *we* are ashamed—for them, for us. The lynching photographs and the photographs from Abu Ghraib *are* as American as apple pie, unfortunately. U.S. democracy has always meant freedom for some, but torment and incarceration—or excarceration—for others.[98] Of course, this is not true only of America. Recalling to mind our brief excursus into Anidjar's work, journalists and scholars have seen in the Abu Ghraib photographs parallels to souvenirs of other wars or prisons: the rebellion of the Indians against the British and the Algerian civil war, for example.[99] The sociological and psychological literature references numerous studies that document and attempt to explain the ease with which ordinary people willingly inflict harm on one another, especially at the behest of authority figures.[100] Given these realities, how apt is it to name one side of the border "animal" and the other "man?" Where is this border, really, and what does it displace or disavow? What abyss does it expose at the heart of modern subjectivity?

Allen Feldman has suggested that Cpl. Graner and his fellow soldiers staged these particular tableaux to create for a moment the control and mastery over the enemy that they were unable to establish on the battlefield. That they stage submission in terms of gender inversion reflects the need to reassert mastery over the (Oriental) other as recompense for the soldiers' own demasculinization by their failure to dominate him where it really counts, he argues. Feldman reads the photos as symptomatic of what he calls the "actuarial gaze," a spectatorial position characteristic of the visual culture of the GWOT that aims to control risk and vulnerability—or at least to reassure the spectator that "we" have "it" under control.[101] In "The Ends of Man," an essay written against the backdrop of the events of the spring of 1968, Derrida spoke of the trembling of man, "played out in the violent relationship of the whole of the West to its other."[102] Without doubt, we find ourselves caught up in what Derrida described more than forty years ago as "the structural solidarity" of "military or economic violence . . . with 'linguistic' violence."[103] The violence and the resulting trauma cut both ways and, as all traumas do, reopens old wounds—wounds that are themselves the result of multiple traumas, including those at the root of subjectivity itself. I submit that it was not only the soldiers who staged the photos but also many—but not all—of *us* who find in the images reassurance that Man is in his rightful place and all is right with the world. And there were—and are—plenty among us who refuse to see, hear, or speak the evil that the Abu Ghraib archive represents.

The images seem to assure "us" of our sovereignty over "them"; thus, one response is to accede to that reassurance and the satisfactions it offers. But look more closely at the photos and fissures in that assurance open up. Insofar as "we" *are* "them"—the detainees, Pvt. England, and the soldiers off-camera—then responding to the photos requires acknowledging the reality of brutal mastery wrought through fragile vulnerability—and fragile vulnerability *to* brutal mastery—as "us." In this light, what has passed for response to the images in the form of political resistance, protest, or outrage must be judged anemic, at best.

But this is not a sufficient response, nor is it all that can be said. The photos also demand that we come to terms with the larger cultural conditions that made them possible in the first place. Some of those conditions arise from our past: the residual effects of Orientalism, of the sexed, raced, and gendered economies that undergird it and extend beyond it. And there is yet more. Former U.S. Secretary of Defense Donald Rumsfeld infamously distinguished between known knowns (things we know we know), known unknowns (things we know we don't know), and things we don't know we don't know. In a public lecture given at Vanderbilt several years ago, Slavoj Žižek added to that list unknown knowns (things we don't [want to] know we know)—that is, things we disavow.[104] Well before the Senate Intelligence Committee's scathing indictment of the CIA's treatment of many of its detainees in the GWOT, the facts about Abu Ghraib, the policies that sanctioned and gave rise to the torments the archive documents, and the names of those who crafted them were readily available to any and all who wanted—or felt obligated—to inform themselves about it.[105] The artist Daniel Heyman was invited along to interviews held in Turkey and Jordan in 2006–2007 of some forty or more former Abu Ghraib detainees conducted by lawyers representing them in U.S. lawsuits. Recasting a traditional courtroom practice, Heyman sketched as the detainees gave their depositions adorning the sketches with transcriptions of their testimony to the specific abuses to which they were subjected. He writes of that experience,

> I can only think that if an artist with two part time jobs could find out the truth of how our country uses torture as a policy in war then every senator, every congressperson, every employee of the executive or the judiciary branch could have found out much more than I did, and found it out much earlier—if they wanted to.[106]

Recall Danner's question one more time: "We must look squarely at the photographs and ask, is what has changed only what we know or what we are willing to accept?"

The photos in both the Abu Ghraib and lynching archives trade in disavowed vulnerability, the very vulnerability that bio-disciplinary power seeks to override. The borders between self and other, us and them, man and woman, black and white, Iraqi and American, human and animal, they suggest, are less secure than some of us might like to think. At bottom, I would suggest, living into whatever awaits us as modernity wanes will require that we find other ways of bearing up under bio-disciplinary power than these. Perhaps we can look into the abyss at the bottom of the fourfold and find resources for new forms of living and living together that better suit our all-too-uncertain future. But first, we need to go deeper into vulnerability and its disavowal by following it into other sites (and sights).

CHAPTER FIVE

BIO-DISCIPLINE AND THE RIGHT TO LIFE

Becoming Terri Schiavo

Perhaps a lot of the opposition to Ms. Schiavo's situation had more to do with the fear of death rather than the sanctity of life.
—George Felos (Mr. Schaivo's lawyer)

We're not doctors, we just play them on C-SPAN.
—Rep. Barney Frank (D-MA)

For millennia, man remained what he was for Aristotle: a living animal with the additional capacity for a political existence; modern man is an animal whose politics place his existence as a living being in question.
—Michel Foucault

IN 1990, MS. Theresa Schiavo was left in a persistent vegetative state (PVS) when her brain was deprived of oxygen for several minutes because of a heart attack brought on by a suspected potassium shortage (originally thought to be caused by undiagnosed bulimia, although her autopsy failed to confirm that).[1] PVS (in which some 10,000–15,000 people in the United States are currently living, by one estimate) is more accurately described as the state of being awake but not aware.[2] The brainstem, which houses the more "primitive" mental functions (e.g., the sleep–wake cycle) still works, but the part of the brain that houses what we call consciousness does not. The person in such a state reacts to noises, opens her eyes, appears to look around, and makes sounds herself, but exhibits no consistency in responding to particular stimuli. Ms. Schiavo's brain injury had deprived her of the ability to swallow without aspirating (effective swallowing requires consciousness); thus, her life was sustained by a feeding tube. Ms. Schiavo became a national celebrity some twelve years after becoming the center of a long legal battle that pitted her husband, who wanted the feeding tube removed arguing (with other witnesses) that she would not want to be kept alive in this condition, against her family of origin, who maintained that her current state (or future, if rehabilitation were provided her) justified keeping the feeding tube in place. Courts at the state and federal level (the Supreme Court refused to hear an appeal) weighed in on the case, siding time and again with Mr. Schiavo. Despite intervention from Congress at the last minute, a judge's order to remove (once again) the feeding tube was carried out on March 18, 2005. Ms. Schiavo died from dehydration on March 31, 2005.

The case was widely covered in many media outlets. Stills and clips from videos of Ms. Schiavo made by her parents, Bob and Mary Schindler, were central to the coverage and to the public's response to the case—and certainly to the mobilization of protestors, pundits, and politicians to what they saw as Ms. Schiavo's defense. Viewing an hour of these videos led Sen. Bill Frist (R-TN), a physician (but not a neurologist) to question the diagnosis of PVS.[3]

The two images of Ms. Schiavo on which I focus here are among those stills. I consider them in relationship to genres of photographs discussed in chapter 2 that have not figured in the intervening chapters: the family snapshot, and freak and medical photography.[4] Recall that family snapshots straddle the border between public and private. They serve to memorialize specific events and loved ones for a particular family, but they do so through a particular form of photographic subjection: what Marianne Hirsch calls the familial gaze. Family photographs arguably follow certain conventions—for example, who hasn't seen, if not posed for, the group photograph at holidays, weddings, or family reunions? By subjecting ourselves and our loved ones to those conventions, we demonstrate to ourselves (and, occasionally, to others) that our family is what all families are supposed to be—at least, at the moment the shutter clicks.

These stills and the movies from which they came, however, are more than keepsakes in the family archive; rather, they became tools in the court of public and political opinion that moved their viewers to take various positions on Ms. Schiavo's situation—and, in some cases, to act on them. Indeed, they were put to evidentiary use to persuade legislators like Sen. Frist (and, likely, right-to-life organizers) to act on the Schindlers' behalf. Thus, although they follow the conventions of family snapshots, they functioned in the public sphere in ways that reprise the intersection between freak photography and medical photography discussed in chapter 2. Although aimed at different audiences and following different conventions, both genres conscript portrait photography to circulate bio-disciplinary power. Medical photography, recall, sought to document (ab)normality by turning bio-disciplinary power's clinical gaze on, for example, sexual deviants and asylum inmates. Thus, clinical photographs of inverts and the insane enabled the organization, classification, and diagnosis—and containment—of abnormality. A form of souvenir photography, freak photography looks back to an important turning point in the emergence and consolidation of bio-disciplinary power. Recall that the demise of the freak shows marked a transition from extraordinary bodies to disability, a problem to be medicalized and fixed. If the audience for medical photographs were medical professionals, freak photographs were sold to and circulated by those whom we might call (*pace* Garland Thomson) proto-"normates." As the lynching photographs entrained their viewers into whiteness, so freak photography inculcated its audience into normalcy by placing (ab)normality on display. Like the other photographs considered so far, the stills of Ms. Schiavo considered as family photographs or as freak photography circulate bio-disciplinary power channeled by the fourfold of Man and his others—sexed, raced, animal, and divine.

As with the photographs considered in previous chapters, the stills of Ms. Schiavo came to the public's attention as part of an imagetext—media reports of the political, legal, and familial controversy over Ms. Schiavo's fate. The rather cold and clinical description I provided earlier of the particular becomings—medical, familial, legal, and political—that brought Ms. Schiavo to public attention reflects the tone of much of the media reportage. But tracking and tracing those becomings (along with those that preceded it) in what follows will be anything but a cold and clinical process. The imagetexts about the controversy over Ms. Schiavo moved many well outside her family to take sides or to take action, although of different kinds and for different reasons. Press coverage focused on the drama staged by prolife religious activists and their (mostly Republican) political allies in both the state of Florida and our nation's capital. Significantly, given the photographic genres the stills of Ms. Schiavo evoke, her case also caught the attention of disability rights activists, although they received less mainstream press coverage during the weeks that the story dominated the news.[5]

People in the disability rights movement were divided about whether to take a position regarding Ms. Schiavo's situation. The distinction disability theorists and activists make between impairment (the physical, mental, or emotional conditions that complicate living for those who have them) and disability (the social condition created by society's failure to accommodate impairments) helps contextualize the disagreement.[6] Impairments vary enormously; thus, the accommodations that, when provided, enable people to creatively adapt to living well with cerebral palsy or with autism, for example, vary greatly, too. Because the controversy over Ms. Schiavo's situation concerned depriving her of the accommodations, support, and care she needed, her case evoked issues central to the disability rights movement, some of its activists argued. But the exceptional nature of her impairment made others reluctant to take it on. Certain other impairments negatively affect consciousness, but PVS eliminates it.[7] Some advocates feared that taking up Ms. Schiavo's cause would only reinforce commonplace (and misleading) associations of disability with utter debility and dependency and of living with disability as a form of life not worth living.[8] That disability activists found themselves in such a conundrum reflects bio-disciplinary power's effects (channeled by the fourfold) on our time and place, as we'll see. Indeed, considering the stills of Ms. Schiavo and the complex of issues (affective and ethical, theoretical and practical, philosophical and theological) that they open up and open onto will expose us in new ways to the deep ambivalence of bio-disciplinary power's hold not only over Ms. Schiavo's situation but over all of us.

Becoming Terri Schiavo, Part I: Photographic Ambivalence

The first of the two stills of Terri Schiavo that will occupy us here is the image of her that viewers came to know best in those months and weeks that the controversy escalated (figure 5.1). In it, we are offered a close-up of Ms. Schiavo's slightly ruddy face, head tilted back, mouth slightly agape, eyes heavy lidded. Combined with her expression and posture, the Peter Pan collar and pastel colors of her housedress accentuates the appearance of child-like innocence and vulnerability, likely moving viewers to pity, sorrow, or sympathy for her. But her gaze is also discomfiting. Her eyes, the putative window into the soul, they say, occlude more than they reveal. She looks into the camera's lens—or does she? It is not clear that she sees—or even whether she sees. (Indeed, the autopsy report showed that she was blind.)[9] Is she returning someone's gaze? The videographer's? A family member's or caregiver's perhaps? Is she attempting to

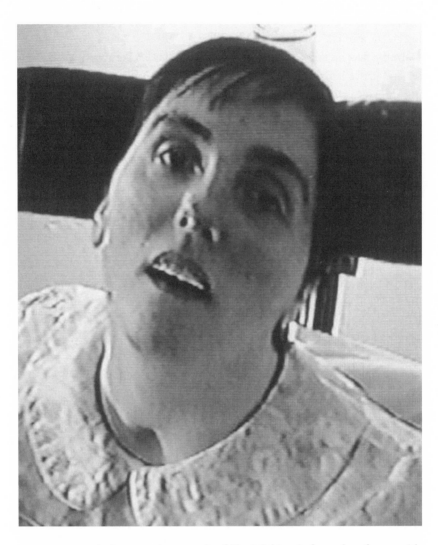

FIGURE 5.1 A close-up photograph of Terri Schiavo's face taken from a videotape from August 11, 2001, and released by the Schindler family on Tuesday, October 14, 2003, in Pinellas Park, Fla. The forty-one-year-old Schiavo suffered brain damage in 1990 when her heart temporarily stopped beating because of an eating disorder. The Supreme Court refused Monday, January 24, 2005, to reinstate a Florida law passed to keep Schiavo hooked to a feeding tube, clearing the way for it to be removed.

communicate something to the videographer? Her family? Is she responding to the camera's presence? To anything at all?

In the second still (figure 5.2), Mrs. Schindler leans toward her daughter and kisses her on the cheek. Ms. Schiavo's eyes close in its receipt giving the viewer a peaceful and familiar vision of the loving bond between
mother and daughter. That Ms. Schiavo closes her eyes eliminates the
discomfiting experience from the first image of being caught (by proxy) in
the circuit of her gaze. Much, but not all. For Ms. Schiavo's posture and
expression remain largely unchanged; her head has turned slightly to her
right, but her neck remains awkwardly outstretched, her mouth agape.
That her eyes are closed suggests that Ms. Schiavo may have registered
the contact as a gesture of affection and took comfort in it. But no matter
how hard we look at the image before us, we cannot be sure.

Consider these images, first, through the confluence of genres I discussed previously. The presence of mother and daughter in figure 5.2
marks it as obviously a family photograph, but so might the intimacy of
figure 5.1 (especially when accompanied by figure 5.2). The unguarded
openness with which Ms. Schiavo returns the camera's gaze in the first
image suggests an intimate familiarity with the videographer—at least, at
first glance. The kiss in the second image signals not only Ms. Schindler's
love and concern for her daughter, but familial tranquility. The image
does not hint at the familial discord and conflict outside the frame. For
all we know, Mr. Schiavo could have been the videographer. According to
Hirsch, this is a hallmark of family snapshots; they "show us what we wish
our family to be, and therefore what, most frequently it is not."[10]

Taken together, the images are difficult to read. Their intimacy fits the
genre of the family snapshot, but Ms. Schiavo's posture and gaze invites
scrutiny of another sort altogether. The intimacy of the stills is at odds with
the objectivity and distance of either medical or freak photography, yet their
subject matter—especially given the context of Ms. Schiavo's situation—
opens them up to the clinical or exoticizing gazes associated with those
genres. Without the social prohibitions (such as they are) that might apply
were we to encounter Ms. Schiavo in person, the gaze becomes a stare.[11]
Like Sen. Frist (although without the cover of medical credentials), we, too,
find ourselves staring into the frame struggling to come to terms with what
it presents to us, that is, to discern Ms. Schiavo's state of being and of mind.
But more to the point, even if we were to meet Ms. Schiavo in person,
her brain injury had deprived her, we're told, of the intellectual and social

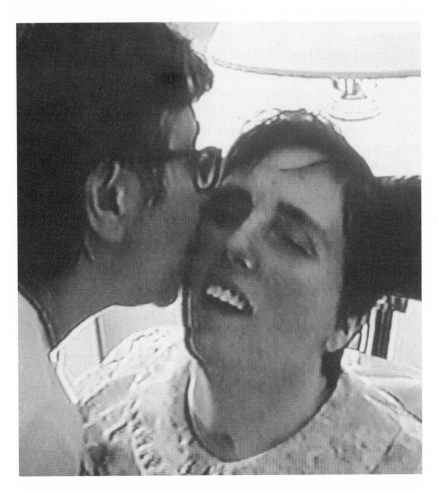

FIGURE 5.2 Terri Schiavo, right, gets a kiss from her mother, Mary Schindler, in this August 11, 2001, image taken a from videotape and released by the Schindler family on Tuesday, October 14, 2003, in Pinellas Park, Florida. The forty-one-year-old Schiavo suffered brain damage in 1990 when her heart temporarily stopped beating because of an eating disorder. The Supreme Court refused Monday, January 24, 2005, to reinstate a Florida law passed to keep Schiavo hooked to a feeding tube, clearing the way for it to be removed.

capacities necessary to look back at us. The stills, then, reveal with particular acuity the social and physical vulnerability of Ms. Schiavo's situation. In many ways—not least in rendering Ms. Schiavo so visually vulnerable—the stills offer us in concentrated visual form the dilemma of her situation.[12]

As with the photographs studied heretofore, I am particularly interested in the iconic dimensions of these images: what they open up and onto through what they index. Both images haunt the viewer with what haunts them. They confront us with a peculiar sense of Ms. Schaivo's present absence or absent presence borne by her posture and the opacity of her gaze. It easy to imagine some family members seeing in that absent presence signs of the Terri Schiavo they love and want to restore to (some measure of) health. It is also easy to imagine others seeing in that present absence a loss whose irrevocability must be accepted and allowed to finalize itself. In a sense, then, the stills take photographic ambivalence to a new level, which affects their political impact. For these images came to serve as what Hariman and Lucaites describe as circuits of political affect in the various public contexts in which Ms. Schiavo's fate was debated.[13] The Schindlers and their allies circulated them quite intentionally as aesthetic resources that would support the legal, political, or legislative resolution they sought—and with considerable, though hardly total, success. Many were indeed moved to take up their cause, but many were otherwise moved by the images and the larger controversy—familial, legal, and legislative—that they also open up and onto.

I am not the first to consider Ms. Schiavo's case in relationship to biopower. Tracking the effects of the various readings given of Ms. Schiavo's body on the handling of her case, Terri Beth Miller argues, exemplifies the depth of normativity's reach into and grasp on medicalized subjects as described by Foucault in *Birth of the Clinic*.[14] John Protevi, Jeffrey Bishop, and Eric Santner all take Ms. Schiavo's situation to be emblematic of the dangers of biopolitics and thus biopower.[15] Santner and Bishop find Giorgio Agamben's concepts of "bare life" and the sovereign exception (developed as a critique of Foucault) illuminative of those dangers.[16] Protevi, who takes up Ms. Schiavo's situation as a test case for his theory of what he calls "political affect" (itself grounded in the work of Gilles Deleuze and Felix Guattari), finds Foucault's perspective more adequate to Schiavo's situation than Agamben's.

That Ms. Schiavo's case existed at all—much less that it became front page news—reflects biopower's distinctive relationship to life and death.

Recall that, in the modern *episteme*, "life (*la vie*)" replaces "nature" as epistemological object. An order of things emerges that divides the organic from the inorganic, separating things that are born, reproduce, and die from things that do not. "Natural history" is replaced with nature *as* history. Each living thing bears within itself the (inherited) seeds of its own becoming and its own eventual demise. Biopower embodies this epistemic shift as a way not only of knowing, but also of being and doing aimed specifically at human life. Biopower differs from those forms of power that predate and are marshaled to serve it (sovereign power and disciplinary power) in target, form, and aspect. In lieu of the sovereign's right to kill, biopower claims the right to make live or allow to die. In the name of the people, it works on and through the individual (aided and abetted by disciplinary power), but its ultimate targets are populations, its aim the survival and flourishing of the race.

Biopower manifests in a new relationship to death, as well, recall. Death recedes from the public into the private realm reflecting, Foucault suggests, sovereign power's subordination to biopower. Instead of a transition from the power of the monarch to God, death now constitutes the outer limit of life and thus of biopower's reach. In seeking to extend life (for certain members of the race) and manage dying (the focus of Bishop's inquiry), biopower extends itself as far as it can toward its limit. Here, biopower entrains sovereign power to consign some to death either by passively standing by (e.g., allowing disease to run its course) or by actively targeting certain populations—those purportedly rife with abnormality—for management or extinction. Biopower also conscripts disciplinary power to its service. As we've seen in the previous chapters, abnormality manifested itself most markedly as excessive sexual desire, wrongly directed desire, and the inappropriate behaviors that issued therefrom. Conjoining bodies and populations, sexuality (itself a product of biopower) became a primary mechanism through which abnormality was managed and through which it was discovered and contained or eliminated in the first place. Two of the institutions that figure most prominently in the becomings that brought Ms. Schiavo to public attention—the family and the medical establishment—become key sites for the exercise of bio-discipline's managerial powers. What we've come to think of as the "normal family"—an economically secure unit made up of mom, dad, and their (2.5 well-adjusted [read heteronormed]) kids—becomes the micro target of population management. Through the clinic, the asylum, and the hospital, life and death are medicalized and managed, controlled and contained.

Like the previous chapters, this one will likely read as a cautionary tale about bio-disciplinary power but of a more ambivalent sort. Recall the description with which I began of how Ms. Schiavo came to be in a persistent vegetative state. That she survived the cardiac event at all manifests biopower's benevolent (which is not to say unambivalent) exercise. The considerable advances in modern medicine in recent decades (from cardiopulmonary resuscitation [CPR] to defibrillators to feeding tubes themselves and well beyond) mean that, to a degree unprecedented in human history, human beings hold the power of life and death in their hands— power that had been considered God's. Physicians and other medical professionals, yes, but with the advent of fairly widespread access to training in CPR and now to defibrillators, the rest of us (especially in developed economies), too. We can *all* play doctors on C-SPAN. We have the capacity now not only to keep alive those in a PVS but also to sustain bodily life after the brain has died (a routine event in hospitals that allows the harvesting of organs for transplant).[17] This same expanded capacity exists at the beginning of (human) life as well as at its end. (Of course, our power over life and death extends well beyond human life, a point to which I'll return in the next chapter.) A fetus is now viable at twenty-four to twenty-eight weeks, which has complicated the debates over (what political discourse configures as) the right to life.[18] We cannot wish those technologies away; they frequently make possible lives—and lives of enhanced quality—that otherwise would not be (at least, for those to whom these technologies are extended, which is a relatively small portion of global humanity). But the outcome of these exercises of biopower cannot be predicted in advance. In extending human life, we have also created new forms of it—of which living in a PVS is one. The benefits of biopower's benevolence are many, to be sure, but its persistent drive to sustain life—a drive to which we are all beholden—sometimes presents us with situations of great (emotional, ethical, and often financial) challenge. No doubt, many readers will have their individual stories—I certainly have mine. Although our stories may have elements in common, each is unique; most, however, remain (relatively) private. In Ms. Schiavo's case, private tragedy became public spectacle.

As public spectacle, however, Ms. Schiavo's situation manifests additional dimensions of bio-disciplinary power's ambivalent—and even malevolent—effects. Recall that she was twenty-six years old at the time of

her heart attack. Hers was a wifely life cut short before it had the opportunity to reproduce; it took the form of human life (white, middle class,
heterosexual) that bio-disciplinary power particularly sought to nurture.
Recall, as well, the suspicion (unsupported by her autopsy) that undiagnosed bulimia led to the potassium insufficiency that prompted the
cardiac arrest. Per Susan Bordo's *Unbearable Weight*, bulimia and other
eating disorders are psychiatric diagnoses that index gender trouble.[19]
Like their predecessor, hysteria, eating disorders articulate the demands
and contours of contemporary gender conformity. How ironic, then, that
the legal decision about whether Ms. Schiavo should live or die centered
around a feeding tube.[20]

Of course, power begets resistance, and biopower is no exception. The
spread of mechanisms of normalization, Foucault tells us, provoked simultaneously the assertion of demands for freedom from its constraints—
waged, significantly, in the name of life. To be specific, in the name of
the right to life. In the conclusion of *History of Sexuality, Vol. 1* entitled
"Right of Death and Power Over Life (*"Droit de mort et pouvoir sur la
vie"*)," Foucault limns "the 'right' to life" as a right "to one's body [*au
corps*], to health, to happiness, to the satisfaction of needs, and beyond all
the oppressions or 'alienations,' the 'right' to rediscover what one is and
all that one can be."[21]

Becoming Terri Schiavo, Part II: Biopolitics and the Right to Life

Here, we arrive at the familial, legal, political, and philosophical heart of
the controversy over Ms. Schiavo's situation. The conflict between the
Schindlers and Mr. Schiavo was between two different visions of how best
to realize Ms. Schiavo's right to life. The Schindlers asserted on her behalf
Ms. Schiavo's right to her body and the satisfaction of her needs, and
to what happiness she might enjoy. Indeed, the Schindlers envisioned a
future for her in which she could, with the help of rehabilitation, exercise
the option of discovering what she might yet be. Mr. Schiavo, on the
other hand, asserted Ms. Schiavo's right to (be "allowed" to) die (now
rather than later) as itself an exercise of her right to life, including to her
body, the satisfaction of her needs, and whatever happiness she might
enjoy (although unlike the Schindler's, he accepted the diagnosis of PVS).
Although right-to-life activists quickly and vocally aligned themselves with

the Schindler's, many nonpartisans who simply watched the controversy play out in the media aligned themselves with Mr. Schiavo, quickly concluding that were *they* to become Terri Schiavo, they wouldn't want to be kept alive "like that."[22]

For people living with disabilities, however—especially those dependent on feeding tubes, catheters, and the like themselves—the situation was much more complicated. As theologian Sharon Betcher notes, disability is equated with degeneracy and subjected to the demand for normalcy. People living with disabilities are thus expected to "organize themselves toward the values of publically acceptable appearance, independent function, and productivity, the key values of capitalist economics."[23] For many, Ms. Schiavo's situation was their worst nightmare; because her life was no longer productive, it was no longer of value, so should be cast aside and cast off. From this perspective, her consignment to death read as premature, cruel, and unjustified. Other people living with disabilities, however, rejected any analogy between their situation and Ms. Schiavo's case, asserting that they *would* prefer death to being kept alive in such a state. The American Association of People with Disabilities (AAPD) took up Ms. Schiavo's cause because, as they saw it, the principles at stake were central to the disability rights movement. Ms. Schiavo, no more than any otherwise-healthy person living with a severe disability from which they would not recover was not presumptively "better off dead" and to consign her to death without really knowing her wishes *in her present condition* was unconscionable. In spokesperson Andrew Imparato's words, "People with disabilities should be able to determine for themselves what happens to them. Part of self determination is the ability to change your mind if your situation changes."[24] Mr. Imparato went on to accuse Mr. Schiavo of keeping rehabilitation professionals (who could help determine whether she could communicate her wishes and, if so, what they were) from contact with Ms. Schiavo. Of course, it's precisely the having of wishes—much less the ability to communicate them—that her diagnosis, if correct, precluded.

As each and all of these perspectives show, embedded in the logic of the right to life—and to death—is modern subjectivity as a project realized through self-mastery and as self-sovereignty. This is a project in which we are deeply invested, one in which we continue to be entrained and to entrain others. That we construe disability per se as a failure in self-sovereignty to be remedied by biomedicine, according to Betcher, is symptomatic of that investment. Indeed, the question of self-sovereignty is at the center of the medical, legal, political, and philosophical debates over Ms. Schiavo's situation—and necessarily so, as her medical condition had essentially robbed her of it. As Bishop points out, the legal dispute kept recurring not because of any changes in Ms. Schiavo's condition, but because of the crisis her lack of self-sovereignty created. In the absence of family concord, the state—pressured, of course, by proponents for and against keeping her alive—had to step in. But it's not only legislative, judicial, and political bodies to whom self-sovereignty matters; Bishop—a physician as well as a philosopher, note—deems it the linchpin in modern medical management not only of life but of death. The good death, he argues, has become the one chosen by the self-sovereign subject— ideally, on her own behalf, or by a preselected proxy prepared to decide in accordance with her previously stated preferences. Bishop is not talking about (nonphysician assisted) suicide here, but rather the complex reality of medically managed deaths. Medical treatments can often prolong life by holding at bay for some time disease processes and certain of their sequelae, but usually with some cost to the quality of life. Deciding when to abandon treatment and move to what we call palliative care has become (ideally, at least) the patient's decision (informed, of course, by conversations with medical staff). When the patient is no longer capable of making this decision on his or her own, it becomes the family's responsibility. Ms. Schiavo was not suffering from a terminal disease, but hers was now a medically managed life whose end—whenever it came—would be medically managed as well. Because Ms. Schiavo could no longer speak for herself, her body became the sole—and conflicted—site of knowledge about her, Miller notes, to a greater extent even than is usually the case in medicine. Also at the heart of her situation was the question of who could or should make medical decisions on her behalf. Because Ms. Schiavo's family could not reach consensus, other proxies had to be found to stand in her stead.

The particularities of Ms. Schiavo's situation prompt Protevi to turn to Agamben's version of biopolitics for insight—and to compare her situation with that of the Abu Ghraib detainees. In both cases, the state steps in to declare a state of exception—"Terri's Law," let's remember, would have applied only to Ms. Schiavo herself—to the law of the *polis* (represented here by the judicial system's machinations to that point). Trading on her medical condition (which Protevi argues had already reduced her to mere organic life), this decision legally reduced Ms. Schiavo to "bare life" (*zoë* versus *bios*), a form of (human) life subject without constraint to sovereign power, the same condition to which the prisoners in Abu Ghraib (and other "black sites") were consigned when the Bush administration declared them "detainees" and not "prisoners of war," as Santner observes.[25] Whereas consignment to bare life meant torture and abuse for the detainees, it was to mean protection and succor for Ms. Schiavo—at least, in the view of those who sought to keep her alive. But to Protevi and Santner, prolonging Ms. Schiavo's life would have been anything but. Only a name connected Terri Schiavo "the material system, the assemblage of body and tube" in the hospice bed to Terri Schiavo the legal person and the personality, Protevi argues.[26] Keeping the feeding tube in place sustained only the former as neither of the latter existed any longer. And it is the wishes of the personality Terri Schaivo, which Protevi takes as clearly expressed before her medical crisis, that should rule the day. To Santner, reinserting the feeding tube under Congressional mandate would be an act of extreme violence and violation. The feeding tube would become a conduit not only for nutrition and hydration but also for "the invasive force of political power," he writes. "What greater form of subjection is there than to have the will of others impinge directly on our life substance, our existence as living tissue? Those pleading for state intervention into Terri Schiavo's persistence as living tissue are pleading for the most radical form of domination one can imagine." It would, in Santner's view, be a form of "soul death" for Ms. Schiavo, her utter subjection to another's sovereign will.[27]

For all three of these philosophers, however, the import of Ms. Schiavo's case lies not so much with its singularity but with what it reveals about our relationship to biopower and biopolitics. For Santner, it signals that biopolitics has utterly absorbed the theo-logic of sovereignty—torqued now, per the epigraph from Mr. Schiavo's lawyer, by our fear of death. For Protevi, it reveals the inadequacy of a jurisprudence (a theory and politics of law) grounded in notions of autonomy and bodily integrity as sovereign rights. Like disability scholars and activists, he worries that living and dying will be allocated according to determinations of value and productivity. That the people at the heart of the three most famous U.S. right-to-die cases—Karen Ann Quinlan, Nancy Cruzan, and Terri Schiavo—were all middle-class white women, each childless at the time of the onset of her medical crisis, is telling, he argues. For Bishop, Schiavo's case reveals medicine's complicity with biopolitics—and biopolitics, in turn, as the essence of the modern state and of modern political activism around life and death—to which we are all vulnerable. Thinking through that vulnerability and how to protect it from biopolitical violence *cum* biomedical benevolence is the challenge he puts before us.

If Protevi and Santner ultimately support the decision to remove Ms. Schiavo's feeding tube, Bishop finds the biopolitics of both positions troubling. "Conservatives" (Bishop's designation) deemed Ms. Schiavo's "bare life" worthy of protection, whereas "liberals" (Bishop's designation again) asserted the preeminence of quality of life over mere existence. Lost, he argues, is the singular and very real loss to and of Ms. Schiavo herself, which he worries that neither position (or modern biomedicine, for that matter) is able to fully register.

One possible route out of this predicament requires rethinking the mind–body dualism implicit in the biopolitics of Ms. Schiavo's situation. In the concluding chapter to *The Anticipatory Corpse*, Bishop tries his hand at a phenomenology of embodiment that articulates the inextricability of self and body. The body, as we know from the philosopher Maurice Merleau-Ponty, especially, is more than a mechanism or container for the self; rather, it is inextricable from the self. Insofar as our bodies bear our projects forward, Bishop argues, then our individual histories are inscribed in our sinews, muscles, and cells. Indeed, he cites evidence from recent studies in neuroplasticity that provide evidence that environment and social context register physically in the brain. This inextricability of self and body, he argues, must reshape how we think of life and loss, an insight that intersects productively with how we think about disability. As the distinction between disability and impairment reminds us, disabling conditions are not just physical; they are personal and social, historical and temporal—that is, they reach back into our past and forward into our future, who we've been and who we will become. That can take very different trajectories, depending on one's impairment. To (learn to) live with Alzheimer's, for example, is to gradually lose one's access to one's past and to the future projects you imagined for yourself (and, in some cases, ultimately to one's self). To (learn to) live as a paraplegic after a car accident initially involves coming to terms with the loss of one's former way of being-in-the-world. The process of adapting to life in this new condition is a matter of reincorporation in a double sense— of learning how to manage and move (with assistive devices such as a wheelchair) in this changed body, of incorporating this changed body into one's way of being-in-the-world. One's social networks—from the family on out—are also called upon in both cases to make adjustments and adaptations. Responses to that call, of course, can vary widely and are also affectively fraught, as well, as the work of disability scholars cited herein make clear.[28]

Whatever else Ms. Schaivo's situation does, it surely makes us (uncomfortably) aware of the vulnerability of modern subjectivity *cum* self-sovereignty. That vulnerability is simultaneously sociopolitical and physical. Although the project itself disavows this, to launch, sustain, and maintain self-sovereignty requires other people and institutions. Furthermore, to realize subjectivity is to materialize it, which is a project that is inextricable from biopower, the fourfold that channels it, and the gendered, sexualized, and ableized racism (positive and negative) that guides and funds it. But I also think it is important to acknowledge at the outset the seductive draw of self-sovereignty, the linchpin of biopolitics. Bio-disciplinary power giveth and it taketh away, we might say; self-sovereignty, after all, as I argued in chapter 1, is itself the product of bio-disciplinary power channeled by the fourfold. We want the gift of (self-sovereign) life it offers us; we recoil at the prospect of losing that particular kind of life—or (worse, for some of us) having it stripped away by the very source that gave it to us in the first place. But this *is* something to which all human lives are vulnerable—politically, socially, and biologically, as each of the chapters so far have shown. As the Gene Robinson photos demonstrate, access to self-sovereignty in the first place is sociopolitically contingent and renders those denied access (or offered only limited access) physically, socially, and politically vulnerable. As the Abu Ghraib photos demonstrate, one can also be legally stripped of self-sovereignty and given over to abuse and torment. To those insights, Ms. Schaivo's case adds self-sovereignty's vulnerability to catastrophic bodily events. But vulnerability isn't only what disrupts self-sovereignty—it is that through which self-sovereignty comes to be constituted in the first place. Biopower did not first take hold of Ms. Schaivo when she became a patient; in collusion with disciplinary power, it enabled, guided, and indeed shaped her initial becomings. And it did that through the very same channels—bodily, psychic, and social—through which it continued to course after Ms. Schaivo's brain injury. I turn to the work of Judith Butler to track and trace both sides of bio-disciplinary power's role in Terri Schaivo's life and death.

Becoming Terri Schiavo, Part III: Livability and Grievability

Turning to Butler to think about Ms. Schiavo's situation is not without risk, especially given assessments of her work by disability theorists. Best known for her performative theory of gender (initially articulated in *Gender Trouble*), disability is not a topic that Butler has taken up in any systematic way (although she alludes to it on occasion) and the import of her work on gender and embodiment for disability studies is a matter of some contention.[29] Although some disability theorists (e.g., Robert McCruer) ultimately find it productive for thinking disability, others worry that, like other social constructionist theorists, she tends to elide the body's (resistant) materiality in favor of its (plastic) performativity.[30] Moreover, many (including McRuer) see in Butler's work on gender (and much feminist theory) an unacknowledged ableism. Performativity, as Butler develops it, presumes a fully able body, they argue. Disability comes into the picture only as trope and often in problematic ways. This is the case despite the fact that not only is (dis)ability inflected and informed by sexuality, gender, race, and class, but also, as Tobin Siebers points out, the forms of "othering" like racism, sexism, and heterosexism that concern Butler (and other theorists) often are framed discursively as disablements. That is, they deny the ability of sexed and raced others to measure up and thus disqualify them from normative or normal status.

My concern here is neither to indict Butler nor to defend her against these charges. I would agree that, no matter how productive, analogies between the ways we are (un)made by gender and the ways we are (un)made by race, sexuality, or disability—*all*, I would argue, what Butler calls vectors of power—are necessarily limited even as and when they (and they always do) interact with one another.[31] The question that Ms. Schiavo's situation puts before us, moreover, is one of interaction, not analogy. Gender *and* (dis)ability—along with race, class, and sexuality—come together in her (un)makings. All, I will suggest, are able to work in and on Ms. Schiavo through certain vulnerabilities—psychic, social, and bodily—through which we are all (un)made.

Implicitly if not always explicitly, the issue of vulnerability circulates through much of Butler's work, including *Gender Trouble*. It becomes a particular focal point first in the *Psychic Life of Power*, in which Butler inquires into the discursive conditions that make subjectivity possible.[32] In *Precarious Life* and *Frames of War*, the events of September 11 and the wars that it spawned prompt her to explore vulnerability's relationship to violence as a socio- and geopolitical issue.[33] Although analyzing psychic, social, and political vulnerability continues to be her strong suit, I find important resources for thinking through bodily vulnerability in these later works, as well, that hewing close to Ms. Schiavo's case helps uncover.

That this is so doubtless reflects the fact that these later texts are framed by what biopower and biopolitics take under their purview, living and dying. For a human life to be truly and fully livable, it has to be recognizable as a (human) life, Butler argues. Dying a grievable death is a hallmark of social viability; an ungrievable death marks the limit of that viability. Tracking grievability and livability through the current wars places on display the human as what Butler calls "a differential norm"—that is, "a value and a morphology that may be allocated and retracted, aggrandized, personified, degraded and disavowed, elevated and affirmed."[34]

This, it seems to me, helpfully frames the controversy that swirled around Ms. Schiavo in the spring of 2005. What grievability (and thus livability) certain publics attached to Ms. Schiavo's life was, I suspect, connected more to her life before the onset of PVS than to her life with PVS. Ms. Schiavo's status as a white, married (therefore presumptively heterosexual) American woman granted her social recognition and a certain value within our racialized heteronormative system. Unlike the early gay victims of AIDS and the unnamed and unknown (to Americans) non-American war dead (two populations Butler considers at some length), that status would mark Ms. Schiavo's life (especially before the onset of PVS) as valuable. It is no surprise, then, as Protevi notes, that her anticipated death registered as loss to at least a portion of the larger body politic.[35] But that status and value comes at a certain price. We know from Lacanian-inflected psychoanalysis (an important strand of Butler's work on gender) that the place to which one accedes as (straight white) woman in a phallogocentric system is that of object more than subject (of desire and of speech). In a sense, then, Ms. Schaivo's disability trades on the conditions of subjection already realized in her social position and her marital status. The absence of Ms. Schiavo's ability to speak for herself (already attenuated before her injury by virtue of her subject position by this account) hollows out space into which others can become Terri Schiavo, in a sense; that is, they come to stand as her proxies. The list of would-be proxies is lengthy: her husband and friends, her parents, her guardian ad litem, the prolife activists, the disability activists, Sen. Frist. Being spoken for—particularly by those who speak in the name of the (paternal) law (father, husband, priest, senator)—comes with the territory of white womanhood, constituted as passive, pure, and domesticated. These are qualities accentuated by her situation, as the stills of Ms. Schiavo attest.

But Ms. Schiavo's condition also created a crisis within the heteronormative kinship system in which she had come to be. In the first years after the onset of PVS, Ms. Schiavo's parents and husband had cooperated in her care. But they eventually became locked in a legal battle over their daughter and wife. The political drama that unfolded around Ms. Schiavo painted the breech as irrevocable (and apparently rightly so). I want to pause here to acknowledge the breach itself *as* loss and crisis: affective and familial ties were stretched to the breaking point in the name of taking responsibility on behalf of someone no longer capable of assuming responsibility (for) herself. At the heart of that breach lies what Bishop argues the biopolitics of the case fails to reckon with; namely, the loss of all that Terri Schiavo had become at the time of her heart attack, which was a loss not only for her family, but first and foremost for (and of) Ms. Schiavo herself—a loss carried in and by incarnated body-memory and communicated in and by the video stills.

This loss inaugurated a crisis in Ms. Schiavo's family, itself an incarnation of our heteronormative kinship system. This system—and thus its crisis—is not only bodily and affective, as the visual images of Ms. Schiavo remind us; it is also rhetorical, epistemological, political, legal, and juridical. The symbolic transfer of daughter from father to husband had been legally performed years before when the Schiavos married, yet the parents were now challenging that transfer (at one point, they petitioned the court on Ms. Schiavo's behalf to divorce Mr. Schiavo). Indeed, the legal dispute and the public spectacle raise deeply troubling questions. Who has the right to speak *for* Ms. Schiavo—to speak on her behalf? Who can claim to know—*really* know—what she would have wanted? What she wants now? Her husband? Her father? Her mother? Their priest? To whom *does* Ms. Schiavo belong, in the end—if no longer to herself? In her case, the claimants to that position seemed to go viral in those last days as person after person stepped up to one or another microphone to pronounce, to announce, to diagnose, to decide, to attempt to legislate her fate. What right do any of us—especially those of us outside her circle of intimates—have to stand in such a place? As I watched the public spectacle that surrounded Ms. Schiavo in her last days, I found myself, at least, longing for just one would-be Solomon to step back and acknowledge that we *are* not Ms. Schiavo; we are *all* just playing her on C-SPAN.[36]

Becoming Terri Schiavo, Part IV: Subjectivity and Vulnerability

That so many felt they could stand in for Terri Schiavo reflects the general conditions of human subjectivity, as Butler lays them out in *Psychic Life of Power, Precarious Life,* and *Frames of War.* In these texts, Butler explores certain vulnerabilities that (un)make human subjects and the social context in which they come to be. In *Psychic Life of Power,* Butler focuses on the conditions that give rise to subjectivity, a term she reserves there for the linguistic and socially constituted position of the *I.* Subjectivity is not a substantive essence, but an ongoing process of becoming. Its roots lie in the need for social recognition, a primal vulnerability visibly and audibly present in infancy that remains with us throughout life. It is that vulnerability that compels us (or propels us) to respond to those interpellations that call us into being-as gendered, sexed, raced, and individuated, for example. We become subjects in giving ourselves over to subjection, in submitting ourselves to those people and regimes that promise us social recognition and thus viability. This need is so strong that we will even subject ourselves to individuals or regimes that neglect or actively harm us, for any social recognition is better than none at all.

It is precisely in and through this structural vulnerability that we are empowered; power, understood in Foucault's sense as a diffuse network of relations, takes us in and we take it up. Not only juridical power (the terminal form power takes, as Foucault puts it), but more important, the subtle normalizing form of power—bio-disciplinary power channeled through the fourfold, as we've seen—that constitutes and courses through the current regimes of sex, gender, race, and kinship that grant us social identities and status. Normalizing (bio-disciplinary) power is able to work on and through us by exploiting this primal social vulnerability. Our agency, through which we conform or resist, repeat (un)faithfully or repudiate, resides in this nexus of self-submission and self-making. We are this interplay of our sedimented history—some of which we can know or (with help) recall, much of which remains necessarily invisible and inaccessible to us—and novel becoming. Each layer calls on and covers over, for the moment, this constitutive vulnerability. Each recitation of becoming exposes again this vulnerability and provides the opportunity for doing otherwise (to recite is not necessarily to repeat). Becoming a subject is, Butler tells us, "no simple or continuous affair, but an uneasy practice of repetition and its risks, compelled yet incomplete, wavering on the horizon of social being."[37] Our status as subjects, then, is never fully achieved, never fully secured, never fully sovereign.

If *Psychic Life of Power* focuses on the becoming of subjectivity, *Precarious Life* and *Frames of War* turn our attention to its undoing and to the various forms of violent response threats of undoing can provoke. The vulnerability at the heart of *Psychic Life of Power*'s account of subjectivity-as-project is given (rightly) ontological status and a name, precariousness. These two books analyze precariousness's role in September 11 and the wars and atrocities (and responses to same) that constitute its aftermath. These analyses demonstrate that precariousness is not only social but also physical. It plays a constitutive role in our bodily life and our social life; it is that upon which subjectivity, constituted where society and the body meet, is founded and founders. It is that upon which bio-disciplinary power, too, is founded and founders (in individual undoings by death). Indeed, bio-disciplinary power's promise to protect us from vulnerability is in no small part what persuades us to take it in and take it up.

Taking precariousness to heart renders subjectivity ec-centric and ek-static. That is, no *I* is truly the center of its own being; it is hollowed out at its core by vulnerability. Moreover, each *I* stands outside itself insofar as precariousness impels us toward others as sites and sources of bodily sustenance and social recognition. Each *I*, then, is in part a *we* insofar as it is composed of attachments to those who enable us to say "*I*" and provide us (or deny us) access to the resources necessary to live on. Parents and other family members, yes, but also teachers, friends, neighbors, lovers, doctors, nurses, and caregivers. This network extends to the anonymous—and global—*they* of our social world. We are—individually and collectively—made *and unmade* by one another on scales large and small. We experience this unmaking on an individual scale when we grieve the loss of a loved one, but this loss echoes the undoing that love-as-desire launches in the first place, according to Butler. The attacks on September 11, Butler suggests, undid us (some of us more than others) on a social scale; they traded on our attachments at a number of levels and brought home to us the extent of our dependence on far-flung others for our very being, material and social.

These insights into subjectivity and precariousness (and thus into bio-disciplinary power) were born in contexts very different from Terri Schiavo's situation. *Psychic Life of Power* offers an account of a kind of becoming to which Ms. Schiavo lost access (thanks to her brain injury) long before she became a public figure. And *Precarious Life* and *Frames of War* were prompted not by private family tragedy rendered public political theatre, but by what followed in the wake of a frontal assault on the U.S. body politic. Yet I think both provide insights into becoming Terri Schiavo in all of its multivalent senses. In turn, thinking through Ms. Schaivo's situation illumines dimensions of bio-disciplinary power's exercise—and its limits—that otherwise might go unremarked, but that are central to my project here.

Butler's emphasis in *Psychic Life of Power* on subjectivity as acquisition—and a tenuous one, at that—carves out space for articulating subjectivity's emergence *and its disintegration* in the person of Ms. Schiavo. If *Psychic Life of Power* emphasizes subjectivity as a social acquisition, *Precarious Life* and *Frames of War* remind us of the material conditions necessary to that acquisition and its sustenance. Precariousness and precarity are bodily as well as social conditions. As Butler notes frequently in the first two essays of *Frames of War*, precariousness is an inescapable condition of embodiment as such. Although Butler's focus is primarily on precariousness manifest in the body's vulnerability to attacks from the outside (rightly so, given the issues that motivate those essays), Ms. Schiavo's case calls attention to the body's vulnerability *from the inside*, a reality Butler notes frequently in *Frames of War* but does not analyze in detail. Ms. Schiavo's situation enables a profound realization of the ways bodies matter; we are all (un)grounded by the materiality of the body.

I am not here laying the body down like a gauntlet—as though it were, after all, an unsurpassable lumpen and obstinate *thing* that will have the last word no matter what. I agree with Butler's position in *Frames of War*—and Bishop's in *Anticipatory Corpse*—that the body is always already socially and psychically invested; thus, separating the physical from the social and the psychic will not do. Indeed, one thing I find particularly valuable in Butler's work is the way she seeks to keep together the social and the personal, the material and the cultural (if by her own lights not always successfully). Her work reminds us that all of this in concert constitutes a network of contingencies, doings and undoings, makings and unmakings; contingencies, I'm arguing, that bio-disciplinary power channeled by the fourfold works on and through. Internal bodily vulnerability is part and parcel of this larger network of contingency—and of the specific features (systemic and otherwise) that constitute the forms it takes in our time and place. Put in more Butlerian terms, this means that our precariousness—material and social—entails our precarity (Butler's term for the political stakes or consequences of precariousness).

Let me substantiate that insight by retracing the steps of my prior analysis of becoming Terri Schiavo now from the inside out. The brain injury caused by anoxia following cardiac arrest certainly traded on the precariousness of embodiment. It also inaugurated a violent and permanent return to that state of primordial prelinguistic vulnerability— postsubjective rather than presubjective, in Ms. Schiavo's case—that Butler identifies. That this bodily rupture reverberated throughout the social fabric of Ms. Schiavo's life evidences the sociality of bodily precariousness. Insofar as Ms. Schiavo, like all of us, was constituted by "the enigmatic traces of others,"[38] as Butler puts it, those others—known and unknown— are caught up in the seismic aftershocks of Ms. Schiavo's bodily trauma. Those traces, etched as they were into Ms. Schiavo's very being, became the tracks others followed to become Terri Schiavo—that is, to step into that space of subjectivity depleted by Ms. Schiavo's brain injury to claim to speak on her behalf.

Recall that Butler reserves the term *subjectivity* in *Psychic Life of Power* for the sociolinguistic position to which human beings accede, conditions permitting. Ms. Schiavo's situation reminds us that linguisticality presupposes a body simultaneously social and material. The physical ability to speak—whether one vocalizes or signs—requires a body, including a very material (and vulnerable) brain.[39] These material grounds of linguisticality are social all the way down. The social process of acquiring language trains and shapes bodies in certain ways (though not without resistance, of course). Thus subjectivity's status as (tenuous) acquisition is of a piece with the human being's bodily and social precariousness. As I said earlier, it is both founded and founders on precariousness. Thus, we attenuate our understanding of what it means to *live* a human life if we focus only on fully accomplished subjectivity—subjectivity as (putative) self-sovereignty, in other words—and not on what (un)grounds it.

I say, "live a *human* life" quite deliberately. Protevi and Santner come close to losing sight of Ms. Schiavo's humanity when they speak of her as, in Protevi's case, reduced by PVS to "only an organism" or, in Santner's case of Ms. Schiavo as (merely) "living tissue."⁴⁰ Thinking of her in that way makes it perhaps a little too easy to contemplate consigning her to (physical) death—a danger that people living with disabilities confront frequently.⁴¹ As disability theorists and activists often point out, many normates imagine living with disabilities—particularly severe disabilities—as a fate worse than death.⁴² This is a dangerous perspective to take under bio-disciplinary power's reign, given its goal of eliminating abnormalities to nurture the life of the race.⁴³

My insistence on the humanness of Ms. Schiavo's life (and death) is not a stubborn assertion of an absolute, which is *not* to say abyssal, distinction between human and other forms of life—animal and otherwise; quite the contrary. Indeed, although I can only note this in passing here, Butler situates her account of precariousness and precarity in *Frames of War* within the larger rubric of life per se. Livability and grievability both presume life and death just as precarity presumes precariousness. The question of suffering, one of the three frames of war she takes up, pertains not only to *human* lives as casualties of war but also to nonhuman lives. Moreover, "it is precisely as human animals that human beings suffer," she writes.⁴⁴ (I'll return to these questions and issues in chapter 6.) Let me conclude this inquiry into Ms. Schiavo's situation with some reflections on the ethical peril and promise in precariousness and precarity that it brings to light. In *Precarious Life*, Butler writes, "The body implies mortality, vulnerability, agency: the skin and the flesh expose us to the gaze of others, but also to touch, and to violence, and bodies put us at risk of becoming the agency and instrument of all these as well."⁴⁵ Precariousness, after all, "emerges with life itself. . . . We cannot recover the source of this vulnerability: it precedes the formation of the 'I.'"⁴⁶ We are "from the start, given over to some set of primary others" leaving us vulnerable to "a range [of touch] that includes the eradication of our being at the one end, and the physical support for our lives at the other."⁴⁷

To this point only one of the five senses—and for understandable reasons, given its role in our inquiry into these signs and wonders in the first place—has occupied our attention: vision. These passages from *Precarious Life*, however, invoke a different sensory mode—namely, touch as both site of and salve for precariousness. The religious activists gathered outside Ms. Schiavo's hospice were motivated by their desire to preserve "the sanctity of life" and I do not doubt their sincerity. If, however, anyone actually had the opportunity to preserve the sanctity of *Ms. Schiavo's* life within the context of the political, legislative, and media circus of her last days, I would submit that it was the hospice workers who bathed her, turned her, and diapered her from the day she entered their care until the day she died.

I do not intend here to romanticize hospice workers—in general or in this situation, especially. It is one thing, I suspect, to give palliative care to a terminally ill person—especially one who has knowingly chosen that form of care. It may be quite another to give such care to someone whose life is ending by court order and at the center of a political spectacle (about which, one can imagine, Ms. Schiavo's caregivers had their own opinions), circumstances that spring from the crisis of self-sovereignty described earlier. The caregivers' touches could do nothing to restore Ms. Schiavo to health; they could not divine what, if anything, she was thinking or feeling. Deprived as she appeared to be not only of responsibility but also of the ability to respond, the workers had no way of knowing how their touches registered. (That abyssal difference Derrida identifies between human and animal applies between human animals, as well—and not only in this instance.) Yet one can hope that their tactile caring-for—if done well, and with compassion—acknowledged the loss of and to Ms. Schiavo and granted dignity to this particular (human) life in its dying. A dying that was ordered and managed, let's not forget, by biopower and its institutions of which the hospice workers are a part.[48] Perhaps we can find in this form of contact an ethical response to precariousness—and precarity—that is worth our consideration, an opening toward ways of living under bio-disciplinary power as modernity declines. If so, it will not be because touch is immune to the possibility of abuse or neglect, as we'll see in chapter 6. Rather, as I'll argue in the conclusion to this volume, it will be because touch links us to one another (and to other forms of life) in ways that open up and onto opportunities to face up to rather than disavow vulnerabilities, both individual and collective.

CHAPTER SIX

THE PERFECT STORM

Hurricane Katrina

For good or bad, storms start with no history. They are just molecules in chaos that join what is already underway. What matters most after them usually depends on what mattered most before them.

—Kent B. Germany

Who gave them the right to play God?

—Carrie Everett, wife of the late Emmett Everett, patient at Memorial Medical Center

There's nothing that man can do that nature can't overcome. We'll continue to respond to what nature throws at us.

—Maj. Gen. John W. Peabody, Commander, Mississippi Valley Division, Army Corps of Engineers

Death, despite all of medicine's inclinations to the contrary, cannot be mastered technologically, discursively, psychologically, sociologically, or spiritually. When we do attempt to do so, . . . it returns to haunt us.

—R. Burt via J. Bishop, *The Anticipatory Corpse*

I F THE STILLS of Terri Schiavo's face opened onto precariousness and precarity as constitutive of human being, the two photographs that anchor our inquiry into Hurricane Katrina open onto their larger purview and thus to bio-disciplinary power as an attempt to master these constitutive vulnerabilities. Like Terri Schiavo's situation, Hurricane Katrina is as much a social as a physical catastrophe; it is an (un)making shaped as much by human action and interaction as by natural forces, by bio-disciplinary power channeled by the fourfold as much as by the power of wind and water.[1] If Ms. Schiavo's case showed us that human precariousness is both material and social, Hurricane Katrina extends that insight into the ecosystem as a whole and in its various parts (including humanity).[2] Moreover, it will show us that not only is precariousness a condition shared by all living things, so too is its political counterpart, precarity.

In what they index and open up and onto, the photographs to come offer us in concentrated form the "perfect storm" that was Katrina and its aftermath—a natural disaster shaped and exacerbated by long-term effects of the exercise of bio-disciplinary power through its fourfold, a rescue and recovery effort hobbled not only by human ineptitude and apparent indifference but also by cracks in the structures built to manage bio-disciplinary power. Tracking the (un)makings of Hurricane Katrina, the suffering—and resilience—it precipitated through these photographs will take us back down many of the paths we have traveled in previous chapters. In so doing, it will open up additional dimensions to the workings of bio-disciplinary power when it finds itself in crisis. This will allow us to home in on the central theological and philosophical challenges—and opportunities—that we confront as we anticipate modernity's demise.[3]

◆ ◆ ◆ ◆ ◆ ◆

On Monday, August 29, 2005, Hurricane Katrina made landfall on the coast of the Gulf of Mexico. One of the strongest hurricanes ever to form in the Atlantic Ocean, it proved to be "the Big One," the storm that Louisianans (New Orleanians especially) had long dreaded. Chris Landsea, a meteorologist with the National Atmospheric and Oceanic Administration who flew into the storm the Saturday before it reached the coastline, reported that its circulation "covered the entire Gulf of Mexico."[4] Damage to coastal towns and cities in Alabama and Mississippi as well as Louisiana proved catastrophic, but New Orleans occupied the center of national attention due in no small part to the relative intensity of media attention the city received in the immediate aftermath of the deluge. Reporters and photographers for its hometown newspaper, the *Times-Picayune* (which later won a Pulitzer Prize for its storm coverage) and local television and radio stations were joined by their colleagues from national media outlets of all varieties, including the cable news networks. The rest of the country witnessed the storm's devastation and its aftermath, made exponentially worse by the ineptitude of the Federal Emergency Management Agency, which, despite advance warning, did not arrive on the scene for five days after the storm struck.

The archive of visual images of the storm is vast and runs the gamut of contemporary visual technologies. One online archive claims some 2,500 still photographs culled mostly from the cameras of photojournalists. The amount of video footage available online likely represents a fraction of what television stations and news programs hold in storage (especially if one includes unedited footage). Consider, as well, photographs and video shot by those survivors fortunate enough to retain access to cameras in the aftermath of the storm. Multiple images that stand in for and open onto the devastation wrought by Katrina come quickly to mind: of survivors crowded on bridges or rooftops, of a lone looter wading through thigh-deep water balancing a box of groceries or water on his head, of dead bloated bodies floating on the flood waters, of abandoned pets roaming the streets in search of food. Two of those images have particular reso-nance for this project, however. The first is that of a dead body in a wheel-chair located just outside the entrance of the New Orleans Convention Center, which served as a shelter for refugees from the storm (figure 6.1).

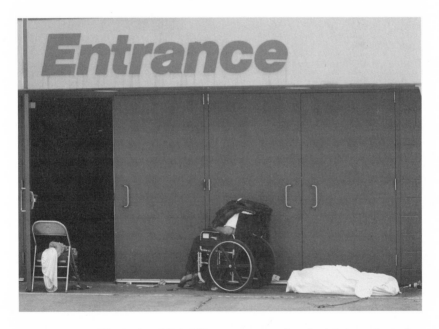

FIGURE 6.1 The body of Ethel Freeman, center in wheelchair, and another body lie covered outside an entrance to the Convention Center in hurricane-ravaged New Orleans in this September 2, 2005, file photo. Herbert Freeman Jr. filed a lawsuit in state Civil District Court in New Orleans, Thursday, August 17, 2006, accusing numerous state agencies and the city of New Orleans of "gross negligence and willful misconduct" in the death of his mother, Ethel.

(AP PHOTO/ERIC GAY, FILE)

This photograph provides a striking contrast to the video stills of Ms. Schiavo discussed in the previous chapter. Instead of a person living with a disability and clearly cared for and about, we confront a dead body—presumably disabled, given that it is in a wheelchair—neglected and abandoned. Instead of a photographic portrait lovingly focused on the subject's face, we encounter from the side and at a distance a body partially covered by a plaid garment of some sort carelessly tossed on top of it—whether to cover the body or simply to relieve the person who discarded it of a garment no longer needed is unclear. In place of the cozy domestic conventions of the family photograph, we encounter this person's body through the conventions of professional photojournalism. The photograph is carefully composed to capture for viewers the tragic ironies of the situation. Focusing his lens on the body in the wheelchair, the photographer Eric Gay has positioned himself and the camera just far enough away to frame them against the entrance to the Convention Center that frames the dead body: two sets of bright red double doors whose function, "Entrance," is announced in bright red letters painted above them and equal in size to the body below. The body looks toward the only one of the four doors that is open—propped open by a metal folding chair. Of the four, it is the door farthest away. Although close enough to seem to be leaning on the (closed) doors, access to what shelter, comfort, and care the building promises is forever denied the dead person. Instead, this body is as casually discarded, it appears, as the white cloth tossed casually across the back of the folding chair nearby or the larger white cloth piled (wait—is there something beneath it?) on the sidewalk behind the wheelchair. Just one more piece of the detritus left in Katrina's wake.

Like the stills of Ms. Schiavo, the presence of a lifeless body in a wheelchair invites a version of the medical gaze associated with freak and medical photography. Who is the occupant of the wheelchair and how did she or he get there? Why was she or he left outside—and by whom? How did she or he die? And what—or who—lies under the white sheet on the sidewalk behind the person in the wheelchair? Regardless of who she or he is (or they are), how could anyone leave someone—alive or dead—alone outside under such conditions?

The second photograph is of a dog making its way alone through a water-covered street in New Orleans (figure 6.2). Like the body in the wheelchair, the dog, too, has apparently been abandoned, although it has managed (so far) to survive. Like the first photograph, this one tells us

FIGURE 6.2 A dog walks along a water-covered street in New Orleans follow-ing the destruction of Hurricane Katrina.

(ANDREA BOOHER/FEMA IMAGE PROVIDED BY IP)

nothing about its subject's past or present. That the wheelchair's inhabit-ant made it to the Convention Center implies that this person had con-nections to family or community. The dog, on the other hand, may have been a pre-Katrina stray or a beloved house pet reluctantly left behind by its owner—perhaps even with enough food and water to last for the few days that the owner imagined would keep them apart, as happened in thousands of cases. The photograph tells us nothing about what happened to the dog. Was it rescued and united with its owner—or perhaps adopted by someone else? Or did it continue to roam the streets of New Orleans until its (timely or untimely, natural or accidental) death?

Like the first still of Ms. Schiavo, but from a greater distance, the dog gazes toward the photographer (and thus toward us). Its gaze, like that of Ms. Schiavo's, obscures as much as it reveals, although for different rea-sons. On the one hand, unlike in Ms. Schiavo's case, the dog seems clearly to register and respond to the photographer's presence. On the other hand, its gaze and its body language communicate an abyssal ambivalence that calls to mind Derrida's reflections on animality. Caught, perhaps, between

desire for sustenance and support and fear of entrapment, its slightly low-
ered head and uplifted tail project resilience and weariness, hope and fear,
submission and dominance. Taking up photographic responsibility, in this
case, confronts us with ethical risk. Would we, like the photographer (at
the moment of shooting, at least) keep our distance from the dog? Or
would we take the risk of a closer encounter and attempt its rescue? And
how might it respond? We have no way of knowing.

The dog's identity and ultimate fate remain unknown, so far as I can
gather, several years on. That is not true of the body in the wheelchair.
Unidentified at the time the photograph was taken, we now know that
the body in the wheelchair is that of Mrs. Ethel Freeman (91 years old at
the time of her death). Her son, Herbert Freeman, Jr. (with the aid of a
neighbor and his boat) brought her to the Convention Center on August
31 because he thought he'd find the care she needed there. Like Ms. Schiavo, Mrs. Freeman relied on a feeding tube for nutrition (sustaining her
life also required a pacemaker). But the Freemans did not find the care
that she needed at the Convention Center. It was not equipped to support
survivors with serious medical conditions. With her son at her side, Mrs.
Freeman died some thirty hours later (on September 1). Officials forced
Mr. Freeman to leave his mother's body behind and evacuate later that
day (ultimately to Birmingham, Alabama). Apparently, his mother's body
remained outside the Convention Center for several days before it was
taken to a morgue in a nearby town. Although Mr. Freeman left a note
inside one of her pockets with his name and phone number, it was seven
weeks before he was reunited with her body.[5] That we know so much
about Mrs. Freeman is itself indicative of the impact of the photograph,
"an iconic image of suffering, represented through disability," Julia Watts
Belser writes.[6] But whereas disability often figures as the natural and individualized, if tragic, consequence of disaster, Mrs. Freeman's photograph
became "an anonymous symbol of the government's slow response to
Hurricane Katrina," according to an article about Mrs. Freeman's funeral.[7]

In and through what they index, both photographs open up and onto
the larger *histoire* of Hurricane Katrina and on what that event reveals
about bio-disciplinary power and its fourfold. At one and the same time,
they call to mind contradictory aspects of that *histoire*—that is, the horrific
suffering and anguish Katrina unleashed, and the creativity, resilience, and
compassion that emerged in response. That Mrs. Freeman's body sits just
outside the entrance to an official storm shelter reads doubly. On the one

hand, it reminds us that the suffering engendered in Katrina's wake was as much a result of human agency as of storm surges. On the other, contextualized by what we now know of her circumstances, the photograph also reminds us of her son's persistence (and her neighbor's help) in trying to care for his mother both before and after her death. His efforts, in turn, call to mind the resilience of many New Orleanians who, in the absence of robust governmental rescue efforts, pulled together to rescue and support each other. Although they rarely made the headlines, stories of citizens using their own boats to rescue one another off of rooftops, of sharing shelter and food, and of setting up security details to protect fellow survivors have emerged in various forms in the months and years since.[8]

The photograph of the dog also reads doubly: as a sign of the suffering many animals endured in the wake of Katrina, but that some managed to avoid thanks to the efforts unprecedented in previous disasters that human beings made to care for them.[9] Creative pet owners smuggled small pets into shelters with them; compassionate rescue workers helped work out care arrangements for them. Despite orders to rescue humans and leave pets behind, numerous accounts have surfaced of rescue workers who, confronted with pet owners ripped apart at the thought of leaving their pets behind, made room for the pets, too.[10] (And, as many photographs document, they frequently rescued abandoned pets themselves.) Motivated in no small part by the amount of press coverage given to animal suffering in the wake of Katrina (accompanied by photographs, of course), individuals and animal rescue organizations mobilized to come to the rescue of animals affected by the storm. Volunteers came from far and near; shelters as far away as Long Island, New York, took in animals from shelters in the Gulf region to make room for Katrina's pet refugees. A veritable aboveground railroad ferried refugee pets to foster homes or new adopted homes around the country. Aided by the Internet, e-mail, and social networking sites, many pets were reunited with their owners in the weeks and months after the storm—often at great emotional cost to those who had cared for them in the meantime.[11] That the dog in the photograph appears alone, however, reminds us of the limits to even these heroic efforts. Thousands of domestic pets perished or were left homeless in New Orleans as a result of Katrina. The loss of farm animals was also significant—and of wild animals ultimately unknowable but undoubtedly extensive.

I have focused, thus far, on Hurricane Katrina's unmaking of New Orleans, but as both John Protevi and Nancy Tuana remind us, the groundwork for that unmaking was laid—quite literally—in the city's founding, in its unique geography and by the geographical and social changes wrought through its settlement and expansion.[12] Bio-disciplinary power channeled by the fourfold is essential to this *histoire*. We tend to think of the United States as a colonial empire—and for good reason— forgetting that it was once colonized itself. Indeed, its history as colonizer and colonized overlap. Those first subjected to colonization on this land were the peoples native to North America. While the British, French, and Spanish inaugurated their subjection, the nascent and emergent United States perpetuated it—and continues to oversee its results. The history of colonialism is integral to New Orleans's past (and its present) in many ways. That this French settlement—occupying land only slightly higher than the waters that precipitated it—became a center for agricultural and slave trade, and ultimately, a uniquely diverse city renowned simultane- ously for its cultural wealth and economic poverty is the result of a conflu- ence of processes and forces not only natural (geographical, hydrological, ecological, even biochemical) and cultural (political, social, and economic) but also, at least in the minds of some, theological.[13]

Founded in 1719 by French settlers, New Orleans was built on a natural levee created by the Mississippi River. Advocates for its founding saw in the area's peculiar geography a certain theo-logic, according to Ari Kel- man.[14] They viewed the Mississippi, this great river that bisected much of North America, as "God's signature carved into the [Mississippi] val- ley."[15] That the river had produced a natural levee so close to where its waters met those of the Gulf of Mexico seemed providential to them. Products made or grown upriver could flow naturally downriver to a new port city built on that levee, which would become a center of trade and commerce. Geography was destiny, they thought. The river would inevita- bly make New Orleans great. In the words of François Xavier Charlevoix, a Jesuit visitor to New Orleans in 1723 quoted by Kelman, "Rome and Paris had not such considerable beginnings, were not built under such happy auspices, and their founders met not with those advantages on the Seine and the Tiber, which we have found on the Mississippi, in compari- son of which, these two rivers are no more than brooks."[16] Architectural historian Karen Kingsley notes that the now-"iconic" (her word) St. Louis Cathedral on Jackson Square centered the settlement—fittingly enough, given this theo-logic.[17] But flooding was also a constant threat to New Orleans and the economic ambitions of its founders. Indeed, in no small part it is the attempts to prevent or control it that set the stage for the catastrophic flooding experienced in Katrina (and its predecessors). The geography that the first settlers encountered has been remade again and again by the (human-made) levee system on which New Orleans has relied for flood control for most of its history. Many of the swamps and wetlands that provided a natural barrier to coastal flooding have been drained in attempts to expand sites for human habitation and to control disease. With the demise of the wetlands, the city became ever more dependent on mechanized means of defense against the water.[18] But the sense of safety that the levees provided proved illusory. Of course, New Orleans had to contend with these means of defense only in times of catastrophe—and the city was spared such in the forty years between Katrina's most recent predecessors, the 1927 flood and Hurricane Betsy in 1965,[19] and then again in the forty years that separated Betsy and Katrina.[20]

In the decades after its founding, New Orleans largely realized the vision its founders had for it. That it became a center for agricommerce (including the slave trade) is an artifact not only of (providential?) geography but of colonial geopolitics—with a biochemical edge. Sugar, a particularly efficient form of energy transfer (from the sun to the human consumer via sugar cane), as John Protevi notes, became a prominent cash crop in the Caribbean colonial economies. Sugar growers—mostly free people of color—fleeing political conflict in and around the French colony of Saint Domingue (on the island of Hispaniola, home to present-day Haiti and the Dominican Republic) moved to Louisiana bringing their African slaves with them.[21] That history is reflected in New Orleans's demographics in which, for example, the black–white binary familiar to most of the United States is replaced by a "trinary" that includes lighter-skinned Creoles or mulattoes and is further stratified by social class.[22] The vibrant musical, gastronomic, and architectural culture for which New Orleans became famous can be traced directly back to its Creole-Caribbean-African roots.[23] (Waves of immigration from Asia, the British Isles, and countries south of the U.S. border have left their impact on New Orleans since its founding, adding to its demographic and cultural complexity.)[24]

New Orleans's agricommercial roots continued to shape the form its denizens' lives took well into the middle of the twentieth century. Like the postbellum Mississippi delta region generally, poverty was higher, educational achievement was lower, and health was poorer in Louisiana than in most of the United States. That reality made New Orleans a prime target in the sixties for President Lyndon B. Johnson's War on Poverty.[25] Historian Kent Germany (see epigraph) argues that the effects of the War on Poverty on New Orleans—and its ultimate failure—were significant.[26] As the social and political order established under Jim Crow was collapsing, many of the initiatives of the War on Poverty helped to fill the vacuum. In addition to providing a significant degree of economic uplift, it helped create a new generation and network of political leaders of color. After the Voting Rights Act of 1965 was passed, the number of African American voters almost doubled, which generated considerable political and economic clout that helped secure this new political class. Over the next fifteen years or so, economic conditions improved in New Orleans—an effect not only of the War on Poverty but also of the burgeoning oil industry in the Gulf of Mexico. But, as was the case in many American cities, the population of New Orleans proper got poorer (and darker) as those who could afford it (including middle-class people of color) left the cities for the suburbs. In 1960, 62 percent of the city's population had been white; by 1980, whites made up only 40 percent of New Orleanians. And then in the eighties the oil boom went bust and, under President Ronald Reagan, federal funds for the War on Poverty all but dried up. The economic gains of the sixties and seventies were reversed. (Racialized outmigration, however, stayed on trend into 2000 when whites accounted for just 28 percent of the population of New Orleans parish). In 1988, faced with the resurgence of (racially inflected) economic inequality, Reagan declared poverty the victor in Johnson's war.

A third industry expanded into the gap left by the collapse of the oil boom and the end of the War on Poverty. Tourism created a service economy that drew on the same labor pool of poor, unskilled people of color that had staffed first agricommerce and, in turn, the oil boom.[27] That industry changed yet again the face of New Orleans as the city's movers and shakers sought to maximize the appeal of New Orleans's storied reputation for the historic, the exotic, and the erotic. In what historian J. Mark Souther dubs its "Disneyfication," the French Quarter (or Vieux Carré), home to some of the oldest buildings in the United States, was cleaned up and (more or less) straightened up.[28] Pursuit of economic growth through urban renewal bolstered the tourist industry by replacing blighted neighborhoods nearby with hotels and a new convention center. With the opening in 1975 of the Superdome, a gigantic state-of-the-art sports and cultural arena, all the pieces were in place to draw visitors and their money to the city year round and for a variety of reasons.[29]

That most of the population of New Orleans lived in poverty was largely invisible to those who temporarily graced the tourist areas with their presence and their money. No less historic (though considerably poorer) neighborhoods like Tremé and the Lower Ninth Ward—home to many of those whose labor (cultural, manual, or domestic) lent the French Quarter its veneer of authenticity—were largely left out of urban renewal schemes and plans. These realities reflected larger national trends. In the years between 1988 and 2005, aided and abetted by increased "geographical, psychological, and institutional" distance between the have's and have not's in New Orleans and elsewhere, Germany argues, "poverty had slipped so far off the national radar that it took the worst storm in a century" to return it to our attention if only for a short while. Not only did the storm expose the fragility of a social fabric woven of racialized economic inequities, but it made visible the effects of a "complicated political bargain" realized not only in New Orleans, but in many U.S. cities. Municipal leaders—and, by extension, most Americans—had, in Germany's words, "made peace with poverty. Unable or unwilling to stop it, they mostly hoped to contain it."[30] To that end, they relied primarily on the "vast law-and-order apparatus" birthed in the sixties.[31]

Hurricane Katrina brought all of these structures and systems—themselves products of and channels for bio-disciplinary power—that had made and remade New Orleans to their knees. The (literal) overtopping of the levee system was (figuratively) repeated over and over again as one and then another system or structure foundered and failed as it was stretched—or pounded—to its limits. Flooding brought with it widespread power failures (governmental as well as electrical), resulting in the now-familiar scenes of survivors—animal and human—stranded on rooftops and bridges, of supposedly widespread looting and lawlessness, of suffering and trauma that shocked many Americans.

Figures 6.1 and 6.2 index and open onto all these dimensions of bio-disciplinary power and its limits. Readers familiar with Hurricane Katrina will know that those most severely affected by it were poor people of color. What has received less attention, however, were the effects of the storm on people living with disabilities many of whom—Mrs. Freeman, for example—were people of color. Although city and state officials made some special arrangements for their transport and shelter, many people with mobility constraints or chronic health problems were trapped in their homes, in skilled nursing facilities, or hospitals. Once again, this is a case of systemic sociopolitical failures not inevitable tragedy.[32]

"Who Gave Them the Right to Play God?": Bio-Disciplinary Power in Crisis

The consequences of the collapse of the systems built to manage bio-disciplinary power for the human inhabitants of New Orleans converge in particularly disturbing ways in the account of events that took place at a hospital, Memorial Medical Center, in uptown New Orleans in the days immediately after the storm as recounted by Pulitzer Prize–winning journalist (and physician) Sheri Fink.[33] The hospital made it through the storm as expected. Although it lost power, its emergency generators kicked in and the staff was able to keep caring for patients at something close to pre-Katrina levels. The morning after the storm, however, water began to rise in the streets outside the hospital. In just a few hours, flooding put the generators out of business altogether, dramatically curtailing the medical care the staff could provide. Plans were made to evacuate the hospital, and the staff improvised a triage system to set the order in which patients would be evacuated. They decided that pregnant women and infants in the neonatal intensive care unit (NICU) should go first (in part because they were most vulnerable to the effects of extreme heat) and the most critically ill would wait. Those with "do not resuscitate" (DNR) orders in their charts (indicating their expressed desire not to receive so-called heroic measures should their health deteriorate) would go last.

The demands on helicopters and boats by rescue needs throughout the city curtailed the evacuation effort significantly. Only about one-third of the hospital's patients were successfully evacuated in that initial effort. Just getting the patients to the evacuation site (an unused helipad across the way) without working elevators proved daunting. In the aftermath, already exhausted medical staff were faced with a disastrous situation, particularly with patients in Memorial's intensive care unit and on the seventh floor of the hospital, leased by another medical company, LifeCare. Many of these patients were critically but not terminally ill, and several were on respirators that ceased to function when the power went off (two of them died before the initial evacuation).

Eventually (two days after the hospital lost power) Memorial's parent company, Tenet HealthCare (based in Houston), realized that their frantic and repeated attempts to get help from governmental agencies for the hospital were going nowhere, and they chartered their own fleet of helicopters (along with some local boats) to complete the evacuation. But the state police in charge of securing the evacuation set an absolute deadline of 5 P.M. for ending it—due, they claimed, to increasing unrest in the city. (Indeed, the combination of rumored unrest and the sound of frequent gunshots had driven some of the staff to arm themselves and the security guards who remained at the hospital.) Faced with the seemingly impossible task of getting all of the patients out by that deadline, the doctors who had taken charge of patient care in the crisis decided that they needed to do something to forestall the suffering of the patients who might be left behind. A combination of morphine and sedation was administered by injection to a number of the more critically ill patients. Forty-five patients died at Memorial—considerably more, the article asserts, than at other New Orleans hospitals of comparable size in Katrina's immediate aftermath. On the basis of the coroner's findings that several of the deaths were homicides, three medical staff members were arrested on charges of second-degree murder, but ultimately none were prosecuted. Only one, Dr. Anna Pou, who administered most of the injections, was brought before a grand jury, which declined to prosecute the case.[34] (Dr. Pou has since mounted a vigorous campaign in various venues to craft guidelines for medical staff in such situations and indemnify them from prosecution except in cases of willful wrongdoing.)

Whether the injections were intended to kill the patients is a matter of dispute; that, in many cases, they hastened or precipitated death is not. It is clear that Dr. Pou and her colleagues turned to the administration of these drugs to forestall the suffering that they believed would necessarily follow from an incomplete evacuation—either, as in Mrs. Freeman's case, from medical conditions that would go untreated or from torments that one doctor, at least, imagined the lawless mobs rumored to be running rampant in the city might visit upon any patients left behind. Whether these doctors were right to do what they did remains contested. The staff itself was divided about it at the time. The participating doctors who consented to be interviewed said they were not troubled by what they had done. One said that he had done for those patients what he would want done for himself under the same circumstances. On the other hand, two of the doctors present that day—both internists—refused to participate. One denounced in no uncertain terms the injections as euthanasia and stormed out of the hospital. The coroner labeled some of the deaths homicides only after consulting with several experts, most of whom concluded the injections violated standards for medical practice. The families of some of those who died under these questionable circumstances filed suit against Tenet. A class action suit was settled out of court for some $25 million.

I go into this much detail about this particular event neither to endorse or condemn the decisions made by these medical professionals, but rather to refocus the process of slow *askesis* involved in tracing the (un)makings that these two photographs open up and open onto—beginning with those who died in the storm and its aftermath. As with Terri Schiavo, it is important to acknowledge the loss to and of Mrs. Freeman, the patients at Memorial (and LifeCare) who died, and their families, friends, and communities. I also want to acknowledge the unmakings engendered by the various forms of suffering—physical, emotional, spiritual, and ethical—that Memorial's medical staff, their patients, and their families endured both during and, I suspect for those who survived, long after those difficult days. Finally, I also acknowledge the larger systemic unmakings that contributed to—and, in some cases, directly created—the conditions in which these losses and forms of suffering occurred. To whatever degree one reads what occurred at Memorial as a breakdown in standards of care, what happened there is inseparable from the breakdowns that occurred outside the hospital walls—in particular, the systemic failures of those government systems created to manage bio-disciplinary power in the first place.

Indeed, what happened at Memorial has much to tell us about what happens when systems erected by bio-disciplinary power are stretched to their breaking point. The institutional conduits for bio-disciplinary power may have failed, but bio-disciplinary power itself continued to flow—still channeled, tellingly, by the fourfold of Man and his others. Look beneath the surface and we see bio-disciplinary power's racism-for and racism-against at work. The triage system according to which the medical staff determined who initially would be evacuated reflects biopower's preference for (re)productive normal life and its consignment of abnormality to death. Recall that fears that abandoned patients would be tormented and killed by imagined lawless mobs helped motivate the doctors to adopt the injection protocol in the first place. In the vacuum left behind, one doctor envisioned lawless mobs of "animals . . . crazy black people who think they've been oppressed for all these years by white people" wreaking havoc on the abandoned patients.[35] Finally, consider the injection protocol itself and its ultimate effects (intended or not). As established in chapter 5, nothing signals Man's displacement of God as putative master over nature than his (also putative) mastery over life and death.

Bio-disciplinary power's racism-for and racism-against comes through in a particularly troubling way in the death of one patient, whose sister is the source of this section's title. Emmett Everett, a 61-year-old 380-pound LifeCare patient of Bolivian descent was awaiting a colostomy for chronic bowel obstruction (a complication associated with paraplegia caused by a spinal stroke at age fifty). As recounted by Fink, Everett's death instantiated exactly what disability activists' fear. He was fully alert and had no DNR order. Yet he was consigned in the triage system to be evacuated with the last group apparently in part because staff members were concerned about their ability to get him to the helipad given his size and impairments. His only complaint the morning of the final evacuation, one staff member recalled, was of dizziness—and that he feared he would be left behind. Everett, too, received an injection and subsequently died.

Here, perhaps, we reach the heart of the matter. Although the circumstances that drove Memorial's medical staff to the injection protocol were certainly exceptional, the logic behind the protocol itself was, at one level, not all that exceptional, as many of their comments make clear. Physician-assisted suicide may be legal only in a few states, at present, but physician-assisted death is not an infrequent occurrence. Easing patients into a more humane (i.e., painless and quick) death to avoid suffering is a common practice in modern palliative care, a set of medical practices aimed at forestalling the pain and suffering of dying. (The concoction injected into the patients at Memorial was based on those practices.) Indeed, the prospect of a more controlled and less painful dying process is doubtless what patients want from palliative care. But the line between easing suffering and hastening death—or even causing it—is in many cases so fine as to be indistinguishable, Bishop notes, a fact confirmed in this instance by the comments of several of the Memorial medical staff.[36]

The morality of this practice within palliative care protocols rests in ensuring the proper exercise of self-sovereignty, Bishop claims. Before the seventies, patients rarely were told when their conditions were terminal, and doctors decided when or whether to end treatment and allow death to take its course. Largely because of complaints from patients and their families, policy and practice shifted the responsibility for such decisions to patients (although, as Bishop notes, these decisions are certainly shaped and guided by input from doctors). The good death is now the chosen death, and this process is set in motion by the patient's decision to forego further treatment in favor of palliative care. Protocols for managing dying include safeguards that aim to ensure that the patient's wishes rule throughout the process (and to protect physicians from liability).

The patients at Memorial were not hospitalized under the protocols established for palliative care, as I noted. And whether those patients whose condition presumably would have allowed it at the time understood the risks and benefits of the injections they were to receive enough to give truly informed consent is an open question. (Indeed, central to Dr. Pou's activism on behalf of formulating standards for disaster care is the acknowledgment that obtaining informed consent under such circumstances is extraordinarily difficult, if not impossible, she claims.) What happened at Memorial, in other words, although for very different reasons, returns us to the conundrum at the root of Terri Schiavo's situation. We confront once again the limits of self-sovereignty as the lifeboat in which we navigate the sometimes-tumultuous waters of modern biomedicine, especially its management of life and death. Ms. Schiavo's case showed us what can happen in the absence of self-sovereignty; Mr. Everett's self-sovereignty appears to have been simply overrun. In both cases, biopower's preferences for the normal and generative over the abnormal and degenerative govern the outcome, which is justified as an exercise in benevolence.

Again, my interest in exploring this dilemma is not to lay blame or deflect it, but to understand what this situation reveals about bio-disciplinary power's exercise in our time and place. What happened at Memorial exposes the vulnerabilities in the structures and strategies that were created by and now manage bio-disciplinary power, including modern subjectivity. The ideal modern subject is Man the Master; he is master over himself, his world, and those "others" who populate it. Access to this position is either attenuated or enabled by such factors as race and ethnicity; class; gender, sex, and sexuality; and (dis)ability. What happened at Memorial, however, reminds us that, although mastery remains the ideal, it is never fully realized even by those given full access to it. As that "strange empirico-transcendental doublet,"[37] Man is not only subject of but subject to modern ways of knowing, being, and doing. As bio-disciplinary power's subject, he embodies its ways of knowing, doing, and being, and as its object, he (like other animals) is subjected to them.

Modern biomedicine trades on this doubled structure in a number of ways. That we rely on the patient as "the decider," if you will, reflects bio-disciplinary power channeled by the fourfold. Even as it cedes responsibility to the self-sovereign subject, masterful (such as it is) management of life and death rests in those schooled in biomedicine's ways of knowing, doing, and being. We patients often subject ourselves (not uncritically, as resistance to the "medicalization" of disability and of gender variance reminds us) to biomedicine and its protocols in the hope of extending life and putting off death—or, when that is no longer possible, avoiding suffering and pain as we die. Because it is inevitably tied to self-subjection, self-sovereignty offers at best limited protection against bio-disciplinary power's exercise and thus its racisms (for or against), whether the acts and decisions that channel it—including those of Memorial's medical staff—are intentionally malevolent or benevolent. But it's not just modern biomedicine that trades on this doubled structure. All of the systems created by bio-disciplinary power—and that, when they're up and running, serve to contain and manage it—do so. The crisis in self-sovereignty is at its heart a crisis in Man's mastery over life and death, and this is the crisis that that runs straight through all of the institutions of bio-disciplinary power that Hurricane Katrina brought to its knees. The problems at Memorial were set in motion by structural failures in transportation and utility systems, of government systems set up to manage disasters, and, of course, of the infrastructure built to manage the particular confluence of earth and water on which New Orleans was built. All are the handiwork of bio-disciplinary power; all manifest its drive to master life and death on scales large and small.

The specter of institutional collapse is something that I greet, at least, with a good deal of ambivalence. On the one hand, insofar as bio-disciplinary power's claims to master life and death underwrite its racisms both for and against, a glimpse of its limits is something to celebrate. On the other, as this chapter in particular has shown, we have come to depend on the "goods and services," if you will, that bio-disciplinary power has crafted in the service of those very racisms. To the degree that the signs and wonders we've been interrogating herald modernity's (imminent or not) passing, the end of bio-disciplinary power is likely to bring with it losses as well as gains, suffering as well as celebration, and calamities as well as opportunities.

Remarking Time, Remaking Space Redux

Our inquiry into these signs and wonders has brought us back, then, where we began: to the question of modernity and its putative end. The end, that is, of ways of knowing, doing, and being that constitute modernity as *episteme* and *ethos*. I remain as resistant now to declaring that end a *fait accompli* as I was at the outset of this project—for reasons that, I trust, the cumulative effect of the intervening chapters make clear. But change of some sort is inevitable; those ways of knowing, doing, and being that constitute modernity are already morphing into what they will become. What that is, precisely, will become fully visible only in retrospect. Still, not only is it difficult to resist anticipating the changes to come, it is important for living into that future that we think ahead. In fact, *The Order of Things* concludes with Foucault's own musings on modernity's end-to-come. At first glance, some of what Foucault says may seem to belie my claim to a Foucauldian ground for my resistance to proclaiming that end as at hand. For example, in naming the so-called linguistic turn in philosophy as heralding philosophy's end, Foucault articulates what will become an oft-cited symptom of postmodernism. More to the point given my interests here is his anticipation of religion's return—in some form. He writes,

> The death of God and the last man are engaged in a contest with more than one round [*ont partie liée*] . . . but since it is in the death of God that he speaks, thinks, and exists, his murder itself is doomed to die; new gods, the same gods, are already swelling the future ocean; man will disappear.[38]

In the introduction to *Signs and Wonders*, I parsed its subtitle, *Theology After Modernity*, through connotations of "after" that are not only temporal but also spatial. "In what sense," I asked, "are we following after modernity—caught up in and by ways of thinking, being, and doing that it brought to birth?" Foucault's reflections here offer a similar perspective insofar as these anticipated ends have modern roots. Although more totalizing in its scope, the groundwork for the linguistic turn was laid in and by modern linguistics, itself an outgrowth of Classical philology; both the

Classical and the modern *epistemes* are orders of *words* and things, remember. The linguistic turn may be a recent phenomenon, but philosophy has been anticipating its own end at least since the late-nineteenth century, Foucault notes. Hegel, Marx, and Feuerbach (not to mention Nietzsche) each understood their own projects as bringing about the end of certain ways of philosophizing. Finally, per the quotation, old and new gods may be "swelling the oceans," but their (re)appearance also just marks the latest round in the contest launched between the gods and Man (the murdered and the murderer) that inaugurated modernity.

And yet, Foucault senses that there is something distinctive about the currently pressing sense of end: "this perilous imminence whose promise we fear today, whose danger we welcome."[39] If the task for the late-nineteenth century was to "establish for man a stable sojourn upon this earth" in the wake of the death of God, the task to come will be framed by the death of Man.[40] And Man's death, should it happen, will occur under circumstances analogous to those that enabled his birth. Man was born in and by "a change in the fundamental arrangements of knowledge," Foucault writes.[41] Were something to happen to cause *those* arrangements to "crumble, as the ground of Classical thought did, at the end of the eighteenth century, then one can certainly wager that *man would be erased [s'effacerait], like a face drawn in sand at the edge of the sea.*"[42]

That Foucault's musings on the end of Man culminate in a visual image is certainly fortuitous, given the central role that visual images have played in the preceding chapters. That the image takes this *particular* shape and form makes it especially salient. To be sure, this image materializes in *words* on paper, but photographs, too, are imagetexts, recall. This particular imagetext serves as an apt pivot point for *Signs and Wonders*. It reprises in concentrated form important insights from this chapter as well as the chapters that precede it even as it anticipates the work to come.

By "the work to come," I mean more than the closing pages of this volume. Finding the resources—intellectual, ethical, and material—that we need to live into the future that is pressing upon us is well beyond the scope of this book. And yet I positioned *Signs and Wonders* as Foucauldian not only in approach but also in its goals. I lured readers into this ascetic plunge into modernity and its putative end with the promise of enlightenment and in the pursuit of freedom. Making good on that promise and that pursuit will require at least a brief turn from the past toward the future, from practices of (de)formation to practices of reformation.

As anticipated in the introduction, making those turns will require a shift from one sensory register (visuality) to another (touch). These turns and shifts are not radical breaks, however, for, like Foucault's ruminations on modernity's ends, they are made possible by what has preceded them—in this case, the preceding chapters.

Figuring Man as a face drawn in sand reminds us that Man's destiny—his birth and his death—lies with forces beyond his control. He will disappear just as he appeared, slowly and anonymously, rendered out of materials—figured here as sand, wind, and sea—that predate him and that will "outlive" him, if you will. Its material figurations recall most immediately the particular convergence of natural forces—earth, water, wind, and sea—with human forces that became Hurricane Katrina. But that figuration also reminds us that, although smaller in scale, the other events discussed herein—the crisis in the Anglican Communion, the torments at Abu Ghraib, the political spectacle that surrounded Terri Schiavo's last days—are also sites where human and natural forces meet. This image-text also reminds us that both human beings and the natural world are subject to change. Sand and sea are anything but stable elements themselves. Always in motion, the sea changes in color, form, and location (tides and currents) depending on the conditions in it and around it. Sand is itself the product of the wind and water's (sea and rain) steady contact with rocks and shells, cliffs and mountains. The old makes way for the new. Even the most destructive incarnations of sand, wind, and sea—hurricanes, for example—unleash new possibilities. These possibilities are as deeply ambivalent as the realities they replace, of course, and not only because they come about through destruction but also because of the radical openness inherent in the new. Imaging Man's end as the result of slow erosion speaks as well to the pace of epistemic change, both past and likely in the future. Finally, that Foucault images Man's end as a process of (de)materialization that is as tactile as it is visual recalls the turn from seeing to touch we made at the conclusion of chapter 5, a turn that, as I will argue in the conclusion to this volume, opens toward ways of knowing, doing, and being that may sustain us as modernity moves toward its end.

CONCLUSION

Marking Time, Making Space

I N THE SPACE and time left to me here, I follow the turns identified in the conclusion to the previous chapter, from modernity's inauguration and consolidation to its (possible) end, from a focus on vision to touch. Recall that these are turns not breaks; they follow organically, if you will, out of the process of *askesis* that we have undergone. A close and patient look into the set of photographs that anchor this text and the events they index has opened up to us (un)makings born in and shored up by the exercise of bio-disciplinary power channeled through the fourfold of Man and his others. These (un)makings are simultaneously discursive and material, sensory and affective, individual and social, local and global, visual and tactile. They affect all of us within reach of bio-disciplinary power (which is to say *all* of us) and the structures that serve to contain and conduct it. Although many of us greet with outrage much of what bio-disciplinary power has wrought, *Signs and Wonders* has shown that we also have grown dependent on its taxonomies and the identities they underwrite, the institutions that inculcate and enforce them, and those that proffer (at least some of) us modernity's goods and services even as they entrain us in its racisms for and against. Thus, we greet modernity's putative end with ambivalence—as befits the heightened sense of ambiguity inherent in this particular what-is-to-come according to Foucault's last reflections in *The Order of Things*. Mustering the resources—also discursive and material, sensory and affective, individual and social, local and global, visual and tactile (and more)—to live into modernity's end is a daunting task, one that we can only begin to envision here. Yet, the new is, we've seen, in no small part a remaking of the old—a literal process of deconstruction if there ever was one. We should anticipate, then, that some resources, at least, are to be found here. My focus, then, will be primarily on articulating resources for knowing, being, and doing otherwise that the signs and wonders that have occupied these pages also open up and open onto.

That said, this look back is also a look ahead, and it is one undertaken with at least some sense of anticipated need in mind. So let me also begin with a bold pronouncement: living into the end of modernity will require, among other things, a new philosophy of life—in both the colloquial sense (of an approach to daily living) and the academic. We need a new ontology and a new *ethos* rooted in shared vulnerability: an ontology that redraws the lines that link and separate forms of life and the living from the nonliving, an *ethos* that enables new ways of relating along and across those redrawn lines. Lest similarities become sameness, this new philosophy of life needs also to acknowledge abyssal differences between.

I am hardly the first to recognize such a need.[1] Emergent forms of scholarship in the humanities and social sciences, including animal studies, posthumanist studies, and the "new materialisms," evidence that.[2] I say "a *new* philosophy of life" not to mark an absolute break with the "old." As we've seen, the "new" is always in part a remaking of what predates and precedes it. Nor, in calling for a new philosophy of life, am I kicking theology to the curb; quite the contrary. As *Signs and Wonders* has shown, to trace the course of modernity's emergence, consolidation, and decline requires tracking a certain theo-logic that undergirds it, one embedded in bio-disciplinary power channeled by the fourfold of Man and his others. It is highly unlikely that the end of modern theo-logic will mean the end of theology per se. The ocean that Foucault imagines slowly eroding Man's face, recall, is full of gods old and new. Yet, if the theo-logic to come has a chance to be something other than one more round in what the translator of *Order* calls the "contest" between God and Man, we need theologians to be engaged imaginatively and creatively—critically and constructively—with not only evaluating but also envisioning new ontological and ethical possibilities. The turns we take here will also open up and onto work by contemporary theologians that bear this out with particular insight and promise. Making the promised shift in sensory registers from vision to touch lays critical groundwork for those possibilities to matter.

Touching Touch I: Touch and Bio-Discipline

At the end of chapter 5, I suggested that the tactile-caring-for provided, one hopes, to Ms. Schiavo by the hospice workers might offer a route toward an ethical response to vulnerability—framed there in Butlerian terms as precariousness and precarity—worth our consideration. Its ethical promise, I noted, did not come because touch was somehow immune to or outside of bio-disciplinary power; hospice care is, as chapter 6 confirmed, an aspect of biomedicine and thus embedded in bio-disciplinary power. Touch's role as a conduit of bio-discipline suggests we should proceed with caution, a stance confirmed by theologian Sharon Betcher. In *Spirit and the Politics of Disablement* touch is focal to her critique of the "optics" through which contemporary liberal Christianity (exemplified here by Marcus Borg's and John Dominic Crossan's popular reconstructions of the historical Jesus) reads gospel narratives wherein Jesus performs healings. Conscripted in and by an optic shaped by our contemporary "cultural cathection to normalcy," we turn these narratives into "medicine shows" rather than critiques of the (literal and metaphorical) mutilations imposed on the colonized by imperial Rome.[3] The power channeled through Jesus's touch is divine rather than bio-disciplinary and its effects arguably political rather than literal. Yet we interpret its achievements in light of our bio-disciplined desires and fears. The masterful touch of the hero-healer Jesus "moves from a body on the clean, intact, and superior side to touch upon the mutilated and dirty" causing all signs of deformity or disability to disappear, we imagine.[4] The blind are made to see (20–20, we presume) and the lame get up and walk (without even a trace of a limp, we presume).

Clearly, then, to mine touch as an ethical resource will take us deeper into its ambiguities and ambivalences. Not only can touch channel either cruelty or comfort; it also limns a site at which theo-logic and bio-discipline meet. Consider touch's role in the photographs and the events they index considered in the preceding chapters. On the one hand, the photographs of the Rt. Rev. Robinson's consecration depict touches that channel the holy and the bio-disciplinary. A laying on of hands made Robinson the first openly gay Anglican bishop (figure 3.2). That he *was* the first openly gay Anglican bishop was signaled photographically when his then-partner handed him the miter, one lover's hands tenderly touching another's (figure 3.1). These benign bio-disciplined touches generated malignant ones when this act of consecration moved others to violence directed at LGBTQI Ugandans and Nigerians by those opposed to their open presence. The lynching photographs (figures 4.1 and 4.2), along with those from the Abu Ghraib archive (figures 4.3 and 4.4), put on graphic display touch as a mechanism of bio-disciplined domination and torment, a death-dealing conduit for violence. Yet a trace of touch's ethical potential remains legible in the contact between one detainee's hip and another's knee in the tableau featured in figure 4.4. Touch regains a more positive valence as it channels bio-disciplined tenderness in the form of a mother's kiss in the second of the stills of Terri Schiavo (figure 5.2) and, we hope, in the care provided to Ms. Schiavo outside the camera's view. The photographs of Mrs. Freeman (figure 6.1) and of the abandoned dog (figure 6.2) taken in the aftermath of Hurricane Katrina offer a poignant portrait of touch's absent presence and present absence in the midst of systemic failures. The fully shrouded body on the sidewalk next to Mrs. Freeman bespeaks touch as a conduit of respect and care, treatment denied Mrs. Freeman's body. The position of the blanket partially covering her body suggests a casual toss, not careful swaddling, a callous or at best careless gesture of touch-from-a-distance. The (unrealized) prospect of physical contact between dog and human in the second photograph (figure 6.2) carries with it promise and threat—to both dog and human. Touch is central to the stories of resilience and rescue that also emerge from Katrina. Human hands reached out again and again to rescue other human beings and, in many cases, animals—aided and abetted, often, by so-called sniffer dogs trained to use their acute sense of smell to locate human survivors (or victims' remains).[5] At Memorial Hospital, medical staff replaced mechanical delivery of certain forms of care (e.g., respirators) with hand-delivered care, in many cases. Those who were evacuated were carried to safety by hand under enormous stress. And yet some of those same hands delivered the injections that eased other patients' suffering—and hastened their deaths.

But touch's relationship to these photographs and thus to bio-disciplinary power is more than a matter of their content. Although we think of (still) photography as solely a visual medium, recall that touch is intimately connected to it, as well. It's the physical contact between finger and shutter that initiates the contact between light and lens—and eventually chemicals and paper (or their digital equivalents)—that creates each photograph in the first place. Per Roland Barthes, it's the materiality of the photograph that makes it a (literal) *memento mori*. Recall, as well, per Margaret Olin, that our contact with photographs as viewers is often as much tactile as it is visual. Photographs touch us—literally and meta-phorically—often as we touch them; when, for example, we sift through a stack of old family photos or encounter the product of photojournalism in a newspaper. We depend on touch to create and to access digital pho-tographs, too; indeed, it's telling that the touch screen inaugurated a new era of technological innovation.[6]

That said, it is the move away from vision to another of the five senses that makes touch compelling. Although touch is hardly exempt from conscription by the various forms of bio-disciplined subjection endemic to the modern *episteme* and *ethos*, vision is its linchpin, as the first two chapters of *Signs and Wonders* demonstrated. Bio-disciplinary power and its fourfold has successfully (which is not to say totally) colonized the visual in the service of its drive toward mastery: over self, over others, over nature, over life, and over death. That drive for mastery, I have sug-gested, is rooted in the disavowal of vulnerability. That vulnerability, like the (un)makings we've been tracking here that trade on it, is simultane-ously discursive and material, sensory and affective, individual and social, local and global, visual and tactile. It is, moreover, a condition shared by all forms of life and the environment that sustains them. Indeed, as we've seen in every chapter, the lines drawn to separate Man from his others limn disavowed vulnerability. Man's claim to forms of mastery modeled after (but not equivalent to) those ascribed to his divine other move him to disavow the vulnerability that he shares with his sexed, raced, and ani-mal others. The structures created to contain and control bio-disciplinary power also aim to master vulnerability. The fractures and fissures in those institutions and structures emerge precisely where mastery meets its limits.

Whatever else we need from a new philosophy of life, we need it to enable us to face up to the very vulnerability that bio-disciplinary power seeks to disavow. The glimpse we caught of touch's promise in chapter 5, recall, was intrinsically linked to a certain absence of mastery. The physical condition that robbed Ms. Schiavo of self-mastery also robbed her care-givers of the ability to know whether their touches met their mark. Might this fracture open onto ways of working with and through vulnerability that resist or bypass modernity's relentless drive toward mastery: ways of knowing, being, and doing better suited to bearing up under modernity's decline? With this quest in mind, then, I turn once again to the work of Jacques Derrida, specifically to his *Le toucher: Jean-Luc Nancy* (in English translation *On Touching—Jean-Luc Nancy*).[7] Derrida's discussion of touch carries its readers to terrain redolent of the fourfold. Touch limns subjec-tivity and its limits (the interplay of immanence and transcendence, body and soul, divinity and humanity, humanity and animality, ethics and *eros*). Sexual difference and racial difference, too, converge where touch appears. Although the sections of *Le toucher* on which I will focus reach back as far as Aristotle and invoke such decidedly premodern figures as the Virgin Mary, the incarnate Christ, and St. John of the Cross (to name a few), they appear in the company of philosophers often deemed postmodern (Lévinas, Nancy, and, of course, Derrida himself).

Touching Touch II: *Le toucher*

An *homage* to fellow philosopher (and former student) Jean-Luc Nancy, Derrida reaches out to Nancy via a series of inquiries on touch in the philosophical tradition, a theme on which Nancy himself has written. Indeed, each gesture toward the tradition gestures toward Nancy insofar Nancy's work on touch becomes a critical lens through which Derrida reads the tradition. I say "reaches out" and "gestures toward" for spe-cific reasons. First, the gap between *Le toucher* and *Jean-Luc Nancy* in the title is, it turns out, indicative of a central insight that emerges from fol-lowing touch through the philosophical tradition. Touch, that most inti-mate (and, it will turn out, arguably essential of senses) beckons toward a contact that is profoundly impossible. Yet, as with other figures of the impossible taken up by Derrida over the years, therein lies its significance. The medium is the message, as is often the case not only in mass media (*pace* Marshall McLuhan) but also for Derrida. As Michael Naas argues, the physical structure of this book mirrors the shape of the analysis that occurs between its pages.[8] Derrida honors Nancy by placing his work in proximity to philosophers from Aristotle to Emmanuel Lévinas, including figures one would expect to encounter (e.g., Merleau-Ponty and Luce Irigaray) and some whose presence surprise. (An example that will be of particular relevance here is Jean-Louis Chrétien, author *of L'appel et la réponse* [*Call and Response*], an analysis of touch in Christianity.)[9] The pages of *Le toucher* are organized into three major parts: "This is—of/to the other" (*Ceci est—de l'autre*), "Exemplary Stories of the 'Flesh'" (*Histoires exemplaires de la 'chair'*), and "Punctuations: 'and you'" ("*Ponctuations: 'et toi'*")—bordered by prefaces and a conclusion and separated by a series of drawings by Simon Hantaï entitled "Salve." Part I considers Nancy's work in the context of other philosophers and thinkers in a series of six fairly lengthy essays. Part III carries further certain themes from earlier analyses in *Le toucher* in three brief and more schematic essays, the last of which concludes by dispersing rather than tying together. Given the enigmatic and untranslatable title "*Salve: postscriptum à contretemps, faute de retouche finale*," this essay marks *Le toucher* as quite literally eccentric: untimely (*contretemps* = outside of time) and unseemly (lacking a final touch-up). These parts are separated by a series of five "tangents" linked together as "Exemplary Stories of the 'Flesh.'" Together with the prefaces and conclusion, the book consists of essays of various lengths and purposes that create a composite of touch.[10]

Because our concerns here are simultaneously philosophical, theological, and ethical, I focus on two portions of *Le toucher* where these three come together: first, Derrida's discussion of the caress in Lévinas, and second, his discussion of the thinker whom I mentioned earlier, Chrétien, which makes up the fifth tangent.[11] In bringing these two portions of *Le toucher* into proximity with one another, I trust that I also extend the book's project in another way. *Le toucher's* structure, it seems to me, takes the form of a book to its limits and, in doing so, embodies touch as (im)possible possibility. The materiality of a book requires that its subject matter be presented in linear form, but these essays (or forays) reach out to one another through and around their immediate neighbors. So, for example, in his account of Chrétien, Derrida explicitly hints at parallels with Lévinas's treatment of touch, but leaves it to the attentive reader to reverse standard convention by reading backward rather than forward. Following this trail from Chrétien to Lévinas exposes a common logic of touch—structured by the fourfold of Man and his others—in the work of two disparate thinkers.

At first glance, the projects of Lévinas and Chrétien seem to have little in common beyond their approach to the theme of touch, in both cases launched from phenomenology, terrain that both treatments also ultimately exceed. Lévinas approaches touch through what is if not an everyday occurrence is at least a common one: the lover's caress of the beloved. Chrétien, on the other hand, approaches touch through what purports to be a unique occurrence: the traditional Christian claim that God became incarnate in Christ. But Lévinas claims that what seems to be the most accessible to us is actually the most elusive. And Chrétien claims that what seems to be the most improbable contact of all is actually the most real. Lévinas and Chrétien, then, start from opposite corners and move (without recognizing it) toward each other: from immanence toward transcendence (in Lévinas's case), and from transcendence toward immanence (in Chrétien's case). Finite-to-finite touch ungrounds what seems to be a fully grounded subject (in Lévinas's case), whereas infinite-to-finite touch grounds the subject-to-be by granting it its essential properties (in Chrétien's case). These two thinkers do not exactly meet in the middle. Yet, as we shall see, Derrida's reading (via Nancy) uncovers a common ground (marked by sexual [in]difference and a certain erotic bearing) that ungrounds both of them.

Touch as Mastery: The Caress

I begin, then, with Derrida's invocation of Lévinas who, like Nancy, has been an important conversation partner for Derrida over the years (and the subject of his own Derridean *homage* a few years before *Le toucher* was written). [12] Our commonsense associations with "caress" might suggest that it is a type of touch, one that yields a distinctive form of pleasure through contact with another (human) being. Because it involves a reaching toward the other, its trajectory starts from within the self (immanence) and moves toward what lies outside the self (transcendence). We take for granted its success; that is, the reaching toward makes contact—flesh to flesh, skin to skin—and achieves satisfaction and release. As contact-with-another, the caress would seem to constitute the most intimate form of what phenomenologists would call intersubjectivity or relationships of one subject to another. The caress seems to proffer to the caresser intimate knowledge of the caressed. In doing so, it promises to unify the orders of sensibility and intelligibility. It seems, on its surface, utterly benign, indeed, utterly good. Perhaps even ethical.

Derrida's reading of Lévinas's analysis of the caress considers two texts: Lévinas's well-known "Phenomenology of Eros" in *Totality and Infinity* (*Totalité et infini*, published in 1961) as well as *Time and the Other (Le temps et l'autre*, published in 1946–1947), a text that precedes by some fifteen years its more famous counterpart.[13] These two texts are linked by a common logic, as well. In both texts, Lévinas reworks and ultimately challenges our commonsense assumptions. In seeking the Beloved (always gendered feminine, Derrida points out), the Lover (always gendered masculine, Derrida points out) is indeed drawn out of himself. The pleasure of the caress is distinct from other pleasures (e.g., eating or drinking), in that it is not solitary. But it is not yet social, thus not yet intersubjective. It envelopes the Lover in the closed circle of the couple, a site that at least holds out the fantasy of fusion and is thus, according to Lévinas, "the exceptional place of the feminine," a point to which I shall return shortly.[14] Fusion is only a phantasm, however, as Lévinas describes the caress. It is the nature of the eternally feminine to remain forever out of reach and thus perpetually virginal. The Lover's quest also fails to achieve satisfaction beyond the level of phantasm. The two—Lover and Beloved, Caresser and Caressed—remain forever locked in a not-yet-embrace. Lévinas describes the caress as constituting a peculiar kind of transcendence: "contact beyond [*au-delà*] contact," a contact that exceeds sensation and knowledge, the order of representation, and the order of intentionality. In short, pursuing the object-to-be-caressed carries the caressing subject to its limits. Derrida quotes Lévinas:

> The caress is a mode of being of the subject where the subject in its contact with an other goes beyond contact. The contact, in as much as it is sensation, breaks with the world of light. But that which is caressed is not touched, properly speaking. It is not the smoothness or warmth of this hand given in contact that the caress seeks. The search for the caress is constituted in its essence by the fact that the caress does not know what it seeks. This "not knowing," this fundamental disorder, is essential to it.[15]

The exposure of limits comes across as both promise and threat. Excess promises insofar as willing dispossession indicates a primordial openness-to-the-other. It menaces insofar as willed dispossession loses control as the Caresser descends into a literal "no-man's-land" (in English, in Lévinas's original) of a vertiginous fusion-not-to-be. In following after the (eternally feminine) Beloved, "caress holds neither a person nor a thing. It loses itself in a mode of being which dissipates itself as though in an impersonal dream without will and without resistance, a passivity and anonymity *already animal or infantile* [emphasis mine]."[16] Tellingly, its immersion in the "false security of the elemental" and in nonknowing—particularly not knowing its mortality—mark the boundary of the not (yet?) human recalling the distinction between Man and his (animal) other within the modern *episteme*.[17]

Elements of Lévinas's analysis of the caress call to mind his analysis of the ethical. Derrida argues, however, that, rather than a site of the ethical (i.e., the Face), Lévinas's description of the caress amounts to an inversion (or even perversion) of the ethical. Both exceed the order of knowing and representation. Both carry the masterful subject toward its limits. The demand of the Face that constitutes the ethical brings the subject up short while the caress culminates in a blind dissipation of both self and other. Both also involve a relationship to death. Whereas the caress yields a forgetting of mortality, the Face presents itself as the demand "Do not kill me."

The limits of the ethical also appear here. The erotic bearing of Lévinas's analysis of the caress is no doubt apparent, and Derrida finds it troubling. He is not, of course, the first to criticize it. Indeed, he refers (in a footnote) to Luce Irigaray's critique of the division it introduces between the feminine and the ethical in "The Fecundity of the Caress."[18] Noting that the caress mirrors the Face suggests to Derrida a set of questions that need to be answered. What is the line, if any, between the transcendence (as excess that renders impossible) inherent in the caress and the transcendence (as ground that makes possible) inherent in the ethical? Insofar as both the caress and the Face gesture toward transcendence, don't they both also gesture toward the ethical? Must the erotic be interrupted for the ethical to take place? Does the structural similarity between the erotic and the ethical link them as tangents of the same impossible possibility? The same desire?

Touch as Mastery: The Incarnation

As noted, Chrétien starts from the opposite corner, as it were. Where Lévinas exceeds phenomenology by following a common everyday experience to its limits, Chrétien exceeds phenomenology by outdoing it. What phenomenology dreams of, theology accomplishes. Phenomenology makes a theoretical mistake when it posits touch between finite human beings as unmediated. Finite-to-finite touch is interrupted by veils and intervals; literal and metaphorical disrobing must precede it. Access to unmediated touch requires that one carry phenomenology toward its limits via a phenomenology of ecstasy and mystical love.

The touch *par excellence* is not the carnal touch, but rather the spiritual touch whose paradigm is the Incarnation, he argues. In the Incarnation, the infinite touches the finite; in becoming flesh, the infinite converts the body from mere flesh to enspirited flesh. Unlike the carnal touch, the touch of the divine is temporally and spatially immediate (that is, eternal and unmediated). Unlike Lévinas's caress, this touch meets its match—at least, on the surface. Chrétien asserts, via Aquinas and John of the Cross, that there *is* mutual contact (call *and* response, to cite the title of his book). Where Lévinas's touch carries the subject to its limits, Chrétien's touch establishes the limits of the subject; that is, it gives to the subject its essential properties. We are used to thinking of the hand of God as a metaphorical appropriation of the human hand. Real physical human touch provides the model for the figurative spiritual touch of the divine. But Chrétien's reading of the Incarnation inverts this assignation of literal and metaphorical. In becoming incarnate in Christ the Son, the merciful hand of God the Father literally reaches out to touch—and through touch to become—human flesh. It is that touch that gives to man his proper hand; the hand that, it turns out, marks man as man. As we have known at least since Heidegger's famous analysis of *Zuhandenheit* in *Being and Time*, handedness grounds man's ability to know, to discriminate, to organize, to see, and to hear.[19] It is these capacities—essential to worldedness—that distinguish man from animal, according to Heidegger and, in turn (as I have argued elsewhere), man from certain of his raced and sexed others.[20]

No doubt, as with Lévinas, certain dynamics of this scene are so obvious as perhaps to go without saying. Derrida notes the anthropo-theo-teleological pattern that dominates this scene. Ontotheology (a system centered around a God whose Word grounds being) and metaphysical humanism—two sides of the same coin, as Derrida notes elsewhere—appear in tandem once again. And just as we might expect, Derrida is not going to let their reappearance go unchallenged. As with Lévinas, Derrida poses a set of questions to expose what remains unthought in Chrétien's project. Is the spiritual touch really as unmediated as Chrétien would like to believe? Are there not passages between that transcend (ground and exceed) Chrétien's assertion of the power of the spiritual touch? Chrétien's theological claim passes first through the philosophical (one gets to Aquinas only through Aristotle). But perhaps more significant for my purposes, Chrétien's theo-logic itself is constituted by a series of passages that he passes by without comment. Derrida notes that Chrétien ignores an essential passage between the infinite and the finite, namely, death. The infinite God becomes truly finite by dying on the cross. The meaning that Christian theology traditionally gives to this death links God, Christ, and sinful man via a prosthetic logic of multiple substitutions. God's death in Christ constitutes a sacrifice that replaces that owed by man to God, thus transforming sinner into saint. That transforming sacrifice is, in turn, commemorated and reenacted in the Eucharistic feast where bread and wine stand (in) for body and blood. God becomes man, the infinite becomes finite, saint becomes sinner, bread becomes body, wine becomes blood, sinner becomes saint: a chain of passages repeated *ad infinitum*.

Derrida also brings to our attention a theo-logic of fiery desire that carries Chrétien's project along. Chrétien figures the touch of the divine as fire; it is a fire that enflames flesh with desire for union with the divine, that provides illumination, but that will not be possessed. The divine fire consumes all attempts to contain it via representation (as icon or idol). The figural logic of Chrétien's text undercuts its surface logic and thus its project of securing the subject by grounding its properties properly in the eternal. Although their projects started out from different places, Chrétien is bound to Lévinas by a shared logic of desire, one that tends toward ecstasy and excess (of representation and possession).

Derrida is not content simply with pointing out the prosthetic logic that runs counter to the surface logic of Chrétien's text. "Tangent V" concludes, as "L'intouchable" does, with questions and allusions that point toward what remains to be thought: What makes possible passages-between? What gives place so that passages between may take place? Here, Derrida invokes *khora*, that enigmatic figure from Plato's *Timaeus* that elsewhere in Derrida's corpus names that which exceeds Christian theo-logic. Chrétien's analysis of touch uses *khora*'s resources (without knowing or at least without acknowledgment) to construct its prosthetic economy, an economy built around sacrifice. Is it possible, Derrida asks, to have an economy of substitution without sacrifice?

Touching Touch III: After Mastery

In keeping with the spirit and the letter of *Le toucher*, let me offer my own tangent: a series of gestures toward what it seems to me this inquiry into touch offers to our attempt to grapple with the challenges posed to us by the signs and wonders considered in this volume. This tangent returns us to the practice of *askesis*—of disciplined attention to, in this case, a logic of (un)making that *Le toucher* describes. On the one hand, *Le toucher* tracks surface logics of touch that generate (putative) mastery. The Lover's caresses pursue successful contact with his Beloved in Lévinas; God's touch grants man his essential and proper ground in Chrétien, the handedness that distinguishes him from his raced and animal others. But touch also undoes those surface logics and, in the process, renders impossible what they purport to pursue. The desire for the Beloved that motivates the caress takes mastery to its limits; the mastery (literally) handed down from God to man is undone by its own prosthetic logic. Touch, then, (un)does the masterful knowing, doing, and being that embodies man's displacement of God and in so doing (un)does the logic that distinguishes man from his (sexed, raced, and animal) others. It clears space for other forms of knowing, doing, and being to take root—forms that figure relationality and thus responsibility differently.

Given theology's imbrication in the logic of mastery that lies at modernity's heart, it will need to contribute to that labor of cultivating those other ways of knowing, being, and doing. Resources that theology can open up and onto will become apparent by delving more deeply into three theological texts that have made only brief appearances in *Signs and Wonders* so far: M. Shawn Copeland's *Enfleshing Freedom*, Sharon Betcher's *Spirit and the Politics of Disablement*, and Mayra Rivera Rivera's *The Touch of Transcendence*. I turn to these three in no small part because of what they share with *Signs and Wonders*.[21] Each explores sites where we have seen bio-disciplinary power's racisms for and against made manifest in especially potent ways. All three texts posit the individualized masterful subject as the centerpiece of a globalized system of domination, exploitation, and oppression that, in Copeland's words, "cannibalizes the bodies, the labor and creativity, and the sexuality and generativity of global 'others'" and is catapulting us toward ecological disaster.[22] All three advocate, in Rivera

Rivera's words "unlearning the self-enclosed *I am*" in favor of ways of knowing, doing, and being rooted in recognition of vulnerability and interdependence.[23]

These three texts also pick up in productive ways on the paths for knowing, doing, and being otherwise opened up by *Le toucher*. Like Derrida, these thinkers draw on sources both premodern and contemporary, theological and philosophical, verbal and visual. In their hands, elements central to mastery's unmaking in Lévinas and Chrétien become resources for remaking. All three projects work out of and work with the desire for connection to others that Derrida shows (un)grounds touch. Each follows that desire along a trajectory that resists the gravitational pull of modernity's drive toward mastery. Instead of disavowing the underlying vulnerability that modernity seeks to master, each advocates working with and through it. In place of an *ethos* of individualism, each advocates an *ethos* of community—that is, one that opens onto an ontology that acknowledges and embraces abyssal differences between humans, if not (yet) all forms of life. Significantly, in each case, what bio-discipline designates as abnormality become resources for that process of working with and working through; resources we tap by working across the bio-disciplined lines that separate "us" from "them."

In its opening pages, Copeland describes *Enfleshing Freedom* in Foucauldian-inflected terms as "a gesture toward a 'critical ontology of the body'" undertaken through a focus on black women's bodies subjected to exploitation and abuse by gendered, sexualized, and racialized brutality.[24] The project of enfleshing freedom "begins in *anamnesis*," Copeland writes, in "the intentional remembering of the dead, exploited, despised victims of history," including the victims of lynching.[25] She rematerializes the horrors of slavery and of lynchings—including the role white Christians played in them—not through photographs but through brief powerful renarrativizations. These imagetexts render legible the scars and wounds, literal and metaphorical, left by those losses on contemporary (individual and collective, physical and social) bodies. *Anamnesis* is not just a memorializing exercise. Copeland also takes us back into this painful past in search of the creative, careful, often-surreptitious ways that enslaved women and men found to enflesh freedom despite the horrors of slavery. We honor their labors in our time and place by going deeper into those scars and wounds, these signifiers of vulnerability, in search of the possibilities for living otherwise that they hold.

Another instance of enfleshing freedom out of torment and death is critical to that process of reclamation: the crucifixion and resurrection of Jesus Christ, as memorialized in the Eucharist. If in *Le toucher* these events were entrained in mastery and its undoing, here they constitute a call to "solidarity," a "cognitive, affective, constitutive, and communicative" praxis of self and community (re)formation rooted in the ancient trope of the mystical body of Christ.[26] Taking in Christ through the Eucharist obligates Christians to take on Christ, "the lynched Jesus, whose shadow falls across the table of our sacramental meal" and whose resurrected body "interrupts the structures of death and sin, of violation and oppression."[27] To take on Christ is itself a process of *askesis*. Taking on the contemporary structures of sin and/as oppression and violation means addressing the material effects of racialized, sexed, gendered, sexualized, and classed subjection in ourselves as well as in our communities.[28] For some, this requires renunciation of "position and privilege, power and wealth."[29] For all, it requires welcoming the "vigorous display" of all of the differences that constitute the human race.[30] Through these practices of solidarity, we enflesh freedom; as Copeland writes, "we are (re)made and (re)marked as the flesh of Christ, as the flesh of his church."[31]

For Betcher, too, Christianity is "at heart a philosophy of desire" manifest in God's love for the world. Living into and out of that desire demands rethinking Spirit "on the slant," Betcher argues—that is, from the perspective of living with a disability (in her case, the amputation of a leg) instead of "on the up-and-up."[32] This is a pneumatology tilted away from the pursuit of eschatological perfection "cathected to the optical illusion of consciousness, the ego-self" and toward the cultivation of a form of compassion rooted not in individual mastery but in "awareness of life's basically communal ground."[33] Read through Betcher, Chrétien's prosthetic logic is a theo-logic of "compulsory holism," in which the prosthesis promises to restore a lost wholeness.[34] Actual prosthetic existence, if you will, becomes in Betcher's hands a resource for contesting that body politics, a contestation that limns an economy of substitution that does not, in fact, end in sacrifice. Living a differently abled life opens up and onto creative ways of knowing, doing, and being through working with rather than against vulnerability, of "wrestling with the exquisite loveliness of and frustration with one's own transient tissues at the same time as she or he wrestles with the physical and psychic cumbersomeness, the severe rigidity, if also acquired grace, of the technologically endowed body."[35] Betcher attests that, "For me, prosthetics, and consequently, incarnation, are about tipping the fierce ambivalence that is mortality toward a love of the futility of it all—toward a love of the flesh and of finitude, I mean."[36] These loves reframe our relationship to vulnerability. Rather than a weakness to be disavowed, it is a reality to be worked through and worked with—lovingly, with humor and patience where possible, and in collaboration with others.

Like Betcher and Copeland, Rivera Rivera describes her project in terms of a theological desire. She seeks to "remobilize[e] the passion and the wisdom of a Christian love for the inappropriable divine Other" to reframe interhuman relations as an "embrace [of] irreducible differences."[37] This embrace is more than metaphorical, as the book's title indicates. Touch becomes more and more central to this project in ways that resonate closely with *Le toucher*. Touch's trajectory opens onto a transcendence that begins as epistemological and ethical, and ultimately becomes ontological and theological. Drawing on the concept of *mestizaje* as developed by Cherríe Moraga and Gloria Anzaldúa, Rivera Rivera argues that all human beings are the sedimented products of multilayered "relations across differences."[38] These relations—some of which we can know and name, others of which are beyond our ken—extend from birth to death and are physical and social, spatial and temporal, biological and historical, wounding and life-giving. These relations make each of us utterly singular, simultaneously interconnected, and totally other to one another. Insofar as we are individually and collectively always in process, we are both temporally and spatially *infini*: unfinished.

In a move that has particular significance for *Signs and Wonders*, Rivera Rivera draws on Spivak's notion of planetarity to extend tactile interrelationality beyond the intra- and interhuman realms to include all that is. Interrelationality takes place on Spivak's planet—the (non)place that gives place, the figure of alterity that we occupy on loan. To more fully mine its ontological (and ethical) potential, Rivera Rivera takes planetarity where Spivak won't (quite) go—into a theological register. When brought into conversation with sources ancient and contemporary (Origen and Ivone Gebara), Christian and Jewish (Nicholas of Cusa and the Talmud), theological and philosophical (Irenaeus and Luce Irigaray), planetarity becomes "God" and "God," in turn, becomes planetary. Divine transcendence configured through planetarity works as much from the inside out as from the outside in. The planetary "God" enfolds all that is in an embrace of abyssal depth and infinite generativity.

That our turn to touch has returned us to planetarity invites some final reflections. Recall from its prior appearance in *Signs and Wonders* that planetarity renders our globe uncanny—that is, unhomelike (*unheimlich*)—which makes finding secure footing on the planet's ever-changing terrain difficult, if not impossible. For some, a planetary God will seem like cold comfort. A planetary God is an uncanny God caught up in and by the shifts and changes under way at any given time as what is gives way to what will be. This is not a God who will swoop down from on high to rescue us from what will be. Yet to seek refuge in such a (nonplanetary) God would be to once again disavow the vulnerability of—*and, with it, the resilience inherent in*—finite and fleshly existence. More to the point, there is support and even comfort to be found in the abyssal depths and infinite generativity of a planetary God, as Rivera Rivera's portrayal makes clear. That said, making good on the promise that inheres in a planetary theo-logic will require more than theological exposition, no matter how persuasive or alluring.

Our plunge into these signs and wonders has, I trust, called attention to our own bio-disciplined subjection through taking up and taking on its ways of knowing, doing, and therefore being. Navigating modernity's end will require (re)invention—of ourselves, of our ways of knowing, doing, and being. Copeland's call to a praxis of solidarity and Betcher's to fleshly improvisation proffer creative ways of knowing, doing, and being that align well with Rivera Rivera's planetary theo-logic. Together they call us to life in community rather than in isolation, on the slant rather than on the up and up, in the embrace of a planetary God rather than waiting on a divine Master; they provide ways of knowing, doing, and being that might just sustain us as we live into modernity's decline.

Certainly, these are not the only forms of knowing, doing, and being that will do or that we will need. Other resources—secular as well as religious, practical as well as intellectual—are indeed out there to be sussed out and fleshed out. Betcher's most recent book, *Spirit and the Obligation of Social Flesh: A Secular Theology for the Global City,* undertakes that task with an eye specifically to resourcing inhabitants of contemporary secular cities (a reference to theologian Harvey Cox's classic book from the seventies)—themselves planetary places—in ways of knowing, doing, and being that can work with and through asymmetrically distributed precarity and precariousness.[39] In addition to disability studies, postcolonial theory, and Christian theology (and Butler and Spivak), this work of "crip/tography" also draws on other religious traditions of thought and practice—Advaita Vedanta, Buddhism, yoga—that have taken root in North America.[40] Wendy Farley, too, merges Christian theology (the so-called medieval mystics figure prominently) with her well-honed knowledge of Tibetan Buddhist contemplative practice in the service of re-formations, as well.[41] Rivera Rivera's latest book *Poetics of the Flesh* turns to this contested category (flesh) to cultivate ways of thinking about embodiment that face up to its vulnerabilities and creative possibilities.[42] This project, like Betcher's latest, limns the border between the secular and the religious, philosophy and theology, self and community, discourse and the body. Of course, whether these ways of knowing, doing, and being will take root among us—and what effects they will have if so—remains to be seen. Living into what is coming—its promises and its perils—will continue to require *askesis*: disciplined attention to forms and practices of (un)making, these and/or others, to which we are inclined to give ourselves over and in which we will be entrained. And, of course, to the signs and wonders—discursive and material, sensory and affective, individual and social, local and global, visual and tactile—that are yet to come.

NOTES

Introduction

1. I foreground a certain kind of (interpellative) identity politics here; one that *Signs and Wonders* explicitly refuses. In what follows, I attend not only to (white) feminist and queer issues (those in which I would presumably have an interest), but also to others, including issues related to (post)coloniality. As Kwok Pui-Lan rightly observes, these issues are intertwined and should be held together more often than they are. See her *Postcolonial Imagination and Feminist Theology* (Louisville, KY: Westminster John Knox, 2005), 137–44.

2. In "What Is Enlightenment?" Foucault suggests that we think of modernity as an attitude rather than an epoch or era. Instead of seeking to fix the boundaries of the modern (both before and after), we might look instead for the struggles this attitude has faced since its inception with various forms of "countermodernity" (Michel Foucault, "What Is Enlightenment?" trans. Catherine Porter, in *The Foucault Reader*, ed. Paul Rabinow (New York: Pantheon, 1984), 32–50; 39; later published in France as "Qu'est-ce que les lumières?" in *Dits et Écrits*, ed. Daniel Defert and François Ewald, Vol. IV (Paris: Éditions Gallimard, 1994), 562–78. In a recent essay, Butler notes modernity's use as a cudgel in international controversies where sex, gender, sexuality, and religion mix. There she notes her own refusal to "traffic in theories of modernity because the concept strikes me as too large . . . [the theories] too general and sketchy to be useful" (Judith Butler, "Sexual Politics, Torture, and Sexual Time," *British*

Journal of Sociology 59, no. 1 [2008]: 1–23, 4). On Jacques Derrida's position on postmodernism, see, for example, his "Response to David Tracy" in *God, the Gift, and Postmodernism*, ed. John D. Caputo and Michael J. Scanlon (Bloomington: Indiana University Press, 2000), 181–84.

3. For more on my views on these matters, see my "Beyond Belief: Sexual Difference and Religion After Ontotheology," *The Religious*, ed. John Caputo (New York: Blackwell, 2003), 212–26; "Theology in Modernity's Wake," *Journal of the American Academy of Religion* 74, no. 1 (2006): 7–15; and "Beyond the God/Man Duo: Globalization, Feminist Theology, and Religious Subjectivity," in *The Oxford Handbook of Feminist Theology*, ed. Mary McClintock Fulkerson and Sheila Briggs (New York: Oxford University Press, 2011), 371–81.

4. To list only a few of the more significant titles, see, for example, William E. Connolly, *Why I am Not A Secularist* (Minneapolis: University of Minnesota Press, 2000); Talal Asad, *Formations of the Secular: Christianity, Islam, Modernity*, 1st ed. (Stanford, CA: Stanford University Press, 2003); and Charles Taylor, *A Secular Age*, 1st ed. (Cambridge, MA: Belknap Press of Harvard University Press, 2007).

5. To be clear, I am not claiming that only moderns distinguished themselves from animals, from the divine, or from one another by means of intrahuman differences. Rather, it is the specific configuration of these differends—and, in turn, the products of that differentiation—that is distinctive to modernity, as we'll see.

6. See Martin Heidegger, "Building, Dwelling, Thinking" in *Poetry, Language, Thought*, trans. Albert Hofstadter (New York: HarperCollins, 1975), 141–60.

7. For more on this, see my "'Through Flame or Ashes': Traces of Difference in Geist's Return" in *Feminist Interpretations of Martin Heidegger*, ed. Nancy J. Holland and Patricia J. Huntington (State College: Pennsylvania State University Press, 2001), 316–33.

8. The recent publication in Germany of Heidegger's "black notebooks" in which he worked out much of his philosophy has raised again questions about how to evaluate his anti-Semitism. I take up the question of animality and race in Heidegger in chapter 5 of my *Deconstruction, Feminist Theology and the Problem of Difference: Subverting the Race/Gender Divide* (Chicago: University of Chicago Press, 1999). For a much more thorough (and up-to-date) inquiry, see Matthew Calarco, *Zoographies: The Question of the Animal from Heidegger to Derrida* (New York: Columbia University Press, 2008). See also Derrida's own extemporaneous thoughts on the subject in "I Don't Know Why We Are Doing This," *The Animal That Therefore I Am*, ed. Marie-Lousie Mallet and trans. David Wills (New York: Fordham University Press, 2008), 141–60.

9. Heidegger capitalizes Being to distinguish its ontological sense from its ontic (being, in the various forms it takes). See Martin Heidegger, *Being and Time: A Translation of Sein und Zeit*, trans. Joan Stambaugh (Albany: State University of New York Press, 1999).

10. For specific references, see the chapters that follow where I engage a wide range of that work.

11. For more on the legistlation itself, see http://medicaid.gov/affordablecareact/affordable-care-act.html.

12. Indeed, for the first time in seventeen years, a Congressional standoff led to a government shutdown in the fall of 2013 that began the very day Obamacare opened for business.

13. Wade Goodwyn, "The Strange Case of Marlise Munoz [*sic*] and John Peter Smith Hospital," *NPR: Policy-ish*, January 28, 2014.

14. I will have more to say about the "iconic" dimension of photographs (often paired in scholarly studies with their "indexical" dimension). For now, though, the ordinary sense in which we speak of certain photos as iconic will suffice. These are photographs that "characterize the way an event will be remembered" (Julianne Hickerson Newton, *The Burden of Visual Truth: The Role of Photojournalism in Mediating Reality* [Mahwah, NJ: Erlbaum, 2001], 96).

15. Amy Allen, "The Anti-Subjective Hypothesis: Foucault and the Death of the Subject," *Philosophical Forum* 31, no. 2 (Summer 2000): 113–30.

16. Much ink has been spilled on Foucault's relationship to modernity and on whether he is postmodern. For a helpful assessment of some of the most important positions in this debate, see Amy Allen, *The Politics of Ourselves: Power, Autonomy, and Gender in Contemporary Critical Theory* (New York: Columbia University Press, 2008), chapter 2. See also Todd May, *The Philosophy of Foucault* (Montreal: McGill-Queen's University Press, 2006).

17. Foucault, "What Is Enlightenment?" 39.

18. I have in mind here Kant's three critiques, the first of which establishes the transcendental subject per se.

19. Foucault's relationship to Kant is a focal point of Allen's read of his position on subjectivity (and hence on modernity). See Allen, *Politics of Ourselves*, especially 23ff.

20. Foucault, "What Is Enlightenment?" 45.

21. Michel Foucault, *La volonté de savoir* (Paris: Éditions Gallimard, 1974); published in English as *The History of Sexuality, Vol. 1: An Introduction*, trans. Robert Hurley (New York: Random House, 1978). Only two other volumes of what Foucault envisioned as a multivolume work were published: *L'usage de plaisir* (Paris: Éditions Gallimard, 1984), translated by Robert Hurley as *The Uses of Pleasure* (New York: Random House, 1985); and *Le souci de soi* (Paris: Éditions Gallimard, 1984), translated by Robert Hurley as *The Care of the Self* (New York: Random House, 1986).

22. No project of Foucault's has been more avidly engaged by religionists than his interrogation into the history of sexuality. This is likely due in no small part to the signal importance of sexuality in contemporary Christianity and, in turn, of Christianity's prominent place in contemporary political life, a topic central to Chapter 3. I will engage a number of those sources in the chapters that follow. Particularly important is Mark D. Jordan's oeuvre starting with

The Invention of Sodomy in Christian Theology (Chicago: University of Chicago Press, 1998). For inquiries specifically into religion's place in Foucault's oeuvre, see Jordan's *Convulsing Bodies: Religion and Resistance in Foucault* (Stanford, CA: Stanford University Press, 2014); James William Bernauer and Jeremy Carrette, *Michel Foucault and Theology: The Politics of Religious Experience* (London: Ashgate, 2004); and Jeremy Carrette, *Foucault and Religion* (New York: Routledge, 1999), a selected anthology of Foucault's writings on religion. A number of African American theologians and ethicists have also drawn on Foucault's work to think about race and sexuality. I engage many of those works in due course.

23. Mark D. Jordan, "Foucault's Ironies and the Important Earnestness of Theory," *Foucault Studies* 14 (September 2012), 7–19.

24. "I would like to write the history of this prison, with all the political investments of the body that it gathers together in its closed architecture. Why? Simply because I am interested in the past? No, if one means by that writing a history of the past in terms of the present. Yes, if one means writing the history of the present." (Michel Foucault, *Discipline and Punish: The Birth of the Prison* [New York: Pantheon, 1978], 31); (*Surveiller et punir: Naissance de la prison* [Paris: Éditions Gallimard, 1975], 39–40).

25. The term has a long history that includes Christian asceticism, but whose roots lie in practices of self-making, if you will, in ancient Greece and Rome. But Foucault also spoke of *askesis* as a contemporary undertaking. As he puts it in the introduction to *The Uses of Pleasure*, philosophical inquiry can and should be "an 'ascesis,' *askēsis*, an exercise of oneself in the activity of thought" that seeks "to learn to what extent the effort to think one's own history can free thought from what it silently thinks, and so enable it to think differently" (*The Uses of Pleasure*, 9 [*L'usage de plaisirs*, 16–17]; quoted by LaDelle McWhorter, *Bodies and Pleasures: Foucault and the Politics of Sexual Normalization* [Bloomington: Indiana University Press, 1999], 186).

26. Edward Farley, *Theologia: The Fragmentation and Unity of Theological Education* (Philadelphia: Fortress, 1983).

27. Wendy Farley, *Gathering Those Driven Away: A Theology of Incarnation* (Louisville, KY: Westminster John Knox, 2011).

28. On this, see the second and third volumes of Foucault's *History of Sexuality*.

29. See, for example, the several anthologies published on this topic, including Kevin J. Vanhoozer, ed., *The Cambridge Companion to Postmodern Theology* (New York: Cambridge University Press, 2003). This is not necessarily a criticism: let me be clear. Postmodernity has gained considerable currency as a descriptor of our contemporary zeitgeist, so to speak; thus, it is important for theologians to respond to it. For an accessible and quite teachable introduction, see Paul Lakeland, *Postmodernity: Christian Identity in a Fragmented Age* (Minneapolis, MN: Fortress, 1997). There are, of course, a variety of theological perspectives (postliberal, process, liberationist, radical orthodoxy) that engage with postmodernity.

30. Here, I am in sympathy with Kathryn Tanner's claim (made by drawing on a postmodern notion of culture) in *Theories of Culture: A New Agenda for Theology* (Minneapolis, MN: Fortress, 1997) that Christian culture does not exist in isolation from other cultural forces; an important correction to some forms of postliberalism.

1. Man and His Others

1. Michel Foucault summarized his central goal as "to create a history of the different modes by which, in our culture, human beings are made subjects" in "Why Study Power? The Question of the Subject," *Michel Foucault: Beyond Structuralism and Hermeneutics,* ed. Hubert Dreyfus and Paul Rabinow (Chicago: University of Chicago Press, 1983), 208.

2. See Michel Foucault, *The Order of Things: An Archaeology of the Human Sciences* (New York: Vintage, 1994), 318; *Les mots et les choses* (Paris: Éditions Gallimard, 1966), 329.

3. For more on Foucault's understanding of power, see Michel Foucault, *The History of Sexuality, Vol. 1: An Introduction*, trans. Robert Hurley (New York: Random House, 1978), 94–97; *La volonté de savoir* (Paris: Éditions Gallimard, 1974), 120–29.

4. Foucault, *Order of Things*, ix.

5. Foucault, *Order of Things*, xi.

6. Foucault, *Order of Things*, xi. For this reason, *The Order of Things* was initially received as an exercise in structuralist analysis—a characterization that Foucault strongly resists in the Foreword (xxiv), among other places (e.g., Michel Foucault, *The Archaeology of Knowledge and The Discourse on Language*, trans. A. M. Sheridan Smith [New York: Pantheon, 1972], 15, 204), and rightly so.

7. I speak of a scaffolding here to try to capture some of the differences between structuralism and Foucauldian archaeology. Scaffoldings are support structures constructed for specific needs in specific contexts. They are a means to an end; once they have served their purpose, they are taken apart and their components are made available for reuse *in different configurations* for other projects. Structuralist analysis, as I understand it, at least, attempted to identify an *enduring* substratum common to all human cultures that, because it enabled cultural productions in all their diversity, could serve as an objective tool of cultural analysis in multiple times and places—one that would bypass bias and illumine genuine commonalities or differences. Although archaeologists unearth structures, they have neither the temporal or spatial permanence that structuralism sought. Moreover, Foucault stops considerably short of attributing *causal* force to them. Indeed, the Foreword makes clear that the question of causal links between the archaeological level and any given scientific project remains an open one. Archaeology is then, in my view, neither "structuralist" or "poststructuralist" (a label often applied to Foucault) but really something

else entirely. For more on this, see Hubert L. Dreyfus and Paul Rabinow, *Michel Foucault: Beyond Structuralism and Hermeneutics*, 2nd ed. (Chicago: University of Chicago Press, 1983), 52ff.

8. Foucault, *Order of Things*, 69; *Les mots et les choses*, 84.

9. Foucault, *Order of Things*, 318, translation slightly modified: "L'homme, dans l'analytique de la finitude, est un étrange doublet empirico-transcendantal, puisque c'est un être tel qu'on prendra en lui connaissance de ce qui rend possible toute connaissance" (*Les mots et les choses*, 331).

10. Foucault, *Order of Things*, 315; *Les mots et les choses*, 326.

11. Foucault, *Order of Things*, xv; *Les mots et les choses*, 7.

12. Foucault, *Order of Things*, 277; *Les mots et les choses*, 289.

13. The full title of Nietzsche's well-known genealogy is indicative: Friedrich Nietzsche, *On the Genealogy of Morals: A Polemic, By Way of Clarification and Supplement to My Last Book, Beyond Good and Evil*, trans. Douglas Smith (New York: Oxford University Press, 1996).

14. Cf. *History of Sexuality, Vol. 1*, Pt. V, "Right of Death and Power over Life" [*La volonté de savoir*, "Droit du mort et pouvoir sur la vie"], and Lecture Ten, 17 March 1976, in *"Society Must Be Defended": Lectures at the Collège de France, 1975–76*, trans. David Macey (New York: Picador, 2003) for Foucault's most prominent discussions of biopower.

15. Foucault, Lecture Ten, 17 March 1976, *"Society Must Be Defended,"* 242.

16. For a particularly helpful take on this issue, see Denise Kimber Buell, "Early Christian Universalism and Modern Forms of Racism," *The Origins of Racism in the West*, ed. Miriam Eliav-Feldon, Benjamin Isaac, and Joseph Ziegler (New York: Cambridge University Press, 2009), 109–31.

17. See, for example, Mark D. Jordan, *The Ethics of Sex* (Malden MA: Blackwell, 2002); Bernadette Brooten, *Love Between Women: Early Christian Responses to Female Homoeroticism* (Chicago: University of Chicago Press, 1996); Denise K. Buell, *Why This New Race? Ethnic Reasoning in Early Christianity* (New York: Columbia University Press, 2005); and Dale B. Martin, *The Corinthian Body* (New York: Yale University Press, 1999). For a comprehensive account of Western history that tracks the emergence of modern "race" via tracing the history of whiteness, see Nell Irvin Painter's *The History of White People* (New York: W. W. Norton, 2010). See also Grace Elizabeth Hale, *Making Whiteness: The Culture of Segregation in the South, 1890–1940* (New York: Random House, 1998).

18. Indeed, each of the scholars I referenced in the prior note are careful to mark both the differences and the continuities. Of particular note, though, is Buell's way of framing the relationship of past and present versions of race and racism. Against the claim that notions of race as fixed and hereditary distinguish modern racism, she argues for analogues (if not precise equivalents) in the ancient world, as well. More to the point, given what follows here, is the role fluidity plays *in conjunction with notions of fixity* in both modern and ancient racisms—especially Christian ones. Christian scholars and laypeople ignore that

conjunction to our ethical peril. See Buell, "Early Christian Universalism and Modern Forms of Racism."

19. See Part III.1 entitled "Docile Bodies" in Michel Foucault, *Discipline and Punish: The Birth of the Prison* (New York: Pantheon, 1978) ["Les corps dociles" in *Surveiller et punir: Naissance de la prison* (Paris: Éditions Gallimard, 1975)].

20. Foucault, *Discipline and Punish*, 136; *Surveiller et punir*, 160.

21. Foucault, Lecture Ten, 17 March 1976, "*Society Must Be Defended*," 243.

22. On the asylum, see Michel Foucault, *History of Madness*, trans. Jonathan Murphy and ed. Jean Khalfa (New York: Routledge, 2006), a much-needed full translation of *Histoire de la folie a l'age classique* (Paris: Éditions Gallimard, 1972). On the clinic, see *The Birth of the Clinic: An Archaeology of Medical Perception* (New York: Vintage, 1994), a translation of *Naissance de la clinique* (Paris: Presses Universitaires de France, 1963).

23. Nazi Germany is the epitome of this and is the primary example Foucault has in mind in "*Society Must Be Defended*."

24. In addition to the introduction, only two volumes—the first on ancient Greece, the second on ancient Rome—made it to publication: *L'usage de plaisir* (Paris: Éditions Gallimard, 1984), trans. Robert Hurley as *The Uses of Pleasure* (New York: Random House, 1985) and *Le souci de soi* (Paris: Éditions Gallimard, 1984), trans. Robert Hurley as *The Care of the Self* (New York: Random House, 1986). According to Ann Laura Stoler, the series was to include a volume on children ("The Crusade for Children," intended as the third in the series) and a concluding volume to be titled "Population and the Races" (Stoler, "A Colonial Reading of Foucault," *Carnal Knowledge and Imperial Power: Race and the Intimate under Colonial Rule*, rev. ed. [Berkeley: University of California, 2010; orig. pub. 2002], 140–61: 155, 149). According to Jeremy Carrette, the fourth volume (entitled "A Confession of the Flesh") was to have been on Christianity. It was apparently well under way when Foucault died in 1984; indeed, a manuscript resides with his estate, which will not publish it (*Religion and Culture*, 2, n. 6; for more, see "Prologue to a Confession of the Flesh"). Part III of *Religion and Culture* contains material relevant to that volume, according to Carrette.

25. This is the title, in French, of Part IV of *La volonté de savoir* ("The deployment of sexuality" in the English translation). *Dispositif*, as Foucault uses it, is notoriously difficult to translate. See Ann Laura Stoler, *Race and the Education of Desire: Foucault's* History of Sexuality *and the Colonial Order of Things* (Durham, NC: Duke University Press, 1995), 36, n. 49, for a useful summary of options employed by various commentators. I find it helpful to concentrate on the denotations associated with *disposer*—to dispose. A *dispositif*—literally, an apparatus, in French—dis-poses the objects in its grasp. It puts them in place and to use in the service of a particular functional order. Those objects can be as varied as social institutions (schools, families), human beings (as sexualized subjects), and scientific studies. In this case, all are brought together in and under an "apparatus" that manages (and produces) sexuality. Roberto Esposito notes

that the Italian philosopher Giorgio Agamben credits the genesis of the term to the Christian concept of *oikonomia* (*dispositio* in Latin). It refers both to the relations among the members of the trinity and the relationship between the second member (Christ) and humanity (Christ serves as the vehicle of divine governance of the human). The term also is applied to the human being as hierarchical union of soul and body, with the soul (ideally) governing the (animal) body. See Roberto Esposito, "The *Dispositif* of the Person," *Law, Culture and the Humanities* 8, no. 1 (2012): 17–30.

26. Foucault, *History of Sexuality, vol. 1, 56*; *La volonté de savoir*, 76.

27. My use of "personage" reflects the original French term in the now famous passage in *History of Sexuality, Vol. 1* in which Foucault describes the emergence of homosexuality as "a personage, a past, a case history [*une histoire*], and a childhood, in addition to being a type of life [*un caractère*], a life form, and a morphology, with an indiscreet anatomy and possibly a mysterious physiology" (43). The French reads "un personage: un passé, une histoire et une enfance, un caractère, une forme de vie; une morphologie aussi, avec une anatomie indiscrete et peut-être une physiologie myterieuse" (*La volonté de savoir*, 59). I follow Lynne Huffer's trenchant critique of the commonplace interpretation of this claim as marking a transition from "acts" to "identities" an interpretation rooted partially in the substitution of a comma for a colon after "a personage [*un personnage*]." See her *Mad for Foucault: Rethinking the Foundations of Queer Theory* (New York: Columbia University Press, 2010), 67–79. Huffer includes a lengthy quotation from the original text and provides her own translation (68–69). I say "characters" following Mark Jordan in his recent *Recruiting Young Love: How Christians Talk About Homosexuality* (Chicago: University of Chicago Press, 2011), xv–xvii. Both terms limn the boundaries between the body and soul, normativity and resistance, truth and fiction. They remind us simultaneously, I hope, of the constructed and fluid nature of our human taxonomies (including the late-nineteenth-century taxonomy of perversions that Foucault cites) and their targets (us) while also preserving the space between such taxonomic structures and real people that is necessary to account for our capitulation and our resistance. On this, see Judith Butler, *Gender Trouble: Feminism and the Subversion of Identity* (New York: Routledge, 1990) about which more will come.

28. On premodern Western sexualities, see Jordan, *Invention of Sodomy* and *Ethics*. On premodern colonial sexualities (a topic to which I'll return in chapter 3), see Stoler, *Race and the Education of Desire*.

29. Foucault, Lecture Ten, 17 March 1976, *"Society Must Be Defended,"* 252.

30. Kelly Brown Douglas, *Sexuality and the Black Church: A Womanist Perspective* (New York: Orbis, 1999); Cornel West, *Prophesy Deliverance! An Afro-American Christianity* (Louisville, KY: Westminster John Knox, 1982; reprinted with a new preface, 2002). Womanist ethicist Emilie Townes also draws productively on Foucault's notions of imagination and countermemory (reconfigured via Gramsci and others) to ground her inquiry into the cultural production of evil in *Womanist Ethics and the Cultural Production of Evil* (New

York: Palgrave Macmillan, 2006). More recently, Anthony B. Pinn has turned to Foucault to frame his project on (black) embodiment as theological conundrum and resource. See Anthony B. Pinn, *Embodiment and the New Shape of Black Theological Thought* (New York: New York University Press, 2010). As *Signs and Wonders* was going to press, I became aware of Alexander G. Weheliye's *Habeas Viscus: Racializing Assemblages, Biopolitics, and Black Feminist Theories of the Human* (Durham, NC: Duke University Press, 2014). Weheliye finds biopolitical discourse as practiced by Foucault, the Italian philosopher Giorgio Agamben, and their American disciples woefully inadequate to the realities of race and racism in the United States. He is particularly critical of the way this discourse displaces that of black scholars in the cult of high theory—especially black feminist scholars like Hortense Spillers and Sylvia Wynter—whom he rightly claims as true theorists in their own right. He seems unaware (not surprisingly, given the fragmentation in the humanities) of the body of work I have just cited. It would be interesting to know what Weheliye would make of it—and of *Signs and Wonders*, for that matter. My thanks to Elias Ortega-Aponté for the reference.

31. Brown Douglas, *Sexuality and the Black Church*, 13. As Huffer notes, Angela Davis has made a similar critique of *Discipline and Punish*. Foucault fails to attend sufficiently to the role gender and race play in the carceral system in general and the effects of slavery and its aftermath on which bodies the American system targets for containment. See Huffer, *Mad for Foucault*, 6.

32. J. Kameron Carter, *Race: A Theological Account* (New York: Oxford University Press, 2010). Carter uses the lectures to revisit and rework West's genealogy of modern race and racism and as a launching pad for his own. Carter makes an important argument for a (Christian and anti-Semitic) theological foundation to the modern ideology of race and racism. My project here is complementary to his in a number of ways, but different in its specific focus on how modern race and racisms—in at least some of their variety—are inculcated and incorporated. For other takes on the relationship between religious difference and modern racisms, see Gil Anidjar, *Semites: Race, Religion, Literature* (Stanford, CA: Stanford University Press, 2007) and *The Jew, The Arab: A History of the Enemy* (Stanford, CA: Stanford University Press, 2006) and David Chidester, *Savage Systems: Colonialism and Comparative Religion in Southern Africa* (Charlottesville: University of Virginia Press, 1996).

33. See Foucault, *"Society Must Be Defended"* and *Security, Territory, Population: Lectures at the Collège de France, 1976–77*, trans. Graham Burchell (New York: Picador, 2007). The French texts were edited by Mauro Bertani under the direction of François Ewald and Alessandro Fontana, and published by Éditions de Seuil/Gallimard in 1997 and 2004, respectively. For a thorough summary of the former (written before their translation into English), see John Marks, "Foucault, Franks, Gauls: *Il faut défendre la société*: The 1976 lectures at the Collège de France," *Theory, Culture and Society* 17, no. 5 (2000): 127–47. Thanks to Eduardo Mendieta for that reference.

34. Foucault, Lecture Five, 4 February 1976, "*Society Must Be Defended*," 100ff.

35. In 1775, he lists Hun and Hindustani; in 1785, "the yellow Indians . . . and the copper-colored red Americans" (cited and then quoted by LaDelle McWhorter, *Racism and Sexual Oppression in Anglo-America: A Genealogy* [Bloomington: Indiana University Press, 2009], 83). J. Kameron Carter argues that the term *race* drops out of Kant's discussion of whiteness after 1775; in coming to define the norm(al), whiteness ultimately becomes not-a-race.

36. On this point, see Carter, *Race: A Theological Account*, along with *The Idea of Race*, ed. Robert Bernasconi and Tommy Lott (Indianapolis, IN: Hackett, 2002), cited by Carter, p. 388, n. 8. Kant is if anything even more central to the account Carter offers of the (theological) genesis of modern race and racism than to McWhorter's more biopolitical account.

37. Race war discourse also appears in debates over slavery, as McWhorter demonstrates. Jefferson's belief that land could not be shared by two races—especially whites and blacks (his terminology) given their history of antagonism and exploitation—was the real motivation of his desire to end slavery and the slave trade (McWhorter, *Racism and Sexual Oppression in Anglo-America*, 94–95).

38. McWhorter, *Racism and Sexual Oppression in Anglo-America*, 100.

39. As we will see, racial taxonomies shift and change with time and place not only across but also within *epistemes*. I will not track the ins and outs of these shifts in the United States as closely as McWhorter does. For simplicity's sake, I will refer to Nordics or Nordics and their descendants—biological and ideological.

40. Indeed, Carter credits Christianity's desire to separate itself from its Jewish origins with providing the genesis of modern notions of race and practices of racism. See especially chapters 1 and 2 of *Race: A Theological Account*. For accounts of how Irish Catholics and other immigrant groups became "white," see Painter, *History of White People*.

41. See especially chapter 1, "The Drama of Race: Towards a Theological Account of Modernity," in Carter, *Race: A Theological Account*, 39–78.

42. Sander Gilman, "The Hottentot and the Prostitute: Toward an Iconography of Female Sexuality," *Difference and Pathology: Stereotypes of Sexuality, Race, and Madness* (Ithaca, NY: Cornell University Press, 1985), 76–108. Baartman was an African woman who was put on exhibit throughout much of Western Europe from 1810 to 1814. Of particular interest was Baartman's outsized (by Western standards) rump. Her "condition," so common as to be unremarkable among her native people, the San, had a Western medical diagnosis: steatopygia (Berndt Lindfors, "Ethnological Show Business: Footlighting the Dark Continent," in *Freakery: Cultural Spectacles of the Extraordinary Body*, ed. Rosemarie Garland Thomson [New York: New York University Press, 2008], 208). For much more on the science of race and its effects on the delineation, expansion, and consolidation of the white race, see Painter, *History of White People*.

43. Painter provides a particularly powerful example in the case of Deborah Kallikak (a name made up by Henry Goddard, who ran the institution where Miss Kallikak was confined). Using the Stanford–Binet intelligence test, Goddard

determined she was a "moron," a trait he claimed reflected a long line of degeneracy of various forms (manifested as prostitution, criminality, and ill health) in the branch of this family from which she was descended (Painter, *History of White People*, 271–73). Both Painter and McWhorter relate the story of the first forced sterilization in the United States (of a young white woman named Carrie Buck). Her case was the subject of a court challenge engineered by advocates for her sterilization to allow it to establish a precedent—which it did. McWhorter notes that, in its wake, tens of thousands were sterilized all over the country. Eventually the practice was applied to black Americans as well, including the legendary civil rights organizer Fannie Lou Hamer (McWhorter, *Racism and Sexual Oppression in Anglo-America*, 213–15).

44. Stoler's initial encounter with the lectures was through the scratchy audiotapes at Saulchoir Library in Paris and subsequently in Italian transcription/translation (Stoler, *Race and the Education of Desire*, 56–57).

45. Stoler, *Carnal Knowledge*, 97; *Race and the Education of Desire*, 15. My focus here will be on the fourfold, but Stoler lists other features of modernity that other scholars have found to have colonial roots, including the panopticon. See Stoler, *Carnal Knowledge and Imperial Power*, 146.

46. Stoler, *Carnal Knowledge*, 152ff.

47. Stoler, *Race and the Education of Desire*, 199.

48. Stoler, *Race and the Education of Desire*, 105, n. 5. As I did with McWhorter, I will follow Stoler's terminology for these identities: colonizer versus colonized, European versus native, Dutch versus Javanese.

49. The affective dimensions of the colonial order varied with one's place in that order. Mixed race children and their parents paid a particularly high price here. See especially Stoler's account of a Frenchman's attempt to redeem his *métis* son from a prison sentence for assaulting a German man and her chapter on the *métissage* in *Carnal Knowledge*. Contemporary ethnographic research that Stoler and her colleagues conducted with Javanese who were domestic servants in colonial households is another case in point. Europeans raised in Dutch colonial households recall their relations with their Javanese *babus* (nursemaids), especially, with deep—and, as they recall it, mutual—affection. But the recollections of the former domestics with whom Stoler and colleagues spoke offer no evidence of that reciprocity. In part, this may reflect the traditional Javanese prohibition on discussing emotion. That some former slave caregivers in the United States interviewed by the Works Progress Administration spoke with some affection of their former charges might bear that out (on this see Emilie Townes, *Womanist Ethics and the Cultural Production of Evil* [New York: Palgrave Macmillan, 2006], 33). But the asymmetrical and exploitive conditions of their employment in these capacities doubtless tempered whatever affection either might have felt.

50. Whatever ties of affection might come to bind a Dutch colonial man to his Javanese concubine, the relationship was exploitive in design and outcome. Colonial men incurred no obligation—legal or financial—to these women or to

any children their union produced. In those times and places where the colonial state allowed such children a claim on citizenship (or its equivalent), that claim required the father's imprimatur.

51. Stoler, *Carnal Knowledge*, 48. Marriage between colonials and colonized was also legalized during this time. This change in marital policy did not reflect the supplanting of nonegalitarian views of the Javanese with egalitarian—quite the contrary. The native wives of colonials were granted European status, but not the husbands of colonial women. This reflected the view that, in desiring colonized men in the first place, colonial women had already "gone native" and fallen victim to degeneracy, marking them as not truly European in the first place.

52. Stoler, *Carnal Knowledge*, 6.

53. Stoler notes that cultural practices predominated over medical ones in the policing and protecting of Europeanness in the colonies. Sterilization and institutionalization were less common than in metropolitan contexts, in other words.

54. Edward W. Said, *Orientalism* (New York: Pantheon, 1979), 42; quoted by Stoler, *Carnal Knowledge*, 65. One can see in the persistence of concerns about climate, geography, and mere proximity to natives the residue of the Classical origins of modern race and racisms; an important reminder of how epistemic change works as well as of race's malleability and flexibility.

55. Note, for example, the proliferation of identities that congeal in different ways around sex, sexuality, and gender reflected in the now ubiquitous acronym LGBTQI. Note as well the increasing inadequacy of our racial and ethnic categories as families become increasingly interracial.

56. This was true in the Dutch Indies, as well, according to Stoler, as is evident particularly in the treatment of *métis* children born of indigenous mothers and European fathers. Authorities thought nothing of removing them from the care of their native mothers. To be in her care was already a form of abandonment—to unmitigated nativism. Not only was she thought unwilling (and more to the point unable) to nurture whatever proto-Europeanness might be flowing through these children's veins (along with native blood), that there might be any genuine maternal ties binding native mother and *métis* child never seemed to cross the minds of colonial authorities.

57. I can only note in passing once again the ever-growing body of scholarship that is calling into question standard narratives of secularization as marking modernity and of any strong line demarcating the secular from the religious. For some of my own thoughts on this question, see my "Beyond Belief: Sexual Difference and Religion After Ontotheology," in *The Religious*, ed. John Caputo (New York: Blackwell, 2003), 212–26; "Theology in Modernity's Wake," *Journal of the American Academy of Religion* 74, no. 1 (2006): 7–15; and "Beyond the God/Man Duo: Globalization, Feminist Theology, and Religious Subjectivity," in *The Oxford Handbook of Feminist Theology*, ed. Mary McClintock Fulkerson and Sheila Briggs (New York: Oxford University Press, 2011), 371–81.

58. See, for example, Talal Asad, *Genealogies of Religion: Discipline and Reasons of Power in Christianity and Islam* (Baltimore, MD: Johns Hopkins University

Press, 1993); and Tomoko Masuzawa, *The Invention of World Religions: Or, How European Universalism Was Preserved in the Language of Pluralism* (Chicago: University of Chicago Press, 2005).

59. For a theological account of the role of "religion" (as a category) and religious differences (especially those between Christianity and Judaism) in modernity's generation, see (once again) Carter, *Race: A Theological Account.* Buell, "Early Christian Universalism and Modern Forms of Racism," suggests yet earlier antecedents of the confluence of Christianity, Judaism, and racism in ancient notions of peoplehood.

60. Stoler, *Carnal Knowledge*, 101.

61. Late in colonial regimes, being Christian also allowed certain natives and *métis* children access to quasi-European status.

62. Stoler, *Carnal Knowledge*, 126. Recall, however, that who counts as "European" is very much in question during this time; a fact borne out by two photographs of classes that accompany this insight in Stoler, *Carnal Knowledge*, 125–26. The captions both mark the students as "European," but where one features only "white" students, the other features a mix of complexions.

63. Stoler, *Carnal Knowledge*, 254, n. 156. Painter documents the role of Christian ministers and laypeople in the policing of degeneracy in the United States among Anglo-Saxons in chapter 18 of *The History of White People.*

64. I adopt this terminology in part for expediency (to avoid repeating biopower and disciplinary power over and over), but only for this context. I include the hyphen to remind us always that they are two different forms of power united in pursuit of certain ends at certain times and in certain places. I am not claiming that biopower and disciplinary power always and everywhere intertwine.

2. Photography and/as Bio-Discipline

1. In the closing chapter of *The Disciplinary Frame: Photographic Truths and the Capture of Meaning* (Minneapolis: University of Minnesota Press, 2009), John Tagg argues that frames are liminal spaces that purport to separate "art" from ordinary objects. As such, they seem to withdraw from the scene. And yet, as he shows (drawing on Jacques Derrida's discussion of frame as *parergon* in *The Truth in Painting*, trans. Geoffrey Bennington and Ian McLeod [Chicago: University of Chicago Press, 1987]), the frame is a kind of Foucauldian *dispositif* whose disciplinary function is part and parcel of the scene it helps to organize (in this case, "art"). My use of frame here and in what follows carries this same sense. The frames I speak of are part and parcel of bio-disciplinary power and its exercise.

2. I am not, moreover, the only theologian to engage with scholarship on photography. In two recently published essays (based on her Harvard dissertation), Sarah Sentilles attends to the place of theological discourse and rhetoric in the work of Roland Barthes and Susan Sontag, thinkers whose work figures

herein, as well. See her "The Photograph as Mystery: Theological Language and Ethical Looking," *Journal of Religion* 90, no. 4 (October 2010): 507–29; and "Misreading Feuerbach: Susan Sontag, Photography and the Image World," *Literature and Theology* 24, no. 1 (2010): 38–55. Sentilles confines herself, for the most part, to excavating that discourse and accounting for its relevance. The project I undertake here is considerably more ambitious (and perhaps foolishly so), as will become clear. At the close of her essay on Barthes, Sentilles observes that theology's attunements to mystery and to ethical concerns position it to make a productive contribution to visual culture theory. I share this view; indeed, this project is one attempt to make good on it.

3. Henri Bergson, *Matter and Memory,* trans. Nancy Margaret Paul and W. Scott Palmer (New York: Zone, 1991), originally published in French as *Matière et Mémoire* (Paris: Presses Universitaires de France, n.d.); Maurice Merleau-Ponty, *Phenomenology of Perception*, trans. Donald Landes (New York: Routledge, 2012), originally published in French as *Phénoménologie de la perception* (Paris: Éditions Gallimard, 1945); Gilles Deleuze, *Cinema 1: The Movement-Image*, trans. Hugh Tomlinson and Barbara Habberjam (New York: Athlone, 1986) and *Cinema 2: The Time-Image*, trans. Hugh Tomlinson and Robert Galeta (New York: Athlone, 1989), originally published as *Cinéma 1: L'Image-mouvement* (Paris: Les Éditions de Minuit, 1983) and *Cinéma 2: L'Image-temps* (Paris: Les Éditions de Minuit, 1985); and Derrida, *The Truth in Painting* and *Athens, Still Remains: The Photographs of Jean-François Bonhomme*, trans. Pascale-Anne Brault and Michael Naas (New York: New York University Press, 2010). For an interesting take on the "anti-ocularcentrism" of twentieth-century French thought, see Martin Jay, *Downcast Eyes: The Denigration of Vision in the Twentieth Century* (Berkeley: University of California Press, 1993), about which more later.

4. For a sampling of this important figure's thought, see Jean-Luc Marion, *The Visible and the Revealed*, trans. Christina M. Gschwandtner et al. (New York: Fordham University Press, 2008). The English translation adds two essays to the volume originally published in French as *Le visible et le révélé* (Paris: Les Éditions du Cerf, 2005).

5. Cf. W. J. T. Mitchell, *Iconology: Image, Text, and Ideology* (Chicago: University of Chicago Press, 1987); *Picture Theory: Essays on Verbal and Visual Representation* (Chicago: University of Chicago Press, 1995); and *What Do Pictures Want? The Lives and Loves of Images* (Chicago: University of Chicago Press, 2005).

6. Guy Debord, *Society of the Spectacle*, trans. Ken Knabb (London: Rebel, 2006). A longer version of the Feuerbach quotation serves as epigraph for DeBord, as well (6).

7. Jean Baudrillard, *Simulacra and Simulation*, trans. Sheila Faria Glaser (Ann Arbor: University of Michigan Press, 1994); originally published in France as *Simulacres et simulation* (Paris: Éditions Galilée, 1981). See also the first epigraph for this chapter, in which Susan Sontag quotes Ludwig Feuerbach, *The*

Essence of Christianity (1843), a text written two years after the invention of the camera (Susan Sontag, *On Photography*, 1st ed. [New York: Picador, 2001], 153).

8. Roland Barthes, "Rhetoric of the Image," *Image-Music-Text*, trans. Stephen Heath (New York: Farrar Strauss and Giroux, 1977), 38.

9. Michel Foucault, *Discipline and Punish: The Birth of the Prison* (New York: Pantheon, 1978), 217; *Surveiller et punir: Naissance de la prison* (Paris: Éditions Gallimard, 1975), 252.

10. See in particular Jacques Rancière, *The Future of the Image* (New York: Verso, 2009 [reprint]) and Mitchell's *What Do Pictures Want?* Rancière offers a potent critique of (post)modernism as an epochal marker in standard narratives of art history. His primary concern is to rethink the relationship between art and politics in more productive ways than those narratives allow. For more on Rancière, see the editor's introduction to Jacques Rancière and Stephen Corcoran, *Dissensus: On Politics and Aesthetics* (New York: Continuum, 2010), a collection of previously published essays. See also Joseph J. Tanke, "What Is the Aesthetic Regime?" *Parrhesia* 12 (November 2011): 71–81.

11. See "Vital Signs: Cloning Terror," chapter 1 in *What Do Pictures Want?* 5–27. See also W. J. T. Mitchell, *Cloning Terror: The War of Images, 9/11 to the Present* (Chicago: University of Chicago Press, 2011), which will figure prominently in chapter 4. According to Mitchell, the collection of snapshots taken by American soldiers of their mistreatment of the prisoners in their charge is part and parcel of this war of images. He connects this war to cloning in a number of suggestive ways.

12. My "that-there-then" riffs off of Roland Barthes's "that-has-been" (*ça-a-été*) in *Camera Lucida: Reflections on Photography* (New York: Hill and Wang, 1981). Barthes is emphasizing the photograph's relationship to the past (a central theme of the book). In addition to temporality, my phrasing highlights the materiality and spatiality of the photograph's relationship to its object.

13. I am borrowing—and, in a sense, repurposing—this term from Jay, *Downcast Eyes*, 9ff.

14. Jonathan Crary, *Techniques of the Observer: On Vision and Modernity in the Nineteenth Century* (Cambridge: Massachusetts Institute of Technology Press, 1990). A word here about the status of this visual subject: In *Picture Theory*, W. J. T. Mitchell criticizes Crary for simultaneously claiming too little and too much for the status of the observer. Too much insofar as Crary posits the observer as the linchpin in a sea change in modernity's scopic regime that encompasses all forms of what we now call visual culture (art, cinema, as well as photography). Too little insofar as Crary acknowledges a gap between this figure and any actual spectator—and thus bypasses questions of race, ethnicity, and class. Mitchell sees in Crary's argument a capitulation to the temptation of metanarrative, if you will, to which Crary falls victim despite his best intentions. I lack the expertise to engage Mitchell's critique in full, but I do think it important to situate my reading of Crary in relationship to it. I read *Techniques of the Observer* as an extension of my reading of Foucault in the previous

chapter. Crary's "observer" is to the visual order what Foucault's "man" is to the order of things; it is a *dispositif*, a discursive position produced by and thus embedded in the specific epistemic change I've been tracking. Given the claims I am making about the relationship between the visual order and the epistemic order, the observer is, like Man, inseparable from the other elements of the fourfold. As will become clear from what follows, the observer's emergence is deeply bound up with these orders' attempts to regulate race, class, and gender. That there are other forms of visual subjectivity—either emergent or leftover from the previous scopic regime—that coexist with the observer would not be surprising given the account of epistemic change I offered previously. That said, as a discursive position, it constitutes one of the framing elements available for (and likely involved in) the constitution of any particular seeing subject. It will, in turn, be inflected by other framing elements (like race, gender, and class).

15. Jay, *Downcast Eyes*, 404.

16. Jay, *Downcast Eyes*, 404.

17. Jay, *Downcast Eyes*, 404.

18. In his more recent book, *Suspensions of Perception* (Cambridge: Massachusetts Institute of Technology Press, 1999), Crary turns his attention to a genealogical account, of sorts, of attention as a central feature of modern subjectivity. Here, he argues that the changes in scopic regime that *Techniques* documents are part of a larger multisensory shift. It's a compelling argument, but one that goes beyond the scope of my interests here. I do want to note, however, that to the degree that *Signs and Wonders* takes its mark from the visual, it may seem to participate in visual culture studies' tendency to focus on the visual to the exclusion of the other senses and sometimes to the exclusion of embodiment per se; a tendency that Crary criticizes. I trust the reader will see, as the argument unfolds, places and ways in which *Signs and Wonders* breaks with this tendency.

19. Jay, *Downcast Eyes*, 5.

20. Jay, *Downcast Eyes*, 5.

21. John Berger, *Ways of Seeing* (London: Penguin, 1972), 16; quoted by Jay, *Downcast Eyes*, 54.

22. Jay, *Downcast Eyes*, 39.

23. One can see the effects of this shift in philosophical thought in this period. According to Crary, Goethe and Schopenhauer were both influenced by the physiological study of vision. For both, the fact that we "see" with our eyes closed cuts the cord of referentiality but in a different way than in Kant's transcendental schema. As readers of Kant's first critique know well, the transcendental space–time schema makes knowledge possible. The labor of synthesis, however, is primarily mental–intellectual (speculative, to use Kant's language), not physiological. For Schopenhauer, the transcendental schema is replaced, as it were, by the new physiology of sight. "What is representation? A very complicated physiological occurrence in an animal's brain, whose result is the consciousness of a picture or image at that very spot" (Schopenhauer, *The World as Will and Representation*, Vol. 2, 191; quoted by Crary, *Techniques*, 77).

24. See Crary, *Techniques,* 88.

25. Stereoscopy is the forerunner of three-dimensional technology. See William Welling, *Photography in America: The Formative Years, 1839–1900 – A Documentary History* (New York: Crowell, 1978), 23. My thanks to Brandy Daniels for this insight and this source.

26. For a fine (and accessible) survey of the history of photography, see Graham Clarke, *The Photograph* (New York: Oxford University Press, 1997). His account of its early history and its early reception informs much of what follows.

27. Walter Benjamin, "The Work of Art in the Age of Mechanical Reproduction" (1936) in Walter Benjamin, *Illuminations: Essays and Reflections,* ed. Hannah Arendt, trans. Harry Zohn, first Schocken paperback ed. (New York: Schocken, 1969). Art had inherited the aura from religious relics, Benjamin claimed. Benjamin worried—and rightly so—that photography's reproducibility coupled with its connection—however fraught—to reality made it an especially effective propaganda tool, as well.

28. As Alan Trachtenberg's account of the initial reception of daguerreotypes in the United States demonstrates, verisimilitude was not necessarily the ideal, especially for photographic portraiture. Photography's ability to capture an idealized essence of the person was very much in question early on—in a double sense. On the one hand, its technology and its look were redolent of magic; thus, it had about it an air of the uncanny. Its dependence on light and chemical changes also limited its ability to conform to artistic insight into the photographed subject. Thus, much thought and skill went into figuring out how to work the technology to achieve the desired effect of idealization. See "Prologue" to Trachtenberg's *Reading American Photographs: Images as History, Matthew Brady to Walker Evans* (New York: Hill and Wang, 1989).

29. Obviously, hindsight reveals that the announcements of painting's death were premature —as was the consignment of photography to the lowbrow. Art photography eventually came into its own—as the object of curatorial care, art historical scholarship, and market commodification. Indeed, from the beginning, the relationship between photography and painting has been more symbiotic than oppositional. As Abigail Solomon-Godeau (among others) has argued, photography proved to be influential on modernist (and postmodernist) painting and sculpture—and vice versa. The distinction between art photography and nonart, she argues, rests on a Cartesian bifurcation between the "technological body and aesthetic soul" (*Photography at the Dock: Essays on Photographic History, Institutions, and Practices* [Minneapolis: University of Minnesota Press, 1991], xii).

30. It is in part the play between image and reality that prompts a turn to theological rhetoric by Barthes, John Berger, and Susan Sontag to account for photographic meaning making (and its limits), Sarah Sentilles argues. Rancière dismisses Barthes's seeming literalism as remythologization that, intentionally or not, compensates for his stripping of photographs of their claim to (mere) literal referentiality in *Mythologies* (Rancière, *Future of the Image,* 10).

31. Solomon-Godeau, "Who Is Speaking Thus? Some Questions About Documentary Photography," in *Photography at the Dock*, 180–81. See also Jacques Lacan's take on photography and/as subject formation in *The Four Fundamental Concepts of Psycho-Analysis*, ed. Jacques-Alain Miller, trans. Alan Sheridan (Harmondsworth, England: Penguin, 1979). For a potent summary put to work, see John Tagg, "The Plane of Decent Seeing: Documentary and the Rhetoric of Recruitment," in *Disciplinary Frame*, 75ff.

32. One thinks, for example, of the complex chain of provenance of many family photographs from garage and estate sales to antique malls.

33. Solomon-Godeau, "Introduction," *Photography at the Dock*, xvii.

34. Tagg, *Disciplinary Frame*, 15. For this reason, Tagg speaks in this book of photographies rather than photography. His point is well taken, as we'll see. Cumulatively, however, these local and relatively discrete deployments have, I think, yielded photography as a more global scopic and discursive regime. What follows will attend both to the (very) local and the more global.

35. Solomon-Godeau, "Introduction," *Photography at the Dock*, xxviii.

36. Solomon-Godeau, "Introduction," *Photography at the Dock*, xxviii.

37. The term, extended (appropriately) to photography, originates in Roland Barthes's account of literary realism as the cumulative effect of various rhetorical strategies. See Barthes's "The Reality Effect" in Roland Barthes, *The Rustle of Language*, trans. Richard Howard (University of California Press, 1989), 141–48.

38. On this, see, for example, Clarke, *The Photograph*.

39. George Eastman invented the Kodak camera and the roll of film in the 1880s. That technology, however, was rather expensive at that time ($25). His later invention, the Brownie, sold for only $1. Amy Louise Wood, *Lynching and Spectacle: Witnessing Racial Violence in America, 1890–1940* (Chapel Hill: University of North Carolina Press, 2009), 284, n. 10.

40. Clarke, *The Photograph*, 45.

41. Robert Sobeieszek, "Historical Commentary," *French Primitive Photography* (New York: Aperture, 1970), 5; cited by Jay, 141. This is the catalog for the exhibition by the same title held November 17–December 28, 1969, at the Alfred Stieglitz Center.

42. Solomon-Godeau, "A Photographer in Jerusalem, 1855: August Salzman and His Times," *Photography at the Dock*, 150–68.

43. Solomon-Godeau, "A Photographer in Jerusalem," *Photography at the Dock*, 155.

44. Solomon-Godeau, "A Photographer in Jerusalem," *Photography at the Dock*, 155, emphasis mine.

45. Solomon-Godeau, "A Photographer in Jerusalem," *Photography at the Dock*, 159.

46. John Tagg, *Burden of Representation: Essays on Photographies and Histories*, 1st ed. (Minneapolis: University of Minnesota Press, 1993), 4–5.

47. Tagg, *Burden of Representation*, 99.

48. Tagg essentially adds the art museum and the discipline of art history (along with other scholarly approaches to "culture") in the closing chapter of *Disciplinary Frame*.

49. Other techniques run the gamut from the codification of strategies for observing individuals to the new science of statistical analysis. Other technologies range from the monumental to the mundane; new forms of architecture to the vertical file cabinet. On this, see Tagg, "The One-Eyed Man and the One-Armed Man: Camera Culture and the State" in *Disciplinary Frame,* especially 20–21.

50. Tagg, *Burden of Representation,* 76.

51. Tagg, *Burden of Representation,* 64.

52. Photographs took their place alongside anatomical drawings and charts in many studies of sexual aberration. The extensive studies Alice Dreger and Anne Fausto-Sterling offer of the role of sexually ambiguous bodies in "the invention of sex," to follow Dreger's title, both note this (and include examples). Cf. Dreger's *Hermaphrodites and the Medical Invention of Sex* (Cambridge, MA: Harvard University Press, 1998). Fausto Sterling wrote that many intersexed people report being photographed by medical personnel during examinations. She includes just one photograph, of an XX infant with "masculinized" genitalia (Anne Fausto-Sterling, *Sexing the Body: Gender Politics and the Construction of Sexuality* [New York: Basic, 2000], 47, fig. 3.1).

53. Jennifer Terry, *An American Obsession: Science, Medicine, and Homosexuality in Modern Society,* 1st ed. (Chicago: University of Chicago Press, 1999).

54. Terry, *An American Obsession,* 178.

55. The committee included the City Corrections Commissioner for New York and a Harvard anthropologist with particular expertise in "'race mixture' and the physique types of criminals" (178). Terry gives the full list of committee members (185). For more on liberal protestants' support of the nascent gay rights movement in the first half of the twentieth century, see Heather White, *Reforming Sodom: Protestants and the Rise of Gay Rights* (Chapel Hill: University of North Carolina Press, 2015).

56. Terry, *An American Obsession,* 221.

57. Five photos deviate from these conventions. One features a male subject posed exactly like the others, but wearing women's underwear (Terry, *An American Obsession*, fig. 5, 203). The other four photos feature a different (male) subject (figs. 6–8, 203). The first of those presents him nude facing forward. In the second, he is fully dressed in a wig and a flowing gown seated sideways and seductively folded into himself. The other two photographs document for the viewer that the first and second photographs are of the same person. In the third, he holds up the gown to reveal first his genital area; in the fourth, his buttocks. Terry notes that these photos indicate the degree to which sexual variance was conceived of in terms of gender deviance.

58. Terry, *An American Obsession,* 196.

59. Terry, *An American Obsession,* 217.

60. Terry, *An American Obsession,* 217.

61. Terry, *An American Obsession,* 217.

62. Ann Laura Stoler, *Carnal Knowledge and Imperial Power: Race and the Intimate Under Colonial Rule* (Berkeley: University of California Press, 2010), fig. 2, 3.

63. Stoler, *Carnal Knowledge and Imperial Power,* fig. 1, 3.

64. That same interplay between rightful domination and (in)subordination registers in the photographs of colonial children or infants alone with servant caretakers (typically the *babu,* in these photographs). See, for example, Stoler, *Carnal Knowledge and Imperial Power,* figs. 25 and 26, 172. Whatever threat native caretakers posed to their charges is arguably (though perhaps barely) contained by the watchful eye of the photographer.

65. Rosemarie Garland Thomson, *Extraordinary Bodies* (New York: Columbia University Press, 1997), especially chapter 3.

66. Garland Thomson, *Extraordinary Bodies,* 63.

67. Cf. Garland Thomson's recent *Staring: How We Look* (New York: Oxford University Press, 2009), which is an analysis of the specific kind of "gaze," if you will, that we "normates" (her neologism for able-bodied people) tend to impose upon people with (visible) disabilities.

68. Garland Thomson, *Extraordinary Bodies,* 59.

69. For more on the freak show, see Rosemary Garland Thomson, ed., *Freakery: Cultural Spectacles of the Extraordinary Body* (New York: New York University Press, 1996).

70. Both Ida B. Wells-Barnett (best known as an antilynching activist) and Frederic B. Douglass expressed strong objections both to freak shows and freak photography, according to Deborah Willis and Carla Williams, *The Black Female Body: A Photographic History* (Philadelphia: Temple University Press, 2002), 74–76; cited by womanist theologian Shawn M. Copeland, *Enfleshing Freedom: Body, Race and Being* (Minneapolis, MN: Fortress, 2010), 140, n. 25.

71. Garland Thomson, *Extraordinary Bodies,* 58. She takes the term from David Hevey, "The Enfreakment of Photography," in *The Disability Studies Reader,* 3rd edition, ed. Lennard J. Davis (New York: Routledge, 2010), 332–47.

72. See Garland Thomson, *Extraordinary Bodies,* 158, n. 39.

73. Garland Thomson, *Extraordinary Bodies,* 73–74.

74. The theo-logic of enfreakment (or monstrosity, to use one of its antecedents) goes back as far as Augustine, according to theologian Sharon Betcher. See *Spirit and the Politics of Disablement* (Minneapolis, MN: Fortress, 2007), 53–54.

75. Copeland, *Enfleshing Freedom,* 140, n. 26. As Copeland and Garland Thomson both report, Stephen Jay Gould encountered three jars of Baartman's remains in 1982 (Garland Thomson, *Extraordinary Bodies,* 158, n. 52). For more on Baartman, see Rachel Holmes, *African Queen: The Real Life of the Hottentot Venus* (New York: Random House, 2007), cited by Copeland.

76. Garland Thomson cites the 1993 volume of the *American Journal of American Genetics* as her source for this information (*Extraordinary Bodies,* 56). I have more to say about Garland Thomson's work in chapter 5.

77. Tagg, *Burden of Representation,* 92.

78. See the website for *Freeze Frame: Eadweard Muybridge's Photography of Motion,* an exhibition of the Smithsonian Institute's National Museum of American

History (October 7, 2000–March 15, 2001), curated by Michelle Delaney, Marta Braun, and Elspeth Brown. http://americanhistory.si.edu/muybridge.

79. This accomplishment—the breaking down of fluid motion into its parts—is no mean photographic feat, especially given the technology available to Muybridge. This was not a matter of pointing and shooting with a motion picture camera; such a device had yet to be invented. Rather, Muybridge constructed an assemblage of multiple still cameras carefully placed and precisely timed to shoot a sequence of photographs of the body-in-motion. As Shawn Michelle Smith argues, however, reading these photographs as bodies-*in-motion* depends as much on what lies just outside the frame (e.g., the spaces between) as on what's inside it. That includes what viewers bring to the experience of viewing, including assumptions about sequentiality. Shawn Michelle Smith, "The Space Between: Eadweard Muybridge's Motion Studies," *At the Edge of Sight: Photography and the Unseen* (Durham, NC: Duke University Press, 2013), 75–98. Recent research has revealed that Muybridge's photographs as published and as initially exhibited were selectively cut out of the longer sequence and even cropped. Thus, although they purported to be mere records of an all-but-instantaneous that-there-then, they were not (*Freeze Frame*, http://americanhistory.si.edu/muybridge).

80. Eadweard Muybridge, *Animal Locomotion: An Electrophotographic Investigation of Consecutive Phases of Animal Movements* (Philadelphia: University of Pennsylvania, 1887). All of the plates were subsequently reproduced in *Muybridge's Complete Human and Animal Locomotion* (Mineola, NY: Dover, 1979). Muybridge's photo series was likely the model for Marcel Duchamp's famous (and initially controversial) painting, "Nude Descending a Staircase (No. 2)," a case in point of the influence of photography on modern art. See Ann Temkin, Susan Rosenberg, and Michael Taylor, with Rachel Arauz, *Twentieth Century Painting and Sculpture in the Philadelphia Museum of Art* (Philadelphia: Philadelphia Museum of Art, 2001), 27. The raced, sexualized, and gendered dynamics of these photographs and their reception as analyzed by Smith in "The Space Between" embody the dynamics I am delineating in this chapter.

81. Or not. Solomon-Godeau notes that workers who couldn't conform to the bodily practices mandated by time and motion studies were fired ("Introduction," *Photography at the Dock*, xxiii).

82. See Martin Heidegger, *Being and Time: A Translation of Sein und Zeit*, trans. Joan Stambaugh (Albany: State University of New York Press, 2010), 141ff.

83. Cf. translator's note at the beginning of Barthes's *Image-Music-Text*, trans. by Stephen Heath (New York: Hill and Wang, 1977), 10.

84. This vocabulary (indexicality and iconicity) is itself evidence of the consolidation of photographies into photography as a discursive regime, one produced and used largely by scholars, especially art historians, I gather. This chapter will show that indexicality and iconicity are caught up in and by bio-disciplinary power. Thus, what follows aligns well with Tagg's claim that art history is itself a disciplinary frame.

85. Benjamin's take on mechanical reproduction is best described, I think, as ambivalent rather than negative. Aura's loss was not necessarily something to be mourned, but something to be observed and noted. With that loss comes widened access to the means of (re)production, which also potentially democratized it (the very capacity that the Nazis exploited with particular success, ironically). Moreover, photographic technologies opened up new ways of looking and seeing. In that sense, close-up and slow motion photography did for vision what psychoanalysis did for self-understanding; it offered new insight. Caroline Duttlinger tracks aura's relationship to photography across Benjamin's larger corpus and argues much more substantively than I can here for a more complex relationship between the two. See her "Imaginary Encounters: Walter Benjamin and the Aura of Photography," *Poetics Today* 29, no. 1 (2008), 79–101.

86. The photographs were recently the centerpiece of an exhibit at the Seaport Museum in New York City curated by Bonnie Yochelson. Cf. her *Alfred Stieglitz' New York* (New York: Skira Rizzoli, 2010). As Solomon-Godeau notes, photography's entrance into the canon of high art also coincided with the beginning of the decline of high modernism and the ultimate emergence of postmodernist artistic practices characterized by an ironic stance toward originality, among other things. See, for example, "Photography After Art Photography" and "Living with Contradictions" in *Photography at the Dock,* 103–23 and 124–48.

87. What goes around comes around, as they say. Prominent contemporary art photographers like Cindy Sherman and Sherrie Levine ironically (and powerfully) riff on documentary conventions in their work. Sherman (the subject of a 2012 retrospective at the Museum of Modern Art) is perhaps best known for her series *Film Stills* in which she "stars" in scenes she has created that mimic perfectly the generic conventions of the movie still—and, in doing so, plays with photography's "reality effect" and the canons of photographic (self-)portraiture (though unrecognizable as herself, Sherman-in-costume is the subject of each of the photographs). Levine works in a number of mediums, but her best-known photographic work is her series "After Walker Evans," which consists of art-quality photographs of some of documentary photographer Walker Evans's most famous photographs. Sherman and Levine were both included in the Metropolitan Museum of Art's 2009 exhibition, *The Pictures Generation, 1974–1984.*

88. The fortieth anniversary of the taking of this photo (June 8, 2012) occurred during the writing of these pages. See "Iconic Vietnam War 'napalm girl' photograph turns 40," (Associated Press, *Chicago Sun-Times,* June 4, 2012). I say more about this later in the chapter.

89. Robert Hariman and John Louis Lucaites, *No Caption Needed: Iconic Photographs, Public Culture and Liberal Democracy* (Chicago: University of Chicago Press, 2007).

90. Susan Sontag, *Regarding the Pain of Others* (New York: Picador, 2003), 26. These very conventions depend on certain developments in photographic technology that make the taking of pictures under duress possible (e.g., the lightweight portable camera, fast speed film) as Clarke notes (*The Photograph*, 159). War photography as we know it came into its own with Vietnam, Sontag argues. Only with that war do we get war photographs utterly free of (the suspicion of) staging—and that is crucial to the moral weight they carry (57). But that very realism also complicates the political effects of war photography from Vietnam. Seeing on television and in their daily papers the grit and pain of war in its everydayness likely made it harder for Americans to sustain belief in the nobility of the cause, according to Hariman and Lucaites, *No Caption Needed* (cf. especially 177). Clarke sees a shift in war photography, too, toward depicting "a sense of underlying meaninglessness. . . . There seems, in that sense, little left to photograph, even though there is everything to record" (*The Photograph*, 161). It is perhaps no wonder, then, that the Bush administration established much firmer control over the presence of photojournalists in the wars in Iraq and Afghanistan by "embedding" them with the military and by forbidding photographs of the coffined American war dead. (As Clarke notes, censorship of war photography has been standard practice since the Civil War.)

91. The conditions of selection I describe earlier in this chapter also apply to these photographs. Lange reportedly shot several images of this family that day and selected this one (likely in conversation with an editor) for publication in the San Francisco paper. Ut along with other photojournalists present shot other photos of the attack, although by his account, he stopped shooting to address Phuc's cries of pain. (That day was the beginning of a long relationship between the two of them that, despite a number of twists and turns along the way, persists to the present. See Tiffany Hagler-Geard, "The Historic 'Napalm Girl' Pulitzer Image Marks Its 40th Anniversary," *Picture This: ABC News*, June 8, 2012.) As Hariman and Lucaites report, the editorial decision to run this photo was quite deliberate, given the general prohibition against full frontal nudity in photojournalism (cf. Hariman and Lucaites, *No Caption Needed*, 173–76). The ABC News website includes other photographs taken of that event, but none carry the affective punch of "Accidental Napalm."

92. Key figures include Brian Massumi (see, for instance, "The Autonomy of Affect," in *Cultural Critique* 31 [1995], 83–109), whose take on affect is influenced by Deleuze and Guattari. Cf. Gilles Deleuze and Felix Guattari, "Precept, Affect, and Concept," *What Is Philosophy?*, trans. Hugh Tomlinson and Graham Burchell (New York: Columbia University Press, 1994), 163ff. Other important contributors include Eve Kosofsky Sedgwick, Teresa Brennan, Lauren Berlant, and Sarah Ahmed. For a sample, see Melissa Gregg and Gregory Seigworth, eds., *The Affect Theory Reader* (Durham, NC: Duke University Press, 2010). For a particularly important contribution to the study of religion and film that is informed by affect theory, see Gail M. Hamner, *Imaging Religion in Film: The Politics of Nostalgia* (New York: Palgrave Macmillan, 2012).

93. Cf., for example, the title of John Protevi's recent book, *Political Affect: Connecting the Social and the Somatic* (Minneapolis: University of Minnesota Press, 2009), which traces the corporate (and thus corporeal) threads of affective connection provoked by recent events, including Hurricane Katrina and Terri Schiavo's case. I will return to this text in later chapters.

94. See "*Studium* and *Punctum*" (chapter 10) in Barthes, *Camera Lucida*, 25–27.

95. Recent scholars challenge certain of Barthes' distinctions between *stadium* and *punctum*. Shawn Michelle Smith argues that the *punctum*, too, is socialized, as evident in the racist inflections present in Barthes's descriptions of his own visual responses to certain photographs ("Race and Reproduction in *Camera Lucida*" in *At the Edge of Sight*, 23–38). Noting that Barthes reads a certain photograph as "touching" suggests to Margaret Olin that both *studium* and *punctum* can move us. They differ in degree, in other words, but not in kind. To be (metaphorically) pricked is to be (metaphorically) touched, in other words. See Margaret Olin, *Touching Photographs* (Chicago: University of Chicago Press, 2012), 58. I'll return to Olin's larger claim about photographs and touch in the concluding chapter.

96. Sontag, *Regarding the Pain of Others*, 81.

97. Sontag, *Regarding the Pain of Others*, 91ff.

98. Solomon-Godeau dates the term's emergence (as distinct from art photography) to the twenties, but notes that Jacob Riis's *How the Other Half Lives* (1890), a book of photographs depicting life among the poor in New York tenements that helped generate relief movements on their behalf, is usually deemed its first instantiation ("Who Is Speaking Thus?" *Photography at the Dock*, 173ff.) According to Sally Stein (cited by Solomon-Godeau), Riis's photographs were mechanisms of surveillance, containment, and social control put to the service of the imperatives of "Americanization." Cf. Sally Stein, "Making Connections with the Camera: Photography and Social Mobility in the Career of Jacob Riis," *Afterimage* 11, no. 10 (May 1983), 9–16. The photographs illustrate Riis's searing textual critique of tenement conditions couched in terms quite similar to those of Quarry Hill, as the introduction makes plain. Notably, Riis's critique closes with an appeal to Christianity (as Christianity provided much of the impetus behind the reform movements of the nineteenth and early twentieth centuries). See Jacob Riis, *How the Other Half Lives: Studies Among the Tenements of New York* (New York: Charles Scribner's Sons, 1914), 1–5.

99. Tagg, *Disciplinary Frame*, 73.

100. Tagg, *Disciplinary Frame*, 72–73.

101. Cf. Tagg's reflections on documentary photography and its limits as propaganda for the New Deal in "The Plane of Decent Seeing: Documentary and the Rhetoric of Recruitment," in *Disciplinary Frame*, 51–94. Most scholars are skeptical of claims for documentary photography's moral purity (a key point in "Who Is Speaking Thus?") and see inherent limits to its political effects. Although documentary photographs may inspire reform, revolution seems beyond their ken. Thanks to social media, the role of a video of the self-immolation of a Tunisian street vendor in launching the so-called Arab spring may

suggest otherwise. Marc Fisher, "In Tunisia, Act of One Fruit Vendor Sparks Wave of Revolution Through Arab World," *Washington Post*, March 26, 2011.

102. The term *snapshot* was imported into emergent photographic discourse from hunting; it originally meant a gunshot that went off too soon. In her study of lynching photographs, Amy Wood notes instances in which Southern merchants played off of this convergence. One in Waco, Texas, sported a sign that read "GO KODAKING . . . GO HUNTING" (Wood, *Lynching and Spectacle*, 97).

103. Hence his claim that *punctum* constitutes the photograph as a partial object in psychoanalytic terms. For an intriguing take on Barthes and this photograph, see Olin, *Touching Photographs*, chapter 2, in which she argues (among other things) that the photograph itself may ever have existed. See also Shawn Michelle Smith's discussion of Barthes's response to that photograph in "Race and Reproduction," *At the Edge of Sight*, 23–25.

104. Sontag, *On Photography*, 10.

105. Sontag, *On Photography*, 8.

106. Sontag, *On Photography*, 8–9.

107. Sontag, *On Photography*, 9.

108. Marianne Hirsch, *Family Frames: Photography, Narrative, and Postmemory* (Cambridge, MA: Harvard University Press, 1997), 8.

109. Olin, *Touching Photographs*, 197.

110. Mitchell, *Cloning Terror*, 113. Whether they will stand the test of time as have the photos in Hariman and Lucaites, *No Caption Needed* remains an open question, of course.

111. Because I attended to the fate of Thompson and Phuc earlier, I will note in passing the counterfeit claim to being the "Hooded Man" asserted by another prisoner. For the details, see Errol Morris, "Will the *Real* Hooded Man Please Stand Up?" *New York Times*, August 15, 2007. The real hooded man testified at the inquiry into the abuses at Abu Ghraib and then vanished.

112. This is the title of chapter 7 of Mitchell's *Cloning Terror*. This archive includes not only the photographs and video clips (only a small number of which were made public) that serve to anchor it, but also all of the material artifacts of various forms (textual and visual), genres (journalistic or official investigations, documentaries, protest art, etc.) produced in the wake of their discovery.

113. Neither image is reproduced per se in *Cloning Terror,* but a number of appropriations of them for protest art (by artists and by political cartoonists) are.

114. Other than the presence of Mr. Andrews (which still requires explanation), there is nothing in the photographs of Gene Robinson's consecration themselves that distinguishes this consecration from any other; one needs the photograph's context to know what one is looking at, so to speak.

115. Hariman and Lucaites, *No Caption Needed*, 29.

116. Hariman and Lucaites, *No Caption Needed*, 29.

117. Hariman and Lucaites, *No Caption Needed*, 36.

118. See his book by that title (Protevi, *Political Affect*).

119. Hariman and Lucaites, *No Caption Needed*, 37.

120. Cf. Mark Danner, *Torture and Truth: America, Abu Ghraib, and the War on Terror* (New York: New York Review of Books, 2004). Art historian Stephen Eisenman notes that, as time passed, polls showed that Americans became increasingly accepting of what happened at Abu Ghraib. He attributes this attitude in part to what he calls "the Abu Ghraib effect" (Stephen F. Eisenman, *The Abu Ghraib Effect* [London: Reaktion, 2007]), an acculturated response to suffering with roots in Western art and its iconography of suffering. I'll return to this issue (and to Eisenman's thesis) in a later chapter.

121. Ariella Azoulay, *The Civil Contract of Photography* (New York: Zone, 2008). My thanks to Gail Hamner for pointing me to this resource.

122. Azoulay, *The Civil Contract*, 89.

123. For more on the relationship between the photographic contract and the social contract, see Azoulay, *The Civil Contract*, 108ff.

124. Azoulay notes, however, that the disenfranchised and those at the bottommost rungs of the social ladder are more often photographed than photographer.

125. Hariman and Lucaites, *No Caption Needed*, 29.

126. Sontag, *Regarding the Pain of Others*, 40.

127. Mitchell, *Cloning Terror*, 114–16; 150–59. A 2004 editorial cartoon about Abu Ghraib, "Abu Ghraib Nam," by Dennis Draughon published in *The Scranton Times* and discussed in both *Cloning Terror* and *No Caption Needed* exploits that commonality. The cartoonist reproduces the scene of "Accidental Napalm" with one significant difference: behind Kim Phuc as though he were her shadow is the hooded man. That placement links all three as victims of state-sanctioned unjust violence (recall that Jesus was crucified as an enemy of Rome) through the similarity in the position and posture of their suffering bodies. See Hariman and Lucaites, *No Caption Needed*, fig. 37, 202 and Mitchell, *Cloning Terror*, fig. 3, 5.

128. I say "call to mind" here and not "resemble" because of the similarities and differences between the body positions of the subjects of these photographs and depictions of Christ. On this, see especially Mitchell's discussion of "Hooded Man" in the last chapter of *Cloning Terror* entitled "State of the Union." Mitchell also takes note of the complex and conflicted affective responses one might have to "Hooded Man" as a result.

129. At one point or another, many of the scholars discussed herein (Barthes, Sontag, Berger, and Hariman and Lucaites) turn to religious or theological terminology to describe some feature of photographic practice (not photographic content), which is arguably symptomatic of this larger cultural reality.

130. Indeed, both Hariman and Lucaites and Sontag describe the role of photographs in political life and family life, respectively, as a form of ritual. Hariman and Lucaites use it to name the role that photojournalism plays in the presentation and consumption of news. Regardless of the source, mode, or mechanism of its delivery (radio being the exception), the news is presented to its consumers either in the form of or accompanied by photography (still or moving). No American newspaper, at least—even the *Wall Street Journal*, where the space devoted to words traditionally far exceeds that for photographs—would give us a front page absent a photograph "above the fold," as they say.

131. This is not the time or place to get into that literature, but allow me to at least point out some of the more prominent voices and seminal texts in the discussion beginning with Pierre Bourdieu, *Outline of a Theory of Practice*, trans. Richard Nice (New York: Cambridge University Press, 1977); Catherine Bell, *Ritual Theory, Ritual Practice* (New York: Oxford University Press, 1992); and Michel de Certeau, *The Practice of Everyday Life* (Berkeley: University of California Press, 1984), to mention just a few. That body of literature is integral to discussions of modernity and secularity that I referenced in the introduction.

132. The alert reader who also knows the work of Judith Butler will hear in these words allusions to her important work on performativity and gender, among other matters. Butler's work will figure prominently in later chapters.

133. Shawn Michelle Smith's *At the Edge of Sight* offers an intriguing series of reflections on a different kind of photographic transcendence. On the one hand, she notes that photographic technology often reveals things we cannot (or do not) see with the naked eye (as we say). This was, in fact, part of what people found fascinating about it early on. On the other hand, photographs open up and open onto what exceeds and grounds them: desire for the now-deceased beloved (as in the nineteenth-century practice of spirit photography) or for the eroticized other (cf. the photographs of F. Holland Day); for social recognition in the face of systemic racism (cf. the photographs of Augustus Washington); and for the resurrection of an agrarian past (cf. Chansonetta Stanley Emmon's photographs).

134. Mitchell, *What Do Pictures Want?* 10.

135. Mitchell, *What Do Pictures Want?* 9. Sontag speaks of family snapshots as talismans of absent loved ones, as magical invocations of their lost presence (*On Photography*, 8–9).

3. Bio-Discipline and Globalization

1. Laurie Goodstein, "Openly Gay Man Is Made Bishop," *New York Times*, November 3, 2003 (front page). The second photograph was published on p. A-16 of the print edition.

2. Goodstein, "Openly Gay Man Is Made Bishop," *New York Times*. The *Times* did not report the content of the Rev. Fox's speech, but World Net Daily, a conservative news aggregator, reports that it read as follows (before he was cut short by the presiding bishop): "Research on homosexuality reports that 99 percent engage in oral sex; 91 percent engage in anal sex. Eight-two percent engage in rimming—the touching of the anus of one's partner with one's tongue." Les Kinsolving, "Censoring the Facts About Homosexuality," World Net Daily, November 8, 2013. www.wnd.co/2003/11/21670.

3. A snapshot of a representative slice of the global episcopacy would look somewhat different. Mary-Jane Rubenstein notes that of the 736 bishops who met at their decennial gathering in 1998 in Lambeth, England (about which more anon), 224 were African and 95 Southeast Asian. She also notes that eleven

were women, although she does not specify their ethnicity or geographical provenance. See Rubenstein, "An Anglican Crisis of Comparison: Race, Gender, and Religious Authority, with Particular Reference to the Church of Nigeria," *Journal of the American Academy of Religion* 72, no. 2 (2004): 341–65, 342.

4. The American church's numbers are down from 2.3 million in 2003, the year Robinson was consecrated, the *Times* reports. Laurie Goodstein, "Episcopalians Approve Rite to Bless Same-Sex Unions," *New York Times*, July 10, 2012. Willis Jenkins gives the population of the Nigerian province at 15 million. See his "Episcopalians, Homosexuality, and World Mission," *Anglican Theological Review* 86, no. 2 (Spring 2004): 293–312, 295. Phillip Jenkins claims 20 million. See his *The Next Christendom: The Coming of Global Christianity* (New York: Oxford University Press, 2002), 59.

5. What follows incorporates in substantially revised form portions of two previously published essays listed here in alphabetical order: Ellen T. Armour, "Blinding Me with (Queer) Science: Religion, Sexuality, and (Post?)Modernity," *International Journal for Philosophy of Religion* 68, no. 1–3 (2010): 107–19; "Planetary Sightings? Negotiating Sexual Differences in Globalization's Shadow," in *Planetary Loves: Postcoloniality, Gender and Theology*, ed. Stephen Moore and Mayra Rivera (New York: Fordham University Press, 2010), 209–24.

6. Gayatri Chakravorty Spivak, *Death of a Discipline* (New York: Columbia University Press, 2003). See especially chapter 3, "Planetarity." I turn to Spivak's planetarity because of its resonances with other aspects of this project. "To be human is to be intended toward the other," she writes. "We provide for ourselves transcendental figurations of what we think is the origin of this animating gift: mother, nation, god, nature. These are names of alterity, some more radical than others. Planet-thought opens up to embrace an inexhaustible taxonomy of such names, including but not identical with the whole range of human universals: aboriginal animism as well as the spectral white mythology of post-rational science. If we image ourselves as planetary subjects rather than global agents, planetary creatures rather than global entities, alterity remains underived from us; it is not our dialectical negation, it contains us as much as it flings us away. And thus to think of it is already to transgress, for, in spite of our forays into what we metaphorize, differently, as outer and inner space, what is above and beyond our own reach is not continuous with us as it is not, indeed, specifically discontinuous. We must persistently educate ourselves into this peculiar mindset" (73).

7. I use the language of heirs and former subjects (rather than former empires and colonies) to mark out the peculiar space occupied by the United States. It originated as a union of former British colonies that, although never a territorial empire exactly, exerts itself around the globe in a mode often experienced and described as "imperial."

8. There is, of course, a large body of scholarship on globalization that goes well beyond Spivak's work here. Of particular import is the trilogy by Michael Hardt and Antonio Negri that was launched with *Empire* (Cambridge, MA: Harvard

University Press, 2000), followed by *Multitude: War and Democracy in the Age of Empire* (New York: Penguin, 2005) and concluded with *Commonwealth* (Cambridge, MA: Belknap Press of Harvard University Press, 2009). Readers who know their work may note points of contact between what I say about globalization in the following paragraphs and may wonder why I don't take it up directly here, especially given that they draw on Foucauldian categories and have a good deal to say about religion. For a helpful assessment of the role of religion in *Empire*, in particular, see Chris Fox, "From Representation to Constituent Power: Religion, or Something Like It, in Hardt and Negri's *Empire*," *Journal for Cultural and Religious Theory* 9, no. 2 (Summer 2008): 30–42. Globalization per se is not my primary concern here, although the concept is helpful to think with and through in this context. I would, however, like to commend Miranda K. Hassett's discussion of the relationship between the dynamics in the Anglican Communion and the literature on religion and globalization. See her introduction to *Anglican Communion in Crisis: How Episcopal Dissidents and Their African Allies are Reshaping Anglicanism* (Princeton, NJ: Princeton University Press, 2007). She argues that, among other things, the conflict pits two different visions of globalization against one another. Those opposed to LGBT inclusion often advocate for and seek to instantiate what she calls "accountability globalism," a version of communion that holds all to a normative shared theological vision. Conversely, those in favor often advocate for and seek to instantiate "diversity globalism," a version of communion that locates unity in the appreciation of differences as goods in themselves. For a constructive contribution to the question of whether the Anglican Communion—or any (post) colonial communion—can achieve a form of being-with that can truly reckon with difference, see Mary-Jane Rubenstein, "Anglicans in the Postcolony: On Sex and the Limits of Communion," *Telos* 143 (Summer 2008): 133–60. I will have more to say about both of these texts later in this chapter.

9. Spivak's planet resembles other uncanny sites that also give place: the womb (according to Luce Irigaray) and *khora* (according to Jacques Derrida). On this convergence, see Mayra Rivera Rivera, *The Touch of Transcendence: A Postcolonial Theology of God* (Louisville, KY: Westminster John Knox, 2009), especially the last chapter. I'll have more to say about this book later.

10. These figures come from the Anglican Communion's website (http://www .anglicancommunion.org/identity/about.aspx).

11. Rubenstein sees this controversy as intrinsically connected to others that predate it, including particularly that over the ordination of women. See "An Anglican Crisis of Comparison" as well as "Anglicans in the Postcolony." Like me, she views this event as playing out on a globalized landscape shaped by the legacies of colonialism. In many ways, our analyses overlap as I'll make clear in subsequent references to her work, although, apart from a brief reference to Foucault and *scientia sexualis* ("Anglicans in the Postcolony," 150), Rubenstein does not make the links to bio-disciplinary power that I do. Instead, she inquires after the possibilities for rethinking community offered by Jean-Luc Nancy.

12. Events have continued to unfold. As a follow-up to Lambeth 1998, the Archbishop of Canterbury convened the Lambeth Commission in 2003 to study the issues further. That commission produced the Windsor Report in 2004, which recommended a moratorium on further consecrations of openly gay bishops because of the threats such actions pose to Anglican unity; see Lambeth Commission on Communion, *The Windsor Report 2004* (Harrisburg, PA: Morehouse, 2004), 54. The 2008 Lambeth Conference was relatively quiet compared with 1998, though changes were afoot through other channels. December 2008 saw the founding of the Anglican Church in North America as an alternative province to the U.S. and Canadian churches (see http://anglicanchurch.net). It held its first churchwide assembly in Texas in June 2009. In July 2009, the bishops of the Episcopal Church voted by an overwhelming majority to open all ministries of the Church to openly gay and lesbian people. See Laurie Goodstein, "Episcopal Vote Reopens a Door to Gay Bishops," *New York Times*, July 14, 2009. If this move violated the spirit of the call for a moratorium, the consecration later that year of the Rev. Canon Mary D. Glasspool, a lesbian, as bishop suffragan of the Episcopal Diocese of Los Angeles violated its letter. Matthew Hay Brown, "Md. Priest Becomes First Lesbian Episcopal Bishop" *Baltimore Sun*, December 5, 2009. I make note of more recent developments later in this chapter.

13. Hassett, *Anglican Communion in Crisis*, 105.

14. See Jenkins, *The Next Christendom*. Although on decline (in numbers) in much of the developed world, Christianity continues to attract new adherents in much of the developing world according to demographic statistics Jenkins cites (2–3).

15. A scene from Lambeth that was repeatedly broadcast on British television could effectively stand in as an iconic representation of this way of depicting the conflict. The Rt. Rev. Chukwuma, bishop of the Enugo diocese in Nigeria, attempted an impromptu exorcism of the Rev. Richard Kircher, a British priest who was the general secretary of the Lesbian and Gay Christian Movement. Jeremy Carrette and Mary Keller offer an astute analysis of this event that complements the framework of my project very well. See Jeremy Carrette and Mary Keller, "Religions, Orientation and Critical Theory: Race, Gender and Sexuality at the 1998 Lambeth Conference," *Theology and Sexuality* 11 (1999): 21–43.

16. See Lamin Sanneh, *Whose Religion Is Christianity? The Gospel Beyond the West* (Grand Rapids, MI: Eerdmans, 2003). Both Sanneh and Jenkins were present at Lambeth 1998, according to Hassett. Indeed, Hassett reports that experience prompted Jenkins to undertake the research project that eventually became *The Next Christendom* (Hassett, *Anglican Communion*, 74).

17. For more on Jenkins's views see, in addition to *The Next Christendom*, Jenkins's *The New Faces of Christianity: Believing the Bible in the Global South* (New York: Oxford University Press, 2006).

18. Terry Brown, ed., *Other Voices, Other Worlds: The Global Church Speaks Out on Homosexuality* (London: Darton, Longman and Todd, 2006). I say "Anglicans

and Episcopalians" here because the boundaries of the Episcopalian church extend into the global South (e.g., mostly South and Latin America, but also Micronesia and Taiwan) reflecting the history of its missionary activity. Although they doubtless also contain a diversity of views within their borders, the dioceses outside the United States have not played a significant role in the current controversy so far as I'm able to determine. Recently, the Brazilian church (formerly affiliated with the Episcopal Church) experienced its own version of what is happening in the United States. A faction of the diocese of Recife, Brazil, under the leadership of its bishop, attempted a break with the Brazilian church (which took disciplinary action) over its inclusive stance on homosexuality and Anglicanism. That led to a property dispute that was resolved in the Brazilian Church's favor by the Brazilian courts. However, it left a large faction in Recife (aligned with the Anglican Communion of North America) quite unhappy. See George Conger, "Civil Court Ruling for Recife Schism," *The Church of England Newspaper*, August 28, 2013.

19. Cited by Rubenstein, "Anglicans in the Postcolony," 136–38. She, too, sees this as complicating, even invalidating, the standard portrait of the conflict as North versus South.

20. See James Solheim, "International Reaction to Gene Robinson's Consecration in New Hampshire Mixed," *Anglican Communion News Service*, November 6, 2003.

21. In using "LGBT persons," I follow nomenclature used by Kapya Kaoma, "Globalizing the Culture Wars" (Somerville, MA: Political Research Associates, 2009). Although the controversy is over "homosexuality," bisexual and transgender people are caught up in its wake—as, indeed, they are here (often along with intersexed and queer or questioning folk, to complete the version of the acronym to which we in the United States are most accustomed). I'll have much more to say about all of this, including the importation of Western taxonomic categories, as the chapter unfolds.

22. For more on Akinola, see Lydia Pohlgreen and Laurie Goodstein, "At Axis of Episcopal Split, an Anti-Gay Nigerian," *New York Times*, December 25, 2006.

23. Cited by Willis Jenkins in "Episcopalians, Homosexuality, and World Mission," 306–7. In a collect written in response to the consecration of Bishop Robinson, the Archbishop of Uganda wrote, "We grieve because we remember the pain that has come from similar *imperial* actions in the past" (297). For more on Uganda, neocolonialism, and the role money is playing, see Kawuki Mukasa, "The Church of Uganda and the Problem of Human Sexuality: Responding to Concerns from the Ugandan Context," in Brown, *Other Voices, Other Worlds*, 168–78.

24. Noting that the Episcopal Church's financial contribution to the Anglican Communion is the largest, Archbishop Drexel Gomez of the Province of the West Indies (part of the global South) said, "as much as we need the money, the gospel must come first. We are prepared to suffer" (Solheim, "International Reaction"). For a fulsome discussion, see chapter 7 of *Anglican Communion*

in Crisis. Following are a few highlights: in April 2004, the Council of Anglican Provinces of Africa voted to reject funding from the Episcopal Church in
the United States of America (Hassett, *Anglican Communion*, 239). Trinity
Church, Wall Street, has ended its support of a theological education program
in Rwanda (Hassett, *Anglican Communion*, 217). What I will call Northern
"traditionalists" (I explain the terminology in a subsequent note) have apparently stepped into these breaches (or perhaps caused them) by offering funds of
their own, according to Hassett.

25. Ruth Gledhill, "For God's Sake," *The Times* (London), July 5, 2007.

26. Akinola and colleagues have condemned homosexuality as not only "inhuman"
but also as "'un-African and unscriptural'" (Dickinson Adeyanju, "Homosexual Priests: Nigerian Anglicans Will Not Succumb to Pressure from the West,
Says Akinola," *The Guardian* [Nigeria], July 30, 2007; quoted by Rubenstein,
"Anglicans in Postcolony," 136). See also the "Statement on Homosexuality by
the Anglican Province of Rwanda," issued January 31, 1998, in which the signa-
tories (all diocesan bishops) write, "We know that some Westerners have intro-
duced homosexual practices in the Great Lakes Region of Africa, but we, as
Africans, repudiate the practice and do not wish it to be seen in our Province."

27. Ann Laura Stoler, "A Colonial Reading of Foucault," *Carnal Knowledge and
Imperial Power: Race and the Intimate under Colonial Rule,* rev. ed. (Berkeley:
University of California, 2010; orig. pub. 2002), 97; and *Race and the Educa-
tion of Desire: Foucault's* History of Sexuality *and the Colonial Order of Things*
(Durham, NC: Duke University Press, 1995), 15.

28. Westerners (or, better, our forebears) have not always mapped sexual behavior according to our modern notion of sexual identity, for that matter. In the
Greco-Roman culture in which Christianity came into being, for example, one's
legitimate sexual partners—and one's proper role in sex acts—were determined
by one's place in a social hierarchy. An elite man, for example, could have licit
sex not only with his wife, but also with his male and female slaves. Doing so
posed no challenge to his masculinity—as long as he was the penetrating partner, not the receiving partner. Although ancient Greeks and Romans associated
certain sexual practices and positions (males who are penetrated, females who
penetrate) with gender transgression, they did not expect to see such practices necessarily reflected in one's everyday manner and style of dress. Moreover, they associated certain male same-sex bonds with virility and warned men
against the effeminizing effects of too much sex with women. For more on
this, see, for example, Dale B. Martin, *The Corinthian Body* (New Haven, CT:
Yale University Press, 1995); certain essays in his *Sex and the Single Savior: Gender and Sexuality in Biblical Interpretation* (Louisville, KY: Westminster John
Knox, 2006); and Bernadette Brooten, *Love Between Women: Early Christian
Responses to Homoeroticism* (Chicago: University of Chicago Press, 1996). Ken
Stone's essay, "The Garden of Eden and the Heterosexual Contract" in *Bodily
Citations: Religion and Judith Butler,* ed. Ellen T. Armour and Susan St. Ville
(New York: Columbia University Press, 2006), 48–70, includes a helpful list of

references to a larger body of scholarship on sexuality in the ancient world (see p. 67, n. 9).

29. David Greenberg, *The Construction of Homosexuality* (Chicago: University of Chicago Press, 1988), chapter 2. Cited by Kevin Ward, "Same-Sex Relations in Africa and the Debate on Homosexuality in East African Anglicanism," *Anglican Theological Review* (Winter 2002): 81–111. See also Will Roscoe and Stephen O. Murray, *Boy-Wives and Female Husbands: Studies in African Homosexualities* (New York: Palgrave Macmillan, 2001), which Ward also cites; and Martin Duberman, Martha Vicinus, and George Chauncey, Jr., *Hidden from History* (New York: Meridian, 1990).

30. The colonialist laws have remained on the books since, but were rarely enforced. In 2014, both Uganda and Nigeria passed new laws that are much harsher in a number of ways. See, for example, Sudarsan Raghavan, "Ugandan Leader Signs Harsh Anti-Gay Bill Despite Warning from Obama Administration," *Washington Post*, February 24, 2014.

31. Ward, "Same Sex Relations in Africa," 101–2.

32. Kevin Ward, "Marching or Stumbling Towards a Christian Ethic?" in Brown, *Other Voices, Other Worlds*, 133–34. The histories Ward documents substantiate Charles Long's observation that "sites of colonial contact" provoked "religious crises that required colonizer as well as colonized to orient themselves vis-à-vis each other" (cited and employed by Carrette and Keller, "Religions, Orientation and Critical Theory," 34).

33. The Anglican Church's role in these experiments allows us to add yet another dimension to Stoler's claim. Historian and ethicist Mark D. Jordan (whose earlier work I draw on later in this chapter) has argued recently that Christian churches have ceded Christian speech about sex to *scientia sexualis*, a development he traces in the United States to the mid-twentieth century. See Mark D. Jordan, *Recruiting Young Love: How Christians Talk About Homosexuality* (Chicago: University of Chicago Press, 2011). Perhaps the British colonies anticipate that surrender, as well.

34. Rubenstein, "An Anglican Crisis of Comparison," 349.

35. A word here about terminology. I will refer to the two opposing positions (and those who hold them) as "traditionalist(s)" and "progressive(s)." I choose this terminology for specific reasons in each case. For one thing, as we've seen, "conservative" and "liberal" are problematic, although common and even useful, rubrics. Hassett uses them but is careful to delineate what they mean (see *Anglican Communion*, 40). "Traditionalist" captures, I hope, the fact that more is at stake for those opposed to LGBT inclusion than sexuality. Moves toward inclusion violate a variety of "traditions" that its opponents hold dear, as we'll see. "Progressive" similarly nods to the view, especially among its Northern advocates, that LGBT inclusion is simply the latest move along a trajectory of progress toward realizing God's desire for greater social justice in the world. I also want to mark here a certain lightness of touch (and a light touch of irony) that I hope might attend their use. The "traditions"

in the name of which certain Anglicans resist inclusion are as constructed, if you will, as the vision of "progress" that inspires those in favor of inclusion. I remain enough of a Derridean, however, to know that I cannot enforce this lightness on my readers.

36. The first of these was the Anglican Mission in the Americas (AMiA) founded under the episcopal oversight of the archbishop of Rwanda. In 2006, a number of these parishes banded together to form the Convocation of Anglicans in North America (CANA), headed by Martin Minns of Fairfax, Virginia, consecrated as bishop by Akinola. A third structure, the Anglican Church in North America, allegedly hopes to replace—or certainly supplement—the Episcopal Church (U.S.A.) as the American arm of the Anglican Communion. According to their website, ACNA was founded at the urging of the Southern Anglican primates gathered at the first meeting of the Global Anglican Future Pilgrimage and Conference (GAFCon), which was sponsored by the Fellowship of Confessing Anglicans in Jerusalem in 2008. See http://www.anglicanchurch .net/media/Our_Genesis_revised_2.8_.13_.pdf.

37. Akinola dismisses this charge as hypocritical, saying that "he was simply doing what Western churches have done for centuries, sending a bishop to serve Anglicans where there is no church to provide one" (Pohlgreen and Goodstein, "At Axis of Episcopal Split"). Anglican polity itself is a rather loose affair at the global level. See Hassett on the "Instruments of Unity" in *Anglican Communion*, 117.

38. Thus, Sanneh speaks of "world Christianity." He distinguishes it from "global Christianity," which still bears the strong imprint of its Western origins. See Ward, "Marching or Stumbling," for an enlightening account of the "world Christianities" indigenous to Uganda, Nigeria, and South Africa in particular.

39. My information about Mr. MacIyalla comes from a personal e-mail exchange with Rev. Jon Richardson on February 26, 2013. See Changing Attitudes Nigeria, http://davis35.wordpress.com. The original site does not appear to be active any longer, which may reflect MacIyalla's move to the United Kingdom.

40. Hassett, *Anglican Communion*, 91–92. This action was quickly and roundly denounced as an invasion by the North despite vocal protests to the contrary by local organizers. Hassett also notes that positions articulated in certain outlets in the Ugandan press document a wider range of opinion on same-sex sex among the populace at large than the Ugandan Church's official reaction would suggest.

41. Personal e-mail correspondence, February 26, 2013. My thanks to Patrick Cheng for putting me in touch with Rev. Richardson and to Rev. Richardson for sharing information and insight and for permission to cite our exchange.

42. Hassett, *Anglican Communion*, 208. Some explained Ssenyonjo's conduct as an attempt to subsidize his retirement with Northern funds, a practice often encouraged by the Ugandan church, she notes (233). This perception of Integrity Uganda was not helped by the subsequent dispute between the American Episcopalian (and founding member of Integrity USA) Louie Crew and the

archbishop of Uganda. Crew charged the Ugandan church with hypocrisy for continuing to accept Episcopalian money while claiming to have severed all connections to the Episcopal Church after Robinson's consecration. See Ward, "Marching or Stumbling?" 135–36.

43. Laurie Goodstein, "Episcopalians Approve Rite to Bless Same-Sex Unions," *New York Times*, July 10, 2012. The rite approved for same-sex unions is one of the two now approved for same-sex weddings.

44. George Conger, "The Episcopal Church Approves Religious Weddings for Gay Couples After Controversial Debate," *Washington Post*, July 1, 2015.

45. Willis Jenkins, "Ethnohomophobia?" *Anglican Theological Review* 82, no. 3 (Summer 2000): 551–63. That said, progressive dioceses like the diocese of Chicago, for example, have established "companion relationships" with dioceses in the global South, including in Sudan and Mexico. These relationships make explicit provision for interdiocesan visits involving laity as well as clergy. Whether these relationships produce similar effects to those Hassett documents at St. Timothy's I can't say.

46. See, for example, Ifi Amadiume, *Male Daughters, Female Husbands: Gender and Sex in African Society* (London: Zed, 1987), which Rubenstein treats at some length in "Crisis of Comparison." A salient contemporary example would be the use of the figure of the Muslim woman clad in a burqa to marshal support for the war in Afghanistan—an effort in which the organization Feminist Majority became involved. See Saba Mahmood, "Agency, Performativity, and the Feminist Subject" in Armour and St. Ville, *Bodily Citations*, 177–221, 207–8. Spivak coined a sentence that has become emblematic of this problem: "white men are saving brown women from brown men" (Gayatri Chakravorty Spivak, "Can the Subaltern Speak?" *Marxism and the Interpretation of Culture*, ed. Lawrence Grossberg and Cary Nelson [Urbana and Chicago: University of Illinois Press], 271–313; 296).

47. Rubenstein, "Crisis of Comparison," 349, n. 15.

48. Andrew Carey, "African Christians? They're Just a Step Up from Witchcraft," *Church of England Newspaper*, July 10, 1998; cited by Hassett, *Anglican Communion*, 72. Although initially resistant to doing so, Spong eventually apologized for his statement. "David Skidmore, "Bishop Spong Apologises to Africans," *Lambeth Daily*, July 28, 1998: 1; cited by Hassett, *Anglican Communion*, 73.

49. Neva Rae Fox, "Nigerian Primate Seated on International Throne of Cathedral," *Episcopal New Yorker*, July–August 2002, 11, quoted in Rubenstein, "Crisis of Comparison," 360.

50. Rubenstein, "Crisis of Comparison," 360.

51. On GAFCon, see http://gafcon.org. Notably, the Archbishop of Canterbury attended GAFCon's second meeting, held in Nairobi, Kenya, in 2013.

52. Katelyn Beatey, "Women's Ordination: A Crack in the Cathedral?" *Christianity Today*, July 2, 2009.

53. For details, see http://www.episcopalchurch.org/library/topics/church -property-dispute.

54. Rick Gladstone, "Nigerian President Signs Ban on Same-Sex Relationships," *New York Times*, January 13, 2014; Alan Cowell, "Uganda's President Signs Antigay Bill," *New York Times*, February 24, 2014.

55. See the International Gay and Lesbian Human Rights Commission's report, "Voices from Nigeria: Gays, Lesbians, Bisexuals, and Transgendereds Speak Out Against the Same Sex Bill." A prominent Ugandan LGBT activist, David Kato, was murdered in January 2011; Jeffrey Gettleman, "Ugandan Who Spoke Up for Gays Is Beaten to Death," *New York Times*, January 28, 2011. A documentary about Kato has also been released; Katherine Fairfax Wright and Malika Zouhali-Worrall, "They Will Say We Are Not Here," *New York Times*, January 25, 2012. Kato's death is only the tip of the iceberg of harassment and assaults to which LGBT Ugandans (and other LGBT Africans) are often subject, including so-called corrective rape.

56. Owen Bowcott, "Uganda Anti-Gay Law Led to Tenfold Rise in Attacks on LGBTI People, Report Says," *The Guardian*, May 11, 2014. See also Adam Nossiter, "Nigeria Tries to 'Sanitize' Itself of Gays," *New York Times*, February 8, 2014.

57. Chris Johnston, "Uganda Drafts New Anti-Gay Laws," *The Guardian*, November 8, 2014.

58. Cathy Lynn Grossman, "Conservative Anglican Leaders Back Uganda Anti-Gay Law," *Religion News Service*, April 28, 2014.

59. Elias Biryabarema, "U.S. Cuts Aid to Uganda, Cancels Military Exercise Over Anti-Gay Law," *Reuters*, June 19, 2014. The political and human rights calculus—complicated in both cases—is particularly difficult in Nigeria given the presence of Islamist organizations on the continent. The April 15, 2014, kidnapping of 270 Nigerian schoolgirls by Boko Haram aroused a great deal of outrage worldwide including the United States, which prompted the U.S. government to reach out to aid the Nigerian government's search for the girls. Monica Mark, "Missing Nigerian Schoolgirls: Boko Haram Claims Responsibility for Kidnapping," *The Guardian*, May 5, 2014.

60. Mariah Blake, "Meet the American Pastor Behind Uganda's Anti-Gay Crackdown," *Mother Jones*, March 10, 2014.

61. Kaoma, "Globalizing the Culture Wars." Indeed, the cover of Kaoma's report features a photograph of Minns and Akinola. A powerful documentary on the role of evangelical Christianity in Ugandan debates on this issue came out in 2013. For information about the documentary, *God Loves Uganda*, along with a trailer, see http://www.godlovesuganda.com. For more on the relationship between American evangelicals (including some Washington politicians) and Uganda, see Jeff Sharlet, *C Street: The Fundamentalist Threat to American Democracy* (New York: Little, Brown, 2010).

62. Howard Chua-Eoan, "Rick Warren Denounces Uganda's Anti-Gay Bill," *Time*, December 10, 2009.

63. See https://ccrjustice.org/home/what-we-do/our-cases/sexual-minorities-uganda-v-scott-lively.

64. See, for example, Stephen Swecker, ed., *Hard Ball on Holy Ground: The Religious Right v. the Mainline for the Church's Soul* (Boston: Boston Wesleyan Press, 2005); and Jim Naughton, "Following the Money: Donors and Activists on the Anglican Right," a special report from *Washington Window* (May 2006), a publication of the Washington dioceses of the Episcopal Church. My thanks to Lionel Deimel for pointing me to these sources.

65. The pursuit of marriage equality for same-sex couples—and its success—is a case in point. The terms of the debate over same-sex marriage at the Episcopal Church's 2015 General Assembly and its resolution as described by Conger, "The Episcopal Church Approves Religious Weddings," are redolent of our current sexual regime. See also the emergence of so-called queer science, which is seeking a biological cause for homosexuality. For a critique of queer science (or, better, what we seem to want from it), see my "Blinding Me With (Queer) Science" from which a portion of what follows here is taken. I should note that, while the question of nature versus nurture is central to the "culture war" over homosexuality in the United States, things are more complicated in African countries.

66. Carrette and Keller, "Religions, Orientation and Critical Theory," 27–28.

67. Michel Foucault, *The History of Sexuality, Vol. 1: An Introduction,* trans. Robert Hurley (New York: Random House, 1978); originally published in French as *La volonté de savoir* (Paris: Éditions Gallimard, 1974).

68. Mark D. Jordan, *The Invention of Sodomy in Christian Theology* (Chicago: University of Chicago Press, 1998).

69. Sodomy is not the earliest instance of Christian dealings with homoeroticism, although it is a pivot point in the eventual emergence of *scientia sexualis.* The groundbreaking study on early Christianity is John Boswell, *Christianity, Social Tolerance, and Homosexuality* (Chicago: University of Chicago Press, 1980). Although its contributions continue to be appreciated, it is not without its critics. See Bernadette Brooten, *Love Between Women: Early Christian Responses to Female Homoeroticism* (Chicago: University of Chicago Press, 1996). For particularly fine work on New Testament perspectives, see Dale B. Martin, *Sex and the Single Savior: Gender and Sexuality in Biblical Interpretation* (Louisville, KY: Westminster John Knox, 2006).

70. That women could engage in illicit acts with one another was not in question, but whether such acts constituted *sodomia* was at issue. On this point, see Jordan, *The Invention of Sodomy in Christian Theology,* 81. For a substantive treatment of early Christian views on homo-sex between women, see Brooten, *Love Between Women.* Among the many contributions this text makes by attending specifically to this question (neglected by prior studies), one is to note that the medicalization of sexual deviance predates the nineteenth century. Brooten finds evidence that clitoridectomy was practiced as a "cure" for same-sex desire (among other forms of deviance) in the Roman era.

71. Jordan, *The Invention of Sodomy*, 43.

72. Indeed, Jordan's research establishes the emergence of sexual personages well before the nineteenth century, thus providing a corrective to Foucault. In *The Ethics of Sex* (Malden, MA: Blackwell, 2002), Jordan discusses several such personages in Christian theology: the virgin martyr, the Christian wife or husband, for example, as well as the sodomite. Brooten also finds evidence for relatively fixed sexual personages in antiquity.

73. Foucault, *History of Sexuality, Vol. 1*, 43; translation modified. The French reads "un personage: un passé, une histoire et une enfance, un caractère, une forme de vie; une morphologie aussi, avec une anatomie indiscrete et peut-être une physiologie myterieuse" (*La volonté de savoir*, 59)." For more on translation issues with this passage, see chapter 1, n. 27.

74. Foucault, *History of Sexuality, Vol. 1*, 43; *La volonté de savoir*, 59.

75. Foucault, *History of Sexuality, Vol. 1*, 43; *La volonté de savoir*, 59. Our current regime of sex, gender, and sexuality is also of relatively recent provenance. It translates awkwardly, at best, to other times and places. On this point, see the introduction to Jordan's *Ethics of Sex*. As Jordan demonstrates in *Invention of Sodomy*, sodomy (like male homosexuality) was associated with effeminacy, but through the larger category of sin that included it, *luxuria*.

76. Foucault, *History of Sexuality, Vol. 1*, 43; *La volonté de savoir*, 59. Jordan's account of sodomy contests this point. Although sodomy was certainly deemed aberrant, it was no temporary state.

77. Carrette and Keller, "Religions, Orientation and Critical Theory," 32.

78. In addition to the sources cited earlier, see John Boswell, *Same Sex Unions in Pre-Modern Europe* (New York: Vintage, 1994).

79. It is also to speak in terms of vocabulary limited not only in its application across historical periods (e.g., see Jordan, *The Invention of Sodomy*, 9–17) but also in what it obscures about the past and the present. Brooten argues, for example, that many other aspects of social status (one's ethnicity, whether one was free or slave) affected the perception of one's homoeroticism in the ancient world. The same is true in our time and place, as we've seen in this chapter.

4. Regarding the Photographs of Others

1. In *Watching Babylon: The War in Iraq and Global Visual Culture* (New York: Routledge, 2005), Nicholas Mirzoeff offers a provocative and intriguing take on the many visual dimensions of the war in Iraq through the figure (literal and metaphorical) of Babylon (a Long Island town and the ancient biblical city in present-day Iraq). The book was likely in publication when the Abu Ghraib photographs came to light; thus, Mirzoeff makes no mention of them. He does, however, consider the question of photography's role in this war as a war of images. See "Section 2, The Banality of Images," 68–104.

2. On the figure of Saddam Hussein as *unheimlich,* see Mirzoeff, *Watching Babylon,* 85–89.

3. On this, see Tim Sherrock, *Spies for Hire: The Secret World of Intelligence Outsourcing* (New York: Simon & Schuster, 2008). For a review, see Harry Hurt III, "The Business of Intelligence Gathering," *New York Times,* June 15, 2008.

4. In a major policy speech given in late May 2013, Obama moved to redefine the United States's approach to terrorism, including a reduction in drone attacks in Pakistan. He also called for the program to be transferred from the Central Intelligence Agency to military oversight to facilitate increased transparency about and accountability for its use. For more on the speech, see Peter Baker, "Pivoting from a War Footing, Obama Acts to Curtail Drones," *New York Times,* May 23, 2013.

5. John Tagg, *Burden of Representation: Essays on Photographies and Histories.* (Minneapolis: University of Minnesota Press, 1993), 92.

6. Philosopher Falguni Sheth and economist Robert Pratsch question the efficacy and thus the value of the "surveillance state" in this instance in their op-ed "In Boston, Our Bloated Surveillance State Didn't Work" published by *Salon.com* on April 22, 2013. Subsequently (and apparently coincidentally), stories in the British newspaper *The Guardian* (thanks to the now infamous leaker Edward Snowden) revealed that the U.S. government routinely collected enormous amounts of metadata about the web and cellphone activity of people around the globe through a program called Prism. Glenn Greenwald, "NSA Collecting Phone Records of Millions of Verizon Customers Daily," *The Guardian,* June 5, 2013; and Glenn Greenwald and Ewen MacAskill, "NSA Prism Program Taps into User Data of Apple, Google, and Others," *The Guardian,* June 6, 2013. This revelation launched a firestorm of controversy not only for the U.S. government, but for the tech companies involved—all of whom denied authorizing or even knowing about Prism's access to their records. Legislation modified that program in June 2015. Phone companies will continue to collect and store metadata, which the government can still access but only with judicial permission.

7. W. J. T. Mitchell, *Cloning Terror: The War of Images, 9/11 to the Present.* (Chicago: University of Chicago Press, 2011), 112. The archive includes but is certainly not limited to the photographs, but extends to the "body of texts and images, recordings and remembrances" that gravitate around their original production, publication, and inquiry into the abuses they document (both official and unofficial). It also includes the visual iconography on which the photographs draw and the protest art they generated. I will be following his usage of the term in this chapter for both the Abu Ghraib archive and, by analogy, what I'll call the lynching archive.

8. For a comprehensive overview updated to reflect the results of the military investigation, see Salon Staff, "The Abu Ghraib Files," *Salon.com* (March 14, 2006). In December 2014, the Senate Intelligence Committee released to the public the report of its investigation into how prisoners were treated by the Central Intelligence Agency; see Mark Mazetti, "Panel Faults C.I.A. Over

Brutality and Deceit in Terrorism Investigations," *New York Times,* December 9, 2014. It remains to be seen whether the report will result in any indictments or prosecutions of CIA employees or their subcontractors, but it seems unlikely. For one thing, as Anthony D. Romero, executive director of the American Civil Liberties Union notes in an op-ed published in the *New York Times,* the statute of limitations has run out for some (but not all). But more to the point, the Obama administration has shown no appetite for taking legal action. Romero advocates preemptively pardoning the major policy makers and leaders to signal the illegality of the actions taken. Anthony D. Romero, "Pardon Bush and Those Who Tortured," *New York Times,* December 8, 2014.

9. Susan Sontag, *Regarding the Pain of Others* (New York: Picador, 2003), 47.

10. Sontag, *Regarding the Pain of Others,* 7.

11. Sontag, *Regarding the Pain of Others,* 95. Events still in the headlines as this book was going to press are significant here. That police killings in 2014 and 2015 of three African American men (Michael Brown in Ferguson, Missouri; Eric Garner in Staten Island, New York; and Freddie Gray in Baltimore, Maryland) inaugurated nationwide protests (and more) exemplifies photographic ambivalence and what it opens up and opens onto. In all three cases, cell phone videos and photographs were key to the public outcry over the killings and subsequent decisions about whether or not to prosecute the officers involved. Of the three, only Gray's case will be prosecuted. Poll after poll has shown a racial gap (smaller in Garner's case than in Brown's) between those who believe the grand juries acted properly and those who do not. Although doubtless a number of those polled have made up their minds without seeing any videos or photographs, the divide is telling. In the wake of these events, many began calling for police to wear body cameras—and, according to San Diego's CBS News affiliate, a number of police departments around the country quickly heeded the call; see Shannon Handy, "More Local Police Departments Requiring Body Cams," *CBS 8* (San Diego, CA), December 8, 2014. According to other reports, academic research on the effects suggests significant declines in police use of force and in civilian complaints; see, e.g., Sharon Coolidge, "Cincinnati Cops to Get Body Cameras," *Cincinnati Enquirer,* December 8, 2014. All dimensions of this phenomenon evidence simultaneously our investment in photographic truth and our immersion in panoptical culture.

12. Robert Hariman and John Louis Lucaites, *No Caption Needed: Iconic Photographs, Public Culture and Liberal Democracy.* (Chicago: University of Chicago Press, 2007), 36, 37.

13. Portions of my analysis of the Abu Ghraib photographs is drawn from an earlier essay, "Visual Theology: Diagnosing Postmodernity" in *Between Philosophy and Theology: Contemporary Interpretations of Christianity,* ed. Lieven Boeve and Christophe Brabante (London: Ashgate, 2011), 175–92; 176–86; 191–92.

14. Full consideration of the relationship (or lack thereof) between these images and trauma would require engagement with trauma theory, a task beyond the scope of the current project. See Abigail Solomon-Godeau's "Remote Control:

Dispatches from the Image Wars," *Artforum* 42, no. 10 (Summer 2004): 61, 64 on the interplay of (sometimes self) censorship, trauma, and various visual images (including Abu Ghraib) in the wake of September 11.

15. Mark Danner, *Torture and Truth: America, Abu Ghraib, and the War on Terror* (New York: New York Review of Books, 2004), 9.

16. Dora Apel, "Torture Culture: Lynching Photographs and the Images of Abu Ghraib," *The Art Journal* 64, no. 2 (Summer 2005): 88–100; and Hazel Carby, "A Strange and Bitter Crop: The Spectacle of Torture," *Open Democracy: Free Thinking for the World*, October 11 2004; Sontag, "Regarding the Torture of Others," *New York Times Magazine*, May 23, 2004. Other scholars have connected the photographs and the practices they document to similar photographs from other wars, as I will note later in this chapter.

17. For details on the exhibition, see James Allen, Hilton Als, Congressman John Lewis, and Leon F. Litwack, *Without Sanctuary: Lynching Photography in America* (Santa Fe, NM: Twin Palms, 2008). For cogent analysis of the exhibition, see Dora Apel and Shawn Michelle Smith, *Lynching Photographs* (Berkeley: University of California Press, 2007). Smith and Apel have each also authored very fine book-length treatments of lynching photographs, which draw on a wide range of scholarship on lynching itself. See Smith's *Photography on the Color Line: W. E. B. DuBois, Race, and Visual Culture* (Durham, NC: Duke University Press, 2004) and Apel's *Imagery of Lynching: Black Men, White Women, and the Mob* (New Brunswick, NJ: Rutgers University Press, 2004). I'll have more to say about these texts in due course.

18. The online archive is available at http://withoutsanctuary.org.

19. Grace Elizabeth Hale, *Making Whiteness: The Culture of Segregation in the South, 1890–1940* (New York: Vintage, 1998), 202. Hale's book traces the long and complex process by which whiteness as a (normative) identity that transcends certain ethnic, class, and religious divides even as it highlights others came into being and what interests it served. Amy Wood's more sustained focus on lynching (and lynching photographs) adds more detail to lynching's relationship to modernity. Its contemporary critics often saw it as a throwback, but Wood argues that the practice reflected social and economic anxieties about modernity's advent particularly in the South. In short, it "erupted and thrived along that fault line where modernity and tradition collided" (Amy Louise Wood, *Lynching and Spectacle: Witnessing Racial Violence in America, 1890–1940* [Chapel Hill, NC: University of North Carolina Press, 2009], 14).

20. LaDelle McWhorter, *Racism and Sexual Oppression in America: A Genealogy* (Bloomington: Indiana University Press, 2009), 161. A word about nomenclature here. The making of whiteness is also the making of blackness, in a sense, insofar as they are defined in opposition to one another. Thus, I will use "white" and "black" throughout this chapter. I do this with a central insight of critical race theory in mind—that is, that race is "socially constructed." That claim is, in my view, entirely compatible with my claims about bio-disciplinary power and its fourfold. While neither "biological" nor "natural," modern race

materializes in socially and individually embodied ways because that is what bio-disciplinary power demands.

21. Smith and Wood also note the resemblance between lynchings and executions, although only Smith makes the explicit connection to Michel Foucault. See Smith, *Photography on the Color Line*, Loc. 1660. Wood traces the overarching framework of spectacle lynchings back to public executions, which continued in the South into the early decades of the twentieth century (much later than elsewhere in the United States) and typically drew large crowds. She reads lynching as, in part, a reaction against the privatization of state executions—one aspect of its fraught relationship to modernity (*Lynching and Spectacle*, 24ff.). Lynching reprises the role public executions of black criminals played in the making of whiteness, she claims. It also reprises their underlying theo-logic of sin, punishment, and redemption.

22. Quoted by Litwack, "Hellhounds," *Without Sanctuary*, 16, emphasis in the original.

23. Wood claims "one in three lynching victims were emasculated" (*Lynching and Spectacle*, 98), acts she also interprets as demasculinizing and animalizing them (playing off the practice of castration in animal husbandry). That interpretation undercuts her claim that treating genitalia as souvenirs—talismans of black male sexual power, she claims—paradoxically retains something of the victim's humanity, in my view.

24. Wood, *Lynching and Spectacle*, 99.

25. For example, according to historian James Madison, eyewitnesses to the infamous double lynching in Marion, Indiana, featured in the photographs I discuss next reported that some white spectators cried, vomited, and expressed anguish or rage at what was being done. One courageous soul actually did somehow bring a halt to the proceedings before the mob could lynch a third victim, James Cameron. Just as they prepared to hang him, "a man . . . stood on top of a car and shouted for the crowd to desist, declaiming Cameron's innocence. . . . The spent mob was calmed and Cameron was escorted back to jail" (Apel, *Imagery*, 20). Yet, like most lynchings, no one was ever prosecuted. Cameron wrote a memoir about the experience, *A Time of Terror* (Baltimore, MD: Black Classic Press, 1994). For more on Cameron's experience and its aftermath, see Smith's essay "The Evidence of Lynching Photographs" in *Lynching Photographs*, 13–20.

26. Litwack, "Hellhounds," *Without Sanctuary*, 12–13. Lynchings were commonly known as "Negro barbecue[s]" and "nigger hunts," according to Litwack ("Hellhounds," *Without Sanctuary*, 10, 12; quoted by Apel, *Imagery*, 23). Wood notes that lynching photographs resemble most strongly photographs of hunters with their prey (*Lynching and Spectacle*, 94–97).

27. Litwack, "Hellhounds," *Without Sanctuary*, 12.

28. Hale, *Making Whiteness*, 203–4; also cited by Apel, *Imagery*, 24.

29. Wood cites one instance in which the entire black population of Erwin, Tennessee, was purportedly forced to witness a lynching of one of their own (*Lynching and Spectacle*, 208).

30. This includes the theologian James Cone, who grew up with lynching as an ever-present danger. See James H. Cone, *The Cross and the Lynching Tree* (Minneapolis, MN: Fortress, 2011), which I draw on later in this chapter. Seeing the knuckles of a lynching victim on display was a decisive turning point in W. E. B. DuBois's views on race and racism and shaped the form his activism took, as well, a number of sources report.

31. Quoted by Apel, *Imagery of Lynching*, 15.

32. On this, see Apel's discussion of the photograph of a group of young white women and girls looking at the lynched body of Rubin Stacy—under the watchful gaze of adults, of course (Apel, *Imagery*, 40–41). Smith, too, considers this photograph in the context of other photographs that feature women and children as victims or spectators of lynchings (Smith, *Photography on the Color Line*, Loc. 1502–608). This photograph is one of the few in the lynching archive to include a black woman (most likely a nanny, Wood suggests, and thus compelled to be there) among the spectators (*Lynching and Spectacle*, 207). Some lynchings were of black men with whom a white woman had had consensual sex. Fearing retaliation upon being found out, the white women in question screamed rape. See also a story Wood relates on photography's role after the fact in a case of a rape survivor's identification of her attacker (*Lynching and Spectacle*, 82–84).

33. Apel cites evidence that some white children were traumatized by lynchings that they witnessed, and the trauma persisted into their adulthood (Apel, *Imagery*, 15), but she also reports that, inspired by a lynching they had witnessed, a group of young white boys tried to lynch a twelve-year-old black boy—unsuccessfully, thanks to the white woman in whose house the would-be victim sought refuge (Apel, *Imagery*, 38).

34. Quoted by Smith, *Photography on the Color Line*, Loc. 1435.

35. Smith, "Evidence," *Lynching Photographs*, 24.

36. Smith, *Photography on the Color Line*, Loc. 1655.

37. Significantly, both Smith and Wood connect lynching photography to the genres of photography that, as we saw in chapter 2, were central to disciplinary power, namely mug shots and portraiture. Wood argues that lynching photographs essentially combine the two genres insofar as they present us with portraits of both black criminality and white mastery over it. This is a compelling point, but glosses over the significant differences in style and format between these genres and the lynching photographs. Smith, on the other hand, argues that lynching photographs render visible what mug shots presume but do not show. If mug shots position the white bodies that enforce normalcy outside the frame, lynching photographs render those bodies visible. Lynching photographs document "white supremacists attempting to harness a diffuse and dispersed power to the bounds of white bodies" (Smith, *Photography on the Color*

Line, Loc. 1665), which they then turn on those they intend to subjugate. I agree, but would add that the photographs don't simply document power; they circulate it. Thus, their disciplinary import resides not only in their indexicality, but in their iconicity; how they "move" their putative viewer—male or female, black or white—for example, toward triumph or outrage, docility or resistance. And the same photograph can move viewers either direction depending on context, among other things.

38. Quoted by Hale, *Making Whiteness,* 204.

39. Quoted by Hale, *Making Whiteness,* 204.

40. Emmett Till's lynching was a particularly potent catalyst here. Photographs of Till's maimed and mutilated head and face above his funeral-garbed body mobilized political actions both large and small. See, for example, Apel, "Lynching Photographs and Public Shaming" in *Lynching Photographs,* 61–66; Wood, *Lynching and Spectacle,* 265–270; and Cone, *Cross and the Lynching Tree,* 65–69. As Wood points out, Till's photo does not follow the conventions of lynching photographs; it belongs in the genre of mourning portraiture. Indeed, its affective power likely lies in no small part in its juxtaposition of the horror of lynching (what remains of Till's face) with the dignified composure of the mourning portrait (Till's body clothed in his Sunday best lying in a casket). Publishing it as many media outlets did accompanied by a portrait of a behatted and unscathed young Till smiling into the camera (and photographs of his mother doubled over in grief) accentuated its power.

41. Recalcitrant Southern senators were reportedly to blame for Congress's failure here. Significantly, the Senate formally apologized for this failure in 2000, a move prompted by the impact of "Without Sanctuary," according to Smith, "Evidence," *Lynching Photographs,* 39. Lynching declines markedly after 1930, although the practice continued well into the sixties and beyond. In *Imagery of Lynching,* Apel names 1981 as the date of the "last publically acknowledged lynching" (15), the hanging of a black teenager in Mobile, Alabama, by the Ku Klux Klan (KKK). The memory of lynching lives on in the U.S. racist lexicon ready to be mobilized—literally or figuratively—to keep blacks in their place. Moreover, the lynching noose has entered the realm of the iconographic where it materializes all too frequently as a vehicle for racial harassment in the workplace, for example (Apel, *Imagery,* 16–17). Spectacular murders by whites of black men still occur from time to time; the 1998 killing of James Byrd who was dragged behind a truck in Texas is only one example. Sharon V. Betcher notes that Byrd was not only black, but also disabled, although the latter's relevance to his selection for torment rarely gets mentioned (*Spirit and the Politics of Disablement* [Minneapolis, MN: Fortress, 2007], 18).

42. Wells-Barnett was the first to use lynching photographs to that purpose, according to Wood, *Lynching and Spectacle,* 185.

43. Apel traces its publication and circulation history in *Imagery,* 29–30. Historian James Madison has deemed it *"the* generic lynching photograph" (James H. Madison, *A Lynching in the Heartland: Race and Memory in America* [New

York: Palgrave, 2001], 116); quoted by Smith, "Evidence," *Lynching Photographs*, 18. This photograph was the inspiration for the lyrics to "Strange Fruit," the song made famous by Billie Holiday. See David Margolick, *Strange Fruit: Billie Holiday, Café Society, and an Early Cry for Civil Rights* (Philadelphia: Running Press, 2000), 31; cited by James Cone in *The Cross and the Lynching Tree*, 134. n. 38. The lyricist was a white Jewish New Yorker who eventually adopted the sons of Julius and Ethel Rosenberg, who were executed as Communist spies. Cone goes on to discuss the song's role in antilynching activism and the movements for racial justice that it spawned. It also confronted white audiences with the reality of lynching.

44. All three of these volumes treat lynching photography in much more detail than I will be able to here. All three contextualize this archive and the practice of spectacle lynching, in particular, in larger historical and visual contexts. I commend them to you in their own right and as indexes to the larger collection of scholarship on lynching and antilynching activism beginning with such figures as W. E. B. DuBois and Ida B. Wells-Barnett, who lived through lynching's heyday and were moved by it to lives of political and intellectual resistance to racism.

45. James Allen, "Notes on the Plates," *Without Sanctuary*, 176.

46. Apel, *Imagery*, 22.

47. Allen, "Notes on the Plates," *Without Sanctuary*, 176. Apel also traces the ultimately successful efforts of antilynching activists to get him to stop selling the photograph and to get the photograph itself off the market (*Imagery*, 30).

48. Apel, *Imagery*, 21.

49. Smith, *Photography on the Color Line*, Loc. 1630–36.

50. As Wood notes, the legal and critical race theorist Patricia Williams writes about the practice in her own family (Wood, *Lynching and Spectacle*, 208).

51. Judith Butler, *Precarious Life: The Powers of Mourning and Violence* (New York: Verso, 2006). I'll have more to say about this in the next chapter. Apel also makes a brief connection between lynching photographs and Butler's work on precarity and precariousness ("Lynching Photographs," *Lynching Photographs*, 57), although she focuses on the brutal denial of livability (and thus grievability) that the photographs embody. Smith's discussion of the artist Kerry James Marshall's *Heirlooms and Accessories* (2002) is also pertinent to this topic, though to very different effect. *Heirlooms and Accessories* ("Evidence," *Lynching Photographs*, 30, fig. 6) highlights the faces of three of the white women in the foreground of Beitler's photograph. Each woman's head appears in full detail against the whitewashed background of the rest of the photograph. Each head is framed in a locket connected by a delicate gold or silver chain to the lynched bodies behind them. Following the title, Smith reads the lockets as both accessories and heirlooms. "These women have been accessories to a crime," she writes, which is "the heirloom their daughters will inherit" ("Evidence," *Lynching Photographs*, 29). Considering Beitler's photograph through its citation in *Heirlooms and Accessories* prompts reflection on lynching's legacy for white

women given the role of white womanhood in its justification. "What social and psychological effect goes into maintaining the necklace as adornment instead of trap? What must be repressed and hidden, made invisible and unspoken?" ("Evidence," *Lynching Photographs*, 31).

52. Wood, *Lynching and Spectacle*, 209–15. Black-owned newspapers chose, in some cases, to publish family photographs of the victim instead, thus drawing straightforwardly on the conventions of portrait photography discussed in chapter 1—perhaps a more successful subversion of lynching photography than reprinting could be in this context, Wood suggests. Tellingly, a lynching in California of two white men was handled quite differently by both types of presses.

53. Smith, "Evidence," *Lynching Photographs*, 18.

54. A published version of the photograph captioned "'American Christianity'" appeared in the *Chicago Defender*, August 16, 1930. It is reprinted complete with caption in Smith, "Evidence," *Lynching Photographs*, 21.

55. Quoted by Smith, "Evidence," *Lynching Photographs*, 23.

56. "Indiana Mob Murders Two; Police Aid K.K.K. Hoodlums," *Chicago Defender*, August 16, 1930, p. 1; quoted by Smith, "Evidence," *Lynching Photographs*, 20.

57. Smith, "Evidence," *Lynching Photographs*, 21. Apel reports that the sheriff and his deputies tried for hours to persuade the mob to disperse—even resorting to tear gas toward the end. The mob eventually overruns the officials, grabs the three men in their custody, and proceeds to kill Shipp before leaving the jail with the other two. This would be consistent with the *Defender's* report that the sheriff identified six of the lynchers, but the circuit court judge would not authorize charges against them (*Imagery*, 82, n. 28).

58. Smith, "Evidence," *Lynching Photographs*, 20.

59. "Indiana Mob Murders Two," p. 1; see Smith, "Evidence," *Lynching Photographs*, 20. Indeed, Nazi Germany used lynching photographs throughout the thirties to condemn U.S. hypocrisy for indicting their racist practices (Wood, *Lynching and Spectacle*, 203).

60. Cone, *Cross and the Lynching Tree*, 31–32.

61. Litwack, "Hellhounds," *Without Sanctuary*, 21.

62. Cone, *Cross and the Lynching Tree*, 7.

63. Cone, *Cross and the Lynching Tree*, 7.

64. Cone, *Cross and the Lynching Tree*, 7.

65. Wood, *Lynching and Spectacle*, 48. Wood finds this theo-logic more evocative of the violence of Christian visions of the Last Judgment than the Crucifixion. However, her assessment of its import for blacks and whites respectively dovetails in many ways with Cone's (see chapter 2 of *Lynching and Spectacle*). This is not surprising, in my view, given that the theo-logic of sin, redemption, and retribution often connect Christology and eschatology.

66. Wood, *Lynching and Spectacle*, 50.

67. Cone, *Cross and the Lynching Tree*, 103. Much of Cone's book tackles lynching as a problem of suffering with many layers. On the one hand, experiencing the lynching of loved ones caused family members to question their faith even as

some found solace in knowing that a crucified Christ understood their pain and loss as a fellow sufferer. In thinking through this complexity, Cone attempts to both honor the redemptive power of this connection and to avoid the sacralization (and heroicization) of suffering that can come with it. Sacralizing or heroicizing suffering can end up justifying suffering *as* redemptive; effectively a cross to be borne. This has particularly problematic consequences for black women, as womanist theologians and ethicists like Delores Williams and Emilie Townes point out. Shawn Copeland's *Enfleshing Freedom: Body, Race, and Being* (Minneapolis, MN: Fortress, 2009) threads this needle with particular insight, in my judgment. I will turn to her book in the concluding chapter of this volume. A particularly cogent critique of this problem has been made by Victor Anderson in *Beyond Ontological Blackness* (New York: Continuum, 1999). Anderson's more recent work turns productively to the theme of the grotesque as a way to navigate these tricky waters. See Anderson, *Creative Exchange: A Constructive Theology of African American Religious Experience* (Minneapolis, MN: Fortress, 2008).

68. Cone, *Cross and the Lynching Tree*, 103. A later issue (December 1919) of *The Crisis* develops this logic in both photographic and story form, according to Cone. The photograph—of another lynching—is titled "The Crucifixion in Omaha." It appears with a story by W. E. B. DuBois that revisits Luke's account of the birth of Jesus as a black child born to a black mother in the context of white racist America (Cone, *Cross and the Lynching Tree*, 104; see also Wood, *Lynching and Spectacle*, 187–88).

69. Nicholas Mirzoeff, *The Right to Look: A Counterhistory of Visuality* (Durham, NC: Duke University Press, 2011).

70. Cone, *Cross and the Lynching Tree*, 163. Cone is referring, of course, to Michelle Alexander's important recent book, *The New Jim Crow: Mass Incarceration in the Age of Colorblindness* (New York: New Press, 2010).

71. This may be changing, given the resurgence of discussion of prison reform and abolition of the death penalty across the United States recently.

72. Cone, *Cross and the Lynching Tree*, 164.

73. This photograph may call to mind another photograph from the Abu Ghraib archive of several hooded and naked detainees lined up with their backs to a wall appearing, in some cases, to masturbate while Pfc. England points to them and laughs. I discuss this photograph in "Visual Theology," 182ff.

74. Stephen F. Eisenman, *The Abu Ghraib Effect* (London: Reaktion, 2007), 28.

75. Although Butler doesn't offer a detailed reading of any of the photographs from the Abu Ghraib archive themselves, they figure prominently in her recent book, *Frames of War: When Is Life Grievable?* (New York: Verso, 2009). Indeed, they are the focus of the second chapter, "Torture and the Ethics of Photography: Thinking with Sontag," which takes on Sontag's agnosticism, if you will, about photography's power to move us. I'll have more to say about *Frames* in the following chapter. For now, however, let me note that Butler, too, affirms that the

Abu Ghraib photographs offer their viewers a "visual 'trace' of the human in a condition of torture" (*Frames*, 78).

76. In *The Abu Ghraib Effect*, Eisenman traces this *pathosformel* from its highbrow (by our current standards) past to its lowbrow present (e.g., in Bond films and the television series *24*). The connections he draws between Abu Ghraib and current popular culture both complement and would benefit from Wood's reflections on lynching photography's role in the creation and commodification of spectacle.

77. Eisenman, *Abu Ghraib Effect*, 17.

78. Here, I echo Mitchell's brief but important comment on Eisenman's thesis: the Abu Ghraib photographs cite the visual vocabulary of the *pathosformel*, but not its aesthetic values or conventions (*Cloning*, 116).

79. Edward Said, *Orientalism* (New York: Vintage, 1979; 25th Anniversary edition. reprinted with new Preface, 2003).

80. Edward Said, "Preface to the 25th Anniversary Edition," *Orientalism* (2003), xv–xxx. There is, moreover, a relatively direct connection between Abu Ghraib and Orientalism. Seymour M. Hersh notes that Raphael Patai's *The Arab Mind*, a text that typifies the Orientalist perspective, according to Said (*Orientalism*, 309ff), was "the bible of the neocons on Arab behavior" ("Torture at Abu Ghraib," *Chain of Command: The Road from 9/11 to Abu Ghraib* [New York: HarperCollins, 2004], 39).

81. Gil Anidjar, *The Jew, the Arab: A History of the Enemy* (Stanford, CA: Stanford University Press, 2003).

82. Anidjar's "Abrahamic" is of Derridean provenance. See Jacques Derrida, *Acts of Religion*, ed. Gil Anidjar (New York: Routledge, 2002).

83. Said, *Orientalism*, 206.

84. Documented by John C. Lamoreaux, "Early Christian Responses to Islam," in *Medieval Christian Perspectives of Islam: A Book of Essays*, ed. John Victor Tolan, Garland Medieval Case Books 10, Garland Reference Library of the Humanities 1768 (New York and London: Garland, 1996), 14; cited by Rollin S. Armour, Sr., *Islam, Christianity and the West: A Troubled History* (New York: Orbis, 2002), 39.

85. Armour, *Islam, Christianity, and the West*, 58–59.

86. Said, *Orientalism*, 231. A similar logic also worked in reverse in a different context. American sexologists connected female inversion to masculinism manifest in brain size and structure. Lesbian brains, they conjectured, more closely resembled Oriental men's brains than those of women. See Margaret Gibson, "Clitoral Corruption: Body Metaphors and American Doctors' Construction of Female Homosexuality, 1870–1900," in *Science and Homosexualities*, ed. Vernon Rosario (New York: Routledge, 1997), 108–32. Thanks to LaDelle McWhorter for the reference.

87. Said, *Orientalism*, 207.

88. The most famous is perhaps "iRaq/iPod," a poster that incorporated "Hooded Man" into a visual image that referenced both Andy Warhol's famous silkscreens of celebrities like Jacquelyn Onassis and Marilyn Monroe and an advertising

campaign for Apple's iPod. Others include a mural painted in Sadr City that places "Hooded Man" next to the Statue of Liberty enrobed and hooded in KKK gear with the caption "That Freedom for Bosh [*sic*]." See Mitchell, *Cloning Terror*, chapters 6 and 7 for more on protest art as a form of cloning. Prominent painters and sculptors also produced protest art based on the images. Mitchell includes examples by Richard Serra (fig. 31, 138) and Fernando Botera (fig. 32, 139). Also of note are Martha Rosler's "Bringing the War Home: House Beautiful, New Series (2004)" and the late Gerald Laing's "War Paintings: 2002–Present," which include paintings based on the photograph of England and the leashed prisoner. My thanks to David McCarthy for pointing me to these references.

89. Jacques Derrida, "The Animal That Therefore I Am (More to Follow)," trans. David Wills, *Critical Inquiry* 28, no. 2 (2002): 369–418; originally published as "L'animal que donc je suis (à suivre)" in *L'animal autobiographique: autour de Jacques Derrida*, ed. Marie-Louise Mallet (Paris: Galilée, 1999), 251–301. Some of what follows was published initially in my "'Man' and His 'Others,'" *Bulletin de la Société Americaine de Philosophie de Langue Française* 15, no. 1 (Spring 2005): 1–11 and subsequently (in slightly revised form) in my "Visual Theology." For a more thorough inquiry into the question of the relationship between animality and humanity in Derrida, see Leonard Lawlor, *This Is Not Sufficient: An Essay on Animality and Human Nature in Derrida* (New York: Columbia University Press, 2007). Lawlor attends to the volume in which Derrida expands considerably on the essay/lecture I treat here. That volume, entitled (in French) *L'animal que donc je suis* (Éditions Galilée, 2006) was published in English as *The Animal That Therefore I Am*, trans. David Wills and ed. Marie-Louise Mallet (New York: Fordham University Press, 2008).

90. For more on the connection to Genesis, see Armour, "Visual Theology," 188ff. A full discussion of the theological dimension of Derrida's inquiry into animality would require going well beyond the bounds of this chapter. For some reflections that take up that question in relationship to questions of war (including a brief reference to September 11), see Lawlor, *This Is Not Sufficient*, 11–24. The problematic of animality is taken up again notably in Derrida's recently published seminars, including *The Beast and the Sovereign, Vols. I and II*, trans. Geoffrey Bennington (Chicago: University of Chicago Press, 2009 and 2011, respectively), where it appears in conjunction with questions of divine, state, and subjective sovereignty as well as the question (again) of life and the living.

91. Derrida, "Animal," 12; "L'animal," 263.

92. Derrida, "Animal," 32; "L'animal," 282.

93. Derrida, "Animal," 32; "L'animal," 283.

94. In "'Man' and His 'Others'" and in "Visual Theology," I refer to *l'animot* as an *episteme* (without comment). That now seems to me problematic given the claims Derrida makes for *l'animot's* longevity. To call it an *episteme* would obscure the very different associations animality carries in different times and places even within "the West" (on this, see Foucault's *History of Madness*, trans.

Jonathan Murphy and ed. Jean Khalfa [New York: Routledge, 2006], for example). It was in no small part *l'animot*'s modern material effects as just outlined that prompted that association. They now tempt me to call it a *dispositif*, a temptation that I will hereby resist in no small part to avoid raising the specter of the complex relationship between a Foucauldian perspective and a Derridean one, not to mention between Foucault and Derrida themselves. John Tagg is more courageous than I. He applies this term—in the fully Foucauldian sense—to the Derridean frame (or *parergon*) of Derrida's *The Truth in Painting*, trans. Geoffrey Bennington and Ian McLeod (Chicago: University of Chicago Press, 1987). See John Tagg, *The Disciplinary Frame: Photographic Truths and the Capture of Meaning* (Minneapolis: University of Minnesota Press, 2009), 246.

95. Indeed, in her own analysis of the Abu Ghraib photographs, Judith Butler notes that "it is precisely as human animals that humans suffer" (*Frames of War*, 75) and goes on to mark the suffering of animals that war causes. The overlap between animal and human points up the need for a new ontology of life, a question to which I will return in the conclusion to this volume.

96. Derrida, "Animal," 29; "L'animal," 279.

97. Said, *Orientalism*, 155.

98. On this, see Eduardo Mendieta and Angela Davis, *Abolition Democracy: Beyond Empire, Prisons, and Torture: Interviews with Angela Davis* (New York: Seven Stories, 2005). See also Mirzoeff, *Watching Babylon*, "Section 3: The Empire of Camps."

99. Amitav Ghosh notes the resemblance between the Abu Ghraib photographs and those of Indian prisoners (themselves sometimes subjected to something like extraordinary rendition and exported to prisons elsewhere) from the British Raj. See Amitav Ghosh, "The Theater of Cruelty," *The Nation* (July 18, 2005). On the comparison to Algeria (which extends far beyond the photos), see Neil McMaster, "Torture: From Algiers to Abu Ghraib," *Race and Class* 46, no. 2 (October 2004): 1–21. For a particularly thoughtful consideration of these photos within the larger context of war photography in general, see Haim Bresheeth, "Projecting Trauma: War Photography and the Public Sphere," *Third Text* 20, no. 1 (January 2006): 57–71. In *Time in the Shadows: Confinement in Counterinsurgencies* (Stanford, CA: Stanford University Press, 2012), Laleh Khalili traces the distinctive forms of detention and confinement deployed not only in GWOT, but in a number of other counterinsurgent wars of our time.

100. The experiments conducted by sociologist Sidney Milgram in the sixties are a prime example. See, for example, Arthur G. Miller, Barry E. Collins, and Diana E. Brief, "Perspectives on Obedience to Authority: The Legacy of the Milgram Experiments," *Journal of Social Issues* 51, no. 3 (1995): 1–20, along with other articles in this issue of the journal.

101. Allen Feldman, "On the Actuarial Gaze: From 9/11 to Abu Ghraib," *Cultural Studies* 19, no. 2 (March 2005): 203–26.

102. Jacques Derrida, "The Ends of Man," *Margins of Philosophy*, trans. Alan Bass (Chicago: University of Chicago Press, 1982), 134.

103. Derrida, "Ends of Man," 135. We should perhaps also note that Derrida began his address by informing his audience that he stipulated his attendance at this event on being able to state openly his solidarity with civil rights and antiwar activists. Receiving those assurances, he came, although he muses that this indicates how little bother such expressions (perhaps especially out of a foreigner's mouth) create for the powers-that-be. All of this is emblematic of the "form of democracy" ("Ends of Man," 114), he says.

104. Slavoj Žižek, "Between Fear and Trembling: On Why Only Atheists Can Believe," Vanderbilt University, November 3, 2006.

105. Apel helpfully traces and tracks in "Torture Culture" much of what the media had made public at the time of its writing (2004, I presume). *New Yorker* reporter Seymour M. Hersh's *Chain of Command: The Road from 9/11 to Abu Ghraib* (New York: Harper Collins, 2004) and Danner's book, *Torture and Truth*, came out in 2004. Danner's book is itself primarily a veritable archive—photographic and documentary—of Abu Ghraib (what preceded it, what made it possible, and the investigations that followed up on it). See also Jane Mayer, *The Dark Side: The Inside Story of How the War of Terror Turned Into a War on American Ideals* (New York: Anchor, 2008; reprinted with a new foreword in 2009). Portions of *The Dark Side* first appeared in *The New Yorker*. For film documentaries on Abu Ghraib, see Errol Morris's "Standard Operating Procedure" and Rory Kennedy's "Ghosts of Abu Ghraib."

106. Daniel Heyman, "It Is Difficult." *Portraits of Iraqis*, 2004–2008, http://www .danielheyman.com/projects_works_iraq.htm. The Rhode Island School of Design mounted an exhibition of the portraits (entitled "I Am Sorry It Is Difficult to Start") in 2013. Some of the works included in the exhibition can be seen as the backdrop to a lecture Heyman delivered at a symposium connected to the exhibition, which is available online at http://www.brown.edu/campus -life/arts/bell-gallery/events/2013/04/05/art-and-war-iraq-symposium. Thanks to David McCarthy for pointing me to Heyman's work.

5. Bio-Discipline and the Right to Life

1. The details of her case have been reported in numerous articles. My source is the report of her court-appointed guardian ad litem dated January 1, 2003. For a more thorough tracking of the legal history, see John Protevi, *Political Affect: The Social and the Somatic* (Minneapolis: University of Minnesota Press, 2009).

2. See Benedict Carey, "Inside the Injured Brain, Many Kinds of Awareness," *New York Times*, April 5, 2005. Dr. Sanjay Gupta places the estimate at 10,000–25,000 people (CNN Morning Show, March 31, 2005).

3. Charles Babington, "Frist Defends Remarks on Schiavo Case," *New York Times*, June 17, 2005. Some of the videos are still available at the website for the Terri

Schiavo Foundation, which the Schindler family founded to carry on the right-to-life cause in their daughter's memory; see http://www.terrisfight.org. Protevi tracks the (mis)use of Ms. Schiavo's (contested) diagnosis in the courts of law and of public opinion quite closely.

4. I am dealing only with stills and not with the movies themselves and thus will apply to them the theoretical approach developed in chapter 2 (supplemented as appropriate here). The scholarship on family home movies of which I am aware is largely congruent in perspective with much of what I have to say about family snapshots as a genre and about their larger social function. The advent of cheap technology for moving picture making (for which Kodak was also responsible) made possible amateur filmmaking in general, including (but not limited to) home movies. Thus, scholars of home movies typically consider them in relationship to both amateur and professional filmmaking, both of which are outside the purview of my project. For more on home movies, though, see especially James M. Moran, *There's No Place Like Home Video* (Minneapolis: University of Minnesota Press, 2002); Karen Ishsizuka and Patricia R. Zimmerman, *Mining the Home Movie: Excavations in Histories and Memories* (Sacramento: University of California Press, 2007); and Patricia R. Zimmerman, *Reel Families: A Social History of Amateur Film* (Bloomington: Indiana University Press, 1995).

5. See Rick Lyman, "Protestors with Hearts on Sleeves and Anger on Signs," *New York Times*, March 28, 2005, on the protests by members of Not Dead Yet, a disability rights group focused particularly against euthanasia. The (*de facto*) alliance between disability rights activists and the religious right aroused concerns of many activists. See, for example, debates in Ragged Edge Online (http://raggededgemagazine.com). Thanks to Dee McGraw for pointing me toward this material.

6. Cf., for example, Anita Silvers, "Reconciling Equality to Difference: Caring (f) or Justice for People with Disabilities," *Hypatia* 10, no. 1 (Winter, 1995): 30–55; Rosemarie Garland Thomson, "Integrating Disability, Transforming Feminist Theory," *NWSA Journal* 14, no. 3 (2002): 1–32; and P. Conrad, "Medicalization and Social Control," *Annual Review of Sociology* 18 (1992): 209–32. At the heart of this distinction is a critique of the medicalization of disability as more concerned with normalizing than creative accommodation. A similar critique of the medicalization of gender nonconformity occurred early in the trans and intersexed communities for similar reasons. See, for example, Alice Domurat Dreger, *Hermaphrodites and the Medical Invention of Sex* (Cambridge, MA: Harvard University Press, 1998) and "Should There Be Only Two Sexes?" in Anne Fausto-Sterling's *Sexing the Body: Gender Politics and the Construction of Sexuality* (New York: Basic, 2000), chapter 4. Recently, however, the main body of intersexed activists has allied itself with medicalization for complex reasons (and not without some ambivalence). Cf. Alyson Spurgas, "(Un)Queering Identity: The Biosocial Production of Intersex/DSD," *Critical Intersex*, ed. Morgan Holmes (Surrey, England: Ashgate, 2009), 97–122. My thanks to Erin Bergner for this information and this source.

7. A new term, "unabled," has come into currency as a descriptor for those whose cognitive capacities are severely compromised. For some cautionary notes about this distinction, see Alison Kafer, *Feminist, Queer, Crip* (Bloomington: Indiana University Press, 2013), 67–68.

8. Consider, for example, the positions of philosophers Peter Singer and Martha Nussbaum (infamously drastic, in his case; much more nuanced in hers). Singer, a well-known animal rights activist, has argued that the centrality of "rationality, autonomy, and self-consciousness" (Singer, *Practical Ethics* [Cambridge, MA: Cambridge University Press, 1979], 131; quoted by Toibin Siebers, *Disability Theory* [Ann Arbor: University of Michigan Press, 2008], 92) to what it means to be human legitimates ending the lives of those who constitutively lack those capacities, a position that has been strongly resisted by disability theorists and activists. Nussbaum posits a "capability threshold" below which one becomes a "former" human being—to whom rights are granted only by charity. PVS exemplifies that state because all of the capabilities that define the human (which go well beyond Singer's narrow list and include some that we share with nonhuman animals) are obliterated. She does not spell out what the consequences would be for human beings in such a condition, although she is much more cautious about ending human lives than Singer. She acknowledges, for example, that the good life for human beings may be more compatible with pain and decrepitude than for other (nonhuman) animals. Moreover, her aim is to provide a stronger philosophical scaffolding for supporting people with disabilities and their caregivers—categories in which all of us will find ourselves at some point, she acknowledges. See Martha Nussbaum, *Frontiers of Justice: Disability, Nationality, Species Membership* (Cambridge, MA: Harvard University Press, 2006), especially chapters 2 and 3.

9. Timothy Williams, "Schaivo's Brain Was Severely Deteriorated, Autopsy Says," *New York Times*, June 15, 2005. The autopsy confirmed the diagnosis of PVS, although it did not confirm bulimia as the (presumed) indirect cause of her heart attack. Photos from the autopsy that showed severe brain atrophy (at the time of her death, her brain weighed approximately half of what's usual for a normal adult) were also released.

10. Marianne Hirsch, *Family Frames: Photography, Narrative and Postmemory* (Cambridge, MA: Harvard University Press, 1997), 8.

11. Being subjected to the stare is a common experience for people with disabilities and, as Sharon V. Betcher points out, for colonized and racialized people, as well. Being "fixed in the gaze or caught in the stare," she writes, threatens to epidermalize (*pace* Franz Fanon) the disabled or colonized person "collapsing the psychic room of personhood" to what the surface of the skin renders visible (Betcher, *Spirit and the Politics of Disablement* [Minneapolis, MN: Fortress, 2007], 5). In *Staring: How We Look* (New York: Oxford University Press, 2009), Garland Thomson argues that, with practice and deliberation (and by trading on the prohibitions against staring), people with disabilities have developed strategies to convert this form of entrapment into a site/sight of

productive encounter, at least on occasion. This is not an easy task, of course, nor does "productive" mean that the encounter ends in some kind of mutual enlightenment, say. But, turned into what Garland Thomson calls "beholding" (the title of chapter 12 of *Staring*), it can result in a reclamation of agency and dignity, of social capital and standing. Staring can be mobilized for political purposes. In the recent civil war in Sierra Leone, for example, soldiers amputated the arms of children as a gesture of intimidation. U.S. advocates for the children (who were brought to the United States to be fitted for prostheses) "carefully orchestrated" staring encounters between the children and Americans to arouse sympathy and support (financial and otherwise) for the children (Garland Thomson, *Staring*, 127–28). Prostheses themselves are as often about "passing" as about restoring function. Disguising the loss of an arm or leg with an aesthetic double offers relief from stares, a benefit sometimes worth the cost in energy of wearing it. Sometimes, but not always. Disability scholar and activist Dr. Theresa Degener, featured prominently in *Staring*, rejects wearing prosthetic arms opting instead for elegant professional clothes that work with her body as it is, allowing it to move in the ways she's adapted and adopted for functionality. For a powerful analysis of what we might call prosthetic ambivalence, see Betcher, *Spirit and the Politics of Disablement*, 90–104. Visuality is central to this ambivalence as the medicalization of disability conspires with the social demand for normalizing the disabled body, as Garland Thomson analyzes in *Staring*.

12. It is important to remember that photographs and other visual images can be turned to recuperative or resistive ends. The artist Doug Auld, whose series of portraits of burn survivors, "State of Grace," Garland Thomson discusses, uses his artistic skills to attempt to counter the social stigma that comes with disability ("Looking Away, Staring Back," in Garland Thomson, *Staring*, 79–86).

13. Robert Hariman and John Louis Lucaites, *No Caption Needed: Iconic Photographs, Public Culture and Liberal Democracy* (Chicago: University of Chicago Press, 2007), 37.

14. Terri Beth Miller, " 'Reading' the Body of Terri Schiavo: Inscriptions of Power in Medical and Legal Discourse," *Literature and Medicine* 28, no. 1 (Spring 2009): 33–54.

15. See Protevi, "Terri Schiavo: The Somatic Body Politic" in *Political Affect*, 115–39; Jeffrey Bishop, "The Sovereign Subject and Death" in *The Anticipatory Corpse: Medicine, Power, and the Care of the Dying* (Notre Dame: University of Notre Dame Press, 2011), 197–222, and "Biopolitics, Terri Schiavo, and the Sovereign Subject of Death," *Journal of Medicine and Philosophy* 33, no. 6 (2008): 338–57; and Eric Santner, "Terri Schiavo and the State of Exception," *University of Chicago Press Blog*, March 29, 2005. Protevi also considers Hurricane Katrina in the same volume. I attend to that dimension of his argument in chapter 6.

16. Agamben takes issue with Foucault's account of the relationship between sovereignty, life, and modernity. Sovereignty's relationship to life hasn't only been

about the power to kill; it's also about the power to (allow to) live—inside or outside the polis. Moreover, sovereign power remains more robust under bio-power than Agamben thinks Foucault allows. This is evident in the creation and maintenance of detention camps of which the paradigm are the Nazi concentration camps. See Giorgio Agamben, *Homo Sacer: Sovereign Power and Bare Life*, trans. Daniel Heller-Roazen (Stanford, CA: Stanford University Press, 1998) and *The State of Exception*, trans. Kevin Attell (Chicago: University of Chicago Press, 2005).

17. We laypeople may think that the pronouncement of death simply acknowledges a biological reality, but in many cases, it produces that reality. Indeed, as Bishop argues in chapter 4 of *The Anticipatory Corpse*, we have the power to determine the line between life and death. The very notion of brain death developed out of the practice of organ donation—itself a practice that blurs the line between life and death.

18. See the recent case of Marlise Muñoz discussed in the introduction to this volume. Recent research in the development of premature babies provides an interesting perspective in the legacies of the mind–body dualism. Many studies have shown that premature infants are far more likely to have developmental or learning disabilities, anxiety disorders, and so on than infants carried to term. The development of neural pathways takes place via interactions between the infant and its environment. Research suggests that the problem may lie in the radical differences between the womb and most neonatal intensive care units (NICU), which inhibit the normal paths brain development would take in the womb. Dr. Heidelise Als, a developmental psychologist at Harvard Medical School, has transformed NICU practices as a result of her research. See Paul Raeburn, "A Second Womb," *New York Times Magazine*, August 15, 2005. Intriguingly, Als got her start studying primatology and paleontology. Her own experiences raising a developmentally and emotionally disabled son were also influential. The skills she used to learn to communicate with him helped her "read" premature infants. Similarly, the animal behaviorist Temple Grandin, who has transformed slaughterhouse practices, credits her autism with enabling her to "read" cows' affective responses to their environments. See Temple Grandin and Catherine Johnson, *Animals in Translation: Using the Mysteries of Autism to Decode Animal Behavior* (New York: Scribner, 2005).

19. Susan Bordo, *Unbearable Weight: Feminism, Western Culture and the Body* (Berkeley: University of California Press, 1993; reprinted in 2003 with a new preface).

20. Also rendered ironic (and troubling) is the existence of the so-called feeding tube diet, popular in Europe, which a Florida physician also offers. It is particularly attractive to brides-to-be as a weight loss measure. See Linda Lee, "Bridal Hunger Games: Losing Weight in Time for the Wedding," *New York Times*, April 13, 2012.

21. Michel Foucault, *The History of Sexuality, Vol. 1: An Introduction*, trans. Robert Hurley (New York: Random House, 1978), 145; *La volonté de savoir* (Paris: Éditions Gallimard, 1974), 191.

22. Indeed, many were moved by Ms. Schiavo's situation to write living wills that attempted to prescribe and proscribe measures to be taken should they become too incapacitated to decide such things for themselves. This led Singer to observe that, because the controversy prompted so many to legally codify that very wish, it would likely result in more feeding tubes being removed rather than fewer. See Peter Singer, "Making Our Own Decisions About Death: Competency Should Be Paramount," *Free Inquiry* 25, no. 5 (2006): 36–38.

23. Betcher, *Spirit and the Politics of Disablement*, 72.

24. Mary Johnson, "After Terri Schiavo: Why the disability rights movement spoke out, why some of us worried, and where to we go from here?" http://www .raggededgemagazine.com/focus/postschiavo0405.html#imparato.

25. Santner, "Terri Schiavo." Protevi argues that Ms. Schiavo's medical crisis performed the initial reduction to bare life. Because bare life remains first and foremost a political category for Agamben, Protevi finds his philosophical perspective limited.

26. Protevi, *Political Affect*, 131. The law here seems to accord with Protevi. Legally, one can be declared "civilly dead," according to Miller, which is defined as "the state of a person who, though possessing natural life, has lost all civil rights and as to them is considered civilly dead" (*Black's Law Dictionary*, quoted by Miller, "'Reading' the Body of Terri Schiavo," 45). That declaration, I gather, precedes the appointment of a proxy, in the absence of advance directives, to stand in for the civilly dead subject. Such a status equates the (putatively permanent) loss of consciousness with loss of autonomy and thus with loss of life, Miller observes.

27. Santner, "Terri Schiavo." His observation brings into sharp relief the U.S. response to the hunger strike by the Guantanamo detainees in the late spring and summer of 2013. Against their clearly expressed will, prison authorities ordered military doctors to force-feed the hunger strikers using the same technology, the feeding tube, that sustained Ms. Schiavo's life. See "Gitmo Is Killing Me," an op-ed by Samir Naji al Hasan Moqbel, one of the prisoners subjected to that treatment published in the *New York Times*, April 14, 2013.

28. For analyses of both dimensions, see, for example, Betcher, *Spirit and the Politics of Disablement*, 90–104, and "Crip/tography," the first chapter of her more recent book, *Spirit and the Obligation of Social Flesh: A Secular Theology for the Global City* (New York: Fordham University Press, 2013), 26–49.

29. Judith Butler, *Gender Trouble: Feminism and the Subversion of Identity* (New York: Routledge, 1990). Butler has made a more substantive filmic foray into the topic of disability. In the portion of a film on contemporary philosophers devoted to her (*The Examined Life*, dir. Astra Taylor, 2008), Butler engages with a young disability studies scholar as they navigate the Mission District in San Francisco; Butler on foot, the younger scholar in her wheelchair.

30. Robert McCruer, *Crip Theory: Cultural Signs of Queerness and Disability* (New York: New York University Press, 2006). See as well Ellen Samuels's 2002 survey of Butler's status in the field, "Critical Divides: Judith Butler's Body Theory and the Question of Disability," *NWSA Journal* 14, no. 3 (2002): 58–76. Siebers

is also critical of Butler's tendency to focus on the psychic and the social over the material—a tendency that much recent humanist theorizing about embodiment shares. See Siebers, *Disability Theory*, chapters 3 and 4, especially 75–80. Notably, Butler herself acknowledges this limitation: "I confess, however, that I am not a very good materialist. Every time I try to write about the body, the writing ends up being about language" (Judith Butler, *Undoing Gender* [New York: Routledge, 2004], 198).

31. I am adding disability to Butler's list. See the Introduction to *Bodies That Matter: On the Discursive Limits of Sex* (New York: Routledge, 1993). In his most recent book, *The End of Normal: Identity in a Biocultural Era* (Ann Arbor: University of Michigan Press, 2013), disability theorist Lennard Davis argues that diversity may be replacing normality as the regnant order of humanity—except in the case of disability, which is still essentialized and fixed. I am persuaded that disability receives differential treatment both by our culture at large and within academia; it is not recognized as a form of diversity. I'm not persuaded, however, that diversity's arrival heralds the (approaching) end of normal—at least, not any time soon. That is an impossible claim to sustain given the differential treatment of black lives evident in mass incarceration and the recent police killings of Michael Brown, Eric Garner, and Freddie Gray. That said, Davis is right that neoliberal capitalism has found ways to market, say, hip-hop culture and gay culture (think "Queer Eye for the Straight Guy") rendering acceptable (certain forms of) blackness and queerness in ways that has not happened for disability (except in rare cases). And, in academic circles, at least, we understand raced, sexed or gendered, and sexual identities as matters of (embodied) performance that are variable and malleable rather than fixed, a status also rarely accorded to disability. But diversity's emergence reads to me, rather, as normalization's expansion—or morphing—rather than its contraction.

32. Judith Butler, *Psychic Life of Power: Theories in Subjection* (Stanford, CA: Stanford University Press, 1997).

33. Judith Butler, *Frames of War: When Is Life Grievable?* (New York: Verso, 2009) and *Precarious Life: The Powers of Mourning and Violence* (New York: Verso, 2006).

34. Butler, *Frames of War*, 76.

35. I use this term here in its ordinary sense, but also in Protevi's more expansive use of it in *Political Affect* and its predecessor *Political Physics* (New York: Athlone, 2001). My analysis, too, I think (though from a slightly different angle) shows Terri Schiavo's to be a political body. Indeed, it suggests we are all (caught up in) bodies politic—from top to bottom, stem to stern.

36. It would be important and productive, I think (although outside the scope of my project here), to analyze this dynamic of Ms. Schiavo's case in light of critiques raised of extending charity to people with disabilities. See Betcher, *Spirit and the Politics of Disablement*, chapter 5; and Julia Watts Belser, "Disability and the Social Politics of 'Natural' Disaster: Toward a Jewish Feminist Ethics of Disaster Tales," *Worldviews: Global Religions, Culture, and Ecology* 19, no. 1

(2014): 51–68. My thanks to the author for sharing an advance copy of this essay with me. I'll have more to say about it in the next chapter.

37. Butler, *Psychic Life of Power*, 30.

38. Butler, *Precarious Life*, 46.

39. That body need not be of flesh and blood. Note recent technological advances that allow people in advanced stages of ALS (more commonly known as Lou Gehrig's disease) who have lost the ability to move any muscle to communicate via a computer interface connected to electrodes implanted in the brain.

40. Protevi, *Political Affect*, 131; and Santner, "Terri Schiavo." In speaking this way, they expose the persistent difficulty that embodiment poses to modern philosophical anthropology. Consciousness continues to constitute the line between the human and the nonhuman. A human being without consciousness ceases to be human and becomes no more than a body. Yet consciousness is bodily and material. Neurological injuries of all sorts manifest as impairments to consciousness, and not just what we know, but who we recognize, how we interact (inhibitions can disappear), even what we know of our bodies (strokes can leave survivors utterly unaware of the paralyzed side of their bodies). The late neurologist Oliver Sacks has written about many of these phenomena for a popular audience. See his *The Man Who Mistook His Wife for a Hat and Other Clinical Tales* (New York: Simon & Schuster, 1970) among others.

41. As the French historian of disability, Henri-Jacques Stiker notes, normates' responses to people with disabilities are often fraught with fear and loathing. But this fear is different, he argues, from the fear of death (as invoked by Mr. Felos in this chapter's first epigraph). That fear is "of a void, of loss" while the fear of disability is the "fear of the different" (Henri-Jacques Stiker, *A History of Disability*, trans. William Sayers [Ann Arbor: University of Michigan, 1999], 8), a fear that prompts in some a desire to kill. "Let us admit the very primordial function that the disabled fill. They are the tear in our being that reveals its open-endedness, its incompleteness, its precariousness. Because of that, because of that difference, they can . . . be considered expiatory victims, scapegoats," Stiker writes (*A History of Disability*, 12). My thanks to Sharon Betcher for the reference.

42. Cf., for example, Bob Fredericks, "Paralyzed Man Woken from Coma Chooses Death," *New York Post*, November 6, 2013. For a complex and nuanced account of living with quadriplegia, see Robin Marantz Henig, "A Life or Death Situation," *New York Times*, July 17, 2013.

43. Personal decisions made on one's own behalf are one thing, but political decisions that affect others are another. As Diane Coleman of *Not Dead Yet* has observed, "The right wing wants to kill us slowly and painfully [with limits on health programs such as Medicare and Medicaid]; the left wing wants to kill us quickly and call it compassion." Quoted by Ceci Connolly, "Schiavo Raised Profile of Disabled (Questions Swirl About End of Life Issues)," *Washington Post*, April 2, 2005.

44. Butler, *Frames of War*, 75.
45. Butler, *Precarious Life*, 26.
46. Butler, *Precarious Life*, 31.
47. Butler, *Precarious Life*, 31.
48. For an example of the kind of care I have in mind, see Gina Kolata, "At These Hospitals, Recovery Is Rare, but Comfort Is Not," *New York Times*, June 23, 2014.

6. The Perfect Storm

1. Although distinct in its approach, the analysis I'll offer of Hurricane Katrina herein has much in common with the general perspective on Hurricane Katrina offered by philosophers John Protevi and Nancy Tuana and theologian Anthony Pinn. Fundamental to all three accounts is the insight we gain from Katrina and events like it to the "viscous porosity" (Nancy Tuana, "Viscous Porosity: Witnessing Katrina" in *Material Feminisms*, ed. Stacy Aliamo and Susan J. Hekman [Bloomington: Indiana University Press, 2008], 188–213) that constitutes our relationship to the world we inhabit. That porosity is simultaneously material and social, historical and immediate, physical and affective. All three see in Katrina an object lesson in vulnerability and responsibility that we ignore at our peril. See John Protevi, "Hurricane Katrina: The Governmental Body Politic" in *Political Affect: Connecting the Social and the Somatic* (Minneapolis: University of Minnesota Press, 2009); Tuana, "Viscous Porosity: Witnessing Katrina," 188–213; and Anthony Pinn, *Embodiment and the New Shape of Black Theological Thought* (New York: New York University Press, 2010), 146–205.

2. I am not the first to connect (dis)ability and environmental concerns in general and with Hurricane Katrina. Sharon V. Betcher's short essay, "Of Disability and the Garden State," *Religious Studies News Spotlight on Theological Education* (March 2013) articulates the consequences of viscous porosity in a particularly powerful way. There, she argues for the mutually transformative import of tracing the connections between environmental issues and disability on both environmental and disability studies, including theology. I return to Betcher's work in the concluding chapter of this volume. Citing critiques by disability theorists of the way (biblical and extrabiblical) "disaster tales" (51) deploy disability as a tragic individualized consequence of disaster, Julia Watts Belser argues that such narratives reconsolidate and renaturalize the divide between the normal and the disabled, thereby obscuring the body politics (if you will) that shape disasters like Katrina. See Julia Watts Belser, "Disability and the Social Politics of 'Natural' Disaster: Toward a Jewish Feminist Ethics of Disaster Tales," *Worldviews: Global Religions, Culture and Ecology* 19, no. 1 (2014): 51–68.

3. In considering Hurricane Katrina in such close proximity to Terri Schiavo's case, I repeat a move made by Protevi in *Political Affect*. Recall from my engagement

with Protevi in the previous chapter that the philosophical approach he takes is more Deleuzian than Foucauldian (or Butlerian), but it is copacetic with mine in several ways. For one thing, his focus on political affect aligns well with my interest in photographic affect. Indeed, photographic affect is a form of political affect. In "connecting the social and the somatic," to quote *Political Affect*'s subtitle, certain photographs create various forms—or levels—of bodies politic that connect individuals to collectives large and small (families, prisons and schools, voluntary organizations, nation states), a claim analogous to Azoulay's concept of photographic citizenship discussed in chapter 2.

4. Willie Drye, "Hurricane Katrina: The Essential Time Line," *National Geographic News,* September 14, 2005.

5. Associated Press, "2 Months Later, Victim of Katrina Is Laid to Rest," *NBCNews.com,* November 16, 2005.

6. Belser, "Disability and the Social Politics of 'Natural' Disaster," 62.

7. Associated Press, "2 Months Later." This may make Mrs. Freeman a rarity in the *histoire* of the role figures of people with disability have played in disaster narratives that Belser critiques. Instead of remaining the picture of tragic and individualized inevitability, Mrs. Freeman became an icon of political and social failure. That said, that she was a person with a disability—and was photographed in a wheelchair—is hardly incidental to the photograph's impact. Belser cites Lakshmi Fjord, who argues wheelchairs serve as "prosthetics" for the presumed tragedy of disabled existence in general. See Lakshmi Fjord, "Disasters, Race, and Disability: [Un]Seen Through the Political Lens on Katrina," *Journal of Race and Policy* 3, no. 1 (2007): 46–66; cited by Belser, "Disability and the Social Politics of 'Natural' Disaster," 62. Without doubt, that sense of tragedy is essential to the photographic affect of Mrs. Freeman's photograph and thus contributes to its iconic status.

8. See, for example, Barry Jean, Marcia Gaudet, and Carl Lindahl, eds., *Second Line Rescue: Improvised Responses to Katrina and Rita* (Oxford: University Press of Mississippi, 2013). Two of the essays in a special issue of the *Journal of American History* (about which more will follow) document the essential role two churches played in communal efforts at rebuilding after Katrina. Another documents the remarkable organizational work done by a coalition of New Orleans's women. See Donald E. DeVore, "Water in Sacred Places: Rebuilding New Orleans's Black Churches as Sites of Community Empowerment," *Journal of American History* 94, no. 3 (December 2007): 762–69; Karen J. Leong et al., "Resilient History and the Rebuilding of a Community: The Vietnamese American Community in New Orleans East," *Journal of American History* 94, no. 3 (December 2007): 770–79; and Pamela Tyler, "The Post-Katrina, Semiseparate World of Gender Politics," *Journal of American History* 94, no. 3 (December 2007): 780–88. In addition, there are a number of fine documentary films about both sides of Katrina's aftermath, including Spike Lee's *When the Levees Broke: A Requiem in Four Acts* (2006) and Carl Deal and Tia Lessin's

Trouble the Water (2008), the heart of which is film footage shot by a gritty survivor, Kimberly Rivers, using her camcorder.

9. See, for example, Deborah Blumenthal, "Shelters for Pets Fill with Furry Survivors," *New York Times,* September 8, 2005.

10. Indeed, among the more remarkable things about Hurricane Katrina's aftermath was the sea change it inaugurated in animal rescue operations in natural disasters. Disaster planning in the United States now routinely includes arrangements to shelter domestic pets. Of course, this new practice is driven as much (or more) by concern for their human owners as by concern for the pets. For more on this, see Cheri Barton-Ross and Jane Baron-Sorenson, *Pet Loss and Human Emotion: A Guide to Recovery* (New York: Routledge, 2007).

11. Several documentary films have been made about the animal rescue efforts after Katrina. Among them are *Dark Water Rising: Survival Stories of Hurricane Katrina Animal Rescues,* directed by Mike Shiley (Shidog Films, 2006), which follows the rescuers themselves capturing them at their best and their worst. It allows a sobering glimpse into the horror that Katrina spawned. See as well the award-winning documentary film *Mine,* directed by Geralyn Pezanoski (Smush Media, 2009) for a compelling and moving account of some of the reunions, but also of the conflicts created between original owners who located their pets a few years after someone else had adopted them. In addition to their affective source in the attachments we often make with pets, these conflicts have roots not only in the law (which defines pets as property), but also, the film suggests, in issues of race and class.

12. See Protevi, *Political Affect,* 163–83; and Tuana, "Viscous Porosity," 194ff. Although there are certainly overlaps, we each highlight different aspects of New Orleans's past (including its recent past) and we make different philosophical connections—but to similar ends, as noted earlier. I commend their accounts to you, as well, especially for what distinguishes them from mine.

13. Much of what follows is drawn from the articles in the special issue of the *Journal of American History* devoted to Hurricane Katrina mentioned (and cited) earlier, which is largely a compilation of papers from a conference sponsored by the University of South Alabama in 2007. This issue is special not only in the usual sense, but in the remarkable mix of disciplines, clear-eyed analytical insight, and deep pathos it contains—to be expected, perhaps, given the personal connections many of the authors had to Katrina and the Gulf coast.

14. Ari Kelman, "Boundary Issues: Clarifying New Orleans's Murky Edges," *Journal of American History* 94, no. 3 (December 2007): 695–703.

15. Kelman, "Boundary Issues," 695.

16. Kelman, "Boundary Issues," 695.

17. Karen Kingsley, "New Orleans Architecture: Building Renewal," *Journal of American History* 94, no. 3 (December 2007): 716–25.

18. As Kelman reports, Congress commissioned Charles Ellet in 1852 (after the flood of 1849) to study the flooding problem in New Orleans and propose a

solution. In that report, Ellet argued that building ever-higher levees and draining the swamps only exacerbated the city's vulnerability. Instead, he suggested a mix of levees, outlets, and artificial wetlands, a recommendation that failed to gain any traction (Kelman, "Boundary Issues," 198–99)—perhaps, in part, because of the yellow fever epidemic of 1853. That event may have strengthened drives to drain the wetlands for sanitary reasons (if, that is, they understood yellow fever to be caused by mosquitos, which seems unlikely given how racialized the etiology articulated by town fathers for the disease was).

19. Katrina's impact on New Orleans was all too reminiscent of Betsy's in both the destruction it wrought (and who bore the brunt of it) and the displacements that followed. See Juliette Landphair, "The Forgotten People of New Orleans": Community, Vulnerability and the Lower Ninth Ward," *Journal of American History* 94, no. 3 (December 2007): 837–43.

20. Unfortunately, the city seems to have embraced once again the notion that it can "engineer itself out of harm's way," that it really can establish a secure boundary between nature and culture, the nonhuman and the human realms— "a myth," Kelman concludes, "that will not die, no matter how many of New Orleans's residents do" ("Boundary Issues," 703).

21. I say "African slaves" rather than "slaves of African descent" because the labor conditions in the Caribbean were so brutal that slaves rarely survived long enough to reproduce. They were replaced by new imports from Africa.

22. Protevi, *Political Affect,* 171. Although often referred to as black by outsiders, Ray Nagin, New Orleans's mayor during and immediately after Katrina, is a case in point. Although not from the Creole political class, as mayor, he played a familiar Creole role: that of mediator between (poorer, less politically powerful) blacks and (wealthier, more powerful) whites, Protevi claims. Arnold R. Hirsch argues that Nagin's reelection, which was decided largely along racial lines, marked the political triumph [not necessarily one to be celebrated] of America's traditional binary system over New Orleans's trinary—and then some—system, which had been in decline for some time. Dubbing this the "canary in the miner's helmet" (Hirsch, "Fade to Black: Hurricane Katrina and the Disappearance of Creole New Orleans," *Journal of American History* 94, no. 3 [December 2007]: 761), he worries that it signals the demise of Creole culture that, because of the displacements in Katrina's wake, faces the challenge of survival in diaspora. Hirsch, who holds an endowed chair in New Orleans history at the University of New Orleans, makes this claim after tracing a good deal of the complex history of race relations in New Orleans from its founding to the present.

23. And to the river. Commodities were not the only things traded up and down the Mississippi and across and around the Gulf. That New Orleans (along with other towns on the Mississippi like Memphis, for example) proved fertile ground for the emergence of new forms of music reflects a trade in forms of cultural expression. Floods, too, were involved. Zydeco, for example, was the creation of New Orleans musicians displaced to Texas, according to Roger

Wood, the author of *Texas Zydeco* (cited by Bruce Boyd Raeburn, "'They're Tryin' to Wash Us Away': New Orleans Musicians Surviving Katrina," *Journal of American History* 94, no. 3 [December 2007]: 812–19, 818), which exposed them to new musical influences. Musicians who have returned from this one (only a fraction of pre-Katrina numbers as of 2007) are active in fundraising and restoration efforts, Raeburn notes.

24. See, for example, Leong et al., "Resilient History," and Elizabeth Fussell, "Constructing New Orleans, Constructing Race: A Population History of New Orleans" in *Journal of American History* 94, no. 3 (December 2007): 846–55.

25. This was not the first time that the U.S. government had taken an interest in New Orleans. Alecia P. Long notes that New Orleans was the first U.S. city to benefit from the FDR administration's new commitment to building public housing. See her "Poverty Is the New Prostitution: Race, Poverty, and Public Housing in Post-Katrina New Orleans," *Journal of American History* 94, no. 3 (December 2007): 795–803. During World War II, the port of New Orleans became for a brief time a hub for the burgeoning military-industrial complex, J. Mark Souther notes in his "The Disneyfication of New Orleans: The French Quarter as Façade in a Divided City," *Journal of American History* 94, no. 3 (December 2007): 804–11. New Orleans lacked the skilled labor needed to staff an increasingly high-tech industry, though, he observes.

26. Kent B. Germany, "The Politics of Poverty and History," *Journal of American History,* 94, no. 3 (December 2007): 743–51.

27. Germany, "The Politics of Poverty and History," 749. According to Fussell, sociologists have long documented that low-skilled jobs tend to go to stigmatized minorities. Ongoing racialized inequities in educational access and quality post–Jim Crow helped ensure the continued presence of such a labor pool (mostly black low-wage workers) in the metro area before Katrina. The labor trend continued post-Katrina, she argues, but with a twist. With so much of the black labor pool displaced, the work of reconstruction turned to Latino/as as laborers who are often subjected to substandard working conditions for substandard wages. (This is not the first time that New Orleans has turned to immigrant workers for such a purpose. The construction of the New Basin Canal that connects the Central Business District and Lake Pontchartrain was deemed too life-threatening for slaves so Irish immigrants were recruited for those jobs.)

28. Souther, "The Disneyfication of New Orleans," 804–11. Traces of the exotic and the erotic remained in pre-Katrina French Quarter, but most of the trade in prostitution and so on was relegated to adjacent areas of the city (the famed Storyville and so-called black Storyville). See Long, "Poverty Is the New Prostitution," 795–803.

29. In the aftermath of Katrina, the traumatic images of the Superdome as shelter of last resort made the arena an icon of the suffering New Orleanians endured— and, ultimately, of recovery when it was subsequently restored in time for the

2006 NFL season. That so much money went toward its restoration also elic-
ited controversy, as Kingsley also notes (Kingsley, "New Orleans Architecture,"
n. 11).

30. Germany, "Politics of Poverty," 750. Two other essays in the special issue of the
Journal of American History provide accounts of the effects of these dynamics
on specific New Orleans's neighborhoods from the nineteenth century to 2007.
Long's essay focuses Storyville ("Poverty Is the New Prostitution") and Landphair's on the Lower Ninth Ward ("Forgotten People").

31. Germany, "Politics of Poverty," 750. In 2012, the *Times-Picayune* dubbed Louisiana the "world's prison capital," according to National Public Radio ("How
Louisiana Became the World's 'Prison Capital,'" *NPR News,* June 5, 2012). One
of every eighty-six adults is incarcerated, a rate "three times higher than Iran's
and ten times higher than Germany's," it reports. Louisiana is home to the
notorious Angola prison, which regularly makes news for various unsavory reasons, but the story focuses on less-well-known rural prisons run (or at least
supervised) by local sheriffs.

32. See, for example, the case of Benilda Caixeta, a quadriplegic New Orleanian
who drowned in her apartment after calling for two days to arrange a ride to the
Superdome via the Paratransit system, which was unreliable in good weather,
according to Congressional testimony quoted by Belser, "Disability and the
Social Politics of 'Natural' Disaster," 62–63.

33. Sheri Fink, "The Deadly Choices at Memorial," *ProPublica,* August 27, 2009.
Originally published in the *New York Times Magazine.* Fink was awarded the
2010 Pulitzer Prize in Investigative Journalism for the story. Fink has also
published a book-length account of the events entitled *Five Days at Memorial:
Life and Death in a Storm Ravaged Hospital* (New York: Crown Publishers,
2013).

34. For Dr. Pou's attorney's response to Fink's article, see http://www.drannapou
.com/legalreply.html.

35. Rumors of this sort were rampant in the days after Katrina prompting pundits
to evoke a return to a Hobbesian state of nature, Protevi notes (an evocation
he aptly criticizes on several grounds). The reality appears to have been much
less apocalyptic and much more complicated. The more extreme rumors—of a
prison revolt, of dead children found in a freezer with their throats cut—proved
false. Moreover, although predatory behavior by gangs did occur, gangs also
pitched in to help secure neighborhoods and rescue stranded survivors. See
Protevi, *Political Affect,* 175–83.

36. Fink's account of the death of another patient, described as "a heavyset African
American man" (*Five Days,* 292) seems less ambiguous. Unlike most of the
other patients subjected to the injection protocol, he survived its administration. Additional morphine injections also failed to still his breathing. After "he
chanted Hail Mary's" (*Five Days,* 292) with an accompanying nurse, Dr. John
Thiele, the physician administering the injections, placed a towel over the man's
face, she reports. He was dead less than a minute later.

37. Michel Foucault, *The Order of Things: An Archaeology of the Human Sciences* (New York: Vintage, 1994), 318; and *Les mots et les choses* (Paris: Éditions Gallimard, 1966), 331.
38. Foucault, *Order of Things*, 385; *Les mots et les choses*, 396.
39. Foucault, *Order of Things*, 385; *Les mots et les choses*, 396.
40. Foucault, *Order of Things*, 385; *Les mots et les choses*, 396.
41. Foucault, *Order of Things*, 387; *Les mots et les choses*, 398.
42. Foucault, *Order of Things*, 387 (emphasis mine); *Les mots et les choses*, 398.

Conclusion

1. Notably, Judith Butler is among those to issue such a call. She has also taken some preliminary steps to extend her insights in some of these directions. See her "On This Occasion . . ." in *Butler on Whitehead: On the Occasion,* ed. Roland Faber, Michael Halewood, and Deena Lin (Lanham MD: Lexington, 2012), 3–18.
2. See, for example, *New Materialisms: Ontology, Agency and Politics,* ed. Diana Coole and Samantha Frost (Durham, NC: Duke University Press, 2010); Mel Y. Chen, *Animacies: Biopolitics, Racial Mattering, and Queer Affect* (Durham, NC: Duke University Press, 2012); Kelly Oliver, *Animal Lessons: How They Teach Us to Be Human* (New York: Columbia University Press, 2009); Kalpana Rahita Seshadri, *HumAnimal: Race, Law and Language* (Minneapolis: University of Minnesota Press, 2012); Rosi Braidotti, *The Posthuman* (Malden, MA: Polity, 2013); and Donna Haraway, *When Species Meet* (Minneapolis: University of Minnesota Press, 2006) and her groundbreaking *Simians, Cyborgs, and Women: The Reinvention of Nature* (New York: Routledge, 1991). Theologians and scholars of religion are also taking up these topics. See, for example, Brent Waters, *From Human to Posthuman: Christian Theology and Technology in a Postmodern World* (New York: Ashgate, 2006), and *Divinanimality: Animal Theory, Creaturely Theology* (New York: Fordham University Press, 2014); and Clayton Crockett and Jeffrey W. Robbins, *Religion, Politics, and the Earth: The New Materialism* (New York: Palgrave Macmillan, 2012).
3. Sharon V. Betcher, *Spirit and the Politics of Disablement* (Minneapolis, MN: Fortress, 2007), 69, 71, 76.
4. Betcher, *Spirit and the Politics of Disablement,* 85.
5. Also noteworthy is the number of New Orleanians who chose to memorialize the losses inflicted by Katrina through getting tattoos. Indeed, the demand for tattoos in post-Katrina New Orleans was so strong that a number of professional tattoo artists moved there temporarily to meet the demand. See Marline Otto, "The Mourning After: Languages of Loss and Grief in Post-Katrina New Orleans," *Journal of American History* 94, no. 3 (December 2007): 828–36. Tattooing is but one of the bodily practices of mourning that combine the tactile and the visual that Otto tracks here.

6. It is worth noting that ancient Greeks and Romans understood vision as tactile—and thus an opening to connections between (at least certain types of) people (for good or ill) and a source of self-knowledge and route for self-making. See Shadi Bartch, *The Mirror of the Self: Sexuality, Self-Knowledge, and the Gaze* (Chicago, IL: University of Chicago Press, 2006). My thanks to Denise Kimber Buell for reminding me of this. For an important example of the role of tactile vision in early Christian theology, see Buell's "Imagining Human Transformation in the Context of Invisible Powers: Instrumental Agency in Second Century Treatments of Conversion," *Metamorphoses: Resurrection, Body and Transformative Practices in Early Christianity*, ed. Turid Karlsen Seim and Jorunn Oklund (New York: Walter de Gruyter, 2009), 249–70.

7. Jacques Derrida, *On Touching—Jean-Luc Nancy*, trans. Christine Irizarry (Stanford, CA: Stanford University Press, 2005); originally published in French as *Le toucher, Jean-Luc Nancy* (Paris: Éditions Galilée, 2000). My discussion of *Le Toucher* is a slightly revised version of a portion of my "Touching Transcendence: Sexual Difference and Sacrality in Derrida's *Le toucher*," *Derrida and Religion: Other Testaments*, ed. Kevin Hart and Yvonne Sherwood (New York: Routledge, 2005), 351–62.

8. Michael Naas, "In and Out of Touch: Derrida's *Le toucher*," *Research in Phenomenology* 31 (2001): 258–65; 258–59.

9. Jean-Luis Chrétien, *L'appel et la réponse* (Paris: Minuit, 1992).

10. Naas suggests that the five tangents represent the five fingers of the hand or the five senses. Perhaps the other five essays could be considered the fingers of the other hand, as well.

11. See Derrida, *Le toucher*, chapter 4, "The Untouchable or the Vow of Abstinence" [*L'intouchable ou le voeu d'abstinence*], 81–108; "Tangente V," 273–329.

12. See Jacques Derrida, *Adieu to Emmanuel Lévinas*, trans. Pascale-Anne Brault and Michael Naas (Stanford, CA: Stanford University Press, 1999); originally published in French as *Adieu à Emmanuel Lévinas* (Paris: Éditions Galilée, 1997).

13. Emmanuel Lévinas, "Phenomenology of Eros," *Totality and Infinity*, trans. Alphonso Lingis (Pittsburgh: Duquesne University Press, 1969), 256–66; originally published in French as *Totalité et infini: Essais sur l'exteriorité* (The Hague: Martinus Nijhoff, 1961); and *Time and the Other*, trans. Richard Cohen (Pittsburgh: Duquesne University Press, 1985); originally published in French as *Le temps et l'autre* (Paris: Arthaud, 1947).

14. Lévinas, *Le temps et l'autre*, 82; quoted by Derrida, *Le toucher*, 92, my translation.

15. Lévinas, *Le temps et l'autre*, 82; quoted by Derrida, *Le toucher*, 92, my translation.

16. Lévinas, *Totalité et infini*, 236, my translation; quoted by Derrida, *Le toucher*, 103. See Lévinas, *Totality and Infinity*, 59.

17. Lévinas, *Totalité et infini*, 236, my translation; quoted by Derrida, *Le toucher*, 103. See Lévinas, *Totality and Infinity*, 59.

18. Luce Irigaray, "Fécondité de la caresse (Lecture de Lévinas. *Totalité et infini,* Section IV, B, "Phénoménologie de l'éros," *Éthique de la différence sexuelle* (Paris: Éditions de Minuit, 1984), 173–99; published in English as "The Fecundity of the Caress: A Reading of Lévinas, *Totality and Infinity,* 'Phenomenology of Eros'," in *An Ethics of Sexual Difference,* trans. Carolyn Burke and Gillian C. Gill (Ithaca, NY: Cornell University Press, 1994), 185–217. Irigaray's critique of Lévinas figures prominently in Mayra Rivera Rivera's *Touch of Transcendence: A Postcolonial Theology of God* (Louisville, KY: Westminster John Knox, 2009), which I turn to shortly. See also Mayra Rivera Rivera, "Ethical Desires: Toward a Theology of Relational Transcendence," in *Toward a Theology of Eros: Transfiguring Passion at the Limits of Discipline,* ed. Virginia Burrus and Catherine Keller (New York: Fordham University Press, 2006): 255–70.

19. Martin Heidegger, *Being and Time: A Translation of Sein und Zeit,* trans. Joan Stambaugh (Albany: State University of New York Press, 1999), I.iii.A.15–17, 62–76. Earlier, Heidegger establishes touch as a capacity unique to *Dasein.* He notes that although we routinely ascribe touch to objectively present things (as in "the chair touches the wall"), "two beings which are objectively present within the world and are, moreover, *worldless* in themselves, can never 'touch' each other, neither can 'be together with' the other" (I.II.12, 51–52).

20. Only *Dasein* is world-making; animals are poor in world, Heidegger argues To be poor in world, though, is not to be utterly without world; stones, however, are worldless. Martin Heidegger, *Fundamental Concepts of Metaphysics: World, Finitude, Solitude,* trans. William McNeill and Nichoolas Walker (Bloomington: Indiana University Press, 1995), section 47, 196ff.

21. Space does not allow me to treat it here, but I want to call attention to Molly Haslam's *A Constructive Theology of Intellectual Disability: Human Being as Mutuality and Response* (New York: Fordham University Press, 2011). There, Haslam (a physical therapist and theologian) critiques the usual formulation of the *imago dei* as rationality arguing in favor of relationality instead. She is drawn there because of her work as a physical therapist with people with severe intellectual disabilities. The phenomenology she offers at the outset of her experience of relationality in that context is one in which touch is integral. Given the foundational role this phenomenology plays in the theology she goes on to develop, her work, too—although quite different in the philosophical and theological resources it engages—would also be relevant here.

22. M. Shawn Copeland, *Enfleshing Freedom: Body, Race, and Being* (Minneapolis, MN: Fortress, 2010), 66.

23. Rivera Rivera, *Touch of Transcendence,* 107.

24. Copeland, *Enfleshing Freedom,* 8. The phrase "critical ontology of the body" is from Paul Anthony Farley's "The Black Boy as Fetish Object," *Oregon Law Review* 26 (1977): 531. Copeland links it to Michel Foucault's "critical ontology of ourselves" referenced in "What Is Enlightenment?" in *The Foucault Reader,* ed. Paul Rabinow and trans. Catherine Porter (New York: Pantheon, 1984).

25. Copeland, *Enfleshing Freedom,* 100.

26. Copeland, *Enfleshing Freedom*, 94.

27. Copeland, *Enfleshing Freedom*, 126.

28. For a more explicitly contemplative approach to this very same task of re-formation, see Wendy Farley's *Gathering Those Driven Away: A Theology of Incarnation* (Louisville, KY: Westminster John Knox, 2011).

29. Copeland, *Enfleshing Freedom*, 82.

30. Copeland, *Enfleshing Freedom*, 82.

31. Copeland, *Enfleshing Freedom*, 83.

32. Betcher, *Spirit and the Politics of Disablement*, 3, 116.

33. Betcher, *Spirit and the Politics of Disablement*, 116.

34. Betcher, *Spirit and the Politics of Disablement*, 97.

35. Betcher, *Spirit and the Politics of Disablement*, 103.

36. Betcher, *Spirit and the Politics of Disablement*, 103.

37. Rivera Rivera, *Touch of Transcendence*, 2, 5.

38. Rivera Rivera, *Touch of Transcendence*, 95.

39. Sharon V. Betcher, *Spirit and the Obligation of Social Flesh: A Secular Theology for the Global City* (New York: Fordham University Press, 2014).

40. Betcher introduces this term on p. 29 of *Social Flesh*, but its full meaning takes some time to unfold. This (iconic) neologism offers us in concentrated form what this work of circumambulation seeks to do—that is, to decode the complexities of urban life, to map out routes for their navigation by drawing on resources to be found there. Exploring these questions from the perspective of "crip" existence ("crip" is to the disability movement what "queer" is to the LGBTQI movement) is crucial to it.

41. See Wendy Farley, *The Wounding and Healing of Desire: Weaving Heaven and Earth* (Louisville, KY: Westminster John Knox, 2005) and *Gathering Those Driven Away*. Her theology, like Rivera Rivera's though grounded in different Christian sources, is rooted in a compelling vision of divine abyssal love.

42. Mayra Rivera Rivera, *Poetics of the Flesh* (Durham, NC: Duke University Press, 2015).

BIBLIOGRAPHY

Adeyanju, Dickinson. "Homosexual Priests: Nigerian Anglicans Will Not Succumb to Pressure from the West, Says Akinola." *The Guardian* (Nigeria), July 30, 2007.

Agamben, Giorgio. *Homo Sacer: Sovereign Power and Bare Life*, trans. Daniel Heller-Roazen. Stanford, CA: Stanford University Press, 1998.

——. *State of Exception*, trans. Kevin Attell. Chicago: University of Chicago Press, 2005.

Alexander, Michelle. *The New Jim Crow: Mass Incarceration in the Age of Colorblindness*. New York: New Press, 2010.

Allen, Amy. "The Anti-Subjective Hypothesis: Foucault and the Death of the Subject." *The Philosophical Forum* 31, no. 2 (2000): 113–30.

——. *The Politics of Ourselves: Power, Autonomy, and Gender in Contemporary Critical Theory*. New York: Columbia University Press, 2008.

Allen, James, John Lewis, Leon F. Litwack, and Hilton Als. *Without Sanctuary: Lynching Photography in America*. Santa Fe, NM: Twin Palms, 2008.

Amadiume, Ifi. *Male Daughters, Female Husbands: Gender and Sex in African Society*. London: Zed, 1987.

Anderson, Victor. *Beyond Ontological Blackness*. New York: Continuum, 1999.

——. *Creative Exchange: A Constructive Theology of African American Religious Experience*. Minneapolis, MN: Fortress, 2008.

Anidjar, Gil. *The Jew, The Arab: A History of the Enemy*. Stanford, CA: Stanford University Press, 2006.

——. *Semites: Race, Religion, Literature*. Stanford, CA: Stanford University Press, 2007.

Apel, Dora. *Imagery of Lynching: Black Men, White Women, and the Mob*. New Brunswick, NJ: Rutgers University Press, 2004.

——. "Torture Culture: Lynching Photographs and the Images of Abu Ghraib." *Art Journal* 64, no. 2 (2005): 88–100.

Apel, Dora, and Shawn Michelle Smith. *Lynching Photographs*. Berkeley: University of California Press, 2007.

Armour, Ellen T. "Beyond Belief: Sexual Difference and Religion After Ontotheology." In *The Religious*, ed. John Caputo, 212–26. Malden, MA: Blackwell, 2003.

——. "Beyond the God/Man Duo: Globalization, Feminist Theology, and Religious Subjectivity." In *The Oxford Handbook of Feminist Theology*, ed. Mary McClintock Fulkerson and Sheila Briggs, 371–81. New York: Oxford University Press, 2011.

——. "Blinding Me with (Queer) Science: Religion, Sexuality, and (Post?) Modernity." *International Journal for Philosophy of Religion* 68, no. 1–3 (2010): 107–19.

——. *Deconstruction, Feminist Theology and the Problem of Difference: Subverting the Race/Gender Divide*. Chicago: University of Chicago Press, 1999.

——. " 'Man' and His 'Others.' " *Bulletin de la Société Americaine de Philosophie de Langue Française* 15, no. 1 (Spring 2005): 1–11.

——. "Planetary Sightings? Negotiating Sexual Differences in Globalization's Shadow." In *Planetary Loves: Postcoloniality, Gender, and Theology*, ed. Stephen Moore and Mayra Rivera Rivera, 209–24. New York: Fordham University Press, 2010.

——. "Theology in Modernity's Wake." *Journal of the American Academy of Religion* 74, no. 1 (2006): 7–15.

——. " 'Through Flame or Ashes': Traces of Difference in Geist's Return." In *Feminist Interpretations of Martin Heidegger*, ed. Nancy J. Holland and Patricia J. Huntington, 316–33. State College: Pennsylvania State University Press, 2001.

——. "Touching Transcendence: Sexual Difference and Sacrality in Derrida's *Le Toucher*." In *Derrida and Religion: Other Testaments*, ed. Kevin Hart and Yvonne Sherwood, 351–62. New York: Routledge, 2005.

——. "Visual Theology: Diagnosing Postmodernity." In *Between Philosophy and Theology: Contemporary Interpretations of Christianity*, ed. Lieven Boeve and Christophe Brabante, 175–92. London: Ashgate, 2011.

Armour, Rollin S. *Islam, Christianity and the West: A Troubled History*. New York: Orbis, 2002.

Asad, Talal. *Formations of the Secular: Christianity, Islam, Modernity*. Stanford, CA: Stanford University Press, 2003.

——. *Genealogies of Religion: Discipline and Reasons of Power in Christianity and Islam*. Baltimore, MD: Johns Hopkins University Press, 1993.

Associated Press. "Iconic Vietnam War 'Napalm Girl' Photograph Turns 40." *Chicago Sun-Times*, June 4, 2012.

Associated Press. "2 Months Later, Victim of Katrina Is Laid to Rest." *NBC News*, November 16, 2005.

Azoulay, Ariella. *The Civil Contract of Photography*. New York: Zone, 2008.

Babington, Charles. "Frist Defends Remarks on Schiavo Case." *Washington Post*, June 17, 2005.

Baker, Peter. "Pivoting from a War Footing, Obama Acts to Curtail Drones." *New York Times*, May 23, 2013.

Bartch, Shadi. *The Mirror of the Self: Sexuality, Self-Knowledge, and the Gaze*. Chicago: University of Chicago Press, 2006.

Barthes, Roland. *Camera Lucinda: Reflections on Photography*, trans. Richard Howard. New York: Hill and Wang, 1981.

——. *Image-Music-Text*, trans. Stephen Heath. New York: Hill and Wang, 1977.

——. *The Rustle of Language*, trans. Richard Howard. Berkeley: University of California Press, 1989.

Barton-Ross, Cheri, and Jane Baron-Sorenson. *Pet Loss and Human Emotion: A Guide to Recovery*. New York: Routledge, 2007.

Baudrillard, Jean. *Simulacra and Simulation*, trans. Sheila Faria Glaser. Ann Arbor: University of Michigan Press, 1994.

Beatey, Katelyn. "Women's Ordination: A Crack in the Cathedral?" *Christianity Today*, July 2, 2009.

Bell, Catherine. *Ritual Theory, Ritual Practice*. New York: Oxford University Press, 1992.

Belser, Julia Watts. "Disability and the Social Politics of 'Natural' Disaster: Toward a Jewish Feminist Ethics of Disaster Tales." *Worldviews: Global Religions, Culture, and Ecology* 19, no. 1: 51–68.

Benjamin, Walter. *Illuminations: Essays and Reflections*, ed. Hannah Arendt and trans. Harry Zohn. New York: Schocken, 1968.

Berger, John. *Ways of Seeing: Based on the BBC Television Series*. London: Penguin, 1972.

Bergson, Henri. *Matter and Memory*, trans. Nancy Margaret Paul and W. Scott Palmer. New York: Zone, 1991.

Bernasconi, Robert, and Tommy Lott, eds. *The Idea of Race*. Indianapolis, IN: Hackett, 2002.

Bernauer, James William, and Jeremy Carrette. *Michel Foucault and Theology: The Politics of Religious Experience*. London: Ashgate, 2004.

Betcher, Sharon V. "Of Disability and the Garden State." *Religious Studies News Spotlight on Theological Education*, March 2010.

——. *Spirit and the Obligation of Social Flesh: A Secular Theology for the Global City*. New York: Fordham University Press, 2014.

——. *Spirit and the Politics of Disablement*. Minneapolis, MN: Fortress, 2007.

Biryabarema, Elias. "U.S. Cuts Aid to Uganda, Cancels Military Exercise Over Anti-Gay Law," ed. Doina Chiacu and Cynthia Osterman. *Reuters*. June 19, 2014.

Bishop, Jeffrey P. *The Anticipatory Corpse: Medicine, Power, and the Care of the Dying*. Notre Dame, IN: University of Notre Dame Press, 2011.

——. "Biopolitics, Terri Schiavo, and the Sovereign Subject of Death." *Journal of Medicine and Philosophy* 33, no. 6 (2008): 338–57.

Blake, Mariah. "Meet the American Pastor Behind Uganda's Anti-Gay Crackdown." *Mother Jones,* March 10, 2014.

Blumenthal, Deborah. "Shelters for Pets Fill with Furry Survivors." *New York Times,* September 8, 2005.

Bordo, Susan. *Unbearable Weight: Feminism, Western Culture and the Body,* 10th anniversary edition. Berkeley: University of California Press, 2003.

Boswell, John. *Christianity, Social Tolerance, and Homosexuality.* Chicago: University of Chicago Press, 1980.

Bourdieu, Pierre. *Outline of a Theory of Practice,* trans. Richard Nice. New York: Cambridge University Press, 1977.

Bowcott, Owen. "Uganda Anti-Gay Law Led to Tenfold Rise in Attacks on LGBTI People, Report Says." *The Guardian,* May 11, 2014.

Braidotti, Rosi. *The Posthuman.* Malden, MA: Polity, 2013.

Bresheeth, Haim. "Projecting Trauma: War Photography and the Public Sphere." *Third Text* 20, no. 1 (2006): 57–71.

Brooten, Bernadette. *Love Between Women: Early Christian Responses to Female Homoeroticism.* Chicago: University of Chicago Press, 1996.

Brown, Matthew Hay. "Md. Priest Becomes First Lesbian Episcopal Bishop" *Baltimore Sun,* December 5, 2009.

Brown, Terry, ed. *Other Voices, Other Worlds: The Global Church Speaks Out on Homosexuality.* London: Darton, Longman and Todd, 2006.

Buell, Denise Kimber. "Early Christian Universalism and Modern Forms of Racism." In *The Origins of Racism in the West,* ed. Miriam Eliav-Feldon, Benjamin Isaac, and Joseph Ziegler, 109–31. New York: Cambridge University Press, 2009.

——. "Imagining Human Transformation in the Context of Invisible Powers: Instrumental Agency in Second Century Treatments of Conversion." In *Metamorphoses: Resurrection, Body and Transformative Practices in Early Christianity,* ed. Turid Karlsen Seim and Jorunn Oklund, 249–70. New York: Walter de Gruyter, 2009.

——. *Why This New Race? Ethnic Reasoning in Early Christianity.* New York: Columbia University Press, 2005.

Butler, Judith. *Bodies That Matter: On the Discursive Limits of Sex.* New York: Routledge, 1993.

——. *Frames of War: When Is Life Grievable?* New York: Verso, 2009.

——. *Gender Trouble: Feminism and the Subversion of Identity.* New York: Routledge, 1990.

——. "On This Occasion. . . ." In *Butler on Whitehead: On the Occasion,* ed. Roland Faber, Michael Halewood, and Deena Lin, 3–18. Lanham, MD: Lexington, 2012.

——. *Precarious Life: The Powers of Mourning and Violence.* New York: Verso, 2006.

——. *Psychic Life of Power: Theories in Subjection.* Stanford, CA: Stanford University Press, 1997.

——. "Sexual Politics, Torture, and Sexual Time." *British Journal of Sociology* 59, no. 1 (2008): 1–23.

——. *Undoing Gender.* New York: Routledge, 2004.

Calarco, Matthew. *Zoographies: The Question of the Animal from Heidegger to Derrida*. New York: Columbia University Press, 2008.

Cameron, James. *A Time of Terror: A Survivor's Story*. Baltimore, MD: Black Classic Press, 1994.

Carby, Hazel. "A Strange and Bitter Crop: The Spectacle of Torture." *Open Democracy: Free Thinking for the World*, October 11, 2004.

Carey, Andrew. "African Christians? They're Just a Step up from Witchcraft." *Church of England Newspaper*, July 10, 1998.

Carey, Benedict. "Inside the Injured Brain, Many Kinds of Awareness." *New York Times*, April 5, 2005.

Carrette, Jeremy. *Foucault and Religion*. New York: Routledge, 1999.

Carrette, Jeremy, and Mary Keller. "Religions, Orientation and Critical Theory: Race, Gender and Sexuality at the 1998 Lambeth Conference." *Theology and Sexuality* 11 (1999): 21–43.

Carter, J. Kameron. *Race: A Theological Account*. New York: Oxford University Press, 2010.

Chen, Mel Y. *Animacies: Biopolitics, Racial Mattering, and Queer Affect*. Durham, NC: Duke University Press, 2012.

Chidester, David. *Savage Systems: Colonialism and Comparative Religion in Southern Africa*. Charlottesville: University of Virginia Press, 1996.

Chrétien, Jean-Luis. *L'Appel et la réponse*. Paris: Minuit, 1992.

Chua-Eaon, Howard. "Rick Warren Denounces Uganda's Anti-Gay Bill." *Time*, December 10, 2009.

Clarke, Graham. *The Photograph*. New York: Oxford University Press, 1997.

Cone, James H. *The Cross and the Lynching Tree*. Minneapolis, MN: Fortress, 2011.

Conger, George. "Civil Court Ruling for Recife Schism." *Church of England Newspaper*, August 28, 2013.

——. "The Episcopal Church Approves Religious Weddings for Gay Couples After Controversial Debate." *Washington Post*, July 1, 2015.

Connolly, Ceci. "Schiavo Raised Profile of Disabled (Questions Swirl About End of Life Issues)." *Washington Post*, April 2, 2005.

Connolly, William E. *Why I Am Not a Secularist*. Minneapolis: University of Minnesota Press, 2000.

Conrad, Peter. "Medicalization and Social Control." *Annual Review of Sociology* 18 (1992): 209–32.

Coole, Diana, and Samantha Frost, eds. *New Materialisms: Ontology, Agency and Politics*. Durham, NC: Duke University Press, 2010.

Coolidge, Sharon. "Cincinnati Cops to Get Body Cameras." *Cincinnati Enquirer*, December 8, 2014.

Copeland, Shaun M. *Enfleshing Freedom: Body, Race and Being*. Minneapolis, MN: Fortress, 2010.

Cowell, Alan. "Uganda's President Signs Antigay Bill." *New York Times*, February 24, 2014.

Crary, Jonathan. *Suspensions of Perception: Attention, Spectacle, and Modern Culture.* Cambridge: Massachusetts Institute of Technology Press, 2001.

——. *Techniques of the Observer: On Vision and Modernity in the Nineteenth Century.* Cambridge: Massachusetts Institute of Technology Press, 1990.

Crockett, Clayton, and Jeffrey W. Robbins. *Religion, Politics and the Earth: The New Materialism.* New York: Palgrave Macmillan, 2012.

Danner, Mark. *Torture and Truth: America, Abu Ghraib, and the War on Terror.* New York: New York Review of Books, 2004.

Debord, Guy. *Society of the Spectacle,* trans. Ken Knabb. London: Rebel, 2006.

De Certeau, Michel. *The Practice of Everyday Life,* trans. Steven F. Rendall. Berkeley: University of California Press, 1984.

Deleuze, Gilles. *Cinema 1: The Movement-Image,* trans. Hugh Tomlinson and Barbara Habberjam. New York: Athlone, 1986.

——. *Cinema 2: The Time-Image,* trans. Hugh Tomlinson and Robert Galeta. New York: Athlone, 1989.

Deleuze, Gilles, and Felix Guattari. *What Is Philosophy?* trans. Hugh Tomlinson and Graham Burchell. New York: Columbia University Press, 1994.

Derrida, Jacques. *Acts of Religion,* ed. Gil Anidjar. New York: Routledge, 2002.

——. *Adieu to Emmanuel Levinas,* trans. Pascale-Anne Brault and Michael Naas. Stanford, CA: Stanford University Press, 1999.

——. *The Animal That Therefore I Am,* ed. Marie-Louise Mallet and trans. David Wills. New York: Fordham University Press, 2008.

——. "The Animal That Therefore I Am (More to Follow)," trans. David Wills. *Critical Inquiry* 28, no. 2 (2002): 369–418.

——. *Athens, Still Remains: The Photographs of Jean-François Bonhomme,* trans. Pascale-Anne Brault and Michael Naas. New York: New York University Press, 2010.

——. "The Ends of Man." In *Margins of Philosophy,* trans. Alan Bass, 109–36. Chicago: University of Chicago Press, 1982.

——. *On Touching—Jean-Luc Nancy,* trans. Christine Irizarry. Stanford, CA: Stanford University Press, 2005.

——. "Response to David Tracy." In *God, the Gift, and Postmodernism,* ed. John D. Caputo and Michael J. Scanlon, 181–84. Bloomington: Indiana University Press, 2000.

——. *The Truth in Painting,* trans. Geoffrey Bennington and Ian McLeod. Chicago: University of Chicago Press, 1987.

DeVore, Donald E. "Water in Sacred Places: Rebuilding New Orleans' Black Churches as Sites of Community Empowerment." *Journal of American History* 94, no. 3 (2007): 762–69.

Douglas, Kelly Brown. *Sexuality and the Black Church: A Womanist Perspective.* New York: Orbis, 1999.

Dreger, Alice Domurat. *Hermaphrodites and the Medical Invention of Sex.* Cambridge, MA: Harvard University Press, 1998.

Dreyfus, Hubert L. and Paul Rabinow. *Michel Foucault: Beyond Structuralism and Hermeneutics,* 2nd edition. Chicago: University of Chicago Press, 1983.

Drye, Willie. "Hurricane Katrina: The Essential Time Line." *National Geographic News,* September 14, 2005.

Duberman, Martin, Martha Vicinus, and George Chauncey, Jr. *Hidden from History.* New York: Meridian, 1990.

Duttlinger, Carolin. "Imaginary Encounters: Walter Benjamin and the Aura of Photography." *Poetics Today* 29, no. 1 (2008): 79–101.

Eisenman, Stephen F. *The Abu Ghraib Effect.* London: Reaktion, 2007.

Esposito, Roberto. "The *Dispositif* of the Person." *Law, Culture and the Humanities* 8, no. 1 (2012): 17–30.

Farley, Edward. *Theologia: The Fragmentation and Unity of Theological Education.* Philadelphia: Fortress, 1983.

Farley, Paul Anthony. "The Black Boy as Fetish Object." *Oregon Law Review* 26 (1977): 457–531.

Farley, Wendy. *Gathering Those Driven Away: A Theology of Incarnation.* Louisville, KY: Westminster John Knox, 2011.

——. *The Wounding and Healing of Desire: Weaving Heaven and Earth.* Louisville, KY: Westminster John Knox, 2005.

Fausto-Sterling, Anne. *Sexing the Body: Gender Politics and the Construction of Sexuality.* New York: Basic, 2000.

Feldman, Allen. "On the Actuarial Gaze: From 9/11 to Abu Ghraib" *Cultural Studies* 19, no. 2 (2005): 203–26.

Fink, Sheri. "The Deadly Choices at Memorial." *ProPublica,* August 27, 2009.

——. *Five Days at Memorial: Life and Death in a Storm Ravaged Hospital.* New York: Crown, 2013.

Fisher, Marc. "In Tunisia, Act of One Fruit Vendor Sparks Wave of Revolution through Arab World." *Washington Post,* March 26, 2011.

Fjord, Lakshmi. "Disasters, Race, and Disability: [Un]Seen Through the Political Lens on Katrina." *Journal of Race and Policy* 3, no. 1 (2007): 46–66.

Foucault, Michel. *The Archaeology of Knowledge and The Discourse on Language,* trans. A. M. Sheridan Smith. New York: Pantheon, 1972.

——. *The Birth of the Clinic: An Archaeology of Medical Perception.* New York: Vintage, 1994.

——. *Discipline and Punish: The Birth of the Prison.* New York: Pantheon, 1978.

——. *History of Madness,* ed. Jean Khalfa and trans. Jonathan Murphy. New York: Routledge, 2006.

——. *The History of Sexuality, Vol. 1: An Introduction,* trans. Robert Hurley. New York: Random House, 1978.

——. *The History of Sexuality, Vol. 2: The Use of Pleasure,* trans. Robert Hurley. New York: Vintage, 1990.

——. *The Order of Things: An Archaeology of the Human Sciences.* New York: Vintage, 1994.

——. *Religion and Culture,* ed. Jeremy Carrette. New York: Routledge, 1999.

——. *Security, Territory, Population: Lectures at the Collège de France, 1976–77,* trans. Graham Burchell. New York: Picador, 2007.

——. "*Society Must Be Defended*": *Lectures at the Collège de France, 1975–76*, trans. David Macey. New York: Picador, 2003.

——. "What Is Enlightenment?" In *The Foucault Reader*, ed. Paul Rabinow and trans. Catherine Porter. New York: Pantheon, 1984.

——. "Why Study Power? The Question of the Subject." In *Michel Foucault Beyond Structuralism and Hermeneutics*, ed. Hubert Dreyfus and Paul Rabinow. Chicago: University of Chicago Press, 1983.

Fox, Chris. "From Representation to Constituent Power: Religion, or Something Like It, in Hardt and Negri's *Empire*." *Journal for Cultural and Religious Theory* 9, no. 2 (2008): 30–42.

Fox, Neva Rae. "Nigerian Primate Seated on International Throne of Cathedral." *Episcopal News Service,* July 16, 2002.

Fredericks, Bob. "Paralyzed Man Woken from Coma Chooses Death." *New York Post,* November 6, 2013.

Fussell, Elizabeth. "Constructing New Orleans, Constructing Race: A Population History of New Orleans." *Journal of American History* 94, no. 3 (2007): 846–55.

Garland Thomson, Rosemarie. *Extraordinary Bodies: Figuring Physical Disability in American Culture and Literature*. New York: Columbia University Press, 1997.

——. "Integrating Disability, Transforming Feminist Theory." *NWSA Journal* 14, no. 3 (2002): 1–32.

——. *Staring: How We Look*. New York: Oxford University Press, 2009.

Garland Thomson, Rosemarie, ed. *Freakery: Cultural Spectacles of the Extraordinary Body*. New York: New York University Press, 1996.

Germany, Kent B. "The Politics of Poverty and History: Racial Inequality and the Long Prelude to Katrina." *Journal of American History* 94, no. 3 (2007): 743–51.

Gettleman, Jeffrey. "Ugandan Who Spoke Up for Gays Is Beaten to Death." *New York Times,* January 28, 2011.

Ghosh, Amitav. "The Theater of Cruelty." *The Nation*, July 18, 2005.

Ghosts of Abu Ghraib. Directed by Rory Kennedy. New York: HBO Documentary Films, 2007.

Gibson, Margaret. "Clitoral Corruption: Body Metaphors and American Doctors' Construction of Female Homosexuality, 1870–1900." In *Science and Homosexualities*, ed. Vernon Rosario, 108–32. New York: Routledge, 1997.

Gilman, Sander. *Difference and Pathology: Stereotypes of Sexuality, Race, and Madness*. Ithaca, NY: Cornell University Press, 1985.

Gladstone, Rick. "Nigerian President Signs Ban on Same-Sex Relationships." *New York Times,* January 13, 2014.

Gledhill, Ruth. "For God's Sake." *The Times*, July 5, 2007.

Goodstein, Laurie. "Episcopalians Approve Rite to Bless Same-Sex Unions." *New York Times,* July 10, 2012.

——. "Episcopal Vote Reopens A Door to Gay Bishops." *New York Times*, July 14, 2009.

——. "Openly Gay Man is Made Bishop." *New York Times,* November 3, 2003.

Goodwyn, Wade. "The Strange Case of Marlise Muñoz and John Peter Smith Hospital." *NPR: Policy-ish,* January 28, 2014.

Grandin, Temple, and Catherine Johnson. *Animals in Translation: Using the Mysteries of Autism to Decode Animal Behavior.* New York: Scribner, 2005.

Greenberg, David. *The Construction of Homosexuality.* Chicago: University of Chicago Press, 1988.

Greenwald, Glenn. "NSA Collecting Phone Records of Millions of Verizon Customers Daily." *The Guardian,* June 5, 2013.

Greenwald, Glenn, and Ewen MacAskill. "NSA Prism Program Taps into User Data of Apple, Google, and Others." *The Guardian,* June 6, 2013.

Gregg, Melissa, and Gregory Seigworth, eds. *The Affect Theory Reader.* Durham, NC: Duke University Press, 2010.

Grossman, Cathy Lynn. "Conservative Anglican Leaders Back Uganda Anti-Gay Law." *Religion News Service,* April 28, 2014.

Hagler-Geard, Tiffany. "The Historic 'Napalm Girl' Pulitzer Image Marks Its 40th Anniversary." *Picture This: ABC News,* June 8, 2012.

Hale, Grace Elizabeth. *Making Whiteness: The Culture of Segregation in the South, 1890–1940.* New York: Random House, 1998.

Hale, Marian. *Dark Water Rising.* New York: Square Fish, 2006.

Hamner, Gail M. *Imaging Religion in Film: The Politics of Nostalgia.* New York: Palgrave Macmillan, 2012.

Handy, Shannon. "More Local Police Departments Requiring Body Cams." *CBS 8 (San Diego, CA),* December 8, 2014.

Haraway, Donna. *Simians, Cyborgs, and Women: The Reinvention of Nature.* New York: Routledge, 1991.

——. *When Species Meet.* Minneapolis: University of Minnesota Press, 2006.

Hardt, Michael, and Antonio Negri. *Empire.* Cambridge, MA: Harvard University Press, 2000.

——. *Multitude: War and Democracy in the Age of Empire.* New York: Penguin, 2005.

——. *Commonwealth.* Cambridge, MA: Belknap Press of Harvard University Press, 2009.

Hariman, Robert, and John Louis Lucaites. *No Caption Needed: Iconic Photographs, Public Culture and Liberal Democracy.* Chicago: University of Chicago Press, 2007.

Haslam, Molly. *A Constructive Theology of Intellectual Disability: Human Being as Mutuality and Response.* New York: Fordham University Press, 2011.

Hassett, Miranda K. *Anglican Communion in Crisis: How Episcopal Dissidents and Their African Allies Are Reshaping Anglicanism.* Princeton, NJ: Princeton University Press, 2007.

Heidegger, Martin. *Being and Time: A Translation of Sein und Zeit,* trans. Joan Stambaugh. Albany: State University of New York Press, 1999.

——. *Fundamental Concepts of Metaphysics: World, Finitude, Solitude,* trans. William McNeill and Nicholas Walker. Bloomington: Indiana University Press, 1995.

——. *Poetry, Language, Thought*, trans. Albert Hofstadter. New York: HarperCollins, 1975.

Henig, Robin Marantz. "A Life or Death Situation." *New York Times,* July 17, 2013.

Hersh, Seymour M. *Chain of Command: The Road from 9/11 to Abu Ghraib.* New York: HarperCollins, 2004.

Hevey, David. "The Enfreakment of Photography." In *The Disability Studies Reader,* ed. Lennard J. Davis, 3rd edition. New York: Routledge, 2010.

Heyman, Daniel. "It Is Difficult." *Portraits of Iraqis, 2004–2008.* http://www.danielheyman .com/projects_works_iraq.htm.

Hirsch, Arnold R. "Fade to Black: Hurricane Katrina and the Disappearance of Creole New Orleans." *Journal of American History* 94, no. 3 (2007): 752–61.

Hirsch, Marianne. *Family Frames: Photography, Narrative, and Postmemory.* Cambridge, MA: Harvard University Press, 1997.

Holmes, Rachel. *African Queen: The Real Life of the Hottentot Venus.* New York: Random House, 2007.

Huffer, Lynn. *Mad for Foucault: Rethinking the Foundations of Queer Theory.* New York: Columbia University Press, 2010.

Hughes, Ron. "Australia Condemns Ugandan and Nigerian Anti-Gay Laws." *Gay News Network Australia*, February 7, 2013.

Hurt, Harry. "The Business of Intelligence Gathering." *New York Times*, June 15, 2008.

International Gay and Lesbian Human Rights Commission. "Voices from Nigeria: Gays, Lesbians, Bisexuals and Transgenders Speak Out Against the Same Sex Bill." New York: International Gay and Lesbian Human Rights Commission, 2006.

Irigaray, Luce. *An Ethics of Sexual Difference*, trans. Carolyn Burke and Gillian C. Gill. Ithaca, NY: Cornell University Press, 1994.

Ishsizuka, Karen, and Patricia R. Zimmerman. *Mining the Home Movie: Excavations in Histories and Memories.* Sacramento: University of California Press, 2007.

Jay, Martin. *Downcast Eyes: The Denigration of Vision in the Twentieth Century.* Berkeley: University of California Press, 1993.

Jean, Barry, Marcia Gaudet, and Carl Lindahl, eds. *Second Line Rescue: Improvised Responses to Katrina and Rita.* Oxford: University Press of Mississippi, 2013.

Jenkins, Phillip. *The New Faces of Christianity: Believing the Bible in the Global South.* New York: Oxford University Press, 2006.

——. *The Next Christendom: The Coming of Global Christianity.* New York: Oxford University Press, 2002.

Jenkins, Willis. "Episcopalians, Homosexuality, and World Missions." *Anglican Theological Review* 86, no. 2 (2004): 293–312.

——. "Ethnohomophobia?" *Anglican Theological Review* 82, no. 3 (2000): 551–63.

Johnson, Mary. "After Terri Schiavo: Why the Disability Rights Movement Spoke Out, Why Some of Us Worried, and Where Do We Go from Here?" http://www .raggededgemagazine.com/focus/postschiavo0405.html#imparato.

Johnston, Chris. "Uganda Drafts New Anti-Gay Laws." *The Guardian,* November 8, 2014.

Jordan, Mark D. *Convulsing Bodies: Religion and Resistance in Foucault.* Stanford, CA: Stanford University Press, 2014.

———. *The Ethics of Sex.* Malden, MA: Blackwell, 2002.

———. "Foucault's Ironies and the Important Earnestness of Theory." *Foucault Studies* 14 (2012): 7–19.

———. *The Invention of Sodomy in Christian Theology.* Chicago: University of Chicago Press, 1998.

———. *Recruiting Young Love: How Christians Talk About Homosexuality.* Chicago: University of Chicago Press, 2011.

Kafer, Alison. *Feminist, Queer, Crip.* Bloomington: Indiana University Press, 2013.

Kaoma, Kapya. "Globalizing the Culture Wars: U.S. Conservatives, African Churches, & Homophobia." Somerville, MA: Political Research Associates, 2009.

Kelman, Ari. "Boundary Issues: Clarifying New Orleans' Murky Edges." *Journal of American History* 94, no. 3 (2007): 695–703.

Khalili, Laleh. *Time in the Shadows: Confinement in Counterinsurgencies.* Stanford, CA: Stanford University Press, 2012.

Kingsley, Karen. "New Orleans Architecture: Building Renewal." *Journal of American History* 94, no. 3 (2007): 716–25.

Kinsolving, Les. "Censoring the Facts About Homosexuality." *WND Commentary*, November 8, 2003.

Kolata, Gina. "At These Hospitals, Recovery Is Rare, but Comfort Is Not." *New York Times*, June 23, 2014.

Lacan, Jacques. *The Four Fundamental Concepts of Psycho-Analysis*, ed. Jacques-Alain Miller and trans. Alan Sheridan. Harmondsworth, England: Penguin, 1979.

Laing, Gerald. *War Paintings 2002–Present.* http://www.geraldlaing.com/index .php/work/warpaintings.

Lakeland, Paul. *Postmodernity: Christian Identity in a Fragmented Age.* Minneapolis, MN: Fortress, 1997.

Lambeth Commission on Communion. *The Windsor Report 2004.* Harrisburg, PA: Morehouse, 2004.

Lamoreaux, John C. "Early Christian Responses to Islam." In *Medieval Christian Perspectives of Islam: A Book of Essays*, ed. John Victor Tolan, 3–31. New York: Garland, 1996.

Landphair, Juliette. "The Forgotten People of New Orleans: Community, Vulnerability and the Lower Ninth Ward." *Journal of American History* 94, no. 3 (2007): 837–43.

Lawlor, Leonard. *This Is Not Sufficient: An Essay on Animality and Human Nature in Derrida.* New York: Columbia University Press, 2007.

Lee, Linda. "Bridal Hunger Games: Losing Weight in Time for the Wedding." *New York Times*, April 13, 2012.

Lennard, David. *The End of Normal: Identity in a Biocultural Era.* Ann Arbor: University of Michigan Press, 2013.

Leong, Karen J., Christopher A. Airriess, Wei Li, Angela Chia-Chen Chen, and Verna M. Keith. "Resilient History and the Rebuilding of a Community: The Vietnamese American Community in New Orleans East." *Journal of American History* 94, no. 3 (2007): 770–79.

Lévinas, Emmanuel. *Time and the Other*, trans. Richard Cohen. Pittsburgh: Duquesne University Press, 1985.

——. *Totality and Infinity*, trans. Alphonso Lingis. Pittsburgh: Duquesne University Press, 1969.

Long, Alecia P. "Poverty Is the New Prostitution: Race, Poverty, and Public Housing in Post-Katrina New Orleans." *Journal of American History* 94, no. 3 (2007): 795–803.

Lyman, Rick. "Protestors with Hearts on Sleeves and Anger on Signs." *New York Times*, March 28, 2005.

Madison, James H. *A Lynching in the Heartland: Race and Memory in America*. New York: Palgrave Macmillan, 2001.

Mahmood, Saba. "Agency, Performativity, and the Feminist Subject." In *Bodily Citations: Religion and Judith Butler*, ed. Ellen T. Armour and Susan St. Ville, 177–221. New York: Columbia University Press, 2006.

Margolick, David. *Strange Fruit: Billie Holiday, Café Society, and an Early Cry for Civil Rights*. Philadelphia: Running Press, 2000.

Marion, Jean-Luc. *The Visible and the Revealed*, trans. Christina M. Gschwandtner. New York: Fordham University Press, 2008.

Mark, Monica. "Missing Nigerian Schoolgirls: Boko Haram Claims Responsibility for Kidnapping." *The Guardian*, May 5, 2014.

Marks, John. "Foucault, Franks, Gauls: Il faut defendre la société: The 1976 lectures at the Collège de France." *Theory, Culture and Society* 17, no. 5 (2000): 127–47.

Martin, Dale B. *The Corinthian Body*. New Haven, CT: Yale University Press, 1999.

——. *Sex and the Single Savior: Gender and Sexuality in Biblical Interpretation*. Louisville, KY: Westminster John Knox, 2006.

Massumi, Brian. "The Autonomy of Affect." *Cultural Critique* 31 (1995): 83–109.

Masuzawa, Tomoko. *The Invention of World Religions: Or, How European Universalism Was Preserved in the Language of Pluralism*. Chicago: University of Chicago Press, 2005.

May, Todd. *The Philosophy of Foucault*. Montreal: McGill-Queen's University Press, 2006.

Mayer, Jane. *The Dark Side: The Inside Story of How the War of Terror Turned Into a War on American Ideals*. New York: Anchor, 2008.

Mazzetti, Mark. "Panel Faults C.I.A. over Brutality and Deceit in Terrorism Investigations." *New York Times*, December 9, 2014.

McCruer, Robert. *Crip Theory: Cultural Signs of Queerness and Disability*. New York: New York University Press, 2006.

McGaughy, Lauren. "Angola Prison Conditions 'Inhumane,' Should Be Subject to Justice Investigation, Richmond Says." *The Times Picayune*, July 12, 2013.

McMaster, Neil. "Torture: From Algiers to Abu Ghraib." *Race and Class* 46, no. 2 (October 2004): 1–21.

McWhorter, LaDelle. *Bodies and Pleasures: Foucault and the Politics of Sexual Normalization*. Bloomington: Indiana University Press, 1999.

——. *Racism and Sexual Oppression in Anglo-America: A Genealogy.* Bloomington: Indiana University Press, 2009.

Mendieta, Eduardo, and Angela Davis. *Abolition Democracy: Beyond Empire, Prisons, and Torture: Interviews with Angela Davis.* New York: Seven Stories, 2005.

Merleau-Ponty, Maurice. *Phenomenology of Perception,* trans. Donald Landes. New York: Routledge, 2012.

Miller, Arthur G., Barry E. Collins, and Diana E. Brief, "Perspectives on Obedience to Authority: The Legacy of the Milgram Experiments." *Journal of Social Issues* 51, no. 3 (1995): 1–20.

Miller, Terri Beth. " 'Reading' the Body of Terri Schiavo: Inscriptions of Power in Medical and Legal Discourse." *Literature and Medicine* 28, no. 1 (2009): 33–54.

Mine: the Movie. Directed by Geralyn Pezanoski. San Francisco: Smush Media, 2009.

Mirzoeff, Nicholas. *The Right to Look: A Counterhistory of Visuality.* Durham, NC: Duke University Press, 2011.

——. *Watching Babylon: The War in Iraq and Global Visual Culture.* New York: Routledge, 2005.

Mitchell, W. J. T. *Cloning Terror: The War of Images, 9/11 to the Present.* Chicago: University of Chicago Press, 2011.

——. *Iconology: Image, Text, and Ideology.* Chicago: University of Chicago Press, 1987.

——. *Picture Theory: Essays on Verbal and Visual Representation.* Chicago: University of Chicago Press, 1995.

——. *What Do Pictures Want? The Lives and Loves of Images.* Chicago: University of Chicago Press, 2005.

Moqbel, Samir Naji al Hasan. "Gitmo Is Killing Me." *New York Times,* April 14, 2013.

Moran, James M. *There's No Place Like Home Video.* Minneapolis: University of Minnesota Press, 2002.

Mukasa, Kawuki. "The Church of Uganda and the Problem of Human Sexuality: Responding to Concerns from the Ugandan Context." In *Other Voices, Other Worlds: The Global Church Speaks Out on Homosexuality,* ed. Terry Brown, 168–78. New York: Church Publishing, 2006.

Muybridge, Eadweard. *Animal Locomotion: An Electrophotographic Investigation of Consecutive Phases of Animal Movements.* Philadelphia: University of Pennsylvania, 1887.

——. *Freeze Frame: Eadweard Muybridge's Photography of Motion.* Curated by Michelle Delaney, Marta Braun, and Elspeth Brown. Washington, DC: Smithsonian Institute's National Museum of American History, October 7, 2000–March 15, 2001.

——. *Muybridge's Complete Human and Animal Locomotion.* Mineola, NY: Dover, 1979.

Naas, Michael. "In and Out of Touch: Derrida's *Le Toucher*." *Research in Phenomenology* 31 (2001): 258–65.

National Public Radio Staff. "How Louisiana Became the World's 'Prison Capital'," *NPR News,* June 5, 2012. http://www.npr.org/2012/06/05/154352977/how-louisiana-became-the-worlds-prison-capital.

Naughton, Jim. "Following the Money: Donors and Activists on the Anglican Right, a Special Report of *Washington Window.*" Washington, DC: Episcopal Diocese of Washington, 2006.

Newton, Julianne Hickerson. *The Burden of Visual Truth: The Role of Photojournalism in Mediating Reality.* Mahwah, NJ: Lawrence Erlbaum Associates, 2001.

Nietzsche, Friedrich. *On the Genealogy of Morals: A Polemic, By way of clarification and supplement to my last book, Beyond Good and Evil,* trans. Douglas Smith. New York: Oxford University Press, 1996.

Nossiter, Adam. "Nigeria Tries to 'Sanitize' Itself of Gays." *New York Times,* February 8, 2014.

Nussbaum, Martha. *Frontiers of Justice: Disability, Nationality, Species Membership.* Cambridge, MA: Harvard University Press, 2006.

Olin, Margaret. *Touching Photographs.* Chicago: University of Chicago Press, 2012.

Oliver, Kelly. *Animal Lessons: How They Teach Us to be Human.* New York: Columbia University Press, 2009.

Otto, Marline. "The Mourning After: Languages of Loss and Grief in Post-Katrina New Orleans." *Journal of American History* 94, no. 3 (2007): 828–36.

Painter, Nell Irvin. *The History of White People.* New York: Norton, 2010.

Pinn, Anthony B. *Embodiment and the New Shape of Black Theological Thought.* New York: New York University Press, 2010.

Pohlgreen, Ludia, and Laurie Goodstein. "At Axis of Episcopal Split, an Anti-Gay Nigerian." *New York Times,* December 25, 2006.

Protevi, John. *Political Affect: Connecting the Social and the Somatic.* Minneapolis: University of Minnesota Press, 2009.

——. *Political Physics.* New York: Athlone, 2001.

Pui-Lan, Kwok. *Postcolonial Imagination and Feminist Theology.* Louisville, KY: Westminster John Knox, 2005.

Raeburn, Bruce Boyd. " 'They're Tryin' to Wash Us Away': New Orleans Musicians Surviving Katrina." *Journal of American History* 94, no. 3 (2007): 812–19.

Raeburn, Paul. "A Second Womb." *New York Times Magazine,* August 15, 2005.

Raghavan, Sudarsan. "Ugandan Leader Signs Harsh Anti-Gay Bill Despite Warning from Obama Administration." *Washington Post,* February 24, 2014.

Rancière, Jacques. *The Future of the Image.* New York: Verso, 2009.

Rancière, Jacques, and Stephen Corcoran. *Dissensus: On Politics and Aesthetics.* New York: Continuum, 2010.

Riis, Jacob. *How the Other Half Lives: Studies Among the Tenements of New York.* New York: Charles Scribner's Sons, 1914.

Rivera Rivera, Mayra. "Ethical Desires: Toward a Theology of Relational Transcendence." In *Toward a Theology of Eros: Transfiguring Passion at the Limits of Discipline,* ed. Virginia Burrus and Catherine Keller, 255–70. New York: Fordham University Press, 2006.

——. *Poetics of the Flesh.* Durham, NC: Duke University Press, 2015.

——. *The Touch of Transcendence: A Postcolonial Theology of God*. Louisville, KY: Westminster John Knox, 2009.

Romero, Anthony D. "Pardon Bush and Those Who Tortured." *New York Times*, December 8, 2014.

Roscoe, Will, and Stephen O. Murray, *Boy-Wives and Female Husbands: Studies in African Homosexualities*. New York: Palgrave Macmillan, 2001.

Rosler, Martha. *Bringing the War Home: House Beautiful, New Series*, 2004. http://www.elgawimmer.com/PopPoliticsPower/pages/06.html.

Rubenstein, Mary-Jane. "An Anglican Crisis of Comparison: Race, Gender, and Religious Authority, with Particular Reference to the Church of Nigeria." *Journal of the American Academy of Religion* 72, no. 2 (2004): 341–65.

——. "Anglicans in the Postcolony: On Sex and the Limits of Communion." *telos* 143 (2008): 133–60.

Sacks, Oliver. *The Man Who Mistook His Wife for a Hat and Other Clinical Tales*. New York: Simon & Schuster, 1970.

Said, Edward. *Orientalism*. New York: Vintage, 1979.

Salon Staff. "The Abu Ghraib Files." *Salon*, March 14, 2006.

Samuels, Ellen. "Critical Divides: Judith Butler's Body Theory and the Question of Disability." *NWSA Journal* 14, no. 3 (2002): 58–76.

Sanneh, Lamin. *Whose Religion Is Christianity? The Gospel Beyond the West*. Grand Rapids. MI: Eerdmans, 2003.

Santner, Eric L. "Terri Schiavo and the State of Exception." *University of Chicago Press Blog*, March 29, 2005.

Sentilles, Sarah. "Misreading Feuerbach: Susan Sontag, Photography and the Image-World." *Literature and Theology* 24, no. 1 (2010): 38–55.

——. "The Photograph as Mystery: Theological Language and Ethical Looking in Roland Barthes's *Camera Lucida*." *Journal of Religion* 90, no. 4 (2010): 507–29.

Seshadri, Kalpana Rahita. *HumAnimal: Race, Law and Language*. Minneapolis: University of Minnesota Press, 2012.

Sharlet, Jeff. *C Street: The Fundamentalist Threat to American Democracy*. New York: Little, Brown, 2010.

Sherrock, Tim. *Spies for Hire: The Secret World of Intelligence Outsourcing*. New York: Simon & Schuster, 2008.

Sheth, Falguni A., and Robert E. Prasch. "In Boston, Our Bloated Surveillance State Didn't Work." *Salon*, April 22, 2013.

Shiley, Mike. *Dark Water Rising: Survival Stories of Hurricane Katrina Animal Rescues*. Portland, OR: Shidog Films, 2006.

Shopenhauer, Arthur. *The World as Will and Representation, Vol. 2*, trans. E. F. J. Payne. Indian Hills, CO: Falcon's Wing, 1958.

Siebers, Tobin. *Disability Theory*. Ann Arbor: University of Michigan Press, 2008.

Silvers, Anita. "Reconciling Equality to Difference: Caring (f)or Justice for People with Disabilities." *Hypatia* 10, no. 1 (1995): 30–55.

Simmons, Rick. "Legal Counsel Reply to NYT: Comments of Rick Simmons, Legal Counsel for Dr. Anna Pou Regarding the New York Times Magazine Posting of August 28, 2009." *Dr. Anna Pou Media*, n.d.

Singer, Peter. "Making Our Own Decisions About Death: Competency Should Be Paramount." *Free Inquiry* 25, no. 5 (2006): 36–38.

——. *Practical Ethics* Cambridge, England: Cambridge University Press, 1979.

Skidmore, David. "Bishop Spong Apologises to Africans." *Lambeth Daily*, July 28, 1998.

Smith, Shawn Michelle. *At the Edge of Sight: Photography and the Unseen.* Durham, NC: Duke University Press, 2013.

——. *Photography on the Color Line: W.E.B. DuBois, Race, and Visual Culture.* Durham, NC: Duke University Press, 2004.

Sobeieszek, Robert. "Historical Commentary." *French Primitive Photography: Alfred Stieglitz Center.* New York: No. 5 Aperture, 1970.

Solheim, James. "International Reaction to Gene Robinson's Consecration in New Hampshire Mixed." *Anglican Communion News Service*, November 6, 2003.

Solomon-Godeau, Abigail. *Photography at the Dock: Essays on Photographic History, Institutions, and Practices.* Minneapolis: University of Minnesota Press, 1991.

——. "Remote Control: Dispatches from the Image Wars." *Artforum* 62, no. 10 (2004): 61–64.

Sontag, Susan. *On Photography.* New York: Picador, 2001.

——. *Regarding the Pain of Others.* New York: Picador, 2003.

——. "Regarding the Torture of Others." *New York Times Magazine*, Mary 23, 2004.

Souther, J. Mark. "The Disneyfication of New Orleans: The French Quarter as Facade in a Divided City." *Journal of American History* 94, no. 3 (2007): 804–11.

Spivak, Gayatri Chakravorty. "Can the Subaltern Speak?" In *Marxism and the Interpretation of Culture*, ed. Lawrence Grossberg and Cary Nelson, 271–313. Chicago: University of Illinois Press.

——. *Death of a Discipline.* New York: Columbia University Press, 2003.

Spurgas, Alyson. "(Un)Queering Identity: The Biosocial Production of Intersex/DSD." In *Critical Intersex (Queer Interventions)*, ed. Morgan Holmes, 97–122. Burlington, VT: Ashgate, 2009.

Standard Operating Procedure. Directed by Errol Morris. New York: Sony Pictures, 2008.

Stiker, Henri-Jacques. *A History of Disability*, trans. William Sayers. Ann Arbor: University of Michigan, 1999.

Stoler, Ann Laura. *Carnal Knowledge and Imperial Power: Race and the Intimate Under Colonial Rule.* Berkeley: University of California, 2010.

——. *Race and the Education of Desire: Foucault's History of Sexuality and the Colonial Order of Things.* Durham, NC: Duke University Press, 1995.

Stone, Ken. "The Garden of Eden and the Heterosexual Contract." In *Bodily Citations: Religion and Judith Butler*, ed. Ellen T. Armour and Susan St. Ville, 48–70. New York: Columbia University Press, 2006.

Swecker, Stephen ed. *Hard Ball on Holy Ground: The Religious Right v. the Mainline for the Church's Soul.* Boston: Boston Wesleyan Press, 2005.

Tagg, John. *Burden of Representation: Essays on Photographies and Histories*. Minneapolis: University of Minnesota Press, 1993.

——. *The Disciplinary Frame: Photographic Truths and the Capture of Meaning*. Minneapolis: University of Minnesota Press, 2009.

Tanke, Joseph J. "What Is the Aesthetic Regime?" *Parrhesia* 12 (2011): 71–81.

Tanner, Kathryn. *Theories of Culture: A New Agenda for Theology*. Minneapolis, MN: Fortress, 1997.

Taylor, Charles. *A Secular Age*. Cambridge, MA: Belknap Press of Harvard University Press, 2007.

Temkin, Ann, Susan Rosenberg, and Michael Taylor, with Rachel Arauz. *Twentieth Century Painting and Sculpture in the Philadelphia Museum of Art*. Philadelphia: Philadelphia Museum of Art, 2001.

Terry, Jennifer. *An American Obsession: Science, Medicine, and Homosexuality in Modern Society*. Chicago: University of Chicago Press, 1999.

Townes, Emilie. *Womanist Ethics and the Cultural Production of Evil*. New York: Palgrave Macmillan, 2006.

Trachtenberg, Alan. *Reading American Photographs: Images as History, Matthew Brady to Walker Evans*. New York: Hill and Wang, 1989.

Trouble the Water. Directed by Carl Deal and Tia Lessin. New York: Elsewhere Films, 2008.

Tuana, Nancy. "Viscous Porosity: Witnessing Katrina." In *Material Feminisms*, ed. Stacy Aliamo and Susan J. Hekman, 188–213. Bloomington: Indiana University Press, 2008.

Tyler, Pamela. "The Post-Katrina, Semi-separate World of Gender Politics." *Journal of American History* 94, no. 3 (2007): 762–88.

Vanhoozer, Kevin J., ed. *The Cambridge Companion to Postmodern Theology*. New York: Cambridge University Press, 2003.

Ward, Kevin. "Marching or Stumbling towards a Christian Ethic?" In *Other Voices, Other Worlds: The Global Church Speaks Out on Homosexuality*, ed. Terry Brown, 133–34. New York: Church Publishing, 2006.

——. "Same-Sex Relations in Africa and the Debate on Homosexuality in East African Anglicanism." *Anglican Theological Review* 84, no. 1 (2002): 81–111.

Waters, Brent. *Divinanimality: Animal Theory, Creaturely Theology*. New York: Fordham University Press, 2014.

——. *From Human to Posthuman: Christian Theology and Technology in a Postmodern World*. New York: Ashgate, 2006.

Weheliye, Alexander G. *Habeas Viscus: Racializing Assemblages, Biopolitics, and Black Feminist Theories of the Human*. Durham, NC: Duke University Press, 2014.

Welling, William. *Photography in America: The Formative Years, 1839–1900*. New York: Crowell, 1978.

West, Cornel. *Prophesy Deliverance! An Afro-American Revolutionary Christianity*. Louisville, KY: Westminster John Knox, 1982.

When the Levees Broke: A Requiem in Four Acts. Directed by Spike Lee. New York: HBO, 2006.

White, Heather. *Reforming Sodom: Protestants and the Rise of Gay Rights.* Chapel Hill: University of North Carolina Press, 2015.

Williams, Roger Ross. "Gospel of Intolerance." *New York Times,* January 22, 2013.

Williams, Timothy. "Schaivo's Brain Was Severely Deteriorated, Autopsy Says." *New York Times,* June 15, 2005.

Willis, Deborah, and Carla Williams. *The Black Female Body: A Photographic History.* Philadelphia: Temple University Press, 2002.

Wolfson, Jay. "A Report to Governor Jeb Bush and the 6th Judicial Circuit in the Matter of Theresa Marie Schiavo." December 1, 2003.

Wood, Amy Louise. *Lynching and Spectacle: Witnessing Racial Violence in America, 1890-1940.* Chapel Hill: University of North Carolina Press, 2009.

Wright, Katherine Fairfax, and Malika Zouhali-Worrall. "They Will Say We Are Not Here." *New York Times,* January 25, 2012.

Yochelson, Bonnie. *Alfred Stieglitz' New York.* New York: Skira Rizzoli, 2010.

Zimmerman, Patricia R. *Reel Families: A Social History of Amateur Film.* Bloomington: Indiana University Press, 1995.

Žižek, Slavoj. "Between Fear and Trembling: On Why Only Atheists Can Believe." Vanderbilt University, Nashville, TN, November 3, 2006.